All of the programs from Appendix C of *dBASE III Plus for the Programmer* are available on diskette for the IBM PC.

You can order a copy of this diskette directly from the author for $25.00, using the form below:

✂- -

Order Form

Shipping information—please print

Name____

Street____

City__________________________State________Zip____________

Date of Order____________________

Please send me:

____ diskettes to accompany *dBASE III Plus for the Programmer* at $25.00 each, $30.00 each if outside U.S. and Canada.

Check method of payment:

❐ check ❐ money order ❐ cash

Credit cards and C.O.D. are not accepted.

✂- -

Mail order to:

Nelson T. Dinerstein
PO Box 596
Hyde Park, UT 84318

Price includes postage, handling, and applicable sales tax.
Price and availability subject to change without notice.

dBASE III
Plus
for the Programmer

Nelson T. Dinerstein
Computer Science Department
Utah State University

Scott, Foresman and Company
Glenview, Illinois *London*

ISBN 0-673-18835-3

Printed in the United States of America.

Library of Congress Cataloging-in-Publication Data

Dinerstein, Nelson T.
dBASE III Plus for the programmer.

Includes index.
1. dBASE III PLUS (Computer program) I. Title.
II. Title: dBASE Three Plus for the programmer.
III. Title: dBASE 3 Plus for the programmer.
QA76.9.D3D544 1987 005.36′9 87-4830
ISBN 0-673-18835-3

3 4 5 6 KPF 92 91 90 89 88

Portions of this book were previously published in *dBASE III for the Programmer: A How-to-Do-It Book*, by Nelson T. Dinerstein, copyright © 1985 Scott, Foresman and Company.

Notice of Liability

The information in this book is distributed on an "As Is" basis, without warranty. Neither the author nor Scott, Foresman and Company shall have any liability to customer or any other person or entity with respect to any liability, loss, or damage caused or alleged to be caused directly or indirectly by the programs contained herein. This includes, but is not limited to, interruption of service, loss of data, loss of business or anticipatory profits, or consequential damages from the use of the programs.

Scott, Foresman Professional Publishing Group books are available for bulk sales at quantity discounts. For information, please contact the Marketing Manager, Professional Books, Professional Publishing Group, Scott, Foresman and Company, 1900 East Lake Avenue, Glenview, IL 60025.

PREFACE

dBASE III Plus represents a major improvement over both dBASE II and earlier versions of dBASE III. Improvements include increased speed, more records in the database files, more fields in the database files, the addition of useful statements and functions to the language, the addition of features for local area networks, and the addition of functions to libraries. The libraries allow the addition of both prewritten and user written routines. Two of the nice extensions are arrays and a library of graphics routines.

The purpose of this book is to show you how to construct high-quality application systems in dBASE III Plus. The book is written in a friendly style and focuses on the material that you will need to build high-quality systems. It is written for the programmer. As such, it is expected that you know how to program in at least one common programming language, but a prior knowledge of dBASE II is not required.

CONTENTS

CHAPTER 2

A dBASE III PLUS PRIMER 6

CHAPTER 3

FUNDAMENTAL dBASE III PLUS PROGRAMMING CONCEPTS 172

CHAPTER

1

Introduction

1.1 BACKGROUND

dBASE III is a product of Ashton-Tate, and is a comprehensive, integrated system for storing, manipulating, and reporting data. It is a full-featured language in that it provides both a complete programming language and a complete set of database operators. You can use the features of dBASE III interactively or in programs, and special features of dBASE III provide additional help to the beginner.

dBASE III is an outgrowth of dBASE II, but you do not need to know anything about dBASE II to learn dBASE III. Since dBASE III has one of the oldest histories of any system in its class, it reflects a well-thought-out design. In addition, the maturity of dBASE III is evident in its ease of use, in its flexibility, and in the power of its operators. Since dBASE III is written in the C language, the addition of new features is facilitated by the C library. You do not need to be a C programmer to take advantage of this flexibility, since these features are provided by Ashton-Tate as an easy-to-use option.

1.2 SYSTEM REQUIREMENTS AND HARDWARE SELECTION

1.2.1 THE TYPE OF COMPUTER

dBASE III is designed to work on a microcomputer that is 100% compatible with the IBM PC, the XT, or the AT. There are a number of microcomputers on the market that satisfy this requirement, but there are also a number that are advertised as being compatible with the IBM products, but really are not. The safe way to purchase a computer is to try the desired software on the computer that you intend to purchase and verify that the software will work.

1.2.2 THE OPERATING SYSTEM

Make sure that your operating system satisfies the requirements of your particular software. In general, if you have PC DOS 2.0 or higher, or MS DOS 2.1 or higher, you should be okay.

1.2.3 MAIN MEMORY

Ashton-Tate recommends at least 256K of main memory, but you will never be happy with your system if you try to run dBASE III with so little memory. Since the cost of main memory has gone down so much in the last few years, it seems unreasonable to use a computer with less than 512K of main memory. In fact, I strongly recommend that you upgrade your computer to 640K if you currently have less than that amount.

1.2.4 DISKS

dBASE III comes on a number of disks (my version came on seven disks), so it just isn't reasonable to use a computer without a hard disk. I recommend that you use a hard disk with at least 20M storage capacity, but I prefer a disk with a capacity of at least 30M.

1.2.5 PRINTER

dBASE III is a real workhorse and you will want a printer to match it. Printers are often rated as light-, medium-, or heavy-duty machines. Look for a real heavy-duty printer—one that will stand up to years of use. Because of the graphics capabilities offered by the optional Graphics Library (part of the *dBASE Tools for C*), you will probably want to get a printer that will allow both normal print and graphics. My choice is a dot matrix printer, one that will allow you to print in three modes: draft, near letter quality, and graphics. Draft mode is used for fast printing, near letter quality is used for a higher quality (but slower) printing, and graphics mode is used to print pictures. I also prefer a printer that is compatible with the IBM Graphics Printer (so that you can do screen dumps as needed) and has a wide carriage. You will occasionally find that you need a wide report, and that a printer with 80 columns of output is just too small. Some of the reports that I have written require 210 columns of output. These require both a wide carriage and compressed print.

1.3 PROTECTION

When dBASE III was first introduced (dBASE III version 1.0), a protection scheme called PROLOK was used. You could run dBASE III, but you needed to insert the original disk in a floppy disk drive to start it. Ashton-Tate found it economically infeasible to continue with this copy protection scheme, since there were so many disks being returned for replacement. A PROLOK protected disk could not be installed on a hard disk unless you used special software to "unprotect" dBASE III. The next protection (SUPERLoK) scheme allowed you to install dBASE III Plus version 1.0 on a hard disk. Once it was installed, you could run dBASE III without a special disk in the floppy disk drive. You can install this version of dBASE III just once on a hard disk, but you can uninstall it and then install it either on another machine or on the same machine at a later date. Version 1.1 of dBASE III Plus is not copy protected, so you can make backups for your own use and installation is greatly simplified.

1.4 SETTING UP YOUR DISKS TO USE dBASE III

I recommend that you create a new directory on your hard disk for dBASE III and that you copy all the desired programs to this directory. If you have a program like EASY PATH from Polygon Software, you can access all of the dBASE III programs from any directory on your disk. This means that you can store dBASE III in one directory and store your programs and data on another directory. If you are running several applications and wish to keep them separate (each set of programs and data is stored in a separate directory), then this strategy is just what you need.

1.4.1 INSTALLING AND RUNNING PROLOK PROTECTED DISKS (dBASE III VERSION 1.0)

Insert the desired distribution disk on drive A, change to drive C, and copy all the programs to your hard disk using the DOS COPY command

```
COPY A:*.*
```

Each time that you wish to run dBASE III, place the original dBASE III System Disk 1 in drive A, go to drive C, enter the command

```
DBASE
```

and then press RETURN.

1.4.2 INSTALLING AND RUNNING dBASE III PLUS, VERSION 1.0, WITH SUPERLoK

Insert System Disk 1 in drive A and then enter the command

INSTALL C:

The installation procedure prompts you to insert distribution disks one at a time in drive A and then copies files from these disks to your hard disk. Not all the files are copied to your hard disk. If you wish to copy some of the remaining files to your hard disk, go to the appropriate directory on drive C and then enter the command

COPY A:complete-file-name

where "complete-file-name" is the complete name of the file on the disk in drive A that you wish to copy to your hard disk. To run dBASE III Plus version 1.0, go to drive C, enter the command

DBASE

and then press RETURN. You do not have to place the original System Disk 1 in drive A.

1.4.3 INSTALLING AND RUNNING dBASE III PLUS, VERSION 1.1, NO COPY PROTECTION

Since this version is not copy protected, you can copy all the dBASE III files, as needed, to your hard disk using the DOS COPY command as described above. Once the copy has been completed, go to drive C and enter the command

DBASE

and then press RETURN.

1.5 THE CONFIG.SYS FILE

The CONFIG.SYS file is used in MS DOS to set certain system parameters. You can use this file to specify both the number of FILES and the number of BUFFERS. I recommend that you insert or modify, as necessary, the two lines

```
FILES=20
BUFFERS=20
```

into this file. I recommend that you use your favorite editor (in nondocument mode) to accomplish this. The CONFIG.SYS file should be placed in the main directory of your hard disk.

CHAPTER

2

A dBASE III Plus Primer

2.1 INTRODUCTION

This primer is designed to provide a brief introduction to some of the language elements in dBASE III Plus. If you are already familiar with dBASE III Plus, you might prefer to skip this chapter. In the following, examples are provided for the most frequently used language elements.

dBASE III Plus is both a sophisticated data management system and a relational database system designed to run on microcomputers. It is a self-contained system, in that dBASE III Plus programs are written in a special language provided as part of the system. The calls to the database functions are part of this language and do not require special subroutine calls.

2.1.1 FILES

Files used by or created by dBASE III Plus are categorized by families. The families and types are given in Table 2.1. Database files contain the actual database records, and index files contain the selected indexes to these database files.

TABLE 2.1

FILE TYPE	EXTENSION	USE
Catalog files	.CAT	A set of related data files. Similar to a subdirectory. Used to group files for a single application.
Command files	.PRG	Application program
Database files	.DBF	Storage of data
Database memo files	.DBT	Storage of memo fields (long strings)
Format files	.FMT	Specifications for custom screen forms
Index files	.NDX	Files that allow fast access to records in database files
Labels	.LBL	Information used by the label command
Memory files	.MEM	Used to store memory variables
Query files	.QRY	Specifications for a filter condition
Report form files	.FRM	Specifications for the printing of a report
Screen files	.SCR	A picture of a screen
Text output files	.TXT	Standard ASCII files that are produced by dBASE III and can be accessed by software from other vendors
View files	.VUE	Specifications for a view of linked database files

2.1.2 VARIABLES AND CONSTANTS

The dBASE III Plus language allows both database record field references and local variable references. Local variables are called memory variables.The names of variables (database and memory) may not exceed 10 characters. They may contain letters, numbers, and underscores, but must start with a letter. A name cannot contain an embedded blank.

The five types of data objects that may be stored in record fields or in memory variables are:

1. *Character strings.* Character strings are delimited by double quotes (" "), single quotes (' '), or brackets ([ ]). The maximum length of a character string is 254 characters. The delimiters are not counted as part of the string.
2. *Dates.* A date is a data item that can be used in two ways. It can be stored and displayed in the normal manner (MM/DD/YY, where MM is the month, DD is the day, and YY is the last two digits of the year) and it can be used in computations. For example, it is possible to compute the number of days from one date to another merely by subtracting the earlier date from the later date. One can also add an integer to a date. For example, 07/01/87 + 10, meaning add 10 days to the first day of July 1987, produces the date 07/11/87.
3. *Numbers.* There are two kinds of numbers in dBASE III Plus, integers and real numbers. Numbers are accurately stored with 15 significant digits.
4. *Logicals (Booleans).* The notation .T. is used to represent TRUE, and .F. is used to represent FALSE.
5. *Memos.* A memo is used to hold large blocks of text. A memo field is actually a variable length character string from 512 to 4096 characters in length. A memo field takes only 10 characters of storage in the data record itself, since the memo field is stored in a separate memo file. The memo field in the database record is used to indicate which record in the memo file is associated with it. There are no variables of type memo, only database fields.

2.1.3 FUNCTIONS

There are a number of functions built into the language. Constants are used in some examples and variables are used in other examples. In most cases, the choice of a constant or a variable is arbitrary. When you are using the function, you may use it with either constants or variables, unless noted otherwise. If a function name is followed by a pair of parentheses and there is nothing in the parentheses in the examples given, then you should not attempt to enter anything in the parentheses either. For example, "DATE( )" is a function that will return the system date. You are not allowed to enter anything between the left and the right parentheses when using this function.

TABLE 2.2 Function Table

TYPE	NAME	DESCRIPTION
Arithmetic	ABS	Absolute value
	EXP	Exponential
	INT	Chop to integer
	LOG	Logarithm
	MAX	Larger of two values
	MIN	Smaller of two values
	ROUND	Round off
	SQRT	Square root
ASCII	ASC	Convert character to ASCII code
	CHR	Convert ASCII code to character
Case	LOWER	Convert to lowercase
	UPPER	Convert to uppercase
Character String	&	Macro expansion
	AT	Substring search
	LEFT	Extract characters from a string
	LEN	String length
	LOWER	Convert to lowercase
	LTRIM	Remove (trim) leading blanks
	REPLICATE	Repeat the character string
	RIGHT	Extract characters from a string
	RTRIM	Remove (trim) trailing blanks

TYPE	NAME	DESCRIPTION
	SPACE	Create a string containing blanks
	STR	Convert number to character string
	STUFF	Insert substring
	SUBSTR	Substring selection
	TRANSFORM	Specify output format
	TRIM	Remove trailing blanks
	UPPER	Convert to uppercase
	VAL	Convert string to a number
Database	BOF	Beginning of file
	DELETED	Deleted record
	EOF	End of file
	FILE	Test for existence of file
	FOUND	Test for result of database search
	LUPDATE	Date of last update
	RECCOUNT	Count records in database
	RECNO	Database record number
	RECSIZE	Size of record
Date	CDOW	Name of day of week
	CMONTH	Name of month
	CTOD	Convert character string to date
	DATE	System date
	DAY	Number of day of month
	DOW	Number of day of week
	DTOC	Convert date to character string
	MONTH	Number of month
	TIME	System time
	YEAR	Four-digit year

TYPE	NAME	DESCRIPTION
Error	ERROR	Return the error number
	MESSAGE	Return the error message
Identification	DBF	The name of the database in USE
	FIELD	The name of the indicated field
	FKLABEL	Identifier of a function key
	FKMAX	Number of programmable function keys
	NDX	Get names of index files in current area
	VERSION	The version number of dBASE III Plus
Input	INKEY	Identifying number of next keypress
	READKEY	Identifying number of key used to exit from full-screen editing
Printer	PCOL	Column of print head
	PROW	Row of print head
Screen	COL	Column of cursor
	ROW	Row of cursor
System	DISKSPACE	Available space on disk
	GETENV	Get content of OS environment variable
	OS	Return the name of the operating system
Tests	IIF	Functional form of the IF statement
	ISALPHA	Test for leading letter
	ISCOLOR	Test for color mode
	ISLOWER	Test first character for case
	ISUPPER	Test first character for case
Time	TIME	System time
Variable	TYPE	Type of data in memory variable

& — *The macro function*

The ampersand (&) is a special character which indicates that the following character string variable is to be replaced with the contents of the character string. This seems to be useful in the following three circumstances:

A. Storing a statement as a string:

EXAMPLE:

```
STORE "? RECNO( )" TO X
&X
```

will cause the number of the current record to be printed on the screen.

B. Changing a character string containing a number to its numeric equivalent:

EXAMPLE:

```
STORE "123.4" TO X
STORE &X TO Y
```

will cause the number 123.4 to be placed in Y.

C. To supply part of a title in a multi-use report:

EXAMPLE:

```
STORE ' "DAILY" ' TO MEMTITLE
SET DEVICE TO PRINT
@ 1,10 SAY &MEMTITLE+" REPORT"
```

will cause the character string "DAILY REPORT" to be sent to the printer and printed at the appropriate place on the page.

ABS(<numeric expression>) — *Absolute value of the number*

Returns the absolute value of the number.

EXAMPLE:

```
. ? ABS(-5)
5
```

ASC(<string>) — *Character to ASCII code*

Returns the ASCII code for the first character of the character string.

EXAMPLE:

```
. ? ASC("AB")
65
```

AT(<string1>, <string2>) — *Substring search*

This function is used to find the position of the <string1> in <string2>.

EXAMPLE:

```
. ? AT("AB","ACABA")
```

will return the value 3, indicating that the character string "AB" starts in position 3 of the character string "ACABA". If <string1> is not contained in <string2>, then the value 0 is returned.

BOF( ) — *Test for the beginning of file*

This function returns the value .T. if the currency pointer is before the first record in the file.

EXAMPLE:

```
. USE TEST
. BOF( )
.F.
. SKIP -1
. BOF( )
.T.
```

This function may be used to stop the scan of a file when moving through the file in reverse order (using SKIP −n).

CDOW(<date variable>) — *Name of the day of the week*

Determine the day of the week from the variable.

EXAMPLE:

If the current date is 01/01/85, then

```
. ? CDOW(DATE( ))
```

returns the value

```
Tuesday
```

CHR(<decimal integer numeric expression>) — *Character from ASCII code*

Return the ASCII character whose code is given by the decimal numeric expression.

EXAMPLE:

In order to reset my printer so that it changes to compressed print mode, I use the code:

```
SET DEVICE TO PRINT
@ 0,0 SAY CHR(15)
```

CMONTH(<date variable>) — *Name of the month*

Returns the name of the month indicated by the date variable.

EXAMPLE:

If the system date is 01/01/85, then

```
. ? CMONTH(DATE( ))
```

will return the value

```
January
```

COL( ) — *Determine column position of cursor*

Returns the number of the column of the cursor on the screen. It is intended for use by a program (.PRG file) to facilitate screen input and output. Once the value has been returned by this function, you can store it in a memory variable in the normal manner.

EXAMPLE:

```
STORE COL( ) TO MYCOLUMN
```

CTOD(<string>) — *Convert character string to a date*

This function is used to convert a character string of the form "MM/DD/YY" or of the form "MM/DD/YYYY" to a variable of type date. If only two digits are used for the year, then the 20th century is assumed. If the year is given as 87, then the year 1987 is assumed.

EXAMPLE:

```
. STORE "01/01/85" TO MEMDATE
. STORE CTOD(MEMDATE) TO REALDATE
```

or

```
. STORE CTOD("01/01/85") TO REALDATE
. ? CMONTH(REALDATE)
January
```

EXAMPLE 2:

```
STORE CTOD(" / / ") TO MEMDATE
```

is a convenient way to create a blank date.

DATE( ) — *The system date*

Returns the system date in the form MM/DD/YY.

EXAMPLE:

```
. ? DATE( )
01/01/87
```

DAY(<date variable>) — *Number of the day of the month*

Returns the day of the week in the form of an integer.

EXAMPLE:

If the system date is 01/10/87, then

```
. ? DAY(DATE( ))
```

displays the value

```
10
```

DBF( ) — *Identify the current database*

Returns the name of the database currently in USE in the current work area.

EXAMPLE:

```
. ? DBF( )
```

will return

```
c:x.dbf
```

if the database file named x.dbf is the one currently in use.

DELETED( ) — *Determine deletion status of current record*

Tests the current record to see if it has been marked for deletion. If so, returns the value .T.; else it returns the value .F. . DELETED( ) corresponds to the dBASE II function *.

EXAMPLE:

To list all the records in the database that have been marked for deletion.

```
. DISPLAY ALL FOR DELETED( )
```

DISKSPACE( ) — *Amount of free space on the disk*

If there is a possibility of running out of room when you write to the disk, use this function to determine the amount of room remaining on the default disk drive before actually writing to the disk.

EXAMPLE:

```
IF DISKSPACE < needed
     . ? "print error message"
ELSE
     * proceed with operation here
ENDIF
```

DOW(<date variable>) — *Number of the day of the week*

Returns the day of the week indicated by the date variable as an integer. 1 is used for Sunday, 2 for Monday, etc.

EXAMPLE:

If the current date is 01/01/87, then

```
. ? DOW(DATE( ))
```

returns the value

```
     5
```

DTOC(<date variable>) — *Convert date to character string*

This is the reverse of the CTOD function, as given above. It changes a date variable to a character string of length 8, with the form MM/DD/YY, even if the year is greater than or equal to 2000. If the year is 2001, then you can use the YEAR function to recover the correct year.

EXAMPLE 1:

```
@ 10,5 SAY "TODAY'S DATE:" + DTOC(DATE( ))
```

EXAMPLE 2:

```
USE INCOME
INDEX ON GLACCTNO + DTOC(INCDATE)
```

EOF( ) — *Test for the end of the file*

If the currency pointer is past the last record in the file, returns the value .T.; else it returns the value .F. . This function is used to determine when a sequential scan of the current database file has passed the last record.

EXAMPLE:

If the current record is the last one in the file, then

```
. ? EOF( )
.F.
. SKIP 1
. ? EOF( )
.T.
```

ERROR( ) — *The error number*

If an error was trapped by an ON ERROR statement, then use this function to return the number of the error. The error number is always an integer. The use of the ON ERROR statement, the ERROR function, and the MESSAGE( ) function can be used to aid in debugging.

EXP(<numeric expression>) — *Exponential*

Returns the value of e raised to the power of the value of the numeric expression (real or integer).

EXAMPLE:

```
. ? EXP(1)
2.72
. STORE 1 TO X
. ? EXP(X)
2.72
. ? EXP(1.0)
2.72
```

FIELD(<integer expression>) — *The name of the field*

The name of the field in the current database file that is indicated by the integer expression is returned in uppercase letters. If the expression is less than 1 or greater than the actual number of fields in the database file, then the NULL string is returned.

EXAMPLE:

```
. ? FIELD(1)
GLRACCTNO
```

FILE('<file name>') or FILE("<file name>") — *Test for existence of a file*

Determine if the named file exists. The file name can be prefixed by both a drive and a path name. For example, TEST.DBF and A:\MYDIR\TEST.DBF are both valid file names. This function returns the value .T. if the file is on the disk; else it returns the value .F. .

FKLABEL(<integer expression>) — *System designator for function key*

Returns the name used by your computer to identify the indicated function key. If your computer uses identifiers that are nonnumeric, you can use this function, in conjunction with SET FUNCTION, to program your own function keys.

EXAMPLE:

On my computer, the values in Table 2.3 were returned:

TABLE 2.3

INTEGER	NAME RETURNED
1	F2
2	F3
3	F4
4	F5
5	F6
6	F7
7	F8
8	F9
9	F10

F1, the HELP key, is not accessible in this manner.

```
. SET FUNCTION FKLABEL(1) TO "LIST ALL OFF;"
```

FKMAX( ) — *Count the number of programmable function keys*

EXAMPLE:

```
. ? FKMAX( )
 9
```

FOUND( ) — *Determine if last search was successful*

If the last FIND, SEEK, LOCATE, or CONTINUE was successful, returns the value .T.; otherwise it returns the value .F. .

EXAMPLE:

```
USE EMPLOYEE INDEX EMPNO
CLEAR
STORE SPACE(3) TO MEMNUM
@ 1,1 SAY "ENTER THE NUMBER OF THE EMPLOYEE" GET ;
  MEMNUM
READ
SEEK MEMNUM
IF FOUND( )
          * process the record
```

```
ELSE
        @ 3,0 SAY "NO RECORD ON FILE FOR THIS NUMBER"
        WAIT
ENDIF
```

GETENV(<string expression>) — *Get the value of indicated environment variable*

Make <string expression> the name of an environment variable to obtain its value.

EXAMPLE:

```
. ? GETENV("PATH")
```

will return the name of the current path.

IIF(<logical expression>, <true expression>, <false expression>) — *Return one of two values, depending on the truth value of the <logical expression>*

This is the functional equivalent of the IF-THEN-ELSE statement in dBASE III Plus. It can be used interactively and in places where a function, but not a multiple line statement, can be used. When the <logical expression> evaluates to .T., then the value of <true expression> is returned, otherwise the value of <false expression> is returned. Since IIF is a function, it can return only one kind (type) of value, so the value of the <true expression> and the value of the <false expression> must have the same data type.

Note:
Ashton-Tate states that the use of the IIF function in a program is faster than the use of the corresponding IF statement, but it appears that the loss of readability makes this use of the IIF function undesirable.

EXAMPLE:

```
IIF(INCDATE < CTOD("01/01/87"), CTOD("  /  /  "), INCDATE)
```

INKEY( ) — *The identifier of the key that was pressed last*

The value returned is an integer between 0 and 255. If there is anything in the type-ahead buffer, the identifier of the next character in that buffer will be returned, and that character is then deleted from the buffer. The value 0 is returned if there is no "next" character. This function is particularly useful for examining the value of a special (non-ASCII) keystroke. Table 2.4 gives the correspondence between the keystrokes and the values returned by the INKEY function.

INT(<numeric expression>) — *Discard fractional portion*

Truncate the number and obtain an integer.

TABLE 2.4

KEYSTROKE	ALTERNATE KEYSTROKE	VALUE RETURNED
→	CTRL-D	4
←	CTRL-S	19
↑	CTRL-E	5
↓	CTRL-X	24
CTRL- →	CTRL-B	2
CTRL- ←	CTRL-Z	26
INS	CTRL-V	22
DEL	CTRL-G	7
HOME	CTRL-A	1
END	CTRL-F	6
PGUP	CTRL-R	18
PGDN	CTRL-C	3
HOME	CTRL-]	29
END	CTRL-W	23
CTRL-PGUP	CTRL --	31
CTRL-PGDN	CTRL- ↑	30

Note the similarity between many of these keystrokes and the WordStar keystrokes.

Note:

If CTRL-S or ← (left arrow) is intercepted by your system as a command to stop output to the screen, then use the command SET ESCAPE OFF to avoid this problem.

EXAMPLE:

```
STORE 123.4 TO X
STORE INT(X) TO Y
```

will place the value 123 in Y.

ISALPHA(<char string>) – *Determine if string starts with a letter*

Returns .T. if first character is a letter; otherwise it returns .F. .

EXAMPLES:

```
. ? ISALPHA("A1")
.T.
. ? ISALPHA("a1")
.T.
. ? ISALPHA("1")
.F.
```

ISCOLOR( ) – *Determine color capability of computer*

Returns .T. if a color board is installed; otherwise it returns .F. .

Note:
This function can be useful if you are writing a system that may be run on a number of different computers. If the computer has color capability, then you may wish to present all the screen displays in color mode. If the computer does not have color capability, then you would probably want to present all the screen displays in monochrome mode. *Caution*: Some computers have a color board installed, but use a monochrome monitor. As a result, you might wish to let the user decide on the type of display, rather than use the ISCOLOR function.

EXAMPLE:

```
IF ISCOLOR( )
     SET COLOR TO GR+,N/W
ELSE
     SET COLOR TO W
ENDIF
```

ISLOWER(<char string>) — *Determine if string starts with a lowercase letter*

Returns .T. if the string starts with a lowercase letter; otherwise it returns .F. .

EXAMPLES:

```
. ? ISLOWER("A1")
.F.
. ? ISLOWER("a1")
.T.
. ? ISLOWER("123")
.F.
```

ISUPPER(<char string>) — *Determine if string starts with an uppercase letter*

Returns .T. if the string starts with an uppercase letter; otherwise returns .F. .

EXAMPLES:

```
. ? ISUPPER("A1")
.T.
. ? ISUPPER("a1")
.F.
. ? ISUPPER("123")
.F.
```

LEFT(<char string>, <length>) — *Extract characters from the left end of a string*

Returns a copy of the first <length> characters in <char string>. If <length> is less than or equal to 0, then the NULL string is returned. If <length> is greater than the number of characters in the string, then all <char string> is returned.

EXAMPLES:

```
. ? LEFT("ABC",1)
A
. ? LEFT("ABC", 4)
ABC
```

LEN(<char string>) – *Determine the length of a string*

Returns the length of the character string. If <char string> is null, then the value 0 is returned.

EXAMPLE:

Assume that X is a memory variable, that FIELDX is a character string field in a database file, and that FIELDX has been defined to have length (size) 10. Then

```
STORE "ABCD" TO X
. ? LEN(X)
```

will print 4 on the screen, but

```
STORE "ABCD" TO FIELDX
. ? LEN(FIELDX)
```

will print 10 on the screen, since the actual contents of FIELDX is "ABCD   ", i.e., the letters ABCD followed by six spaces.

LOG(<numeric expression>) – *Natural logarithm*

Returns the natural logarithm of the numeric expression. This function is the inverse of the EXP function.

LOWER(<string>) – *Convert characters in string to lowercase*

Converts all the uppercase characters in the string to lowercase.

EXAMPLE:

```
. STORE "ABC" TO X
. ? LOWER(X)
 abc
```

LTRIM(<char string>) – *Remove leading blanks*

Removes the leading blanks from a character string and returns a new character string.

Note:
If you convert a number to a character string, you may find that dBASE has inserted leading blanks at the left of the new string. Use this function to remove them.

EXAMPLES:

```
STORE 25.7 TO X
STORE STR(X,10,1) TO Y
. ? Y
          25.7
. ? LEN(Y)
 10
STORE LTRIM(STR(X,10,1)) TO Z
. ? Z
 25.7
. ? LEN(Z)
 4
```

LUPDATE( ) – *Get date that the current database was last updated*

The value returned is a constant of type date.

MAX(<number>, <number>) – *Return the larger of two numbers*

The value returned is the larger of the two values.

MESSAGE( ) – *Get the error message*

If an error occurs and is trapped by an ON ERROR statement, you can use this function to obtain the error message in the form of a character string. Once obtained, you can use it as you would any character string.

MIN(<number>, <number>) – *Return the smaller of two values*

The value returned is the smaller of the two values.

MOD(<number>, <modulus>) – *Return the remainder*

The remainder obtained from the division of <number> by <modulus> is returned.

Note 1:
If <modulus> has the value 0, then dBASE returns asterisks as the value of the number.

Note 2:
If <modulus> is negative, then the value return by the function is negative.

Note 3:
This function can be used to facilitate conversion from one type of measurement to another.

EXAMPLE:

To convert from inches to feet and inches, use the following:

```
@ 1,1 SAY "ENTER THE MEASUREMENT IN INCHES" GET ;
  MEASUREMNT
READ
STORE INT(MEASUREMNT,12) TO FEET
STORE MOD(MEASUREMNT,12) TO INCHES
```

MONTH(<date variable>) – *Number of the month*

Returns the month of the year in the form of an integer.

EXAMPLE:

```
STORE CTOD(" / / ") TO MEMDATE
CLEAR
@ 1,1 SAY "ENTER THE DATE" GET MEMDATE
READ
STORE MONTH(MEMDATE) TO NUMMONTH
```

NDX(<integer>) – *Get the name of the indicated index file*

Returns the name of the indicated index file. The index files are recorded by dBASE and can be displayed using the DISPLAY STATUS command. For a given database file, the name of the nth index in this list corresponds to the name returned by the NDX function with a value of n for the <integer>. The value of <integer> must be between 1 and 7. If the value of <integer> is greater than the number of active indexes for the current database, then the NULL string is returned.

OS( ) – *Get the name of the operating system*

You might wish to test the name of the operating system to determine if it is MS DOS or another system.

EXAMPLE:

```
. ? OS( )
DOS 3.1
```

PCOL( ) — *Current column position of printer*

Returns the number of the last (current) column printed. Used to facilitate certain operations involving the printer. Designed to be used by a program.

PROW( ) — *Current row position of printer*

Returns the number of the last (current) row printed. Used to facilitate certain operations involving the printer. Designed to be used by a program.

READKEY( ) — *Get identifier of key used to exit from editing*

Returns an integer that identifies the key pressed to exit from full-screen editing.

Note:
If the exit was performed without changing the data displayed on the screen, then the value returned is between 0 and 36. If data was changed, then the value returned is between 256 (0 + 256) and 292 (36 + 256). The correspondence between keystrokes and the values returned by the READKEY function are given in the following table. Note the close relationship with the WordStar keystrokes, as also shown in Table 2.5.

RECCOUNT( ) — *Count the records in the current database*

If the file is empty, then the value 0 is returned. All the records in the file are counted, even deleted and filtered records.

RECNO( ) — *Number of the current record of current database*

Return the number of the current database record.

EXAMPLE:

If the database file EMPLOYEE is not empty,

```
. USE EMPLOYEE
. ? RECNO( )
```

TABLE 2.5

KEYSTROKE	ALTERNATE KEYSTROKE	VALUE
←	CTRL-S	0
→	CTRL-D	1
HOME	CTRL-A	2
END	CTRL-F	3
↑	CTRL-E/CTRL-K	4
↓	CTRL-X/CTRL-J	5
PGUP	CTRL-R	6
PGDN	CTRL-C	7
CTRL- ←	CTRL-Z	8
CTRL- →	CTRL-B	9
	CTRL-U	10
	CTRL-N	11
ESC	CTRL-Q	12
(This code is not used)		13
CTRL-END	CTRL-W	14
	CTRL-M	15
RETURN		16
CTRL-HOME	CTRL-]	33
CTRL-PGUP	CTRL- -	34
CTRL-PGDN	CTRL- ↑	35
F1		36
INS	CTRL-V	None
DEL	CTRL-G	None

will cause the number 1 to be displayed on the screen, indicating that the current record number of the database file currently in use is 1.

Warning:
If the file is empty,

```
. ? RECNO( )
```

will still return the number 1, not the expected value of 0. This means that the RECNO function cannot be used to determine the success or failure of an operation or whether a file is empty. Use FOUND( ) or EOF( ), not RECNO( ), to test for the success of a SEEK.

In dBASE II, this was the # function.

RECSIZE( ) — *Get size of record in current database*

If there is no current database, then the value 0 is returned.

REPLICATE(<char string>, <integer>) — *Duplicate a string*

A new character string is created that consists of <char string> duplicated <integer> times.

EXAMPLE:

```
STORE 5 TO X
. ? REPLICATE ("*", X)
```

Note:
Since the LIST function can employ functions in the variable list, this function can be used to produce a bar graph.

EXAMPLE:

If a database file contains a field named FREQ, and you wish to graph the values of FREQ, one bar for each record in the database file, use a statement of the form:

```
LIST ALL FREQ, REPLICATE("*", FREQ)
```

RIGHT(<char string>, <length>) — *Extract characters from the right end of a string*

Returns a copy of the last <length> characters in <char string>. If <length> is less than or equal to 0, then the NULL string is returned. If <length> is greater than the number of characters in the string, then all <char string> is returned. In combination with LTRIM, this function can be used to insert asterisks as leading characters when checks are printed.

EXAMPLE:

```
STORE REPLICATE("*",10) TO X
@ ROW,COL SAY RIGHT(X+LTRIM(STR(VALUE,10,2)), 10)
```

might produce the output

```
***1568.50
```

ROUND(<numeric expression, integer>) — *Round off a number*

Rounds the numeric expression to <integer> decimal places. If <integer> is a negative number, then the number is converted to an integer and the decimal place is moved to the left <integer> places.

WARNING:
The results of rounding a negative number are not what is normally expected.

EXAMPLES:

```
. ? ROUND(1.46,1)
 1.50
. ? ROUND(-1.46,1)
 -1.40
. ? ROUND(154.5,-2)
 200.0
```

ROW( ) — *Determine current row of cursor*

Determine the number of the row in which the cursor is located. Designed to be used by a program.

RTRIM(<char string>) — *Remove trailing blanks*

Remove the trailing blanks from a character string and return a new character string.

Note:
This function is identical in function to the TRIM function.

SPACE(<numeric expression>) — *Create a blank character string*

Creates a character string containing only blanks with the length specified by the numeric expression. If the numeric expression is not an integer, the decimal part is discarded when determining the length of the string.

Note:
It is recommended that you use this function to generate character strings that contain blanks, since you have good control over the exact length of the string. If you use something of the form

```
STORE "      " TO X
```

then you must always count the number of blanks in the string constant every time that you debug or change your program. A statement of the form

```
STORE SPACE(4) TO X
```

clearly simplifies maintenance of the programs.

EXAMPLE:

```
. STORE SPACE(25) TO NEWSTRING
. ? LEN(NEWSTRING)
 25
. STORE SPACE(25.8) TO NEWSTRING
? LEN(NEWSTRING)
 25
```

SQRT(<positive numeric expression>) — *Square root*

Return the square root of the numeric expression.

EXAMPLE:

```
. ? SQRT(9)
 3.00
. ? SQRT(3.14159)
 1.77245
```

STR(<numeric exp>[,<length>][,<decimal>]) — *Convert a numeric expression to a character string*

If neither the <length> nor the <decimal> is specified, then the result of this function is a character string of length 10 that consists of the rounded integer part of the <numeric exp>. If <decimal> is not specified, then the number is always rounded to an integer before it is converted to a character string. If the specified <length> is too small to hold the result, then the new string will be filled with asterisks (*). The parameter <decimal> determines how many of the digits to the right of the decimal will be preserved.

Note:
This function is often used to convert a number to a character string when performing output.

EXAMPLE 1:

```
@ 50,1 SAY "PAGENO:"+STR(PAGENO,3)
```

EXAMPLE 2:

```
. STORE 123.4 TO X
. STORE STR(X,5,1) TO Y
```

will place "123.4" into the location Y.

EXAMPLE 3:

```
. STORE 123.4 TO X
. ? STR(X,1)
*
```

STUFF(<char string1>,<starting position>,<length>,<char string2>) — *Insert a substring into a character string*

All the characters in <char string2> are inserted into <char string1> immediately before the character in the position number <starting position>. The parameter <length> indicates the number of characters in <char string1> that are to be removed when the insertion takes place. If <length> does not equal

LEN(<char string2>), then the string returned by STUFF will have a length different from the length of the original string.

Note:
The original string is not changed by the STUFF function unless you specifically perform this operation with an assignment statement similar to

X = STUFF(X,N1,N2,Y) .

EXAMPLE 1 (REPLACEMENT WITH A STRING OF THE SAME LENGTH):

```
. ? STUFF("ABC",2,1,"X")
AXC
```

EXAMPLE 2 (REPLACEMENT WITH A STRING OF A DIFFERENT LENGTH):

```
. ? STUFF("ABC",2,1,"XY")
AXYC
```

EXAMPLE 3 (DELETION OF A SUBSTRING):

```
. ? STUFF("ABC",2,1," ")
AC
```

EXAMPLE 4 (INSERTION OF A SUBSTRING):

```
. ? STUFF("ABC",2,0,"X")
AXBC
```

SUBSTR(<string>,<starting position>,[<length>]) — *Substring function*

Obtains from <string> a copy of the substring that starts in <starting position> and has length <length>. If <length> is omitted, the substring will start at the indicated position and continue through to the last character of <string>. If <length> is greater than the number of characters in <string> from the <starting position> to the end of the string, then the length of the resultant string will be determined by the actual number of characters obtained from <string>. In dBASE II, this function was the $ substring function.

EXAMPLE:

```
STORE "ABCD" to X
STORE SUBSTR(X,2,2) TO Y
```

will place the value "BC" in Y.

Note:
The function cannot be used as a pseudovariable, i.e., it cannot be used in the following manner:

STORE "A" TO SUBSTR(X,3,1).

To accomplish this task, use the STUFF function.

TIME( ) — *System time*

Returns the system time in the form HH:MM:SS.

TRANSFORM(<char string>, <"PICTURE format">) — *Specify a PICTURE format*

Use this function to specify a character string and then convert it to the desired format for proper output, in those situations where an @ . . SAY statement is not appropriate. For example, use it in ?, ??, DISPLAY, LABEL, LIST, and REPORT statements. Remember to delimit the PICTURE format as you would in an @ . . SAY statement.

EXAMPLE:

```
. LIST ALL NAME, TRANSFORM(SALARY,"#,###,###.##")
```

TRIM(<string>) — *Remove trailing blanks*

Remove the blanks at the end of the <string>. The length of the new string will be reduced by 1 for each blank removed from the end of the <string>. If the original string consisted entirely of blanks, then the length of the TRIMmed string will be 0.

EXAMPLES:

```
. STORE ("A    ") TO B
. ? LEN(B)
5
. ? LEN(TRIM(B))
1
. STORE SPACE(20) TO A
. ? LEN(TRIM(A))
```

```
0
. STORE TRIM("A       ")+TRIM("B       ") TO C
. ? LEN(C)
2
```

Assume that LASTNAME and FIRSTNAME are fields in a database file and that they have sizes 15 and 10, respectively. If you execute the following code:

```
REPLACE LASTNAME WITH "SMITH", FIRSTNAME WITH "TOM"
```

then

```
? LASTNAME+", "+FIRSTNAME
```

will cause:

```
SMITH          , TOM
```

to be printed on the screen.

```
? TRIM(LASTNAME)+", "+FIRSTNAME
```

will cause:

```
SMITH, TOM
```

to be printed on the screen.

TYPE(<expression>) — *Determine the data type of the expression*

This function is used to determine the type of the data in the <expression>. The data types are:

C: Character

D: Date

L: Logical (Boolean)

M: Memo

N: Numeric

U: Undefined

The <expression> must always be delimited. The delimiters may be single quotes, double quotes, or brackets([ ]). The use of the delimiters is shown by the following: '<expression>', "<expression>" and [<expression>]. An expression might be undefined if it contains a variable that is undefined. For example, if A is a memory variable that has never been defined (nothing has been placed into A), then TYPE('A') would return the value U.

Note:
This function cannot be used to evaluate the data type of a macro.

EXAMPLES:

```
. STORE 1 TO X
. ? TYPE('X')
N
. ? TYPE("X")
N
. ? TYPE([X])
N
. ? TYPE('Y')
U
. ? TYPE("1+3")
N
. ? TYPE(["A"])
C
. STORE CTOD("01/01/87") TO X
. ? TYPE("X")
D
```

UPPER(<char string>) — *Convert to uppercase*

All the characters in the string are converted to uppercase.

EXAMPLE:

```
. ? STORE "abc" TO X
. ? UPPER(X)
ABC
```

VAL(<char string>) — *Convert numeric string to integer*

The VAL and macro (&) functions can be used to convert a numeric string to a number. If any of the leading characters in the string are neither numeric nor blank, then the value 0 is returned. If a nonnumeric character is embedded within the number, then everything from the position of the nonnumeric character to the right is ignored. The precise format of the number generated by the VAL function is determined by the SET DECIMALS statement. In general, the VAL function rounds the generated number to the number of decimal places indicated by the SET DECIMALS statement.

EXAMPLES:

```
. STORE 123.45 TO X
. STORE STR(123.4,6,2) TO Y
. ? &Y
123.45
. ? VAL(Y)
123.45
```

VERSION( ) — *Version number of dBASE III Plus in use*

EXAMPLE:

```
. VERSION( )
dBASE III Plus version 1.2
```

YEAR(<date variable>) — *Return the number of the year*

This function will return a four-digit year number.

EXAMPLE:

```
. ? YEAR(DATE( ))
1987
```

2.1.4 Mathematical and Logical Operators

The mathematical operators are:

+	Addition
−	Subtraction
*	Multiplication
/	Division
** or ^	Exponentiation
( )	Parentheses

The relational operators are:

<	Less than
>	Greater than
=	Equal
< > or #	Not equal
< =	Less than or equal
> =	Greater than or equal

The logical operators are:

.AND.	And
.OR.	Or
.NOT.	Not
( )	Parentheses

The string operators are:

+	String concatenation
−	String concatenation, with movement of blanks to the end of the string
$	Substring comparison. A$B is true if A = B or A is contained in B.

Precedence of the arithmetic operators:

1. Unary + or −
2. Exponentiation
3. Multiplication and division
4. Addition and subtraction

Precedence of the logical operators:

1. .NOT.
2. .AND.
3. .OR.

Precedence of the operator types:

1. Arithmetic and string
2. Relational
3. Logical

Evaluation of expressions is performed left to right, and expressions within parentheses are performed first.

2.2 LOGICAL DESCRIPTIONS OF THE LANGUAGE ELEMENTS

Summary of Commands

The summary of commands is given in Table 2.6.

TABLE 2.6 Command Table

CATEGORY	COMMAND	DESCRIPTION
Arithmetic	AVERAGE	Compute arithmetic mean
	COUNT	Count the number of records
	SUM	Compute the sum of database fields
Assembly Language Interface	CALL	Execute a LOADed binary file
	LOAD	Place a binary file in memory
Assistance	ASSIST	Menu help for commands
	DIR	Names of files on current disk
	DISPLAY MEMORY	Names and contents of memory variables
	DISPLAY STATUS	Current information on databases, files, and indexes
	DISPLAY STRUCTURE	Structure of current database
	HELP	Explain dBASE III Plus commands
Database Operations	CLEAR ALL	Close all databases
	CLOSE	Close a file
	COPY	Copy a database
	COPY FILE	Copy any kind of file
	COPY STRUCTURE	Create new database with same structure
	CREATE	Create a database
	DELETE	Mark records for later removal
	ERASE	Delete files from directory
	EXPORT	Copy from a database to a PFS file

CATEGORY	COMMAND	DESCRIPTION
	IMPORT	Copy from a PFS file to a database
	JOIN	A relational database command; combines fields from two records to form a third record
	MODIFY STRUCTURE	Change the structure of a database
	PACK	Physically remove DELETEd records
	RECALL	Reinstate records marked for deletion
	RENAME	Change the name of a file
	SELECT	Make one of up to 10 database files the current file
	SORT	Create a sorted version of the database
	TOTAL	Create a summary database
	USE	Specify a database for use
	ZAP	Remove all records from current database
Data Display	@ . . SAY	Display formatted output
	@ . . TO	Draw or erase box or line
	?	Unformatted output on next line
	??	Unformatted output on current line
	BROWSE	Display or edit records
	DISPLAY	Display field names and contents
	LABEL	Print labels
	LIST	Same as DISPLAY, but no output pause
	REPORT	Produce a report
	TEXT	Output a block of text
Debugging	DISPLAY HISTORY	Display contents of HISTORY file
	LIST HISTORY	Display contents of HISTORY file
	RESUME	Continue executive of program
	SET DEBUG	Print output from SET ECHO
	SET DOHISTORY	Record commands in HISTORY file
	SET ECHO	Echo commands on screen

CATEGORY	COMMAND	DESCRIPTION
	SET HISTORY	Record commands or set file size
	SET PRINT	Echo output from TALK to printer
	SET STEP	Pause after each command
	SET TALK	Display results of a number of dBASE III Plus commands
	SUSPEND	Suspend execution of program
Devices	CLEAR	Erase the screen
	EJECT	Send a form feed to the printer
Editing of Database Records	BROWSE	Display and edit records
	CHANGE	Edit specified fields
	EDIT	Edit contents of record
	REPLACE	Change contents of database fields
	UPDATE	Batch modification of database contents
Event Processing	ON ERROR	Take action if error
	ON ESCAPE	Take action if ESC pressed
	ON KEY	Take action on keystroke
Indexes	INDEX	Create an index
	REINDEX	Rebuild index file
Memory Variables	CLEAR ALL	Initialize system
	CLEAR MEMORY	Erase all memory variables
	DISPLAY MEMORY	Display names and contents of all memory variables
	RELEASE	Erase selected memory variables
	RESTORE	Retrieve memory variables from a save file
	SAVE	Save memory variables in a file
Other Files	COPY FILE	Copy any kind of file
	CREATE LABEL	Create or edit a label form file
	CREATE QUERY	Create a filter condition

CATEGORY	COMMAND	DESCRIPTION
	CREATE REPORT	Create or edit a report form file
	CREATE SCREEN	Create a screen format file
	CREATE VIEW	Create a linkage between files
	MODIFY COMMAND	Create or edit a program
	MODIFY LABEL	Create or edit a label form file
	MODIFY QUERY	Modify a filter condition
	MODIFY REPORT	Create or edit a report form file
	MODIFY SCREEN	Modify a screen format file
	MODIFY VIEW	Modify a linkage between files
Parameter Control	SET the following parameters ON, OFF, or to specific values:	
	ALTERNATE	Use to save output in file
	BELL	ON/OFF during entry of data
	CARRY	Copy contents from last record
	CATALOG	Manipulate a named collection of files
	CENTURY	Display year as four digits
	COLOR	Screen attributes
	CONFIRM	Auto-skip
	CONSOLE	Screen
	DATE	Determine date format
	DEBUG	Copy results of ECHO to printer
	DECIMALS	Specify decimal places for SQRT, LOG, and EXP
	DEFAULT	Specify default disk drive
	DELETED	Skip or process records marked for deletion
	DELIMITERS	Specifies boundary markers for full-screen editing
	DEVICE	Specify that output goes to screen or to printer
	DOHISTORY	Record in HISTORY file

CATEGORY	COMMAND	DESCRIPTION
	ECHO	Echo of commands being executed
	ESCAPE	Abort execution of current process
	EXACT	Equality of two strings requires exact match if ON, partial match if OFF
	FIELDS	Accessibility of fields
	FILTER	Ignore records that do not meet specified conditions
	FIXED	Specify the number of decimal places for all numeric operations as given in the SET DECIMALS command
	FORMAT	Use the format given in a file
	FUNCTION	Set a function key value
	HEADING	Use column headings for AVERAGE, DISPLAY, LIST, and SUM
	HELP	Display help message in case of syntax error
	HISTORY	Record commands or set file size
	INDEX	Specify the current indexes
	INTENSITY	Reverse video
	MARGIN	Adjust the left-hand margin
	MEMOWIDTH	Set output width for memo field
	MENUS	Display full-screen editing menu if appropriate to task
	MESSAGE	Display message beneath status bar
	ORDER	Change controlling index
	PATH	Specify paths to be searched if desired file is not in directory
	PRINT	Echo output other than from @ . . SAY command to printer
	PRINTER	Redirect printer output
	PROCEDURE	Open a procedure file
	RELATION	Link two database files
	SAFETY	Warn if file will be overwritten or otherwise destroyed

CATEGORY	COMMAND	DESCRIPTION
	SCOREBOARD	Display or hide status messages
	STATUS	Display or hide status bar
	STEP	Execute program one line at a time
	TALK	Display results of a number of dBASE III Plus commands
	TITLE	Use or suppress catalog prompt
	TYPEAHEAD	Set number of characters in buffer
	UNIQUE	Used to create an index file with unique index values; used with the INDEX ON command
	VIEW	Open a view file
Positioning of Currency Pointer	CONTINUE	Set pointer to the next record that satisfies the condition in the latest LOCATE command
	FIND	Set pointer to first record with matching index value; index must be character string or number
	GO/GOTO	Set pointer to specified record
	LOCATE	Set pointer to record satisfying a given condition
	SEEK	Set pointer to the first record with matching index value; index may be character string or numeric
	SKIP	Advance or back up pointer
Programming	&&	Comment to end of line
	ACCEPT	Input character string from screen to memory variable
	CANCEL	Abort execution of program
	DO	Execute a program or procedure
	DO CASE	Start a case statement
	DO WHILE	Start a loop
	EXIT	Leave a loop and go to the line immediately following the loop
	IF	The IF-THEN-ELSE
	INPUT	Enter data of various types into memory variable

CATEGORY	COMMAND	DESCRIPTION
	LOOP	Immediately advance to next ENDDO; skip remainder of statements in loop
	NOTE	Comment
	PARAMETERS	Specify the parameter list for a procedure
	PRIVATE	Hide memory variables (make variables local)
	PROCEDURE	Identify the beginning of a subroutine
	PUBLIC	Make memory variables global
	QUIT	Close all files and exit from dBASE III Plus
	READ	Used with @ . . GET
	RETRY	Exit and execute procedure again
	RETURN	End a program or procedure
	RUN	Executes a non-dBASE III program
	STORE	Create a memory variable and enter data into it
	WAIT	Suspend program execution until a key is pressed
Record Insertion	APPEND	Add record to end of database
	INSERT	Insert record into the specified position in the database

Scope of Commands

There are three possible scopes:

1. ALL: all records in the database file
2. NEXT n: the next n records, starting with current
3. RECORD n: nth record only

2.3. THE LANGUAGE ELEMENTS

Note:
In the following language element descriptions, the current database is the one in USE. Nevertheless, it is possible to have up to ten databases open at one time. When working with more than one database, only one is in USE (the current one) at a time. In the descriptions of the elements,

[X] means that X is an optional element of the statement and <X> means that, when the statement is used, the programmer replaces <X> with an appropriate constant or variable. For example,

```
USE <database file> [INDEX <index file>]
```

could appear in a program as:

```
USE EMPLOYEE
```

since the INDEX clause is optional, or as

```
USE EMPLOYEE INDEX EMPNO
```

An ALIAS is an additional name for a database file. The ability to give a file an alias name is very useful to the programmer. For example, suppose that you have two database files in use and that there is a field in each of the two files with a common name. If you wish to unambiguously identify a specific field to work with, you must also identify the database file concerned. This can be done using an alias automatically assigned to the file when it was selected for use in your program.

When a SELECT statement is executed in conjunction with a USE statement, you assign a file to a specific work area. Assume that you have two database files, MYFILE1.DBF and MYFILE2.DBF, and that each contains a field called TEST. Then

```
SELECT 1
USE MYFILE1
SELECT 2
USE MYFILE2
```

assigns MYFILE1.DBF to the user work area 1 and assigns MYFILE2.DBF to user work area 2. To refer to the field named TEST in MYFILE1.DBF, use the extended name

```
A->TEST
```

The extended name is formed from the concatenation of three elements: The alias of the file (actually the alias of the work area), the symbol "->" and the name of the field.

You, as the user of the system, may also assign an alias to a database file. See the USE command later in this section. The alias that you assign may not be used for the above purpose (unambiguous reference). It is used to give an alternate name to a database file for convenience of programming.

Record Selection Criteria: Scope and Condition

In the following <scope> means that you may select any of the possible choices for a scope and FOR/WHILE <condition> means that you may select an appropriate <condition> to use with the word FOR and/or with the word WHILE. If you use both the FOR and the WHILE options, each option has its own <condition>. A FOR condition means that the operation will continue from the first record of the <scope> until the end of the <scope>, with records selected that satisfy the <condition>. A WHILE condition means that the operation will continue from the first record of the <scope> until the <condition> is no longer true. In dBASE III Plus, both the FOR and the WHILE may be used in the same statement. The default for the <scope> varies with the command, but the default, if there is one, is either NEXT 1 or ALL. If the FOR/WHILE option is selected, then the default <scope> is ALL.

The choices for the scope of an operation are:

1. ALL—Examine all the records in the database.
2. NEXT <integer>—Examine the next <integer> records.
3. RECORD <integer>—Examine only the one record with the number <integer>.
4. REST—Examine all the records from the current one to the end of the database.

EXAMPLE 1:

```
COUNT NEXT 5 FOR A > 1
```

means that a count of the next 5 records (the scope) in the database that satisfy the additional restriction that the value of the field A must be greater than 1 (the condition) is desired.

EXAMPLE 2:

```
COUNT ALL WHILE A > 1
```

means that a count of all the records (the scope) in the database until the value of the field A is not greater than 1 (the condition) is desired.

EXAMPLE 3:

```
LIST
LIST ALL
LIST NEXT 3
LIST RECORD 1
LIST REST
```

Output to the Printer

In the DISPLAY, LIST, and REPORT commands, the TO PRINT option means that the output from the command will be directed to your printer. You have the responsibility to make sure that your printer is turned on and ready to accept output before this option is used. You can also cause output to go to the printer through the use of the ^P toggle.

The Skeleton

A <skeleton> is used to select one or more file or memory variable names. The "?" is used as a wild card character for a specific name character and the "*" is used as a wild card character for one or more name characters. The use of the <skeleton> is determined from the context. In the DIR command, the <skeleton> refers to one or more files. In the SAVE command, the <skeleton> refers to one or more memory variables. See Table 2.7 for use of the <skeleton>:

Standard Character String Delimiters

The delimiters for character strings in dBASE III Plus are the double quote ("), the single quote (') and brackets ([ ]). You may use any of them, as long as they are used in pairs.

Statements and Commands

In programming, the term *command* usually refers to an order given interactively, and the term *statement* refers to a line of a program. In dBASE III Plus all the elements of the language can be used as lines of a program and the language elements that can be entered on one (possibly long) line can be used interactively. Since the distinction between a command and a statement tends to blur in dBASE III Plus, the terms *command* and *statement* are used interchangeably in this book. When examples are used to illustrate the use of a command (statement),

TABLE 2.7

SKELETON	MEANING
.	All files on the disk.
?T*.*	All file names that have T in the second position.
X*	All memory variables starting with the letter X.

the dBASE III Plus prompt (the dot) is usually placed before the interactive use of the command and not placed before the command when a programming use is being stressed.

Use of the /?

In some of the statements that follow, you can ask for information concerning the current catalog, rather than perform the indicated operation. For example, the statement

```
ERASE <file name>
```

will delete the indicated file from both the disk and the current catalog, while

```
ERASE ?
```

will list the files that can be ERASEd from the current catalog. When you can choose between a file name and the use of the ? symbol, then options will be indicated in the syntactical description of the statement as follows:

```
ERASE <file name>/?
```

meaning that you can choose to enter either the file name or the ? symbol.

Use of the F1 Help Key

A number of statements use full-screen editing in one form or another. Whenever full-screen editing is used by a statement, you can either hide or display the menu of keystrokes appropriate for that statement by pressing the function key F1. (See figure on p. 50.)

? [<expression>][, <expression>] . . .

Display the value of the expression on the next screen line.

EXAMPLE:

```
. STORE "123" TO X
. STORE "234" TO Y
. ? X
 123
? X,Y
 123         234
```

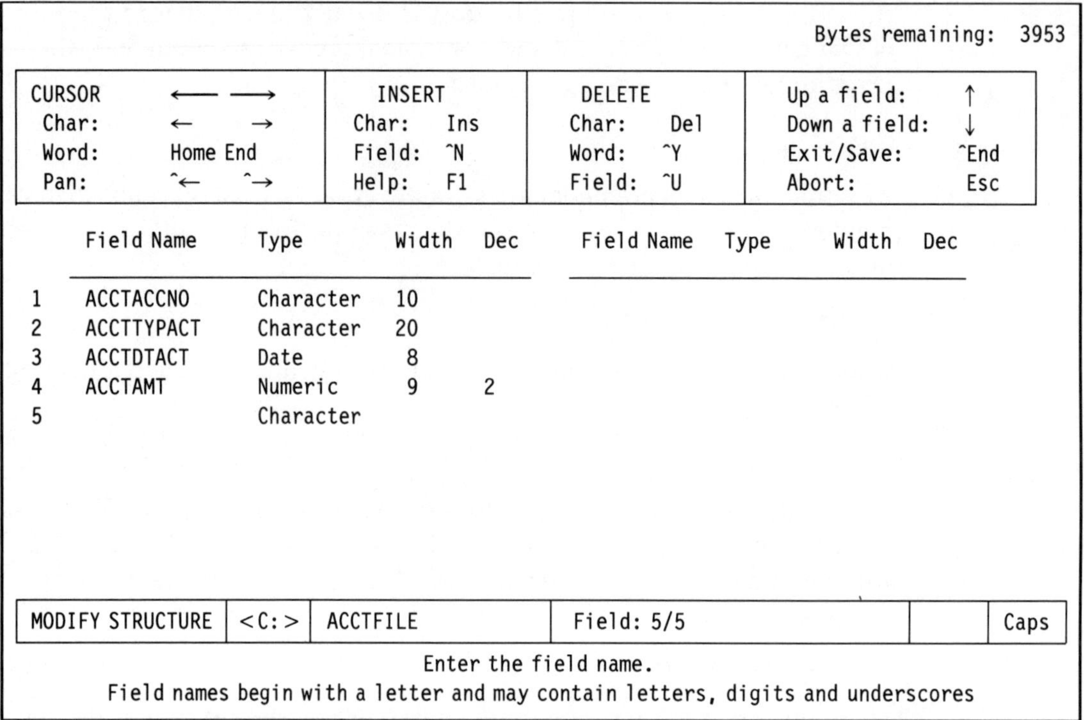

?? [<expression>]

Display the value of the expression on the same screen line.

EXAMPLE:

```
. ? X
. ?? Y
```

will cause the value of Y to appear on the same screen line as the value of X. It is equivalent to:

```
. ? X,Y
```

@ <row, col> CLEAR

Clear (erase) a rectangle on the screen from the first position to the right of the given coordinates to the end of the screen. If x and y are the row and col values, then the actual row number is $x+1$ and the actual column number is $y+1$.

@ <row, col> SAY <exp> [PICTURE <edit string>]

Displays formatted output on the screen or the printer. (See SET DEVICE command for instructions on directing output from @ . . SAY command to the printer.) The coordinates are given in x,y form and the actual row and column numbers used for output are x + 1 and y + 1, respectively. The parameter <exp> can be any dBASE III Plus expression that does not involve data of type memo. When output is sent to the screen, the value of <row> should not exceed 23 and the value of <col> should not exceed 79. Note also that row 0 of the screen is ordinarily used for messages from dBASE. When output is sent to the printer, the value of <col> should not exceed 255.

The <edit string> is used to specify how the output is to be formatted, and it is always delimited (e.g., enclosed in quotes). There are three distinct types of information that can appear in an <edit string>:

1. Data type
2. Insertion characters, and
3. Format functions

Data type and insertion information is provided on a character by character basis. When one of these characters appears in the <edit string>, then the character in the <edit string> specifies either the type of data to appear in that output column or the specific character to appear in that output column. Format functions are not on a character by character basis, but apply to a collection of columns of output. The editing string data typing characters are shown in Table 2.8, the insertion characters are shown in Table 2.9, and the format functions are shown in Table 2.10.

The functions can be combined. For example, if the combined format function XC is used, then DB will be printed after negative numbers and CR will be printed after positive numbers.

A template is any (legal) combination of data type and insertion characters. Format functions and templates may each be used alone or in combination with each other. If the two are used together, there will be one function (possibly a combination) and one template. If a format function is used in an <edit string>, it must come first in the string. If a function is used in an <edit string>, the first character of the <edit string> must be an @.

TABLE 2.8 Characters for Data Typing

9	: Digits and sign for numeric data.
#	: Digits, blanks, and sign.
A	: Letters only.
L	: Logical (Boolean) data only.
N	: Letters and digits only.
X	: Any character.
Y	: Logical (Boolean) data of the form Y, y, N, or n only.
!	: Convert (one character) to uppercase. Same as N for any other character to be printed.
$	: Replace leading zeros with dollar sign.
*	: Replace leading zeros with asterisks.

TABLE 2.9 Characters for Insertion

	: Decimal point.
	: Comma.

TABLE 2.10 Format Functions

A	: Alphabetic characters only. Used with character data only.
B	: Left-justify numbers. Used with numbers only.
C	: Print CR after a positive number. Used with numbers only.
D	: Print the date in the form MM/DD/YY. Can be used with date, character, and numeric data. This is the default format for dates.
E	: Print the date in the form DD/MM/YY. Can be used with date, character, and numeric data.
R	: Literals only.
S<integer>	: Limit the display to <integer> columns. If there is not enough room for the number in the display area, then the number is scrolled horizontally. NOTE: This function is used only with the GET option.
X	: Print DB after a negative number. Used with numbers only.
Z	: Print zero (0) as blanks. Used with numbers only.
(	: Enclose negative numbers in parentheses. Used with numbers only.
!	: Uppercase letters only. Used with character data only.

Occasionally, if you use an <edit string> in an unusual manner, the results are surprising.

EXAMPLE 1:

```
STORE 123.4 TO X
SET DEVICE TO PRINT
@ 5, 5 SAY X PICTURE "999.9"
      OUTPUT: 123.4
STORE "ABCDEF" TO Y
SET DEVICE TO SCREEN
@ 5, 5 SAY Y PICTURE "XXXXXX"
      OUTPUT: ABCDEF
STORE 1234.5 TO X
@ 5,10 SAY X PICTURE "9,999,999.99"
      OUTPUT: 1,234.5
```

EXAMPLE 2:

```
STORE "123 abc" TO SMALL
STORE "123 ABC" TO LARGE
STORE "123.45" TO NUMB
@ 0,0 SAY SMALL PICTURE "9999999"
     OUTPUT: 123 abc
@ 0,0 SAY SMALL PICTURE "!!!!!!!"
     OUTPUT: 123 abc
@ 0,0 SAY NUMB
     OUTPUT: 123.45
@ 0,0 SAY NUMB PICTURE "9999999"
     OUTPUT: 123
@ 0,0 SAY NUMB PICTURE "99999.99"
     OUTPUT: 123.45
@ 0,0 SAY NUMB PICTURE "$$$$$.99"
     OUTPUT: $$123.45
@ 0,0 SAY NUMB PICTURE "!!!!!!!"
     OUTPUT: !!!!!!!
```

EXAMPLE 3:

```
STORE -1 TO X
@ 0,0 SAY X PICTURE '@C'
     OUTPUT: -1
@ 0,0 SAY X PICTURE '@X'
```

```
    OUTPUT: 1 DB
@ 0,0 SAY X PICTURE '@X 999'
    OUTPUT: -1
```

@ <row, col> SAY <exp> [PICTURE <edit string1>] GET <variable> [PICTURE <edit string2>][RANGE <exp1,exp2>]

For an introduction to this statement, see the entry immediately preceding this one. The GET allows the entry of data from a formatted screen. The <variable> immediately after the word GET must be defined before the statement is executed. That is, you must use field names from a database file in USE or initialize a memory variable with a dummy value (such as all blanks or a zero) so that the <variable> name is recognized by dBASE III Plus. To transfer data from the screen either to a memory variable or to a field in a database record, use the READ statement. The number of GETs that precede a READ may not exceed 128. If you forget to use the READ statement in conjunction with an @ . . SAY . . GET, then data will be displayed on the screen, but you will not be able to change it or to enter new data.

In this statement, the SAY provides a prompt (if desired) and the GET is used to display the current value of the <variable> and to obtain a new value. The SAY and the GET clause each have their own PICTURE's, since they are used for two different purposes.

Both templates and format functions may be used in <edit string1> and in <edit string2>.

Note:
In order to use the RANGE option, you must make sure that <variable> has the same type as <exp1> and <exp2>. This means that you will not be able to initialize <variable> with blanks and then make <exp1> and <exp2> numeric. Also remember that you may check the RANGE of numeric and date variables only.

EXAMPLE 1:

```
STORE SPACE(8) TO MEMDATE
CLEAR
@ 5,1 SAY "ENTER THE DATE IN THE FORM MM/DD/YY" GET ;
  MEMDATE
READ
```

Note:
In this case, MEMDATE is an ordinary character string and dBASE does not perform any error checking on the input.

EXAMPLE 2:

```
STORE SPACE(8) TO MEMDATE
@ 5,1 SAY "ENTER THE DATE" GET MEMDATE PICTURE "@D"
READ
```

Note:
In this case, dBASE checks your entry for correct date format, but MEMDATE is still typed as a character string, not as a date.

EXAMPLE 3:

```
STORE SPACE(10) TO X
@ 5,1 GET X PICTURE "9999999.99"
READ
```

Warning:
When the @ . . SAY . . GET is used for the input of real (decimal) numbers using a picture clause in the above manner, you may not enter your own decimal point. You must enter leading zeros or blanks to line up the number to be entered with the existing decimal point. For this and other reasons, I recommend that you do not use a GET with a PICTURE clause for real (decimal) input.

EXAMPLE 4:

```
STORE 0 TO X
@ 5,10 SAY "ENTER THE WEIGHT" GET X PICTURE "9999" ;
    RANGE 2000,3000
READ
```

@ <row1,col1> TO <row2,col2> [DOUBLE]

Draw a box on the screen where <row1,col1> are the coordinates of the upper left-hand corner and <row2,col2> are the coordinates of the lower right-hand corner. The area enclosed by the box is not erased. The border of the box is drawn using a single line, unless the DOUBLE option is used.

EXAMPLE:

```
@ 1,1 TO 23,79 DOUBLE
```

@ <row1,col1> CLEAR TO <row2,col2>

Clear a rectangular area on the screen, where <row1,col1> are the coordinates of the upper left-hand corner of the cleared area and <row2,col2> are the coordinates of the lower right-hand corner.

ACCEPT [<"prompt">] TO <memvar>

Input a character string from the screen to the indicated memory variable. Quotation marks should not be used when the string is entered at the keyboard. The prompt string is optional.

EXAMPLE:

```
CLEAR
ACCEPT "CONTINUE (Y/N)" TO ANSWER
IF SUBSTR(ANSWER,1,1) <> "Y"
        RETURN
ENDIF
```

APPEND [BLANK]

If the BLANK option is not used, then the user is interactively prompted for the input in full-screen editing mode. If the BLANK option is used, then an empty record is appended to the current database. The user can then REPLACE the values in the fields of this record later.

EXAMPLE:

```
USE EMPLOYEE
APPEND
```

will cause a blank record of the type for the EMPLOYEE database file to be presented on the screen. The user may then fill in this record. When the record has been filled in, it is stored in the database file and another record is presented on the screen. To indicate that you wish to stop the append process, type a carriage return or a ^Q as the first character in the first field of the record on the screen.

Note 1:
If the BLANK option is used, an empty record is always appended to the database, even if you enter a ^Q. The APPEND BLANK option does not cause an automatic entry into full-screen editing mode.

Note 2:
The APPEND can be used in conjunction with a FORMAT file in order to use custom screens, but better control is obtained through the use of the APPEND BLANK, display of an empty but formatted record on the screen, and interactive input.

EXAMPLE:

```
USE EMPLOYEE
APPEND BLANK
REPLACE EMPLOYEENO WITH MEMEMPNO, EMPDATE WITH ;
  MEMDATE, . . .
```

Note:
It is not unusual to COPY data to a file from a database in delimited or system defined format and then APPEND it to another database. See the COPY command later in this section.

APPEND FROM <file> [FOR/WHILE <exp>][TYPE][<file type>]

<file> is the name of a database or MS/PC DOS file containing the data to be entered into the current database file. The FOR or WHILE clause indicates the selection criteria. The TYPE <file type> option is used to specify the type of the file that the data will be obtained from. If the TYPE option is not used, a dBASE III Plus database file is assumed. Since dBASE can determine the appropriate extension for each type of file, you do not need to provide an extension with the <file> name. The options for <file type> are:

1. DELIMITED [WITH <delimiter>]—Each line in the file is treated as a collection of data to be transferred into a single record in the current database. Each record is scanned left to right, until a delimiter is encountered. Each group of data is then inserted into the current database record in the next available field. When the current line of the input file is exhausted, a new blank record is appended to the current database file and the process continues. This TYPE is appropriate for files

created by BASIC programs by choosing <delimiter> to the quotation marks. If only the word DELIMITED is used, then dBASE expects the standard BASIC format: the character strings are delimited by double quotes and the fields are separated by commas.

2. DELIMITED WITH BLANK—Use this TYPE to read files where data items in the file have been separated by a single space, and each line of the file is to become a record in the current database file.
3. SDF—Use this TYPE when you wish to read data from a file created by a FORTRAN program. Data is scanned from left to right according to the size of the fields in the database file. For example, if the first field has size 5, then dBASE attempts to copy the first 5 characters from the current line into this field, not using any separators or delimiters at all. If the second field has size 10, then dBASE attempts to copy the next 10 characters into the second field. dBASE III Plus then continues until all of the fields in the current record have been filled or until an end of line (carriage return/line feed) is encountered.
4. DIF—VisiCalc spreadsheet format. Column headers must be removed.
5. SYLK—Multiplan spreadsheet format. The Multiplan must have been saved in row order, not in column order. Column headers must be removed.
6. WKS—Lotus 1-2-3 spreadsheet format. Column headers must be removed.

EXAMPLE:

```
USE EMPLOYEE
APPEND FROM TEMP DELIMITED
```

ASSIST

This command is for the person who wishes to use dBASE III Plus in the interactive mode. A collection of menus is presented on the screen, one menu at a time. The menus prompt the user for the desired input. This function is definitely not recommended for the experienced programmer. It is designed to be used by the nonprogrammer. (See figure on the next page.)

```
Set Up   Create   Update   Position   Retrieve   Organize   Modify   Tools   04:16:53 pm

 Database file
 Format for Screen
 Query
 Catalog
 View
 Quit dBASE III Plus

 ASSIST          <C:>               Opt: 1/6
   Move selection bar - ↑ ↓.  Select - ↵.  Leave menu - ←→.  Help - F1.  Exit - Esc.
                              Select a database file.
```

AVERAGE [<field name list>][<scope>][FOR/WHILE <condition>][TO <memory variable list>]

Compute the average (arithmetic mean). If the <field name list> is empty, then a separate average will be computed for each numeric field in the database record. If the <field name list> is not empty, then there will be one average computed for each field named in the list. If the TO option is used, then the results of the averaging process will be stored in the named memory variables.

Warning:
The number of memory variables that you name in the <memory variable list> must exactly match the number of fields being averaged.

EXAMPLE:

```
USE EMPLOYEE
AVERAGE SALARY TO MEMAVERAGE
```

BROWSE [FIELDS <field name list>][LOCK <integer>] [FREEZE <field>] [NOFOLLOW][NOMENU] [WIDTH <integer>][NOAPPEND]

BROWSE allows full-screen editing of the database in use. There is an options menu that can be called (and recalled) to the screen by pressing F10. There is also a menu of keystrokes that can be called by striking F1. You must exit from the options menu (press ESC) before you can continue editing and viewing the data. F1 is a toggle that either hides or displays the keystroke menu.

Warning:
I consider this function to be very dangerous, since changes are made to records immediately, and there is no emergency abort. It is just too easy to destroy your data. To view the data without any changes, use the DISPLAY or LIST command. To edit your data, use the EDIT, CHANGE, or REPLACE command.

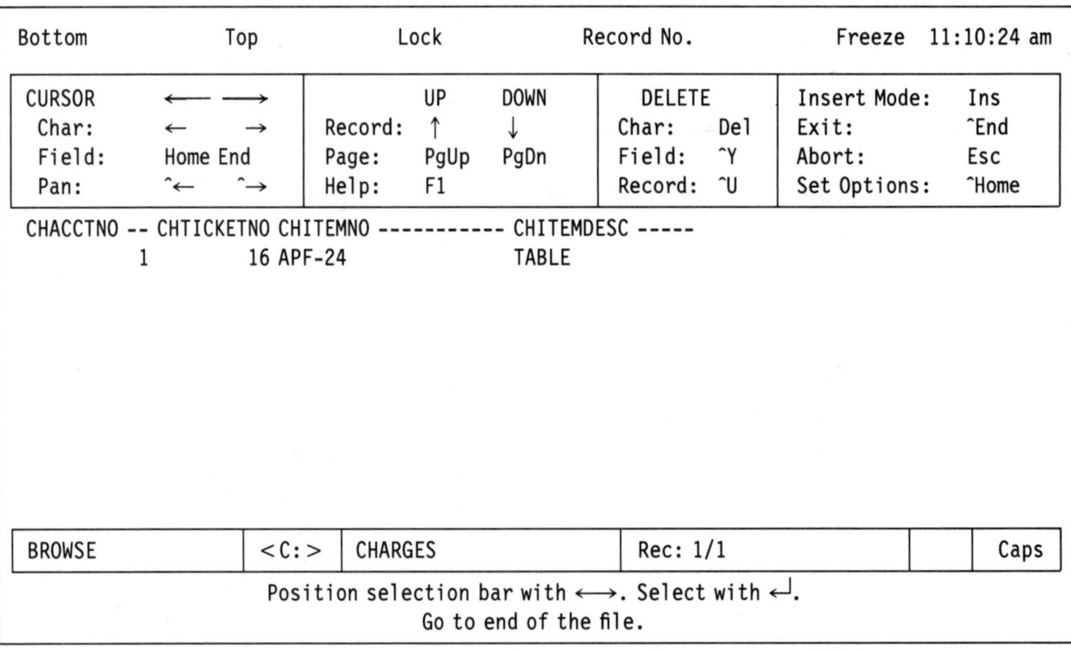

The optional clauses in the statement roughly correspond to the options available in the options menu. The use of each of these clauses appears in Table 2.11.

The options in the menu bar are given in the Table 2.12.

CALL <binary file name> [WITH <char string>/<memory variable>]

The CALL statement is used to execute a binary program that has already been placed in memory using the LOAD statement. <binary file name> is used without any extension. The WITH clause is used to pass parameters to the called routine. See the LOAD statement for more information.

TABLE 2.11

NAME OF CLAUSE	USAGE
FIELDS	Fields and the order of their display.
FREEZE	Specific field to be edited.
LOCK	The fields that are always displayed at the left of the screen. This collection of fields always starts with the first field in the database and consists of a contiguous group.
NOAPPEND	Do not allow user to append a new record.
NOFOLLOW	If an index file is currently associated with the database and you change the value in the key field, then the record changed is immediately moved to its proper position on the screen. If NOFOLLOW has not been selected, then the currency pointer continues to point to the changed record in its new position. If NOFOLLOW has been selected, then the currency pointer remains at the position previously occupied by the changed record.
NOMENU	Do not allow access to the options menu bar.
WIDTH	Limit the display width of each field. The one limitation applies to all fields in the display. You can horizontally scroll the data within the display area.

TABLE 2.12

NAME OF OPTION	USAGE
BOTTOM	Go to the last record in the file.
FIND	Similar to the FIND and SEEK statements.
FREEZE	See the entry for FREEZE in Table 2.11.
LOCK	See the entry for LOCK in Table 2.11.
RECORD NO	Go to the record with the indicated number.
TOP	Go to the first record in the file.

CANCEL

Emergency abort of a command file. Place this statement in the command file (program) and execute it in the event of an error. When this statement is executed, the system is placed in interactive mode. This statement is equivalent to a RETURN from the highest level of your application system.

CHANGE [<scope>] FIELDS <field name list> [FOR/WHILE <condition>]

Allows the user to change the specified fields of records that are within the given scope and that satisfy the given selection criteria (condition). The indicated fields are presented on the screen, one record at a time. The user may then change any or all of the fields presented. The CHANGE command invokes a menu driven, interactive operation. The CHANGE command performs the same function as the EDIT command.

```
Record No.      1

CURSOR      <--  -->          UP     DOWN     DELETE         Insert Mode:   Ins
 Char:      <-    ->  Record: ↑      ↓        Char:    Del   Exit/Save:     ^End
 Word:      Home End  Page:   PgUp   PgDn     Field:   ^Y    Abort:         Esc
                      Help:   F1              Record:  ^U    Memo:          ^Home

CHACCTNO                  1
CHTICKETNO               16
CHITEMNO    APF-24
CHITEMDESC  TABLE
CHMANU      COFFEE TABLE
CHLOCATION  WHSE 1
CHQTY          1.0
CHITEMPR        84.50
CHDOLLARS       84.50
CHDATE      03/05/87
CHDISPDATE    /  /
CHDISPAMT          .
CHRESTYPE
CHRESREPTD
CHACTRESDT    /  /
```

EXAMPLE:

```
USE EMPLOYEE
CHANGE SALARY
```

CLEAR

Clears (erases) the screen and positions the cursor at the upper left-hand corner of the screen. CLEAR also clears all pending GETs.

CLEAR ALL

Closes all files and releases memory variables. Can be used to force the closure of database, index, format, and memo files. For purposes of programming style, I recommend that you use this function in connection with your own application system menus. Whenever you RETURN from a major menu operation, if you execute a CLEAR ALL command in your program, then you know that all the files have been closed, the file headers have been properly updated, the index files have been properly updated, and all the memory variables have been released. The releasing of the memory variables assures that no variables will inadvertently be carried over to another module. The use of this command in conjunction with menus is a matter of programming preference and style. You may occasionally find some situations where it is inconvenient to use the CLEAR ALL command in the manner described above. I suggest the following rule: Use the CLEAR ALL command after each major module of your application unless it makes programming impossible. To selectively close database files, use the CLOSE DATABASES statement. To selectively release memory variables, use the RELEASE statement.

CLEAR GETS

Clears any pending GETs. A GET is pending if an @ . . GET statement has been executed and no READ, CLEAR, or CLEAR ALL has been executed yet. The maximum number of pending GETs is 128, unless you place an entry in the CONFIG.DB file to change this number.

CLEAR MEMORY

Release all public and private memory variables. This statement differs from the RELEASE ALL, which will release only private memory variables in the current module.

CLEAR TYPEAHEAD

Clear out the typeahead buffer.

CLOSE <file type>/ALL

Selectively close all active files of a specific type, or use the ALL option to close all files of all types. The types of files that can be closed using this statement are given in Table 2.13.

Warning:
You cannot selectively close a single database file using this command. To close a single database file, make it the current file and then execute a USE command.

EXAMPLES:

```
CLOSE DATABASES
CLOSE ALTERNATE
CLOSE ALL
```

CONTINUE

Used with the LOCATE command. It re-executes the last LOCATE command, starting the search from the current record. Since the

TABLE 2.13

FILE TYPE	FILES CLOSED
ALTERNATE	Alternate
DATABASES	Databases, index and format
FORMAT	Format
INDEXES	Index
PROCEDURE	Procedure

LOCATE statement has a different currency pointer for each area, you can execute a LOCATE, leave the area, perform other operations, return to the original area, and then execute a CONTINUE as if you had never left the area.

COPY FILE <source file name> TO <target file name>

Used to copy a file of any type to a file of a different name. Both the <source file name> and the <target file name> must be completely specified, i.e., you will need to provide the extension for both files.

EXAMPLE:

```
COPY FILE EMPLOYEE.DBF TO EMPBAK.DBF
```

COPY STRUCTURE TO <file name> [FIELDS <field name list>]

Create a new empty database. The new database has the same structure as the database in use if the FIELDS option is not used. If the FIELDS option is used, the new database has only the fields named in the <field name list>.

EXAMPLE:

```
USE EMPLOYEE
COPY STRUCTURE TO TEMP
```

This will create a new empty database file named TEMP with the same structure as EMPLOYEE.

COPY TO <target file name> STRUCTURE EXTENDED

The result of this command is to create a new database file that has four fields in it. Each record in the new database contains, as data, the name of a field, the type, the length, and the number of decimal places (if appropriate). Instead of creating a database file with the same structure as the current database (using the COPY STRUCTURE command), it creates a new database file whose data reflects the structure of the source database file. In order to create a new database from the structure data contained in this type of file, use the CREATE FROM statement.

COPY TO <target file name> [<scope>][FIELDS <list of field names>][FOR/WHILE <condition>][TYPE][<file type>]

Copy part or all of selected records from the current database file. A new file is always created when this statement is executed; that is, it does not append data to the end of an existing file, but creates a new file. If the TYPE clause is not specified, a new database file is created. The structure of the new database file is determined by the presence or absence of the FIELDS clause. If the FIELDS clause is absent, then the structure of the new database file is the same as that of the source (current) database file. If the FIELDS clause is used, then it determines the structure of the target database. If the TYPE is SDF or DELIMITED, then memo fields are not copied. See the APPEND statement for a list of the allowable file TYPEs. Note that file names A through J are not appropriate as file names, since they are alias names for the areas.

EXAMPLES:

```
USE EMPLOYEE
COPY TO TEMP
```

This will create a new database file named TEMP.DBF with the same contents as EMPLOYEE.

```
COPY TO TEMP DELIMITED
```

This will create an ASCII file named TEMP.TXT. Each of the records in EMPLOYEE will appear as a row in the new file. The fields will be separated by commas and the character strings will be enclosed in quotation marks (''). This type of file is useful when interfacing with BASIC.

```
COPY TO TEMP DELIMITED WITH '
```

The same result as COPY TO TEMP DELIMITED, except that the delimited used in this case will be the single quote (').

```
COPY TO TEMP SDF
```

This will create an ASCII file named TEMP.TXT. Each of the records in EMPLOYEE will appear as a row in the new file. The fields are not separated by commas and the character strings are not enclosed in quotation marks. This type of file is useful when interfacing with FORTRAN.

COUNT [<scope>][FOR/WHILE <condition>][TO <memvar>]

Count the number of records in the current database that satisfy the selection criteria and <scope>. Optionally store the result in the indicated memory variable.

EXAMPLE:

```
USE EMPLOYEE
COUNT FOR DELETED ( ) TO MEMDELCNT
```

will place the number of records marked for deletion in the database file EMPLOYEE into the memory variable named MEMDELCNT.

CREATE <file name>

This command is used interactively. When CREATE is typed at the keyboard, the user is prompted for each of the fields to appear in the record and for the characteristics of each field. The user terminates the record definition by typing a carriage return in response to the new field prompt or a ^End at other places. The allowable keystrokes are displayed at the top of the screen. If you make a mistake, for example, if you select a data type different from one of the legal types, dBASE will signal an error and provide some suggestions for help.

The possible field types are:

C = character string

D = date

L = logical (Boolean)

M = memo

N = numeric

Characters have only a width. A date always consists of 8 characters, and this width is automatically entered for you. Logicals have only a width, and it is always 1. Memos always take 10 bytes in the record. The actual memo data is stored in another file for you. The width of 10 is automatically entered for you when you specify that the field is of type memo. Numbers have a width (which includes the decimal point, the sign, and all decimal digits, if any). If the number is not an integer, then you must indicate the number of places to the right of the decimal. You will be prompted for each of the fields, one at a time. You indicate that you have entered the last field by typing a carriage return in response to the prompt for the next field.

The interactive entry of the definition of a database record is done using full-screen editing operations and with some help in case of errors in entry. Two control characters of particular importance are: ^N and ^U. You may insert a field in a current definition by moving the cursor to the desired field and then entering ^N.

EXAMPLE:

To enter a new fourth field, move the cursor to the definition for the fourth field, type ^N, and then enter the new definition for the fourth field. The old fourth field becomes the new fifth field, etc.

To delete the definition of a field, move the cursor to the field to be deleted and type ^U.

The maximum number of fields in a single dBASE III Plus database file is 128.

CREATE <database file name> FROM <structure file name>

Use this statement to create a new database file from the structure information contained as data in a database file. The file containing the structure information will most likely have been created using the COPY STRUCTURE EXTENDED statement.

CREATE LABEL <label file name>/?

See the MODIFY LABEL command, since CREATE LABEL is identical in function to MODIFY LABEL.

CREATE QUERY <query file name>/?

See the MODIFY QUERY command, since CREATE QUERY is identical in function to MODIFY QUERY.

CREATE REPORT <report form file name>/?

See the MODIFY REPORT command, since the CREATE REPORT is identical in function to the MODIFY REPORT.

CREATE SCREEN <screen file name>/?

See the MODIFY SCREEN command, since the CREATE SCREEN is identical in function to the MODIFY SCREEN.

CREATE VIEW <view file name>/?

See the MODIFY VIEW command, since the CREATE VIEW is identical in function to the MODIFY VIEW.

CREATE VIEW <view file name> FROM ENVIRONMENT

A new .VUE file of with the indicated name is constructed using:

1. The current areas, their databases, and their indexes
2. The relations between the database files
3. The active area
4. The active field list
5. The appropriate format files

DELETE [<scope>][FOR/WHILE <condition>]

Mark the indicated records for later physical removal from the current database.

EXAMPLE:

```
USE EMPLOYEE
GOTO 5
DELETE NEXT 1
```

will mark the indicated record for future deletion.

```
USE EMPLOYEE
DELETE ALL FOR SALARY > = 40000
```

will mark all EMPLOYEE records where the SALARY is ≥40000 for future deletion.

Note:
Physical deletion of records is performed using the PACK statement.

DIR [<drive:>][<path>][<skeleton>]

Display name, number of records, date of last update, and size of the files on the indicated (or default) drive. If <skeleton> is not specified, then only the DBF files are displayed. The <path> option is used to display files in a specific path. The <skeleton> indicates which type of files are to be selected for display.

Warning:
The size of a file displayed by this command may be incorrect if the file has been updated and not yet closed. In this case, CLOSE the file first and then use the DIR command. This command is used in the interactive mode.

EXAMPLES:

```
. DIR
```

Display the names and sizes of all DBF files on the current disk.

```
. DIR *.*
```

Display the names and sizes of all files on the current disk.

```
. DIR *.NDX
```

Display the names and sizes of all index files on the current disk.

```
. DIR G*.*
```

Display the names and sizes of all files on the current disk, where the name starts with the letter G.

```
. DIR ?G????.*
```

Display the names and sizes of all files on the current disk, where the name is exactly 6 characters long and the second character in the name is G.

```
. DIR \INV\*.*
```

Display the names and sizes of all files on the current disk in the path directory named INV.

DISPLAY FILE [LIKE <skeleton>][TO PRINT]

This command is equivalent, in many ways, to the DIR command. The major advantage of this form of the command is the TO

PRINT option, allowing you to echo the output to the printer. This feature is not available in the DIR command.

DISPLAY FILES [ON <drive name:>][TO PRINT]

Same function as the DIR command. Lists the names and sizes of all DBF files on the default or indicated drive.

DISPLAY [<scope>][<expression list>][FOR/WHILE <condition>] [OFF][TO PRINT]

For the records selected from the current database by the <scope> and the selection criteria, display the fields indicated in the <expression list>. Prefix the output with the record number, unless the OFF option is selected. The <expression list> may contain names of database fields alone or in string or arithmetic expressions that can be evaluated. Column titles are provided. If a memo field is not explicitly named in the <expression list>, only the word MEMO will appear in the record DISPLAYed. When a memo field is displayed, the default is to use a width of 50 columns. To change to a different width, use the SET MEMOWIDTH statement. Output to the screen pauses every 20 lines for ease of observation. To DISPLAY records from a file in USE other than the current file, prefix the field names individually with "<alias>->". If you do not wish to see headings when the data is displayed, use the SET HEADINGS OFF statement.

Note:
If you DISPLAY a record with no <expression list>, all of the nonMEMO fields will be displayed. If you specifically name the MEMO field in the <expression list> of the command, then the contents of this field will also be displayed.

EXAMPLES:

```
USE EMPLOYEE
DISPLAY OFF ALL
```

Display all the records in the EMPLOYEE file on the screen. The listing will pause after twenty records have been DISPLAYed on the screen and will continue when indicated by the user. Records marked for future deletion will appear with an "*".

```
USE INVENTORY
DISPLAY B->PARTNO, B->ITEMCOST FOR .NOT. DELETED( )
```

DISPLAY HISTORY [LAST <integer>][TO PRINT]

Display statements listed in the HISTORY file. If the LAST clause is not used, then the entire contents of the HISTORY file is displayed. If the LAST clause is used, then the last <integer> statements in the file are displayed.

DISPLAY MEMORY [TO PRINT]

Display the name, type, and size of each active memory variable. It also shows the number of variables defined, the number of variables available (256 minus the number of memory variables currently used), the number of bytes used, and the number of bytes still available for more memory variables (6000 minus the number of bytes currently used). The maximum number of memory variables is 256 and the maximum number of bytes that can be used by the combination of all memory variables (the sum of the areas of all the memory variables) is 6000. Immediately after a CLEAR ALL, there are no memory variables in use. If you are working interactively (no program in use), then you can use the DISPLAY MEMORY statement at any time. If you are running a program and press ESC you must then indicate that you wish to suspend rather than cancel execution of the program before you can use the DISPLAY MEMORY statement. If you cancel rather than suspend, the memory variables associated with the execution of the program are lost.

DISPLAY STATUS [TO PRINT]

Display the current status of dBASE III Plus. Information is provided for each of the following:

1. For each user work area: the database file name, the work area number, the alias for the database name, relations between databases, the names of all index files currently in use, the names of the open memo files, and the field(s) of the database on which these indexes are based.

2. The name of the current database file.
3. The directory search path.
4. The name of the disk drive to use for file access.
5. The print destination.
6. The current parameter settings.
7. The left margin setting.
8. The current function key assignments.

This command may be of great use in debugging a program.

DISPLAY STRUCTURE [TO PRINT]

Display the structure of the current database. This statement is useful in determining the structure of the database record and in determining the number of records currently in the file. The specific information provided by this command is:

1. The name of the current database.
2. The number of records in the database.
3. The date of the last update to the file.
4. The definition of each field.
5. The number of bytes in each record.

EXAMPLE:

```
USE EMPLOYEE
DISPLAY STRUCTURE
```

DO <file name> [WITH <parameter list>]

Execute the statements contained in the indicated command file. Optionally pass parameters. The type (extension) of the file is assumed to be PRG, unless it is explicitly given. Control returns to the calling program, or to interactive use, when a RETURN statement is encountered or when the end of the file is encountered. The WITII option is used only to assign aliases to variables or constants. This gives you the opportunity to have a variable name in a routine that is different from the corresponding variable in the calling program. You can pass a variable, field name, constant, or expression. When the data is received by the routine, a new name is assigned to the data. The storage location (memory variable) that corresponds to this new name stays in existence until the subroutine has been completed.

Note:
The DO statement cannot call a file that is already open.

EXAMPLE 1:

DO INVENTOR

The program in the file named INVENTOR.PRG will be executed.

EXAMPLE 2:

DO A:INVENTOR WITH PARTNO, SUM, 27*COST

Pass the values of the three parameters to the subroutine named INVENTOR (or more properly, INVENTOR.PRG). The subroutine INVENTOR must start with a PARAMETERS statement (defined later in this section) to assign names to the values passed to it. Remember: the only purpose of passing parameters in this manner is to provide a local alias name for certain data items.

Warning:
The total number of files that can be open (in use) at any one time in dBASE III Plus is 15. Each command file that is executed using the DO is counted as an active (open) file. If your nest subroutine calls too deeply, you will restrict the number of database and index files that can be open. The number of open files (15) includes, but is not limited to, the number of open database, index, format, and command files.

DO CASE

The full form is:

```
DO CASE
     CASE <condition>
             <statements>
     CASE <condition>
             <statements>
             .
             .
             .
     [OTHERWISE]
             <statements>
ENDCASE
```

It is recommended that you always use the OTHERWISE option, so that you write self-protecting programs. You may wish to use the CASE statement as a replacement for deeply nested IF's. You may use virtually any dBASE III Plus statements for a specific CASE, including another DO CASE. If you have nested DO CASE statements, remember to include an ENDCASE for each DO CASE.

A CASE statement is executed as follows. Each of the CASE's is examined in turn, starting with the first. If at least one of the <conditions>'s is true, then only the first one that is true is executed. If none of the expressions are true, then the OTHERWISE clause is executed.

EXAMPLE:

```
WAIT TO CODE
DO CASE
     CASE CODE = "A"
          DO PROCA
     CASE CODE = "B"
          DO PROCB
     CASE CODE = "C"
          DO PROCC
     OTHERWISE
          ? "ILLEGAL CODE ENTERED"
          WAIT
ENDCASE
CLEAR ALL
```

DO WHILE <condition>
<statements>
ENDDO

This is the only form of looping available. Each DO WHILE loop must have its own ENDDO statement to end the loop.

Note:
dBASE examines the first line of a loop (the DO WHILE statement) just once, so you cannot use macro expansion (the & operator) in a DO WHILE statement, if the expression following the & operator changes during the execution of the loop.

EXAMPLE 1 (A COUNTER-CONTROLLED LOOP):

```
STORE 1 TO LOOPINDEX
DO WHILE LOOPINDEX <= 10
    ? LOOPINDEX
    STORE LOOPINDEX+1 TO LOOPINDEX
ENDDO
```

EXAMPLE 2 (A CONDITION-CONTROLLED LOOP):

```
USE EMPLOYEE
DO WHILE .NOT. EOF( )
    ? EMPLOYEENO, EMPNAME
    SKIP 1
ENDDO
```

EDIT <scope> [FIELDS <list of field names>][FOR/WHILE <condition>]

Calls the interactive, full-screen editor for changing the contents of fields in database records. If a record has been DELETEd, but not yet physically removed from the file, the record is presented on the screen with the DEL symbol displayed at the top of the screen. When a record is displayed on the screen for editing, a menu of keystrokes is presented at the top of the screen. F1 is used as a toggle to hide or display this menu. (See figure on the next page.)

To edit a MEMO field, move the cursor to the beginning of the field, enter ^PgDn and then use the same editing control keys as is used in MODIFY COMMAND. To discontinue editing of a memo field, enter ^W or ^PgUp to save the changes and ESC to abort the changes.

For the specifics on the control keys used in full-screen operations, see Section 2.4.

EJECT

Output a form feed to the printer. This is useful at the end of a report. This statement will cause a form feed at the printer whether the current device is SCREEN or PRINTer.

Note:

If your printer is not turned on or is not properly connected, then dBASE will probably lock up.

```
Record No.      1

CURSOR     <--  -->              UP     DOWN      DELETE          Insert Mode:   Ins
 Char:     <-    ->     Record:  ↑      ↓        Char:    Del    Exit/Save:     ^End
 Word:     Home End     Page:    PgUp   PgDn     Field:   ^Y     Abort:         Esc
                        Help:    F1              Record:  ^U     Memo:          ^Home

CHACCTNO                 1
CHTICKETNO              16
CHITEMNO     APF-24
CHITEMDESC   TABLE
CHMANU       COFFEE TABLE
CHLOCATION   WHSE 1
CHQTY           1.0
CHITEMPR          84.50
CHDOLLARS         84.50
CHDATE       03/05/87
CHDISPDATE     /  /
CHDISPAMT             .
CHRESTYPE
CHRESREPTD
CHACTRESDT     /  /
```

EXAMPLE:

```
SET DEVICE TO PRINT
  place "say" statements here
EJECT
SET DEVICE TO SCREEN
```

ENDDO

Marks the end of the current WHILE loop. Anything appearing to the right of the ENDDO on the same line is considered to be a comment.

ERASE <file name>/?

Erase a file from the disk and from the current catalog. Similar to the MS/PC DOS DEL function, except that the full name and extension of the file must be given. No wild card characters may be used with this command, that is, no "*" and no "?" may be used. If the form

ERASE ?

is used, then a directory of the files on the current catalog are displayed.

Warning:
You cannot ERASE an open file.

EXIT

Leave the current DO WHILE loop and go directly to the line immediately following the ENDDO. This command can be used to simplify a quick exit from a loop.

EXPORT TO <file name> TYPE PFS

The contents of the current database file are copied to a PFS in the correct format. The name of the new file is not given an extension. The format for the fields in the new PFS file is determined from one of the following:

1. If the dBASE file (the .DBF file) was created using the dBASE IMPORT command, then the default is to use the associated FORMAT file in the catalog to determine the field format. If you use a SET FORMAT TO <.FMT file name> command, you can change the format information. If you have specifically indicated that you do not wish to use the information in the FORMAT file (as a result of using the SET FORMAT TO command without a FORMAT file being specified), then the dBASE file structure is used.
2. If the dBASE file was not created using the IMPORT command, then you can either specify the format file through a SET FORMAT TO <file name> command or let dBASE use the .DBF file structure to determine the format of the fields in the PFS file.

FIND <character string>

This is one of the two commands that allows use of an index specified in the USE or SET INDEX statement to directly access the first occurrence of a record in a database with a specific key value. (See also the command SEEK.) If use of a variable is desired, use statements of the form:

```
STORE <character string> to MEMVAR
FIND &MEMVAR
```

When using a <character string> constant, it is not necessary to put the string in quotes, unless there are leading blanks. Trailing blanks would only be important if EXACT has been set to ON.

Normally, the time required to find the desired record is extremely fast. If more than one index is in use, the first one in the list of indexes (the primary or controlling index) is used for the FIND. For example, if the statement

```
USE AFILE INDEX B, C, D, E, F
```

is used to establish a current file, the index B is the primary index and is the one used by the FIND statement. This means that when a value is "found," it is the value of the index in B. In the case where B is the primary index, but you desire another index (say C) as the primary index, it is necessary to execute a SET ORDER statement like

```
SET ORDER TO 2
```

If the "FIND" is successful, the value of RECNO( ), the current record number, is set to the number of the record found, EOF( ) will be .F. (FALSE), and FOUND( ) will be .T., that is, have the value TRUE. If the "FIND" is unsuccessful, the value of the function EOF( ) will be .T. (TRUE), and the value of FOUND( ) will be .F. (FALSE). The "FIND" operation always starts at the beginning of the database file (implicit GOTO TOP). Note also that the "FIND" may be used in conjunction with any character string, date, or numeric indexed field.

Note 1:
The FIND and the SEEK differ from the LOCATE in that the LOCATE can be used on an unindexed file. If you attempt to use either the FIND or the SEEK on an unindexed file, an error will occur.

Note 2:
The SEEK statement does not require the use of the & symbol (macro expansion) when dealing with a memory variable. Since macro expansion can slow down execution of a program, and since some compilers do not

allow the use of macro expansion, it is highly recommended that you always use the SEEK rather than the FIND.

EXAMPLE:

```
USE EMPLOYEE INDEX LASTNAME
ACCEPT "ENTER NAME" TO MEMLNAME
FIND &MEMLNAME
IF EOF( )
     ? "NO RECORD ON FILE FOR GIVEN NAME"
     WAIT
ELSE
     .
     .
     .
ENDIF
```

GO/GOTO BOTTOM

Position the currency pointer to the last record in the database. If an index is in use, the last record is the one that is last by the index value.

GO/GOTO [RECORD] <**expression**>

or simply

<**expression**>

Position currency pointer to the record number indicated by <expression>.

GO/GOTO TOP

Position current record pointer to the first record in the database. If an index is in use, the first record is the one that is first by the index value. This statement is useful to make the (logically) first record in the database file the current record. For example, after the COUNT is performed, the currency pointer is at the end of the database file and RECNO( ) is one greater than the number of records in the database. To reset the currency pointer to the beginning of the database, use the GOTO TOP command.

EXAMPLE:

```
USE EMPLOYEE
COUNT FOR DELETED( ) TO MEMCOUNT
IF MEMCOUNT > 0
     GOTO TOP
     DO WHILE (.NOT. EOF) .AND. (.NOT. DELETED( ))
          ? "NAME=", EMPLNAME
          SKIP 1
     ENDDO
ENDIF
```

HELP [<keyword>]

The HELP command with no <keyword> invokes a menu-driven tutorial on the features of dBASE III Plus. HELP with a <keyword> displays information concerning the command indicated by the <keyword>. The information presented may include any of the following:

1. A syntactical description of the command
2. The purpose of the command
3. The use of the command
4. Related commands

(See figure on p. 82.)

EXAMPLES:

```
. HELP
. HELP STORE
```

IF <exp>
<commands>
[ELSE
<commands>]
ENDIF

This is the IF-THEN-ELSE statement. The IF <exp>, the ELSE and the ENDIF must all appear on separate lines. Anything after the ELSE and the ENDIF is considered to be a comment. IF statements can be nested to any level, but there must be an ENDIF corresponding to each IF.

```
                                                                MAIN MENU
                              Help Main Menu

                              1 - Getting Started
                              2 - What Is a . . .
                              3 - How Do I . . .
                              4 - Creating a Database File
                              5 - Using an Existing Database File
                              6 - Commands and Functions









HELP            <C:> CHARGES          Rec  1/1
      Position selection bar - ↑ ↓.  Select - ↵.  Exit with Esc or enter a command.
                           ENTER >
```

EXAMPLE:

```
IF X = "A"
      DO PROCA
ELSE
      IF X = "B"
             DO PROCB
      ELSE
             ? "ILLEGAL VALUE FOR X=", X
      ENDIF
ENDIF
```

IMPORT FROM <file name> TYPE PFS

Create a new dBASE database file from the information contained in a PFS file. The name of the dBASE file is the same as the name of the PFS file, except for the extension name (.DBF). If a catalog is currently open, then the new .DBF file, the new .VUE and the new .FMT files are added to this catalog.

Note:
If you need to have the associated .FMT file opened when you open the .DBF file created in this manner, it is recommended that you use the SET VIEW statement, rather than the USE statement, since the SET VIEW opens both of these files for you.

EXAMPLE:

```
IMPORT FROM MYPFSFIL TYPE PFS
```

INDEX ON <expression> TO <index file name> [UNIQUE]

Create an index on the indicated field (or combination of fields) and place the new index table into the indicated file name. If the name of the index file is given without a version, the version NDX is used. If a file of the indicated name exists, it will be replaced by the new file, so you may easily reindex a database file as needed. To replace an existing index file without assistance prompting from dBASE III Plus, it will be necessary to SET SAFETY OFF. Indexes are useful in conjunction with the FIND and SEEK statements. You may create an index on character strings, dates, and numbers. The length of the field (or combination of fields) that you wish to create an index on is limited to 100 characters.

Note 1:
If you index on just a date, then the index is maintained for you in chronological order. If you index on a combination of a character string and a date, you must use the DTOC function to convert the date to a character string before you can concatenate the string and the date. When the date is converted to a string, you lose the ordering property of the date, since a character string of the form "01/01/88" precedes "01/02/87". As a result, you not only have to convert a date to a character string (when it is used as *part* of an index expression), but you must also change the form of the date string from MM/DD/YY to something of the form YYMMDD.

Note 2:
You can index individually on numerical, string, and date fields. If you index on a combination of different fields, change (as necessary) the types to character strings (as shown in example 2 below) before you attempt to concatenate the names of the fields in the indexing expression.

Note 3:
You cannot index either on a logical field or on a memo field.

EXAMPLE 1:

```
USE EMPLOYEE
INDEX ON EMPLNAME TO EMPLNAME
```

will create a new index on the field EMPLNAME and place this index table into the file EMPLNAME.NDX.

```
USE EMPLOYEE
INDEX ON EMPLNAME+EMPFNAME to EMPNAME
```

will create an index that is the combination of two fields.

EXAMPLE 2:

```
USE EMPLOYEE
INDEX ON HIREDATE TO HIREDATE
USE EMPLOYEE
INDEX ON DEPT+STR(YEAR(HIREDATE)*10000+;
  MONTH(HIREDATE)*100+DAY(HIREDATE),6) TO DEPTHDAT
```

INPUT [<prompt string>] to <memvar>

Get the input from the keyboard and place it into the indicated memory variable. The parameter <prompt> may be either a delimited character string constant or a character string variable. The type of the memory variable is determined from the type of the data input (if the data entered from the keyboard is a character string, it will be necessary to delimit the input data with quotation marks or brackets). If a character string (something in quotes) is entered, the memory variable will contain a character string. If a number is entered, the memory variable will contain a number. Use .T. to indicate the Boolean TRUE and use .F. to indicate the Boolean FALSE, when desired as input. If you type a RETURN in response to the INPUT command, the command is ignored and nothing is stored in <memvar>. When a date is input, it must be input as a character string and then converted to a date using the CTOD function.

Note:

It is necessary to initialize <memvar> before it is used in the INPUT statement. The common technique is to assign a blank or a zero to this memory variable before it appears in the INPUT statement.

EXAMPLE:

```
STORE 0 TO MEMAMT
INPUT "ENTER THE AMOUNT" TO MEMAMT
```

INSERT [BLANK] [BEFORE]

Allows the insertion of a record into the current database. If the BLANK option is used, then an empty record is inserted; else the user is prompted for the field values to be placed into the new record. If a database file contains, say, 20 records and you insert a new record after the 10th record, then records 11 thru 20 are physically moved to make room for the new 11th record.

Warning:
If the BEFORE option is used, a physical rearrangement of the data will take place. It is therefore recommended that you do not use the BEFORE option.

Note 1:
If the database file is currently indexed, then the record is placed at the end of the database.

Note 2:
When a record is placed at the end of a database using the INSERT statement, the INSERT statement works just like the APPEND statement and you will be prompted to enter new records until you indicate that you have no more records to enter (press ^Q, ESC, or RETURN when the new empty record is presented on the screen).

Note 3:
You can use SET CARRY ON to simplify the addition of a new record if the new record contains a high percentage of data duplicated in the previous record. In order for the SET CARRY ON option to work, you must enter the data in the previous record immediately before you INSERT the new record.

JOIN WITH <alias> TO <file name> FOR <condition> [FIELDS <field list>]

Two databases (the current database and the one designated by <alias> are joined to create a third database. The <alias> of a database file as used here is not the work area alias but the database file name alias. The <alias> name can be determined by use of the command DISPLAY STATUS. The alias for a database file name is either the name of the file itself or the <alias> name given it when the USE command was executed. The <condition> indicates which records are to be selected from the two databases, and the FIELDS clause indicates which fields from each of the two databases are to be included in the records of the third database. Each of the records of the current database are compared with each of the records of the WITH database. If the FIELDS clause does not appear, then all fields from both records are preserved. The maximum number of fields allowed in a database, including the third database, is 128. When this statement is executed, a new database is always created. If a catalog is currently in use, it is updated with the name of the new database. For a further description of features of relational database management systems, see *An Introduction to Database Systems*, third edition, by C. J. Date, Addison-Wesley, February 1982.

EXAMPLE:

```
SELECT 1
USE EMPLOYEE
JOIN WITH FAMILY TO TEMP FOR A->EMPLOYEENO;
   =B->FAMEMPNO
```

will concatenate records from the two database files, if EMPLOYEENO in EMPLOYEE equals FAMEMPNO in FAMILY, and will place the concatenated records into the database file TEMP.

Warning 1:
Ashton-Tate recommends that you do not use an alias for the field names of the current database file (EMPLOYEE in the example above), but it seems to work just fine if you do.

Warning 2:
This command will usually consume excessive amounts of both time and disk space. It is therefore recommended that this command not be used in any of your application systems. Use indexes and the FIND or SEEK command to locate records in a database file that are logically associated with records in another database file. Although dBASE III Plus is advertised as a relational database language, it is recommended that you do not use the relational database features in commercial quality applications.

LABEL FORM <label file name>/? [<scope>] [SAMPLE] [FOR/WHILE <condition>] [TO PRINT] [TO FILE <text file name>]

Uses the label format specified in <label file name> file to print or display labels. If no extension is given for <label file name>, LBL is assumed. If no extension is given for <text file name>, TXT is assumed. The SAMPLE option is used to print dummy labels to aid in alignment of the printing. Automatic prompting to continue the printing of the dummy labels or to start printing the actual labels is provided with the SAMPLE option. If you wish to print the labels directly, use the TO PRINT option. If you wish to send the labels to a text (ASCII) file, use the TO FILE option.

LIST [OFF] [<scope>] [<expression list>][FOR/WHILE <condition>][TO PRINT]

Same as DISPLAY, except that no pauses take place when displaying the records in a large database. This is useful for obtaining a hard-copy list of the database records. In the following, it is assumed that you have turned on the printer before the output from the LIST statement.

Note:
If you LIST a record with no <expression list>, all the non-MEMO fields will be displayed. If you specifically name the MEMO field in the <expression list> of the command, then the contents of this field will also be displayed.

EXAMPLE:

```
USE EMPLOYEE
LIST ALL TO PRINT
```

LIST HISTORY [LAST <integer>] [TO PRINT]

Use this command in the interactive mode to aid in debugging. The last <integer> statements that have been executed are displayed on the screen or on the printer for you.

LIST MEMORY [TO PRINT]

This command is identical to the DISPLAY MEMORY command, except that there will be no pause during long output. Useful when output to the printer is desired.

LIST STATUS [TO PRINT]

This command is identical to the DISPLAY STATUS command, except that there will be no pause during long output. It is particularly useful when output to the printer is desired, since no pause takes place during long output.

LIST STRUCTURE [TO PRINT]

This command is identical to the DISPLAY STRUCTURE command, except that there will be no pause during long output. Useful when output to the printer is desired.

LOAD <name of binary file>

Use this statement to place a copy of a binary file (program) in memory to be executed later by a CALL statement. This statement is particularly helpful when you wish to interface dBASE III Plus with a nonstandard hardware device like a bar code reader. In most cases, a nonstandard device comes with its own driver, a program written in assembler language. Just LOAD this program from disk into memory once during the execution of your dBASE program and then execute it as necessary using the CALL statement. The default extension for the binary file is .BIN, but you can include another extension of your own choice.

Notes:

The binary file cannot exceed 32,000 bytes in size. The file must be binary, and dBASE does not verify that it has the correct format. Any assembly language programs that you use must satisfy the following restrictions in order to interface correctly with dBASE III Plus:

1. The first executable instruction must have an offset of zero.
2. The assembly language program must not use memory outside of its beginning and ending addresses.

3. The assembly language program must not change the size of any parameters passed to it by the CALL . . WITH statement in DS:BX.
4. The assembly language program must restore the CS and the SS registers before returning to dBASE III Plus.
5. Return from the assembly language program to dBASE III with the RET FAR command, not with an EXIT. If your assembly language program terminates with an EXIT rather than with a RET FAR, execute the program through the use of the RUN/! statement, rather than through the use of the LOAD and CALL combination.

If you plan on writing your own assembly language programs:

1. Use the following command to assemble your program.

MASM <filename> <filename> NULL NULL

2. Use the following command to link your program

LINK <filename> NULL NULL

3. And then convert your program to binary format using a command of the form

EXE2BIN <filename>

If you have an entry for MAXMEM in CONFIG.DB, it must not be so restrictive that there is not enough room for both dBASE and your LOADed program(s) to be in memory.

LOCATE [<scope>] [FOR/WHILE <condition>]

Search the current database from the record indicated by the <scope> for the first record that satisfies the <condition>. If a record is located in this manner, the currency pointer indicates this record. Type CONTINUE to continue the search to try to locate another record that satisfies the same <condition>. This command is normally used in the interactive mode. If a record satisfying the conditions is found, then the value of FOUND( ) is set to .T. (TRUE); otherwise the value of FOUND( ) will be .F. (FALSE). Use this command interactively to find a record in an unindexed database file.

Warning:
This command can be time-consuming, since it sequentially searches from the current record through the database file for the desired records.

LOOP

Skip the remainder of the statements in the current WHILE loop, but continue the loop. This command is equivalent to "goto the ENDDO at the end of the loop". Depending on your programming style, you may find several applications for this statement.

EXAMPLE:

```
USE EMPLOYEE
DO WHILE .NOT. EOF( )
    IF DELETED( )
        SKIP 1
        LOOP
    ENDIF
        <normal processing goes here>
    SKIP 1
ENDDO
```

will allow you to write programs without deeply nested IF's.

MODIFY COMMAND [<command file name>]

Allows the user to perform full-screen editing of a procedure (program) directly from dBASE III Plus. If the <command file name> is omitted, the user is prompted for the name. If you do not explicitly give the extension, then the extension PRG is assumed. If the file does not exist, it is created. Cursor controls are given in Table 2.14.

If you are using two floppy disk drives, you will probably want to use this editor because you will not have enough room on your disk for dBASE III Plus, some other editor, and your application programs. I personally prefer to use a good word processor (editor) like WordStar, since it is more powerful and provides a number of functions that I like to use, but which are not available with the MODIFY COMMAND.

Warning 1:
If you use WordStar, remember to use it only in nondocument mode when editing dBASE III Plus application programs.

Warning 2:
The MODIFY COMMAND has some limitations that you might find difficult to live with. In particular, lines are limited to 79 characters and

TABLE 2.14

KEYSTROKE	ACTION
Arrow keys	Move the cursor in the indicated direction.
^A, Home	Move the cursor to the beginning of the previous word.
Backspace, Rub	Delete character to the left of the cursor.
^B, ^→	Move cursor to end of line.
^C, PgDn	Next page.
^D	Same as right arrow.
^E	Same as up arrow.
^F, End	Move the cursor to the beginning of the next word.
F1, ^\	Hide/display the keystroke menu.
^G, Del	Delete the character in the cursor position.
^KB	Reformat paragraph.
^KF	Find first occurrence of string.
^KL	Find next occurrence of string.
^KR	Copy the contents of another file into the file being edited. The file read in is inserted into the current file at the cursor position.
^KW	Copy all the current file to another file.
^M, RETURN	Move the cursor to the beginning of the next line.
^N	Insert a blank line immediately after the cursor.
^Q, Esc	Exit and abort any changes.
^R, PgUp	Previous page.
^S	Same as left arrow.
^T	Delete next word.
^V, Ins	Set insert mode on or off.
^W	Exit and save changes.
^X	Same as down arrow.
^Y	Delete the current line.
^Z, ^←	Move cursor to beginning of line.

a file cannot contain more than 5000 characters. Even though Ashton-Tate has included a number of new features (since the original dBASE III), some of the most useful functions of WordStar are still missing. For example, you still cannot copy or move a block of code from one place in a program to another.

Note:
You can modify your copy of dBASE III Plus so that entry of the MODIFY COMMAND statement will automatically call your favorite editor, rather than the Ashton-Tate editor. To do this, make the following entry in your CONFIG.DB file:

TEDIT = <name of your editor>

Since I use WordStar, I have entered the following in my CONFIG.DB file:

TEDIT = WS

In order to facilitate using the editor from dBASE III Plus, I have also included the following statement in my CONFIG.DB file:

F10 = "MODIFY COMMAND "

When I press F10, the MODIFY COMMAND statement is entered for me, and I just need to type in the name of the file that I wish to edit.

Note:
When I first used WordStar in this manner, I found that it was called in document mode. In order to change the parameters for WordStar so that it would be called in nondocument mode by dBASE III Plus, it was necessary to run the WordStar installation program. If you use an editor of your choice in this manner, you may find that you will have to make some changes similar to the one noted here.

MODIFY LABEL <label file name>/?

Use the command to create or modify a label format file. A label format file is used by the LABEL command to display or print labels. If you do not specify the extension of the <label file name>, LBL is assumed. When this command is executed, a menu bar with three menu items is displayed on the screen. The three menu items are: Options, Contents, and Exit. Use Options to specify the size of the label, use Contents to specify the content of each line of the label, and use Exit to terminate the design of the label. To select a nonstandard label size, move the highlight to the appropriate position of the first menu, press RETURN, and enter a new value. (See figure on the next page.)

```
Options                         Contents                         Exit 10:35:09 am

 Predefined size:         3 1/2 x 15/16 by 1

 Label width:                35
 Label height:                5
 Left margin:                 0
 Lines between labels:        1
 Spaces between labels:       0
 Labels across page:          1


 CURSOR:   ←─  ─→        Delete char:  Del   Insert row:    ^N    Insert:     Ins
   Char:   ←    →        Delete word:  ^T    Toggle menu:   F1    Zoom in:    ^PgDn
   Word:   Home End      Delete row:   ^U    Abandon:       Esc   Zoom out:   ^PgUp

 MODIFY LABEL        |<C:>| NAME.LBL        | Opt: 1/7        |      | Caps
            Position selection bar - ↑ ↓.  Select - ↵.  Leave menu - ←→.
            Select a standard label size: (Width x Height by Number across).
```

When you have completed your information for the size of the labels in the first menu, press the right arrow and specify the content of each line of the label. Move the highlight to the desired line of the label, press RETURN to identify the line to be changed, and enter the information to be displayed in the label. If you need to see database structure information at this point, press F10. No matter how you have defined F10 with the SET FUNCTION statement, dBASE knows from the context of your work that you want to see the structure of the current database. Use the arrow keys to cycle through the names of the fields after you press F10. If you highlight a field name and then press RETURN, the name of the field is copied for you to the cursor position in the line of the label that you are editing. You may enter names of fields from the current database file, functions that manipulate the contents of the fields (like the STR to change a number to a character string for label use), and character string constants (delimited).

You may enter more than one item to appear on a line of the label. If you enter, for example, the two fields A and B with the entry

A,B

then the output will be printed as if you had entered

TRIM(A) + ", " + TRIM(B)

Before a label is printed, the system removes blank lines and centers each printed line.

The restrictions of label dimensions are:

Width of label	1–120 characters
Height of label	1–16 lines
Left margin	0–250
Lines between labels	0–16
Columns between labels	1–120
Number of labels across	1–15

The standard size options are shown in Table 2.15.

MODIFY QUERY <query file name>/?

Use this statement to create or modify a filter for a database file or for a view file. In order to activate the filter for a database or view file, use the SET FILTER TO FILE <file name> statement.

When this command is executed, a menu bar with four menu items is displayed on the screen. The menu items are: Set Filter, Nest, Display, and Exit. The Set Filter option is used to create a new filter or modify an existing one; the Nest option is used to specify or

TABLE 2.15

WIDTH	HEIGHT	NUMBER OF LABELS ACROSS
$3\frac{1}{2}''$	$\frac{15}{16}''$	1
$3\frac{1}{2}''$	$\frac{15}{16}''$	2
$3\frac{1}{2}''$	$\frac{15}{16}''$	3
4"	$1\frac{7}{16}''$	1
$3\frac{2}{10}''$	$\frac{11}{12}''$	3

change the order in which the individual statements in the filter condition are evaluated; the Display option is used to view a record to see if the filter has been defined correctly; and the Exit option is used to terminate design of the filter. The options in the menu bar are explained in the following:

```
Set Filter               Nest                 Display                Exit 10:41:45 am
 Field Name
 Operator
 Constant/Expression
 Connect
 Line Number         1

 Line | Field      | Operator          | Constant/Expression | Connect
 1
 2
 3
 4
 5
 6
 7

 MODIFY QUERY    | <C:> | QUERY.QRY        | Opt | 1/2
        Position selection bar - ↑ ↓.  Select - ↵.  Leave menu - ←→.
                Select a field name for the filter condition.
```

Set Filter

A new menu is displayed on the screen. In order to select a function from this menu, such as the entry of a field name as part of a condition, place the highlight on the item and press RETURN. The names of the fields in the database are displayed on the screen. Select a name and press RETURN to enter it in the condition table. You can enter the name of a field, an operator to be used in the condition, a value to be used to test against the content of the specified field, and an optional connector. The connectors are used to provide logical AND, OR, and NOT operators in a complex condition.

The operators that can be used with the different data types are shown in Table 2.16.

When you enter a value to be tested, be sure to enter the correct data type. In particular, if the data is a character string, remember to delimit it. If the data is a date or a number, do not use delimiters.

To change the line number, highlight it, press RETURN, enter the number of the line to be changed <entered>, and then press RETURN.

You can connect a number of conditions through the selection of the CONNECT option. When you select this option, the following choices will be presented on the screen:

No combination

Combine with .AND.

Combine with .OR.

Combine with .AND..NOT.

Combine with .OR..NOT.

In order to logically link a statement in a filter condition with the next one in the table, place an entry in the column named Connect of the current condition. Only records that satisfy the filter condition can be accessed when the filter is in effect.

If you decide to make delete an entire statement in a condition, highlight the name of the field in the Set Filter table and press ^U.

Nest

Use this feature to place parentheses around or remove parentheses from groups of statements in your condition. The statements are numbered and appear in the condition table at the bottom of the screen. The purpose of the parentheses, if used, is to change or clarify the order in which the statements in the condition are to be evaluated. For example, if the statement

```
A .OR. B .AND. C
```

is to be evaluated, should it be evaluated as

```
(A .OR. B) .AND. C
```

TABLE 2.16

CHARACTER STRINGS	DATES OR NUMBERS
= Matches	= Equals
< > Does not match	> More than
Begins with	> = More than or equal
Does not begin with	< Less than
Ends with	< = Less than or equal
Does not end with	< > Not equal to
$ Contains	
Does not contain	
Is contained in	
Is not contained in	
> Comes after	
> = Comes after or matches	
< Comes before	
< = Comes before or matches	

or should it be evaluated as

```
A .OR. (B .AND. C).
```

In general, each of the two versions of the condition gives different results. If you have any doubt concerning the method of evaluation that dBASE will use, I recommend that you use parentheses to guarantee that the evaluation will be performed as expected.

Display
The first record in the database file that satisfies the filter condition is displayed on the screen so that you can see if the filter is being applied correctly.

Exit
You can either save the changes or abort them.

MODIFY REPORT <report form file name>/?

This command is used to create or modify a report form file. The report form file would be used later by the REPORT command to produce a report. Unless you explicitly give the file name extension, the extension of FRM will be assumed. When this command is executed, you will be presented with a menu bar at the top of the screen. In order to make a selection from the menu bar, highlight the desired item and press RETURN. The menu items are Options, Groups, Columns, Locate, and Exit.

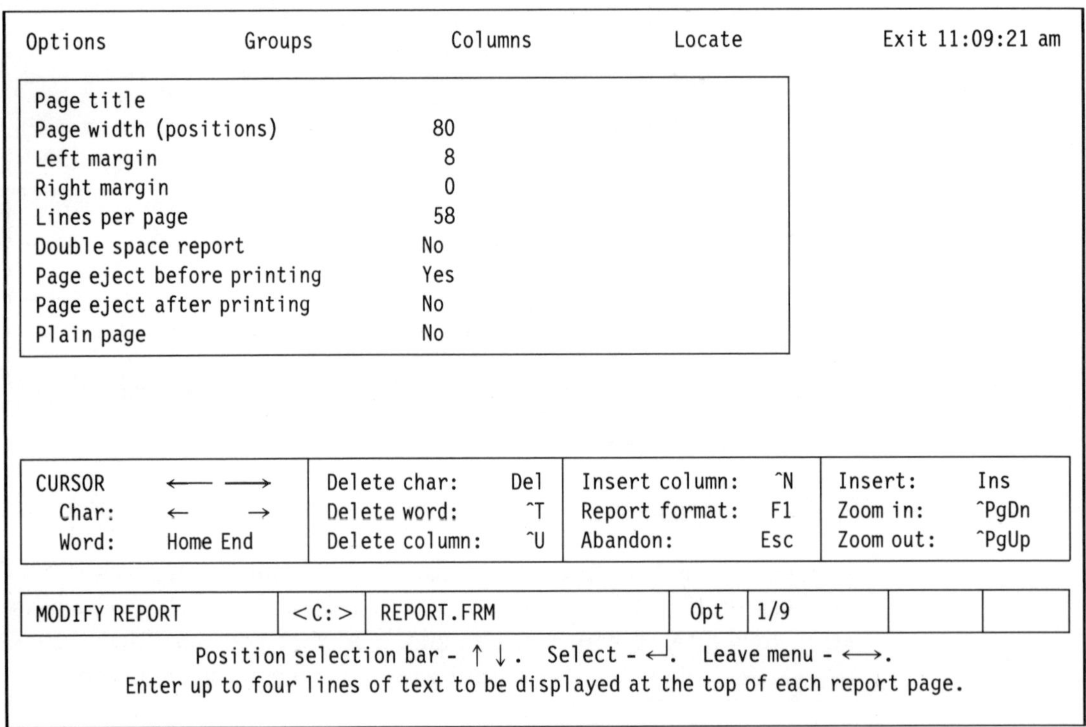

Options is used to specify parameters that apply to the entire report. The particular parameters to be set are:

1. A title for the report: up to four lines.
2. The width of the report page: between 1 and 500 columns.
3. The left and right margins.
4. The number of lines per page: between 1 and 500.
5. Spacing between lines of the report: single or double.

6. Page ejects: before printing the report, after printing the report, and none at all.
7. Plain page: suppress printing of page numbers, system date, and some headings.

The Groups option is used to specify how you want to print headings and summaries associated with groups of data (control groups). You may group data in any reasonable manner. For example, you may group records in your database file by department, but remember that the records in the database must be presented to the REPORT WRITER in the same group order that you specify here. To do this, you must either SORT the database file prior to using the REPORT command or you must specify the appropriate index. Before you use the REPORT command, you must specify the database to be used by the report. At this time, specify the database file name and the index to be used with a USE command.

The Columns option is used to enter specific column information as listed below:

1. *Contents.* The name of a field or an expression that identifies the data to appear in a specific report column.
2. *Heading.* The column heading.
3. *Width.* The width of the display area for the data. The default is to use the actual size of the field in the database file. If you choose a width that is too small for the data, then the data will appear in the same column area on the next line of the report.
4. *Decimal places.* If the number of decimal places to the right of the decimal point is smaller than the actual data, then the data is rounded when output.
5. *Total this column.* It is surprising to find this option associated with Columns rather than with Groups, since it indicates whether a column with numeric data should be subtotaled or not (the default is to subtotal each column containing numeric data). The actual printing of the subtotals is controlled by your entries under the Groups option. Totals are printed for each subgroup, group, and at the end of the report, providing a grand total.

Note:
To delete a column, press ^U (CTRL-U). To add a column before an existing one, press ^N (CTRL-N).

As you specify the column information, dBASE draws a picture of your report at the bottom of the screen, showing the column headings and a coded description of the detail lines (the actual data lines in the report). The symbols used in the coded descriptions are shown in Table 2.17.

You can press F1 for help with keystrokes and F10 for a list of the fields in the database. When you have completed entry of information for a column, press PGDN to move on to the next column. Press PGUP to go back to a previous column.

The Locate option can be used to review your report layout and selectively edit or modify your report. The difference between Columns and Locate is that Columns is oriented to entering the next column for the report and Locate is oriented to entering report information for a specific field in the database. When you select the Locate option, the names of the fields in the database are listed for you. Selection of a name from this list immediately places you in Column mode, ready to enter or edit column information for this specific field.

Exit allows you to terminate your report design and to save or abort any changes made to the report specifications.

MODIFY SCREEN <screen file name>/?

The MODIFY SCREEN statement allows you to draw a picture of a screen display using a full-screen editor and then automatically

TABLE 2.17

CODE	MEANING
>	Right margin
<	Left margin
X	Character data
9	Numeric data that will not be totaled
#	Numeric data that will be totaled
mm/dd/yy	A date—the specific form of the date will depend on your specific date format and the status of SET CENTURY. The default date format is mm/dd/yy.
.L.	Logical data
?	A memo column

convert this picture into a dBASE III Plus program that will draw this screen for you. The picture is stored in an SCR file and the program is stored in an FMT file. You can make changes to the picture as needed, and dBASE will automatically change the FMT file for you. The FMT file is created or modified when you terminate the MODIFY SCREEN function. Once you have created an FMT file in this manner, you can activate it through the use of a SET FORMAT TO statement.

When you invoke the MODIFY SCREEN function, a menu bar will be displayed at the top of the screen. The items in the menu bar are: Set Up, Modify, Options, and Exit. To select an option from the menu bar, highlight the name of the option and press RETURN. If you find that you wish to return from a process to the menu bar, try pressing F10.

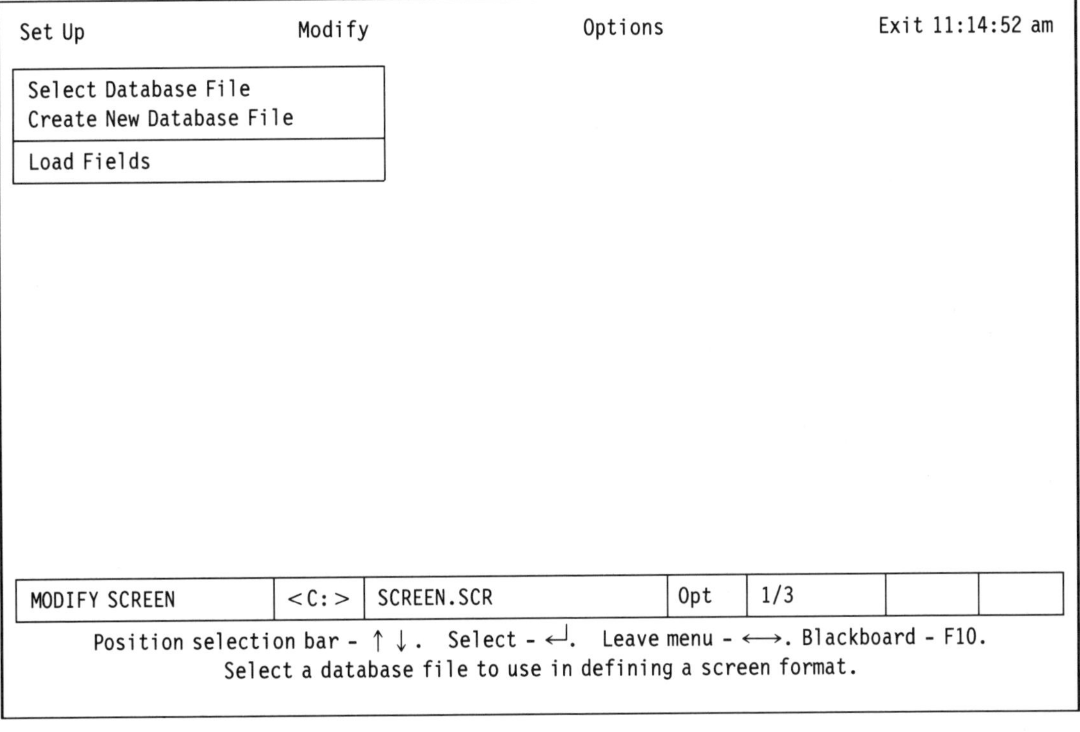

The Set Up option is used to specify the database file to be associated with the screen display. If the one that you desire has not been created yet, you can create it. You can also modify the structure of an existing database file through the use of this option. The workspace for specifying which database fields will be used is called the blackboard. As you select the names of database fields, they are placed on your blackboard. To add new field names, press F10 and select the desired names.

The Modify option allows you to specify each of the following:

1. *Action.* Display the data (SAY) or enter/edit date (GET).
2. *Source.* Specify the name of the active database. If you wish to change the name of the database, you must do this through the Set Up option.
3. *Content.* Specify the name of the field.
4. *Type.* Specify the type of data to be displayed or entered. You can enter character, date, logical, memo, or numeric, but memo can only be used when you enter or edit the data.
5. *Width.* Specify the size of the field.
6. *Decimals.* Specify the number of places to the right of the decimal point.
7. *Picture.* Specify the PICTURE to be used when the data is entered or displayed. See the @ . . SAY statement.
8. *Range.* Specify upper and lower bounds for date or numeric data.

The Options menu allows you to document your screen image through the Create Text File Image function and to draw either a single line or a double line box on any portion of the screen. When you indicate that you wish to draw a box, dBASE places MODIFY SCREEN in box-drawing mode. To draw the box, place the cursor for the upper left-hand corner, press RETURN, place the cursor for the lower right-hand corner, and then press RETURN.

The Exit option is used to terminate MODIFY SCREEN and either save or abort your changes. If you select the Save option, then the new FMT file is generated at this time. If you select the Abandon option, then no FMT file is generated.

The actual placement of the fields on the screen is done on the blackboard. To move between the blackboard and the menu items, press F10. Once you are on the blackboard, you can perform each of the following tasks:

1. *Enter text.* Use the usual full-screen editing keystrokes. Unfortunately, pressing F1 while on the blackboard *does not* display a menu of applicable keystrokes.

2. *Move text.*
   A. Move to the right: position the cursor, press INS, and then press SPACEBAR as needed.
   B. Move to the left: position the cursor and press DEL.
3. *Move fields.* Position the cursor at the field, press RETURN, move the cursor to the new position, and press RETURN again.
4. *Insert a blank line.* Press RETURN.
5. *Enlarge the display area for a field.* Position the cursor at the area and press INS.
6. *Decrease the display area for a field.* Position the cursor at the area and press DEL.
7. *Delete text.* Press DEL.
8. *Delete a field from the blackboard.* Position the cursor and press ^U (CTRL-U).

```
Set Up              Modify              Options              Exit 11:19:05 am







MODIFY SCREEN   | <C:> | SCREEN.SCR           | Pg 01 Row 00 Col 00 |     |     |
          Enter text. Drag field or box under cursor with ←┘. F10 for menu.
                      Screen field definition blackboard.
```

MODIFY STRUCTURE <database file name>

Change the structure of the current database. If you do not explicitly give the extension for the database file name, the extension of DBF is assumed. This command will automatically back up the current database file and then reload it when you have completed your structural modifications. It will be your responsibility to remove the backup file (with the BAK extension) yourself. The backup file will have the structure and contents of the original (unmodified) database file.

You may change any of the following: field name, type, width, or the number of decimal places. The command will attempt to reload the data stored in the backup file in the obvious manner. For example, if you have changed the name of a field, the appropriate data will be placed in the newly named field.

Warning:

If you change both the name and the size of a field, the appropriate data will not be reloaded from the backup file. Use the MODIFY STRUCTURE command to change the name and then use the MODIFY STRUCTURE command again to change the field size.

You may insert a new field in the definition with ^N and delete an existing one with ^U.

Warning:

If you delete a field and then add another one of the same type and size in its place, it is treated as a simple name change.

Use ESC to exit and abort changes, and ^End to exit and save the changes.

An options menu can be displayed on the screen by pressing either ^HOME (CTRL-HOME) or ^] (CTRL-]). This menu contains the following items: Bottom, Top, Field #, Save, and Abandon. Use Bottom to go immediately to the last field in the definition, Top to go immediately to the first field in the definition, Field # to select a specific field to go to, Save to save the modifications, and Abandon to abort the changes. (See figure on the next page.)

MODIFY VIEW <view file name>/?

A view is a logical (virtual) database that consists of data stored in two or more database files. dBASE logically links records together according to specifications that you provide. Once the records are linked together, you can access the data in different files as if it were

```
                                                        Bytes remaining:  3953

CURSOR    <--  -->    |   INSERT        |  DELETE       |  Up a field:    ↑
 Char:    <-    ->    |  Char:   Ins    |  Char:   Del  |  Down a field:  ↓
 Word:    Home End    |  Field:  ^N     |  Word:   ^Y   |  Exit/Save:     ^End
 Pan:     ^<-   ^->   |  Help:   F1     |  Field:  ^U   |  Abort:         Esc

     Field Name    Type        Width   Dec       Field Name   Type      Width   Dec

 1   ACCTACCNO     Character    10
 2   ACCTTYPACT    Character    20
 3   ACCTDTACT     Date          8
 4   ACCTAMT       Numeric       9       2
 5                 Character

MODIFY STRUCTURE | <C:> | ACCTFILE          | Field: 5/5          |      | Caps
                          Enter the field name.
     Field names begin with a letter and may contain letters, digits and underscores
```

physically all together in one file. In a sense, a view is an unnormalized version of the data. If you do not explicitly give the extension for the database file name, the extension of VUE is assumed. Once a view has been constructed, it can be activated through the use of the SET VIEW TO statement.

When you execute the MODIFY VIEW statement, a menu bar containing the following menu items is placed on the screen: Set Up, Relate, Set Fields, Options, and Exit. (See figure on p. 106.)

Set Up

Use this option to select up to nine database files if a catalog is open and up to 10 database files if no catalog is open. The allowable databases are listed on the screen and you select one by highlighting it and pressing RETURN. When you select a database file, the associated index files are then displayed on the screen and you can now select indexes for the database file. If you want to create a view using precisely the database and index files currently open, use the CREATE VIEW FROM ENVIRONMENT statement. If a

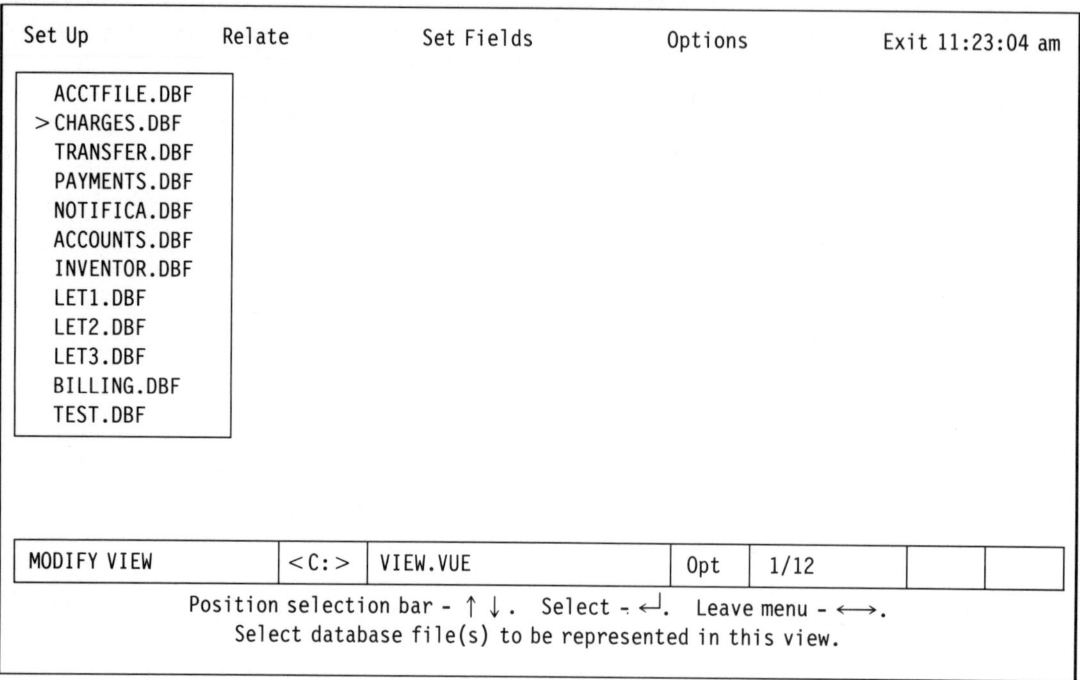

catalog is open, you can have up to nine database files in a chain; otherwise you can have 10.

Relate

Use this option to link database files together in a chain (linked list). The first database file that you select is the controlling file and the first database in the chain. After you have selected the initial database file, you can then select another database file and link the new file to the preceding one. You can continue linking in this manner until you have entered the maximum number of allowable database files in the chain. It is possible to relate files either by data content or by record numbers, but it appears that relating files by record number has inherent problems. For example, what happens if you delete a record from one of the files but not from the other? The records in the two files no longer match as they should, and the linkage between the two files will be incorrect.

To start the list (chain), move to the Relate menu and select a database file from the ones that you listed in the Set Up menu item. As soon as you select one of these files, dBASE then lists the remaining file names. To choose from the remaining files, highlight a name in this new list and press RETURN. You have now indicated that you wish to link your previous choice with your most recent one. dBASE now places a triangle to the right of the most recently selected database file name, waiting for you to specify how to link these two database files together. If you are linking the two databases together by the names of database fields (the recommended method), press F10 to see the names of the fields. Enter the name of the field in the previous database file to be associated with the index in the most recent database file. Press RETURN, and then left arrow to return to the Relate menu. Continue this process until you have specified and linked each database file.

Set Fields
The default is to display all the fields in all the files. If you do not wish to display all the fields in all the files—for example, if your chain has two files in it and you wish to display the duplicated information just once—use this menu item to change the display. Highlight the name of the database file, press RETURN, and then deselect the name of one of the fields by highlighting it and pressing RETURN. When you have deselected as many names as desired, return to the Set Fields menu item by pressing either left or right arrow.

Options
Options allows you to specify a filter and a format file. The filter allows you to simultaneously work with data in one or more of the files in the chain. The format file can be used to tailor the display of the data in the view.

Exit
You can Save or Abandon your modifications to the view.

Warning:
When I tried to use a view, I found that only the initial database file was used, if all the fields were included in the display (the default mode). As soon as I deselected one of the fields from the view, the data was displayed correctly.

NOTE or *

Both of these, when placed at the beginning of a line of the program, allow the insertion of comments. These comments are not echoed at the screen. I like to use the "*" at the beginning of each program to identify it and to indicate unusual items in the program. If you wish to place a comment at the end of a line, place the characters && to the right of the other entry on the line and dBASE will treat anything to the right of the && as a comment.

EXAMPLES:

```
* EMPENTER.PRG
* THIS PROGRAM ENTERS NEW EMPLOYEE RECORDS
SEEK MEMIDNO  && FIND THE RECORD WITH THE SAME IDNO
```

ON ERROR [<statement>]

If a dBASE error occurs, trap the error and execute the indicated statement. To discontinue error trapping, use ON ERROR without the accompanying statement.

EXAMPLE:

```
ON ERROR DO ERRRUTIN
```

ON ESCAPE [<statement>]

If the ESC key is pressed, execute the indicated statement. If both ON KEY and ON ESCAPE are active, ON ESCAPE takes precedence. To discontinue ESC trapping, use ON ESCAPE without the accompanying statement.

EXAMPLE:

```
ON ESCAPE @ 5,0 SAY "The Escape key cannot be used here?
```

ON KEY [<statement>]

If a key is pressed, execute the indicated statement. Remember to remove the character from the input buffer with the INKEY( ) or with the READ statements.

PACK

All the records marked for deletion (by the DELETE command) will be physically removed from the database. All active index files for the current database will automatically be reindexed for you.

EXAMPLE:

```
USE EMPLOYEE INDEX EMPLNO
DO WHILE .NOT. EOF( )
     DELETE NEXT 1 FOR SALARY > 40000
     SKIP 1
ENDDO
PACK
```

will mark selected records for physical removal (the DELETE statement) and then will physically remove them (the PACK statement).

PARAMETERS <parameter list>

Used to assign a local <private> name to the data passed from the calling program. The local data names are treated as local memory variables and are deallocated (RELEASEd) when the subroutine has been completed. If the data item in the calling program is a memory variable and if its value has been changed in the called program (the subroutine), then the change is effective in the calling program. Thus the names in the <parameter list> are treated as local aliases for the data passed to it. This command must appear as the first executable command of the subroutine and must match the WITH option in the DO statement of the calling program. The number of objects in the WITH <parameter list> of the DO command must match the number of objects in the <parameter list> of the PARAMETERS command.

EXAMPLE:

```
* SUBROUTINE FOR TEST.PRG
PARAMETERS LENGTH, WIDTH, HEIGHT, WEIGHT
STORE LENGTH*WIDTH*HEIGHT*5.00 TO WEIGHT
RETURN
```

PRIVATE [ALL [LIKE/EXCEPT <skeleton>]][<memory variable list>]

Used to hide higher level memory variable names from the current program (subroutine) and from any programs called directly or indirectly from the current program. This allows the use of variables that are local to the called program but have the same names as variables at a higher level. If you make a variable name from a higher level program PRIVATE and then reuse the variable name at the current (lower level), then the original type and value are given back to the original variable upon exit from the lower level program and the local memory variables are released at the time of the exit (the new data values are not passed to the higher level program). This command can be used to protect higher level variables from change during the execution of a subroutine.

PROCEDURE <procedure name>

Used to mark the beginning of each utility program in a procedure file. Each of the programs in a procedure file must begin with a PROCEDURE command of the form PROCEDURE <procedure name> and must end with the word RETURN. A procedure name may have length of 1 to 8 characters consisting of letters, numbers, and underscores. Each procedure name must begin with a letter. You may have no more than one procedure file open at any one time. To open a procedure file, use the SET PROCEDURE TO command. To close a procedure file, use the CLOSE PROCEDURE command. The two purposes of a procedure file are to save file access time and to reduce the number of open files. Once a procedure file has been established by your application program, it can be used until the program terminates. You can execute the programs in a procedure file as if they were PRG files in your directory. When you create a procedure file with your editor, give it a PRG extension.

PUBLIC <memory variable list>

Make a memory variable first used in a lower level program accessible at a higher level. Usually, a memory variable must not exist before it is made PUBLIC. The only exception is that a variable that is already PUBLIC may be redeclared as PUBLIC.

QUIT

All the active files and databases are closed, the memory variables are released, and an exit to the operating system is performed. Make this the last command in your application program or the last interactive command if you are using dBASE III Plus in the interactive mode. This is the only safe way to exit from dBASE III Plus. If you exit in any other manner, you might damage files and lose data.

READ [SAVE]

Activates all @ . . GET commands executed since the last READ, CLEAR, or CLEAR GETS. If you have any @ . . GET commands without a READ command, then they will be treated as @ . . SAY commands. When the READ statement is encountered by dBASE, full-screen editing mode is entered. If the SAVE option is used, the GETs are not cleared, so you may READ them again at a later time.

Note 1:
The SAVE option may be of help to you if you wish to continue editing until all the entries are correct.

Note 2:
If you use the SAVE option, you may need to execute a CLEAR GETS before you enter more data with additional @ . . SAY . . GETs, because of the limitation of 128 pending GETs.

RECALL [<scope>] [FOR/WHILE <condition>]

Essentially the inverse of the DELETE statement. This command removes the delete flags from all records in the current database file. The RECALL command will not recover any records that have been physically removed from the database (by the PACK or the ZAP) commands. If SET DELETED is ON, the RECALL statement is ignored. The default scope is NEXT 1, that is, the current record.

EXAMPLE:

```
USE EMPLOYEE
DELETE ALL
```

will mark all the records in the database file for future physical removal.

```
RECALL ALL
```

will remove all the "*" marks placed in any of the records by a DELETE statement.

REINDEX

Use the currently active index files or use the SET INDEX command to establish a new set of index files. Then use the REINDEX command to cause a reindexing of all the active index files for the current database file. If you reindex a file on a field that can have only unique values (SET UNIQUE ON), then a reindex preserves the uniqueness, whether UNIQUE is currently ON or OFF.

EXAMPLE 1:

```
USE EMPLOYEE INDEX EMPNAME, EMPSSN
REINDEX
```

EXAMPLE 2:

```
USE EMPLOYEE INDEX EMPNAME
          .
          .
          .
SET INDEX TO EMPSSN
REINDEX
```

RELEASE [<memvar list>] [ALL [LIKE/EXCEPT <skeleton>]]

Deallocates the space used by the indicated memory variables. This statement is useful in freeing selected memory variables if you run out of available memory variables. In the <skeleton> you may use the wild card characters ? and * . If the current program is a routine called by a higher level program, variables at the higher level are not released, only the ones defined in the current routine.

EXAMPLES:

```
RELEASE ALL
```

releases all active memory variables.

```
RELEASE ALL LIKE T*
```

releases all active memory variables whose names start with the letter T.

```
RELEASE ALL EXCEPT ??T*
```

releases all active memory variables except those that have the letter T in the third position of their name.

```
RELEASE A, B, C
```

releases the memory variables A, B and C.

RELEASE MODULE <name of binary file>

Erase the previously LOADed assembly language program from memory.

RENAME <original file name> TO <new file name>

Used to change the name of an MS/PC DOS file while in dBASE III Plus. You must include the extensions for both files. If a database file that contains a memo field is renamed, you will have to rename the corresponding DBT file yourself.

EXAMPLE:

```
RENAME TEMP.DBF TO TEMP1.DBF
```

REPLACE [<scope>] <field> WITH <exp>[, <field> WITH <exp>...] [FOR/WHILE <condition>]

Used to replace the indicated fields with the values supplied in the corresponding WITH clauses for all the records in the current database indicated by the <scope> and the <condition>. If the <scope> is not supplied, then only the current record is affected.

Note:
You may not use the alias name with the name of the field to be replaced. For example,

```
REPLACE A->X WITH B->X
```

is not allowed, but

```
REPLACE X WITH B->X
```

is allowed.

EXAMPLE:

```
USE EMPLOYEE INDEX EMPLOYEENO
STORE SPACE(5) TO MEMEMPNO
CLEAR
@ 5, 1 SAY "ENTER EMPLOYEE NO" GET MEMEMPNO
READ
SEEK MEMEMPNO
IF EOF( )
    ? "NO RECORD ON FILE FOR GIVEN EMPLOYEE NUMBER"
    WAIT
ELSE
    STORE 0 TO MEMSALARY
    STORE CTOD("  /  /  ") TO MEMDATE
    @ 10,0 SAY "ENTER THE NEW SALARY" GET MEMSALARY
    @ 11,0 SAY "ENTER THE DATE" GET MEMDATE
    READ
    REPLACE EMPSALARY WITH MEMSALARY, EMPDATE ;
        WITH MEMDATE
ENDIF
```

where EMPSALARY and EMPDATE are record fields in the database file EMPLOYEE. Note that the ";" allows the continuation of a statement on the next line.

Note:

If you replace a field that affects an active index, then the replacement automatically updates the indexes affected. If you replace a field that does not affect an index, then no index files are updated.

REPORT FORM <form file name>/? [<scope>] [FOR/WHILE <condition>] [PLAIN][HEADING <character string>][NOEJECT] [TO PRINT]/[TO FILE <text file name>][SUMMARY]

This command allows the printing of a report using the predefined report format contained in the form file. If the extension of the <form file name> is not explicitly given, FRM is assumed.

If the PLAIN option is selected, then the report is printed without page numbers, without a date, and the HEADING appears on the first page only.

Use the HEADING option to enter an additional heading line.

Delimit the <character string> with (") or (') or ([]). You can use either the PLAIN or the HEADING option. If both appear, then PLAIN is used by dBASE.

Use the TO PRINT option to have output go to the printer. In this case you may use the NOEJECT option to suppress the initial form feed at the beginning of the report. Use the TO FILE option to direct output to a text file. A default extension for the file that receives the report is TXT unless explicitly stated.

If you use the SUMMARY option, none of the detail lines of the report are printed or sent to the file. The resultant report will consist only of headings and summary lines. See MODIFY REPORT or a description of headings and summary lines.

Note:
The default scope consists of all the records in the database. When you USE a database file, make sure that the appropriate index is in effect.

RESTORE FROM <file> [ADDITIVE]

You may retrieve memory variables and their values from a file created with the SAVE command. The default extension for the file is MEM. If the ADDITIVE option is used, the new memory variables will be added to the current collection of memory variables. If this option is not used, all memory variables in existence before the RESTORE will be released. Remember that there may not be more than 256 active memory variables and that the total amount of room used by the memory variables may not exceed 6000 bytes, unless you change this limitation in the CONFIG.DB file. When memory variables are RESTOREd from a program, the variables are typed as PRIVATE.

EXAMPLE:

```
RESTORE FROM SAVEFILE
```

RESUME

This interactive command is executed after a running program is interrupted. In most cases, the program will be interrupted as a result of pressing the ESC key. When you press the ESC key, you will be asked to A(bort), I(gnore), or S(uspend) execution of the program.

You can resume execution of the program only if you choose S(uspend). The use of ESC, S(uspend), and RESUME are quite useful in debugging a program, since an ESC followed by a S(uspend) allows you to do a DISPLAY MEMORY to look at memory variables.

RETRY

The RETRY statement is used in a subroutine to force a repeat of the routine. When the RETRY statement is executed, control returns to the calling routine and the subroutine is executed again. This statement can be used to recover from a variety of errors, if it is executed as a result of an ON ERROR situation.

RETURN [TO MASTER]

If the TO MASTER option is not used, then the RETURN causes an exit from a subroutine and control is passed to the program at the line immediately following the point where the subroutine was invoked. If a RETURN from the highest level program is executed, control goes to dBASE III Plus and the "." appears on the screen. If the TO MASTER option is used, then a transfer takes place to the highest level calling program (probably the main menu of your application system). When a RETURN is executed, all PRIVATE variables are released.

EXAMPLE:

```
WAIT "ENTER ANOTHER INVOICE (Y/N)" TO ANSWER
IF UPPER(ANSWER) < > "Y"
     RETURN
ENDIF
```

RUN <file name>

or

! <file name>

Executes a COM or EXE file, or a DOS command like DIR from within dBASE III Plus. When the execution of the COM or EXE file has completed, then control returns to dBASE III Plus. ! provides an alternative form of the command.

Warning:
You may need as much as 512K main memory in your computer for this command to work with a EXE or a COM file, but certain DOS routines may require less than 512K main memory. If you have at least 512K memory installed in your computer, you should not have any trouble with this command. In addition, you will probably need the file COMMAND.CMD on your work disk if you are using two floppy disks.

SAVE TO <file name> [ALL LIKE/EXCEPT <skeleton>]

The names and values of all the indicated memory variables are saved (stored) in the file. Unless otherwise specified, the extension of the file is MEM.

EXAMPLES:

```
SAVE TO SAVEFILE
SAVE TO A:SAVEFILE ALL LIKE MEM*
```

SEEK <expression>

The SEEK command is similar to the FIND command, except that the macro function (&) is not used with memory variables. If the <expression> is a character string constant, it must be delimited. Since the SEEK does not require the use of macro expansion, it is recommended that you always use the SEEK rather than the FIND for two reasons: In some cases the SEEK is faster than the FIND; and some compilers cannot handle macro expansion.

EXAMPLES:

```
SEEK NAME
SEEK "Smith"
```

SELECT <work area/alias>

Make the indicated work area the current work area. The selection may be accomplished by supplying the work area number, work area alias, or the database file alias. If a memory variable is used after the keyword SELECT, then it must be preceded by the & symbol.

EXAMPLE 1:

```
SELECT 1
USE A
SELECT 2
```

```
USE B
DO WHILE .NOT. EOF( )
     STORE AKEY TO MEMKEY
          process record
     SELECT 1
     SEEK MEMKEY
     IF .NOT. EOF( )
          process record
     ENDIF
     SELECT 2
     SKIP 1
ENDDO
```

EXAMPLE 2:

```
SELECT 1
USE EMPLOYEE INDEX EMPLNAME
     .
     .
     .
SELECT 1
     .
     .
     .
SELECT A
SELECT EMPLOYEE
```

EXAMPLE 3:

```
STORE "EMPLOYEE" TO MEMVAR
SELECT &MEMVAR
```

SET

When this statement is executed, a menu bar is presented on the screen. This menu bar allows you to SET a number of dBASE III Plus system parameters. The left and right arrows move from one menu item to another. The up and down arrows move you to different entries in each menu item. You may SET any of the following:

1. All ON/OFF SET commands.
2. Screen colors.
3. Function key assignments.

4. Drive and search path.
5. Alternate, format, and index files.
6. Margin.
7. Decimal places.

Note:
Pay close attention to the messages at the bottom of the screen during the change process. They will give you the instructions on how to accomplish the changes.

```
Options    Screen    Keys    Disk    Files    Margin    Decimals    02:03:02 pm

 Alternate    OFF
 Bell         ON
 Carry        OFF
 Catalog
 Century      OFF
 Confirm      OFF
 Deleted      OFF
 Delimiters   OFF
 Device       SCREEN
 Dohistory    OFF
 Escape       ON
 Exact        OFF
 Fields       OFF
 Fixed        OFF
 Heading      ON
 Help         ON
 History      ON
 Intensity    ON

 Set            |<C:>|              | Opt |1/25    |    |
  Position selection bar - ↑ ↓.  Change - ↵.  Leave menu - ←→. Exit - Esc.
                Specify the dBASE III environment options.
```

SET ALTERNATE ON/OFF DEFAULT: OFF

Echo output screen to a disk file. To use this command, you must first identify the name of the file to receive the output. Information placed on the screen by an @ . . SAY is not echoed to the alternate file.

EXAMPLE:

```
SET ALTERNATE TO OUT
NOTE DISK FILE NAME WILL BE OUT.TXT
SET ALTERNATE ON
        .
        .
        .
SET ALTERNATE OFF
```

SET ALTERNATE TO [<file name>]

This statement is used to select a file name to be used when SET ALTERNATE is ON. The default extension is TXT. If the statement is executed without a file name, then the alternate file is closed. The alternate file can also be closed by using the

```
CLOSE ALTERNATE
```

statement.

EXAMPLE:

```
SET ALTERNATE TO OUT
```

SET BELL ON/OFF DEFAULT: ON

Sound the bell if invalid data has been entered or if an input field has been filled.

SET CARRY ON/OFF DEFAULT: OFF

Repeat data from the record just INSERTed or APPENDed when INSERTing or APPENDing.

SET CATALOG ON/OFF DEFAULT: OFF

Enable/disable access to the current catalog. When access is enabled, a number of statements cause the catalog to be updated. If a catalog is set off, it is still open but not updated.

SET CATALOG TO [<catalog name>/?]

Identify and open a catalog. When this statement is executed, the named catalog is automatically set on. If this statement is executed without a parameter after the word TO, then the current catalog is closed.

Note:
When your first catalog is created, dBASE places a special file named CATALOG.CAT in your current directory. When a catalog is open, you cannot use work area 10—dBASE uses it for its own work. Maintenance of the catalog is automatic, if the catalog has been set on by the SET CATALOG statement.

SET CENTURY ON/OFF DEFAULT: OFF

Include/exclude the first two digits (the century) of the year in any display of dates. This statement also affects all full-screen editing.

EXAMPLES:

```
STORE DATE( ) TO X
? X
 01/01/87
SET CENTURY ON
? X
 01/01/1987
```

SET COLOR ON/OFF DEFAULT: OFF

Select color or monochrome mode.

SET COLOR TO [<standard>[, <enhanced>][, <border>] [, <background>]]

Specify each of the four screen color displays: standard, enhanced, border, and background. The standard and enhanced displays are each specified in pairs of the form C1/C2, where C1 is the foreground color and C2 is the background color. The <background> parameter should be used only on those monitors that cannot set the background color for each individual character on the screen. The <background> parameter can be used to set the background color for the entire screen. If no parameters are used, then color mode is reset to the default colors, white on black. The codes for the available colors are given in Table 2.18.

When a color is entered, you may suffix the color code with *, +, or both. The * indicates blinking and the + indicates high intensity. On the monochrome display, U indicates underline and I indicates inverse video.

Note:
The SET COLOR statement can be of use, if you wish to hide entry of a password. For example, you can use an @ . . SAY . . GET and the statement

```
SET COLOR TO GR,W/W
```

just before a password is to be entered, and then reset the color to the appropriate color, after the password has been entered. When the password is entered using this technique, it will not appear on the screen.

EXAMPLE 1:

```
SET COLOR TO B/G, BG/R
```

will set blue on green as the standard display and cyan on red as the enhanced display (used, for example, when editing).

TABLE 2.18

COLOR	LETTER CODE
BLACK	N
BLANK	X
BLUE	B
BROWN	GR
CYAN	BG
GREEN	G
MAGENTA	RB
RED	R
WHITE	W
YELLOW	GR+

EXAMPLE 2:

```
SET COLOR TO GR,W/W
CLEAR
STORE SPACE(6) TO PASSWORD
@ 1,0 SAY "ENTER THE PASSWORD FOR THE SYSTEM:" GET ;
  PASSWORD
READ
IF PASSWORD < > "ZZXYZ"
    ? "INCORRECT PASSWORD"
    QUIT
ENDIF
SET COLOR TO GR,N/W
```

SET CONFIRM ON/OFF DEFAULT: OFF

When in full-screen edit mode, you must type a RETURN to confirm input and move to the next field.

SET CONSOLE ON/OFF DEFAULT: ON

If OFF, output that normally goes to the screen does not appear there. If the keyboard input is being performed, it will be accepted, but it will not show on the screen. This statement can only be used within a program, has no effect on @ . . SAY statements, and has no effect on error messages.

SET DATE AMERICAN/ANSI/BRITISH/ITALIAN/FRENCH/GERMAN DEFAULT: AMERICAN

Use the SET DATE statement to select a specific format for input and output of dates. If you wish to change the format for all dates, enter the appropriate statement in the CONFIG.DB file. Use the SET DATE statement in your programs for temporary changes. The specific formats are given in Table 2.19.

SET DEBUG ON/OFF DEFAULT: OFF

Output from the SET ECHO command is routed to the printer, instead of the screen.

TABLE 2.19

TYPE	FORMAT
AMERICAN	MM/DD/YY
ANSI	YY.MM.DD
BRITISH	DD/MM/YY
ITALIAN	DD-MM-YY
FRENCH	DD/MM/YY
GERMAN	DD.MM.YY

EXAMPLE:

```
SET TALK ON
SET ECHO ON
SET PRINT ON
SET DEBUG ON
```

SET DECIMALS ON <numeric expression> DEFAULT: 2

Determines the number of decimal places that will be displayed as the result of division, SQRT( ), LOG( ), and EXP( ). For other arithmetic operations, the number of decimal places used in the display is determined from the decimal places in the number(s) involved. The actual value stored in a memory variable or in a database field is not necessarily the same as the displayed value.

EXAMPLES:

```
. SET DECIMALS TO 3
. STORE SQRT(10) TO X
. ? X
        3.162
? 1.00000*X
        3.16227766
```

SET DEFAULT TO <drive> DEFAULT: The current drive when dBASE was executed

All file accesses will be made to the specified <drive>, unless the referenced file name specifically indicates the drive.

EXAMPLE:

```
SET DEFAULT TO B
USE EMPLOYEE
```

refers to the database file B:EMPLOYEE.DBF, but

```
USE A:EMPLOYEE
```

refers to the database file A:EMPLOYEE.DBF.

SET DELETED ON/OFF DEFAULT: OFF

If ON, then records marked for deletion will be ignored by certain dBASE III Plus commands. The INDEX and the REINDEX commands never ignore any record marked for deletion. If DELETED is ON, then all other dBASE III Plus commands will ignore records marked for deletion, except in the case where the first record of the scope is marked for deletion and RECORD <expression> or NEXT <expression> is used to indicate the scope. This parameter will allow you to process your database records without having to check for records flagged for deletion.

Note:
If DELETED is ON, then RECALL ALL does not remove the deletion mark from any of the records in the current database file.

SET DELIMITER ON/OFF DEFAULT: OFF

Fields are delimited by reverse video or by highlighting, when full-screen editing is being used. See, for example, the @ . . GET and the EDIT commands. When DELIMITER is set to ON, then the editing area is still in either reverse video or is highlighted, but the area is now preceded and followed by the appropriate delimiter character. To choose the delimiter characters to be used in this manner, use the SET DELIMITER TO statement.

SET DELIMITER TO [<character string>/DEFAULT]

This command allows you to specify your own field delimiter, that is, a field delimiter other than the colon. If you enter one delimiter, it is used to delimit both ends of the area. If you enter two delimiters, the first is used to delimit the left-hand end of the area and the second is used to delimit the right-hand end. If the DEFAULT option is selected, then the delimiter is reset to the colon.

EXAMPLE 1:

```
. SET DELIMITER TO '/'
. SET DELIMITER ON
```

EXAMPLE 2:

```
. SET DELIMITER TO '[]'
. SET DELIMITER ON
```

SET DEVICE TO PRINT

The output from subsequent @ . . SAY commands will go to the printer.

SET DEVICE TO SCREEN

The output from subsequent @ . . SAY commands will go to the screen. This is the system default.

SET DOHISTORY ON/OFF DEFAULT: OFF

Record/do not record statements from currently executing programs in the file named HISTORY. Any commands that you execute interactively are always added to the HISTORY file. Use DISPLAY HISTORY to display the contents of this file on the screen. Some simple testing of your program can be performed using the HISTORY file. To accomplish this, interactively enter the DISPLAY HISTORY command to show the lines of the program on the screen. Use the up arrow to display the desired statement on the screen, edit the statement, and then press RETURN to execute the statement. If your program has terminated because of a syntax error, you will probably want to suspend execution of your program, rather than cancel it, so that the values of the memory variables will be retained. Table 2.20 shows the (simple) editing keystrokes available when you edit the HISTORY file.

TABLE 2.20

KEYSTROKE	ACTION
Right arrow	Go right one character
Left arrow	Go left one character
Up arrow	Go back one statement
Down arrow	Go forward one statement
Home	Go left one word
End	Go right one word
Backspace	Delete previous character
Del	Delete current character
Ins	Toggle between insert and overwrite modes
Caps Lock	Toggle between uppercase and lowercase

Note:
The default number of lines in HISTORY is 20. To change this number, use the SET HISTORY TO statement. The history file can be quite useful if your program terminates because of an error, but you do not know where in the program (at which statement) the termination occurred.

Warning:
Programs will run more slowly when DOHISTORY is set ON.

SET ECHO ON/OFF DEFAULT: OFF

Display the command line being executed on the screen and/or the printer, depending on the setting of certain output parameters. This command is especially useful when debugging a program. The recommended sequence of commands for debugging a program are:

1. Remove all SET DEVICE TO PRINT and SET TALK OFF commands from the program(s)
2. SET TALK ON
3. SET ECHO ON
4. SET DEBUG ON
5. SET PRINT ON

If you follow this procedure, each command executed and the changes in the values of the memory variables will be printed.

SET ESCAPE ON/OFF DEFAULT: ON

If ESCAPE is set ON, a program can be aborted when ESC (the Escape key) is struck. Once a program has been aborted by the use of the ESC key, it can be restarted from the point of interruption, if you suspend execution when prompted and later enter the RESUME command interactively. If ESCAPE is set OFF, then you cannot abort execution of your program.

SET EXACT ON/OFF DEFAULT: OFF

Determines how the equality of two character strings (constants, memory variables, or database fields) is performed. If EXACT is ON, the length of the two character strings must be the same and the contents, character for character, must be the same in order for the two strings to be equal. If EXACT is OFF, the two strings have different lengths, the shorter string being on the left, and then they are not equal. If the shorter string is on the right and if EXACT is OFF, then the comparison is done on a character by character basis, starting with the leftmost character of each, and continuing until the end of the shortest string is encountered.

EXAMPLES:

```
. SET EXACT OFF
. ? "ABC" = ABCD"
.F.
. ? "ABCD" = "ABC"
.T.
. SET EXACT ON
. ? "ABC" = "ABCD"
.F.
. ? "ABCD" = "ABC"
.F.
```

SET FIELDS ON/OFF DEFAULT: OFF

Use or ignore the fields listed in the SET FIELDS TO statement to access database fields. If FIELDS is set ON, only the fields listed in the SET FIELDS TO statement can be edited or displayed. You can access fields both in the current database and in databases in other areas.

Warning:
If you SET FIELDS ON before using the SET FIELDS TO statement, then no fields will be accessible.

SET FIELDS TO [<list of field names>/ALL]

Specify a list of fields in one or more databases that can be accessed. When FIELDS is set to ON, only the fields in this list can be accessed. This restriction on access applies to display, editing, and also the defaults for a number of statements. If SET FIELDS TO is used without any parameters, that is, if SET FIELDS TO is immediately followed by a RETURN, then all the fields in the active database are removed from the current field list, and so they become inaccessible. The use of another SET FIELDS TO statement will add more fields to the current list.

Note 1:
To include a field from a database in another work area, you can include the name of the alias in the field list or you can move to the desired area and then add the name of the field. It appears that the first technique is the desired one. If you wish to include fields of the same name from two databases, always include the alias.

Note 2:
The SET FIELDS statement affects the dBASE statements that contain a FIELDS clause. Then the SET FIELDS TO statement is used, and the following statements can access several fields from more than one database file (the current database or any or all its descendants):

AVERAGE	EDIT
BROWSE	JOIN
CHANGE	LIST
COPY TO	SUM
COPY STRUCTURE	TOTAL
DISPLAY	

Note 3:
The @ . . GET and the REPLACE commands can access the fields named in the SET FIELDS TO list.

Note 4:
It is recommended that VIEWS and RELATIONS not be used in conjunction with the SET FIELDS TO statement.

Note 5:
The INDEX, LOCATE, SET FILTER, and SET RELATION ignore the SET FIELDS TO list, whether the field list is set on or off.

SET FILTER TO [FILE <file name>/?][<condition>]

When a filter condition is in effect, all the records of the current database file that satisfy the <condition> are ignored by the dBASE commands. If the FILE option is used, then the filter condition is obtained from a file with the given name and with the QRY extension. If the <condition> does not appear in the command and if the FILE option is not used, then the filter is deactivated. A filter is identified with the specific work area in which it was originally invoked. Therefore, each work area may have its own filter condition associated with it. The filter used is the one assigned to the current work area.

Note:
The filter condition is defined with the SET FILTER statement, but it is not activated until you change the currency pointer in the database file.

SET FIXED ON/OFF DEFAULT: OFF

dBASE III Plus functions such as RECNO( ), DOW( ), and LEN( ) always display an integer. Other functions and numeric operations display real (decimal) numbers. If FIXED is OFF, the results displayed by functions and certain arithmetic operations may vary in the number of places displayed to the right of the decimal. If FIXED is ON, the number of places displayed to the right of the decimal will be the number of places established by the SET DECIMALS command. In any event, the SET FIXED command refers only to the way that the data is displayed, not to the way in which it is stored in main memory. When output is displayed with a smaller number of places to the right of the decimal than its storage format, the number is rounded at the indicated position.

Remember:
The default value for SET DECIMALS is 2.

EXAMPLES:

```
. SET FIXED OFF
. ? 1/3
 0.33
. ? 1.0000*1/3
      0.3333
. SET FIXED ON
. ? 1.0000*1/3
      0.33
. ? 1/3
 0.33
```

SET FORMAT TO [<format file name>/?]

Allows the use of a custom screen format for APPEND, CHANGE, EDIT, and INSERT. Unless otherwise specified, the extension for the file name is FMT. If no custom format is specified, the standard format is used. You can close a format file either with the CLOSE FORMAT statement or with the SET FORMAT TO followed by a RETURN. You can use CREATE SCREEN or MODIFY SCREEN to help you develop format files.

SET FUNCTION <numeric exp> TO <character string> [;]

Used to reprogram the function keys. Function key F1 cannot be reprogrammed, but F2 through F10 can. The standard (default) key values are shown in Table 2.21.

If you include a semicolon (;) at the end of your <character string>, the command will be executed immediately after you press the function key. If there is no semicolon at the end of the command, then you will need to press the RETURN key after you press the function key before the command will be executed. You may also enter several commands to be executed when the function key is pressed.

EXAMPLES:

```
. SET FUNCTION 2 TO 'DIR *.*'
```

Press F2 and then the RETURN to obtain a listing of all the files on the default disk.

TABLE 2.21

KEY	VALUE
F1	HELP;
F2	ASSIST;
F3	LIST;
F4	DIR;
F5	DISPLAY STRUCTURE;
F6	DISPLAY STATUS;
F7	DISPLAY MEMORY;
F8	DISPLAY;
F9	APPEND;
F10	EDIT;

```
. SET FUNCTION 2 TO 'DIR *.*;'
```

Press F2 to obtain a listing of all files on the default disk.

```
. SET FUNCTION 10 TO 'CLEAR; LIST STATUS;'
```

Press F10 to erase the screen and list the status.

```
. SET FUNCTION 10 TO "MODIFY COMMAND "
```

Press F10 to initiate the MODIFY COMMAND statement. Then enter the name of the file to edit and press RETURN.

SET HEADING ON/OFF DEFAULT: ON

If HEADING is set to OFF, then no column headings will appear when the commands AVERAGE, DISPLAY, LIST, and SUM are used. If HEADING is ON, then the column headings will be used. The size of the output fields will be the larger of the column heading and the field size.

SET HELP ON/OFF DEFAULT: ON

If there is an error in a command or statement, then you will receive an error message. If HELP is ON, you will also be asked the question "Do you want some help? (Y/N)". If you answer affirmatively, you will be presented with the correct syntax of the statement and a description of its usage. You may then reenter the command.

Warning:
Sometimes the syntax is quite cryptic and less than useful. If you find that dBASE has presented you with the syntax for the wrong statement, press N in response to the query, and then use the HELP command directly. For example, say that you want help with the SET COLOR statement, but dBASE has given you syntax for the general SET statement. Press N, and then enter the command

```
HELP SET COLOR
```

SET HISTORY ON/OFF DEFAULT: ON

Activate/inactivate the history feature. If HISTORY is set OFF, then SET DOHISTORY ON does not work. Since DOHISTORY adds to the current HISTORY file, I see little need for this statement.

SET HISTORY TO <integer> DEFAULT: 20

Specify how many statements can be stored in the HISTORY file. <integer> must be between 0 and 16,000.

SET INDEX TO [<list of index file names>/?]

Used to associate a list of index files with the database file currently in use. Any index files associated with the current database before the command is executed are disassociated. Unless explicitly given, the extension of NDX is assumed for an index file. The first index file in the list is the primary, controlling, or main index. It is the only index used by the FIND and the SEEK commands. It also determines the logical (access) order for sequential access to the database file. When a database file is updated (records are modified, added, or removed), then all of the affected active indexes, not just the primary index, are updated. You may have up to seven index files open at one time for any single database file.

Note:
The SET INDEX TO followed by a RETURN can be used to close all the index files associated with the current database file.

EXAMPLE:

```
USE EMPLOYEE INDEX EMPNAME
          .
          .
          .
SET INDEX TO EMPSSN
SEEK MEMSSN
```

SET INTENSITY ON/OFF DEFAULT: ON

If ON, fields are displayed in reverse video for the full-screen operations like APPEND, EDIT, and INSERT.

SET MARGIN TO <numeric expression> DEFAULT: 0

Sets the left-hand margin for all printed output. Does not affect the screen display. You can use this feature to line up your output (reports) so that you do not have to move the paper when you change from another system (like WordStar) to dBASE III Plus.

SET MEMOWIDTH TO <integer> DEFAULT: 50

Specify the width of the output to be used when a memo field is displayed or printed. The lines that were entered with soft carriage returns at the end of the line are adjusted in length in the normal manner of word processing.

SET MENU ON/OFF DEFAULT: ON

If MENU is ON, then a menu showing the cursor movements will be shown when the full-screen commands are used. In any event, you can use F1 to display or hide the menu. (See figure on the next page.)

SET MESSAGE TO [<character string>]

When this statement is executed, a message is displayed at the bottom of the screen. The <character string> must be delimited and can be no more than 79 characters in length. This statement works only when STATUS is set ON. You can use this statement to display your own help, warning, and error messages.

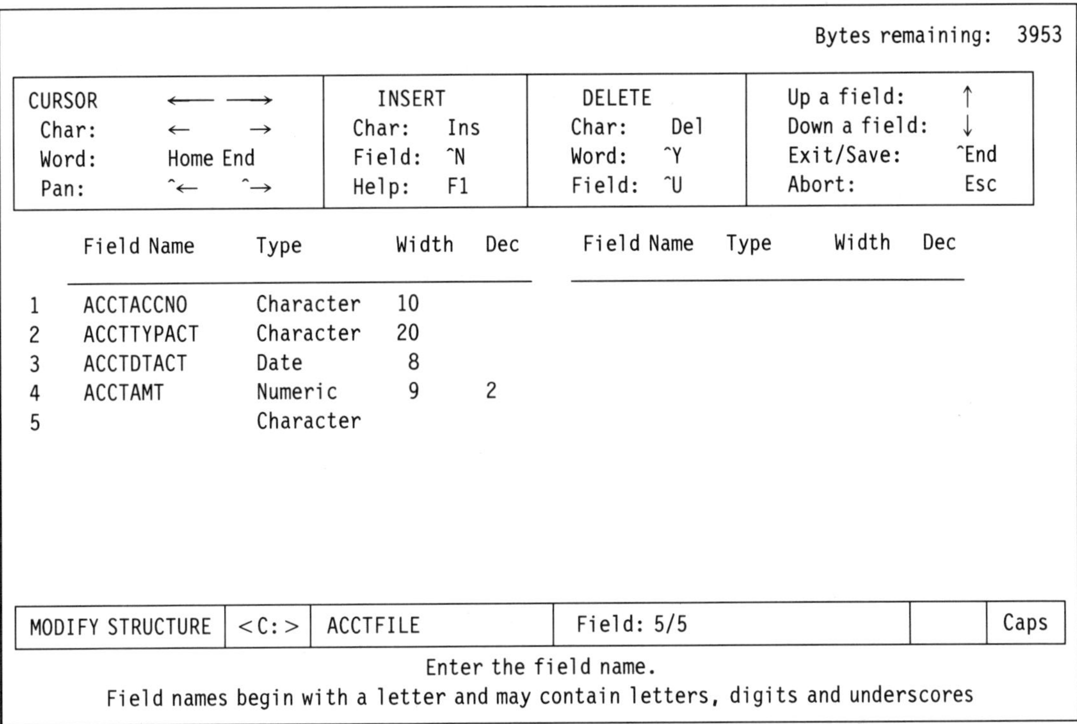

SET ORDER TO [<integer>]

Specify that index number <integer> in the USE or SET INDEX TO statement is to be used as the controlling index for the FIND, SEEK, and the GOTO TOP statements. <integer> must be between 0 and 7. If the value of <integer> is zero (0) or if no parameter is specified, then the database file is accessed as if it were unindexed. This statement is faster than the SET INDEX TO statement, since it neither opens nor closes index files.

Warning:
You cannot refer to an index in this statement unless it has already been open with a USE or with a SET INDEX TO statement.

SET PATH TO [<path list>]

Since dBASE III Plus does not use the PATH that you establish at the DOS level, you can establish a PATH within dBASE for a similar purpose.

SET PRINT ON/OFF DEFAULT: OFF

If PRINT is ON, then all unformatted data output to the screen (other than from the @ . . SAY command) will be echoed to the printer. See also the DEBUG command.

SET PRINTER TO <device name> DEFAULT: LPT1

Designate a device to be used for output. The possible choices are LPT1, LPT2, and LPT3 for parallel output, and COM1 and COM2 for serial output.

SET PROCEDURE TO [<procedure file name>]

Used to establish a procedure file. The file may have up to 32 different procedures in it, and each procedure must start with the PROCEDURE statement. If the extension is not explicitly given for the file name, then the extension PRG is assumed. Only one procedure file may be open at any one time. The use of a procedure file may significantly reduce the number of files open at any one time. See also the PROCEDURE command earlier in this section. To close a procedure file, use the CLOSE PROCEDURE command or the SET PROCEDURE command without any file name.

SET RELATION TO [<key expression> INTO <alias>]

or

SET RELATION TO [<numeric expression> INTO <alias>]

or

SET RELATION TO [<RECNO( )>] INTO <alias>]

Used to establish a linkage from the current database file to another open database file (the linked file). The linked file is identified either by its database alias or by its work area alias. Each active database may have at most one associated relation, so there may be up to 10 active relations. If the SET RELATION command is used without any options, then the relation for the active database file is destroyed (deallocated).

If the <key expression> form is used, then the fields in the <key expression> must exist in the current database file and the linked file must be indexed on the expression. The record in the linked file that is associated with the current record in the current file is the first one with the desired index value. If there is no record in the linked file with the desired index value, then the current record pointer in the linked file is positioned after the last record in the file.

If the <numeric expression> form is used, then the record is selected from the linked file by the record number indicated by the expression. If no record is found, the current record pointer for the linked file is positioned after the last record in the file.

Warning:
When the <numeric expression> form is used, the linked file must not have any indexes currently associated with it.

If the <RECNO( )> form is used, then the linkage between files is based on record numbers. If no record is found, the current record pointer for the linked file is positioned after the last record in the file.

Warning:
When the <RECNO( )> form is used, the linked file must not have any indexes currently associated with it.

EXAMPLES:

```
SELECT 2
USE X INDEX Z
SELECT 1
USE Y
SET RELATION TO Z INTO B, or
SET RELATION TO Z INTO X
SELECT 2
SET INDEX TO
SELECT 1
SET RELATION TO RECNO( ) INTO B
```

SET SAFETY ON/OFF **DEFAULT: ON**

If SAFETY is ON and you have requested an operation that will destroy (overwrite) an existing file, then you must verify that you wish to continue with the operation. The question asked is "<file name> already exists, overwrite it? (Y/N)". If SAFETY is OFF, then the overwrite proceeds without asking the question. You will probably want to SET SAFETY OFF for all your application programs.

SET SCOREBOARD ON/OFF DEFAULT: ON

Display or hide certain messages from dBASE. When STATUS is ON, certain messages are displayed in the status bar. If STATUS is OFF, then these messages appear on line zero (0) of the screen. In addition, some messages are displayed on the line where an error has occurred. If SCOREBOARD is set OFF, then these messages are not displayed. If you set these messages off, you will probably want to replace them with messages of your own.

SET STATUS ON/OFF DEFAULT: ON

Use or do not use the status bar at the bottom of the screen. I suspect that you will want to SET STATUS OFF for most of your applications. When STATUS is OFF and SCOREBOARD is ON, then typical scoreboard information is displayed on line zero (0) of the screen.

SET STEP ON/OFF DEFAULT: ON

Used to execute a program one statement at a time. Make sure that TALK and ECHO are also ON. Then execute the program with the normal DO statement. Each statement in your program and its effect upon memory variables will then be displayed. After each statement is executed, you will be prompted to continue stepping through the program (press SPACEBAR), suspend execution of the program (press S), or cancel execution of the program (press ESC).

SET TALK ON/OFF DEFAULT: ON

The results of many of the dBASE III Plus commands are displayed on the screen. This command is useful for debugging (see also the DEBUG command), but must be OFF when users execute the application program. Set TALK OFF when you are checking out your program, unless you specifically want results echoed to the screen.

SET TITLE ON/OFF DEFAULT: ON

Prompt/do not prompt for a title when a file is added to a catalog.

SET TYPEAHEAD TO <integer> DEFAULT: 20

Specify how many characters are allowed in the typeahead buffer. The value of <integer> must be between 0 and 32,000. SET ESCAPE must be ON to use this statement. In order to completely disable the typeahead buffer, use the following statement

```
SET TYPEAHEAD TO 0
```

SET UNIQUE ON/OFF DEFAULT: OFF

Used to create an index file with no duplicates. Set UNIQUE ON and then index the file using the INDEX ON statement. There will be no more than one entry in the index file for each index value. This command is useful when you wish to obtain an ordered list with no records that have duplicate index values. A SET UNIQUE ON followed by an INDEX ON is equivalent to an INDEX ON . . . UNIQUE.

EXAMPLE:

```
SET UNIQUE ON
USE EMPLOYEE
INDEX ON EMPNAME TO EMPNAME
LIST ALL EMPNAME, EMPADDRESS TO PRINT
```

SET VIEW TO <view file name>/?

Specify a view. A view consists of:

1. Database and index files in specific word areas
2. Relations between database files
3. A specific work area
4. A field list
5. Filters, and
6. Format files

SKIP [<numeric expression>]

or

SKIP [+ <numeric expression>]

or

SKIP [– <numeric expression>]

Move the current record pointer of the current database either forward or backward. If the sign is + or is omitted, then the direction of movement is forward (toward higher record numbers). If the sign is –, then the direction of movement is backward (toward lower record numbers). If an index file is in use, then the SKIP command actually moves the pointer in index file order. For example, if the indexed records are in the order 1,5,2,3,4 and the current record pointer points to record 5, then the current record pointer will point to record 2 after the command SKIP 1 is executed.

If SKIP 1 is executed when the current record is the last record in the file, then EOF( ) will be set to .T. and RECNO( ) will be one greater than the number of the last record in the file.

If SKIP –1 is executed when the current record is the first record in the file, then BOF( ) will be set to .T. and RECNO( ) will be 1.

SKIP 1 is equivalent to SKIP without any number.

Note:

The SKIP statement is used to process a database file sequentially.

SORT <scope> TO [<new database file>] ON <field> [/A][/C][/D] [, <field> [/A][/C][/D] ...][FOR/WHILE <condition>]

Create a new database file from the selected records and fields in the current database file. Arrange the records in the <new database file> in ascending (/A) or descending (/D) order according to the ON clause. If /C is used, then dBASE does not differentiate data by uppercase and lowercase. The default sort order is ascending (same as /A). When the sort is to be performed on more than one field, the fields are listed in decreasing order of importance. Thus, if we wish to sort by name within city, then the ON clause would be

```
ON CITY, NAME
```

Notes:

If the /C is to be combined either with /A or with /B, use only one slash. The parameter then has the form

```
/AC
```

or

```
/BC
```

EXAMPLE:

```
USE EMPLOYEE
SORT TO TEMPEMP ON CITY, NAME
```

STORE <expression> TO <memory variable list>

Used to create and place a value in one or more memory variables. The memory variable is dynamically allocated, that is, the type of the memory variable is the same as the type of the data placed in it. If a memory variable has the same name as a database record field name, then the memory variable can be referred to by using the memory alias. For example, if X is the name of a memory variable and also the name of a database field, then X will refer to the field and M->X can be used to refer to the memory variable.

Note:
An alternate form of the STORE command is:

<memory variable name> = <expression>

EXAMPLES:

```
STORE 2 TO Y
STORE Y+1 TO Y
Y = Y+1
```

SUM [<scope>][<expression list>][TO <memvar list>] [FOR/WHILE <condition>]

Sum the numeric fields indicated in the <expression list>, using the records selected by the <scope> and <condition> and place the results in the corresponding memory variables. If no <expression list> is used, then all numeric fields will be summed. This command does not change the current database records and does not create a new database file.

If TALK is ON and no <expression list> is given, then a small report is presented on the screen that has all the appropriate numeric field names as column headings and the sum of each numeric field as the values in the columns. If the <memvar list> is given, the number of variables in the list must exactly match the number of numeric fields SUMmed, and the results of the SUM will be placed in the corresponding memory variables.

EXAMPLE:

```
. SET TALK ON
. SUM
        4 records summed
   F2      F3
   16      12
. SUM TO X,Y
        4 records summed
   F2      F3
   16      12
. ? X,Y
           16          12
. SET TALK OFF
. SUM F2 TO X
? X
           16
```

SUSPEND

This command is used in a program to halt execution of the program and save the current environment. After a program has been SUSPENDed, you can use RESUME to continue execution from the point of suspension. This command is equivalent to pressing ESC while a program is running and selecting the S(uspend) option when prompted by dBASE.

TEXT

<text characters>

ENDTEXT

The <text characters> will be output to the current device exactly as they appear in the program. The macro function (&) will not be expanded if it appears as one of the text characters. Similarly, any delimiters will be displayed or printed exactly as they occur. This statement may be of use when you desire to output several lines of text material.

TOTAL ON <key field> TO <database file name> [<scope>] [FIELDS <field name list>][FOR/WHILE <condition>]

Sums numeric fields in the current database file and places the result in a second database file. Unless the extension is explicitly given for the second file name used in this command, the extension of DBF will be assumed.

This command causes a sequential scan of the current file. If there is an active index for the current database file, the index order is used. If there is no active index, the physical order is used. The value of the <key field> in the current database file is examined. When the value in the <key field> changes and when the physical or logical end of the current database file is encountered, a record is output to database file named in <database file name>. Thus, the records of the current database file are grouped by the value of the <key field>. Each collection of records, from the first occurrence of a <key field> value until the <key field> value changes, is a group. Exactly one record will be output to the new database file for each group in the current database file.

The TOTAL command always overwrites an existing database file or creates a new one. The structure of the new database file will almost be the same as the structure of the current database file. All of the fields in the current database file will appear in the same order in the second database file and have the same type and size, except for the memo fields. The memo fields that exist in the current database file will not appear in any form in the new database file.

The FIELDS clause indicates the fields that are to be summed. If there is no FIELDS clause, then all the numeric fields in the current database file will be summed. If there are any nonnumeric fields or numeric fields in the current database file that are not summed (the FIELDS clause is used, but the name of one or more fields does not appear in the clause), then the values of these fields in the first record encountered in each group are used in the output record. If there is not enough room in a numeric field in the new database file to hold a numeric sum, then the field is filled with asterisks (*) and you will receive the error message:

```
Numeric overflow (data was lost)
```

When TOTAL is used, a new database with approximately the same structure as the current database is always created. The size of each of the numeric fields in the new database is precisely the same size as the corresponding field in the current database. If the number of significant digits in a sum exceeds the number of digits in the corresponding field, then a numeric overflow will occur.

EXAMPLE:

```
. USE X INDEX F1
. LIST
```

Record #	*F1*	*F2*	*F3*	*F4*
1	A	1	Memo	2
2	A	3	Memo	4
3	A	5	Memo	6
4	B	7	Memo	8
5	B	8	Memo	9

```
. TOTAL ON F1 TO TOTX
. USE TOTX
. LIST
```

Record #	*F1*	*F2*	*F4*
1	A	9	12
2	B	15	17

Warning:
The data in the current database file must be accessed in the correct order or the TOTAL will not work as expected. For example, sort the data or access it using an index on the appropriate field(s).

TYPE <file name> [TO PRINT]

Display or print the contents of an ASCII (text) file. The <file name> must include the extension.

Warning:
Files that have been encoded, such as database and index files, will not be readable.

UPDATE ON <key field> FROM <alias> REPLACE <field1> WITH <exp1> [,<field2> WITH <exp2> ...] [RANDOM]

Uses records from the <alias> database file to update records in the current database file. <key field> must be the name of a field in each of the two database files. Any references to field names in the <alias> database file must be prefixed with the alias name. For example, if X is the name of a field in the <alias> database file and this database file is in area B, then you must refer to this field by the name B->X.

If the RANDOM option is used, the current database file must have an active, primary index on that field, and the <alias> file may be in any order. If the RANDOM option is not used, then both of the databases must either be sorted in the same order on the <key field> or they must both have an active, primary index on the <key field>.

If there is more than one record in the current database file with the same <key field> value, then only the first of these records will be updated.

This command is useful when you wish to update a database in BATCH mode. Enter the transaction records into a new database file with the name of <alias>. Sort or index as appropriate. Then UPDATE the appropriate file. In many situations this technique will save time over an interactive technique.

USE [<file name>/?][INDEX <index file list>] [ALIAS <alias name>]

Open a database file with up to seven active index files in the current work area. If the database file contains memo fields, the associated DBT file will also be opened. If no parameters are used, then the current database and all its associated index files will be closed. If the ALIAS option is not used, the name of the alias will be the same as the name of the database file. If the INDEX option is not used, then the first record in the database file becomes the current record. If at least one index is specified, the current record is the first one specified by the primary index.

EXAMPLE:

```
USE EMPLOYEE INDEX EMPSSN
```

WAIT [<prompt string>] [TO <memory variable name>]

When this command is executed, all processing is halted until a key is depressed. This command can be used to:

1. Request a selection from a menu, or

2. Force a user to see a message on the screen.

The <prompt string> must be delimited (enclosed in quotes). If the <prompt string> option is used, the <prompt string> will be displayed on the screen before input is requested. If a <prompt string> is not used, the default prompt of

Press any key to continue...

will be used. If a nonprintable character is entered in response to the WAIT prompt, then a null character will be stored in the <memory variable>. If the TO option is not used, then the user response will not be stored.

Note:
If ON KEY WAIT TO <memory variable name> is used, the keystroke that caused a branch to the ON KEY statement is placed in <memory variable name> and the WAIT is not executed.

EXAMPLE 1:

```
DO WHILE .T.
    SET DEVICE TO SCREEN
    @  5, 5 SAY "SAMPLE MENU"
    @  6, 5 SAY "-----------"
    @  7,10 SAY "A. EXIT FROM THE SYSTEM"
    @  8,10 SAY "B. FUNCTION 1"
    @  9,10 SAY "C. FUNCTION 2"
    @ 10,10 SAY "D. FUNCTION 3"
    WAIT "ENTER A SELECTION CODE" TO ;
      MEMCODE
    DO CASE
         CASE MEMCODE = "A"
              QUIT
         CASE MEMCODE = "B"
              DO FUNCTION1
         CASE MEMCODE = "C"
              DO FUNCTION2
         CASE MEMCODE = "D"
              DO FUNCTION3
         OTHERWISE
              ?
```

```
                    WAIT "ILLEGAL SELECTION CODE"
          ENDCASE
          CLEAR ALL
      ENDDO
      RETURN
ZAP
```

Physically remove all records from the current database file. Any active index files will automatically be reindexed. If SAFETY is ON, you will be asked to verify that you actually wish to physically remove all the records.

Warning:
Once the records have been physically removed, they cannot be recovered.

2.4 FULL-SCREEN OPERATIONS

Full-screen operations are used with a number of commands, including: APPEND, BROWSE, CHANGE, CREATE, EDIT, INSERT, MODIFY COMMAND, MODIFY STRUCTURE, and READ. When full-screen operations are used in conjunction with data, a form for the entry or changing of the data is presented on the screen and the cursor can be moved about the screen. This form of entry and editing is quite easy to use and greatly simplifies the data entry operations. Full-screen operations are also used with text, in particular with MODIFY COMMAND and with the manipulation of the HISTORY file. The keystrokes used in full-screen operations are presented in Table 2.22. The key is the keystroke recommended to achieve the desired function and the alternate is an alternate keystroke to achieve the same operation.

TABLE 2.22

KEY	ALTERNATE	DESCRIPTION OF FUNCTION
↑	^E	Cursor to previous field or line.
↓	^X	Cursor to next field or line.
←	^S	Cursor one column to the left.
→	^D	Cursor one column to the right.

KEY	ALTERNATE	DESCRIPTION OF FUNCTION
^→	^B	End of line or pan right. REPORT: Scroll file structure display up.
^←	^Z	Beginning of line or pan left. REPORT: Scroll file structure display down.
BACKSPACE	Rub	Delete the character to the left of the cursor.
Del	^G	Delete the character under the cursor.
End	^F	Cursor one word to right.
^End	^W	Exit from editing and save changes.
Esc	^Q	Exit. In APPEND, BROWSE and INSERT, save operations from all but the last record and abort changes to current record. In all other commands, abort all changes.
F1	^\	Toggle help menu on or off. LABEL & REPORT: Show structure.
Home	^A	Cursor one word to right.
^Home	^]	Toggle to display or clear the option menu. EDIT: Initiate editing of a memo field.
Ins	^V	Toggle INSERT mode on and off. When INSERT mode is off, entry of data overwrites existing data.
^KB		COMMAND: Reformat paragraph.
^KF		COMMAND: Find string.
^KL		COMMAND: Find next string after ^KF.
^KR		COMMAND: Copies entire file into current file at the position marked by the cursor.
^KW		COMMAND: Copies entire (current) file to another file.
^N		Insert new field definition, column, row, or line.
PgDn	^C	Cursor to next record or screen display.
^PgDn	^HOME	MEMO: Used to enter or modify a MEMO field for the record that you are currently appending, editing, or inserting. Move the cursor to the MEMO field in the full-screen display of the record and then enter ^PgDn.
PgUp	^R	Cursor to previous record or screen display.
^PgUp	^W	Exit and save operations.

KEY	ALTERNATE	DESCRIPTION OF FUNCTION
RETURN	^M	Cursor to next field or line. APPEND & INSERT: Exit and discontinue entry, if at first character of an empty record. COMMAND: Go to the beginning of the next line. If INSERT is toggled on, also insert a new blank line. EDIT: Exit and save if at last field of record.
^T		Erase word to right of cursor.
^U		BROWSE & EDIT: Mark record for deletion. LABEL: Delete row. REPORT: Delete column. SCREEN: Delete current field or box. STRUCTURE: Delete field definition.
^Y		Erase contents of current field, line, or word.

When you are not in full-screen editing mode, the control characters as shown in Table 2.23 may be used.

TABLE 2.23

KEY	ALTERNATE	DESCRIPTION OF FUNCTION
←		Move one character to the left.
→		Move one character to the right.
↑		Display previous statement.
↓		Display next statement.
BACKSPACE	^H	Go left and delete one character.
CAPS LOCK		Toggle between upper and lower case.
DEL	^G	Delete current character.
END		Go to next word.
HOME		Go to previous word.
NUM LOCK		Toggle numeric keys on and off.
^p		Toggle printer on or off.
RETURN	^M	Carriage return.
^S		Freeze or release the screen (toggle).

KEY	ALTERNATE	DESCRIPTION OF FUNCTION
^T		Delete next word.
^X		Erase the current command line (interactive use only).
^Y		Delete current line.

2.5 CONFIG.DB

CONFIG.DB is a file used by dBASE III Plus to initialize global parameters to be in effect when dBASE is operating. This file effectively allows you to tailor dBASE III Plus to suit your individual tastes. If there is a CONFIG.DB file on the same directory where you are running dBASE III, then this is the file that is used. If there is no CONFIG.DB file on the current directory, dBASE uses the DOS PATH statement (if any) to look for one. This allows you to have no CONFIG.DB file at all, that is, you can use the standard defaults, or you can have a number of CONFIG.DB files, each tailored to a specific situation. Place the standard CONFIG.DB file in your root directory, and place individualized CONFIG.DB files in the same directory as your data files, one CONFIG.DB file for each collection of data files. CONFIG.DB can be used to set each of the following:

1. The dBASE III Plus statement executed (if any) when dBASE is first entered. This option is used by dBASE III Plus only if you activate dBASE without supplying the name of a PRG file on the command line. If you activate dBASE with a DOS command of the form

   DBASE <PRG file name>

   then dBASE does not execute this statement.
2. The values of (the effects of pressing the) function keys.
3. The default settings for a number of parameters, both those that can be set ON and OFF, and those that are assigned a numeric value.
4. The text editor to be used when the MODIFY COMMAND statement is executed. Use the keyword TEDIT.
5. The text editor to be used when a memo field is edited. Use the keyword WP.

6. The amount of space allocated for memory variables. Use the keyword MVARSIZ.
7. The amount of memory allocated for the PICTURE and RANGE options in the @ . . GET statements. Use the keyword BUCKET.
8. The number of GETs that can be active at any one time. Use the keyword GETS.
9. The amount of memory retained by dBASE when a DOS program is executed. Use the keyword MAXMEM.
10. The dBASE prompt symbol. Use the keyword PROMPT.

All the entries in the CONFIG.DB file have the form

```
<keyword> = <value>
```

EXAMPLES:

```
BELL = OFF
BUCKET = 3
```

where the value is a multiple of 1K bytes. The default is 2.

```
COMMAND = ASSIST
F10 = "MODIFY COMMAND"
GETS = 144
```

where the default is 128 and the allowable range is 35-1023.

```
HISTORY = 50
MAXMEM = 272
```

where the default is 256.

```
MVARSIZ = 6500
```

where the default is 6000.

```
PROMPT = DB3>
```

where the default is the period (.).

```
TEDIT = WS
```

where the default is the dBASE III Plus editor.

```
TYPEAHEAD = 30
WP = WS
```

where the default is the dBASE III Plus editor.

2.6 CONFIG.SYS

Use the editor of your choice, possibly the dBASE III Plus editor, to create or modify the CONFIG.SYS file in the root directory of your hard disk (or on your boot disk, if you do not have a hard disk). If you use an editor that can put special control characters in the text file (like WordStar), use it in nondocument mode. Add the following lines to this file or modify existing lines, as necessary:

```
FILES=20
BUFFERS=20
```

Although you can only have a total of 15 files open in dBASE III Plus at any one time, dBASE needs up to five files for its own use. Hence the use of 20 files in CONFIG.SYS. Do not confuse the CONFIG.SYS file with the CONFIG.DB file. The CONFIG.DB file is used only by dBASE III Plus, and only when you activate dBASE. CONFIG.SYS is used only by DOS, and only when you boot the computer.

2.7 MEMO FIELDS

A memo field is defined by entering the letter M as the type of a field in a database. There are no memory variables of type memo. When a field of type memo is created, room is left in the database record for a pointer (10 bytes). The actual memo is stored in an auxiliary database file with the same name as the database file, but with an extension of DBT. The initial size of a record in the DBT file is 0 bytes. If you are using the dBASE III Plus editor, the maximum size of a memo field is 5000 bytes. If you are using a different editor, then the maximum size of the memo field is determined by the editor.

In order to edit a memo field in a database record, EDIT the desired record, place the highlight on the name of the memo field, and press ^HOME. At this point, the editor (either the dBASE III Plus editor or the editor that you specified in the CONFIG.DB file) is invoked and the file being edited contains the memo information. After you have completed entering or changing the memo, exit from the editor of your choice. You will then return to edit mode with the highlight on the memo field. Now choose how to exit from edit mode. If you abort at this stage, the content of or the change to the memo will be lost, since the new memo field is transferred to the appropriate database file (actually the DBT file) when you save the records in the database file, not when you exit from editing the memo field.

In order to display the contents of the memo field, use the DISPLAY or the LIST statements. You can direct output to the screen or to the printer by excluding or including the TO PRINT option. Use the SET MEMOWIDTH statement to specify the width of output when a memo field is displayed or listed. The default is 50, no matter which editor you are using. When a memo field is displayed or listed, the name of the memo field appears as a column header. To suppress this, use the SET HEADINGS OFF statement. In order to print a memo field, use the following sequence of statements:

```
SET HEADINGS OFF
SET MEMOWIDTH TO <desired width>
USE <database name>
GOTO <desired record number>
LIST NEXT 1 <memo field name> TO PRINT OFF
```

Since a character string is limited to 254 characters, you cannot assign a memo field to a character string variable.

2.8 DATES

A dBASE III Plus date is always stored in 8 bytes in an encoded format. The actual storage format is controlled by dBASE, but you can enter and display a date in a wide variety of formats. For a listing of these entry and display formats, see the SET DATE entry in this chapter.

There are a number of functions for the manipulation of dates. They are listed in Table 2.24.

When a date variable is entered or changed, dBASE examines the value for correctness. For example, the month must be an integer between 1 and 12, and the day must be between 1 and the numeric value of the last date of the chosen month. If the month is September (the 9th month), then the value of the day cannot exceed 30. The number of days allowed in February is correctly determined—both for leap years and for nonleap years. When you enter a date into a memory variable, use something similar to

TABLE 2.24

FUNCTION	PURPOSE
CDOW	Return the name of the day of the week.
CMONTH	Return the name of the month of the year.
CTOD	Change a character string to a date.
DATE	Return the system date.
DAY	Return the number of the day of the month.
DTOC	Change a date to a character string.
MONTH	Return the number of the month of the year.
TIME	Return the system time (not really a date function).
YEAR	Return the number of the year.

```
MEMDATE = CTOD("  /  /  ")
```

to initialize the memory variable before you attempt input. This will make the memory variable an object of type date, so that dBASE will verify the correctness of your entry.

You can perform arithmetic on variables and constants of type date as shown in Table 2.25.

TABLE 2.25

OPERATION	RESULT	COMMENTS
date + integer	date	Or integer + date
date – integer	date	
date – date	integer	Number of days between dates

Examples of each of the above are:

```
. ? CTOD("01/01/87") + 1
01/02/87
. ? CTOD("01/02/87") - 1
01/01/87
. ? CTOD("01/01/87") - CTOD("01/01/86")
365
```

You can index on a date field in a database file and dBASE will order the dates in the correct manner. If you wish to index on a combination of fields, one of which is a date field, then you must change the date field to a character string in the INDEX statement and the new string date must then be concatenated with other strings. For example, suppose that we have two fields in our database named MYNAME and MYDATE and that we wish to index on the combination of MYNAME and MYDATE. If we were to use an index statement of the form

```
INDEX ON MYNAME+DTOC(MYDATE) TO MYKEY
```

the index would not allow us to access records in order by date within values of MYNAME because the date would be converted directly into a string. For example, we would have entries like

```
"SMITH 01/01/87"
"SMITH 05/01/86"
```

that clearly are in string order, but are not in date order. When we convert a date to a character string to be used in an index, we must convert the date so that the date order is preserved. This is accomplished by an index statement of the form:

```
INDEX ON MYNAME+STR(YEAR(MYDATE),2)+;
  STR(MONTH(MYDATE),2)+;
    STR(DAY(MYDATE),2) TO MYKEY
```

You can compare two objects of type date, but there are some anomalies involving the date obtained by using CTOD(" / / "), as shown by the following dialog:

```
. STORE CTOD("  /  /  ") TO X
  /  /
. STORE CTOD("01/01/87") TO Y
01/01/87
. ? X < Y
.F.
. ? Y < X
.F.
. ? Y < CTOD("  /  /  ")
.F.
. ? CTOD("  /  /  ") < Y
.F.
```

```
. ? CTOD("01/01/87") < X
.F.
. ? X < CTOD("  /  /  ")
.T.
```

The following dialog is even stranger:

```
. ? X = CTOD("  /  /  ")
.T.
. ? X <> CTOD("  /  /  ")
.T.
. ? X = X
.T.
. ? X <> X
.T.
```

In other words, it just is not safe to use CTOD(" / / ") in a test that compares two dates like those shown above.

There are some instances (in addition to the use of a date in a combination index) when you will need to convert a date to a character string. Consider, for example, the problem of listing all the records in a database file for a specific date. The statement

```
LIST ALL FOR MYDATE = 01/01/86
```

does not work, but either of the following will work

```
LIST ALL FOR MYDATE = CTOD("01/01/86")
LIST ALL FOR DTOC(MYDATE) = "01/01/86"
```

2.9 CATALOGS

A catalog is a file that contains information on a specific set of dBASE files, including: DBF, LBL, FMT, FRM, NDX, QRY, and SCR files. The catalog is maintained by dBASE and is created or activated when you use the SET CATALOG TO statement. A catalog can be deactivated through the use of the SET CATALOG OFF statement. You can associate a description with each catalog and with each database file in a catalog. The master catalog is CATALOG.CAT.

A catalog seems to be most useful in interactive mode. Once a catalog has been established, an interactive user of dBASE:

1. Can ask what catalogs are available on the current directory by entering the command:

   SET CATALOG TO ?

2. Can select one of the listed catalogs by highlighting a name and then pressing RETURN.
3. Can ask what files are available in the current catalog by entering the command:

   USE ?

4. Can select one of the listed files by highlighting a name and then pressing RETURN.

The following dBASE III Plus statements access the current catalog. Special marks are provided with a number of statements to indicate how the statements affect the catalog. These are shown in Table 2.26.

The statements that affect catalogs and their associated marks are shown in Table 2.27.

2.10 LINKING FILES TOGETHER: RELATIONS AND VIEWS

Files can be linked together in a hierarchical organization (tree structure) using the SET RELATION TO statement. If there is a link from database file X to database file Y, the link can be established in two ways: by record number and by common values. I strongly recommend that files be linked only by values, since linkage by record numbers can lead to a multitude of problems.

TABLE 2.26

MARK	AFFECTS
?	Query capability
A	Add entries to catalog
C	Close catalog
D	Delete entries from catalog
R	Rename catalog entries

TABLE 2.27

C	CLOSE ALL	A	IMPORT FROM
C	CLOSE DATABASES	A	INDEX
C	CLOSE FORMAT	A	JOIN
C	CLOSE INDEX	?	LABEL FORM
A	COPY STRUCTURE	C	QUIT
A	COPY STRUCTURE EXTENDED	R	RENAME
A	COPY TO	?	REPORT FORM
A	CREATE	?	SELECT
A	CREATE FROM	C?	SET CATALOG TO
A?	CREATE/MODIFY LABEL	A?	SET FILTER TO
?	CREATE/MODIFY FORMAT	AC?	SET FORMAT
A?	CREATE/MODIFY QUERY	C?	SET INDEX
A?	CREATE/MODIFY REPORT	A?	SET VIEW
A?	CREATE/MODIFY SCREEN	A	SORT
A?	CREATE/MODIFY VIEW	A	TOTAL
D?	DELETE FILE	AC?	USE
D?	ERASE		

If the linkage is from file X to file Y and if the files are linked by values, you must designate a field in X and an index for Y. Then, when you access a record in X, some of the related information in Y is available to you, almost as if it were in X. In order to establish the link between X and Y, first use code similar to the following:

```
SELECT 2
USE Y INDEX YIDNO
SELECT 1
USE X
* THE USE OF AN INDEX FOR Y IS MANDATORY, BUT THE USE
* OF AN INDEX FOR X IS OPTIONAL
```

```
SET RELATION TO XIDNO INTO Y
* NOTE THAT X MUST BE THE CURRENT DATABASE WHEN THE ;
   SET
* RELATION STATEMENT IS USED. IN ADDITION, NOTE THAT
* NO REFERENCE IS MADE TO THE Y INDEX IN THE SET ;
  RELATION
* STATEMENT. THE Y INDEX MUST BE IN EFFECT BEFORE THE ;
  SET
* RELATION STATEMENT. SINCE THE SET RELATION ;
  STATEMENT
* LEAVES THE CURRENCY POINTER AT THE END OF FILE X, IT ;
  IS
* NECESSARY TO RESET THE POINTER.
GOTO TOP
DO WHILE .NOT. EOF( )  && OF FILE X
      ? XCONAME, B->YAMOUNT
      SKIP 1
ENDDO
```

Note how information in file Y is accessed within the program. Look carefully at the output statement in the loop. Notice from the syntax of the statement that there can be no more than one record at a time in Y linked to any particular record in X? The linkage between files can be deactivated using the SET RELATION TO statement, followed immediately by a RETURN (no parameter). The linkage is also deactivated when your application system terminates. In order to establish a more permanent linkage, you need to establish a view.

One way to create a view is to establish the desired environment by selecting the databases to be used, the appropriate indexes, and then entering the SET RELATION TO command to link the files together. Once the environment has been established, use the CREATE VIEW FROM ENVIRONMENT statement. This will create a view that will preserve the linkage. It is also possible to create a view using the CREATE/MODIFY VIEW statement, as described in this chapter. Once a view has been created, you can activate it with the SET VIEW TO statement.

A view has an advantage over a simple relation (linkage), in that it keeps track of all the auxiliary files associated with the databases (simplifying your maintenance operations) and it allows reference to fields in all the database files without reference to area.

Whether you use a simple relation (linkage) or a view, you will still have one problem: if the linkage goes from file X to file Y, no more than one record in file Y can be linked to a record in file X. If we wish to present the data to the user so that each record in X is linked with more than one record in Y, then we need a slightly different approach.

EXAMPLE:

In this example, we use two database files whose structure and content follow:

```
. SELECT 1
. USE Y
. LIST STRU
Structure for database: C:Y.dbf
Number of data records:      4
Date of last update     : 09/25/86

Field    Field Name    Type       Width    Dec
1        YIDNO         Numeric    4
2        YDATE         Date       8
3        YAMOUNT       Numeric    9        2

** Total **                       22
. LIST ALL

Record#    YIDNO    YDATE       YAMOUNT
1          1        01/01/87     2500.00
2          2        01/01/87     3650.95
3          1        06/01/87    50000.00
4          2        06/01/87    49000.00

. SELECT 2
. USE X INDEX XIDNO
. LIST STRU
Structure for database: C:X.dbf
Number of data records:      2
Date of last update: 09/25/86

Field    Field Name    Type         Width    Dec
1        XIDNO         Numeric        4
2        XCONAME       Character     15
3        XADDRESS      Character     30
```

```
4         XTELNO    Character       13
** Total **                         63
. LIST ALL
```

Record#	*XIDNO*	*XCONAME*	*XADDRESS*	*XTELNO*
1	1	PRIME MOVER	MAIN STREET, ANY CITY	(800)555-1212
2	2	BIG COMPANY	MAPLE STREET, ANOTHER CITY	(800)555-5555

```
. SET RELATION TO YIDNO INTO X
. LIST ALL OFF
```

YIDNO	*YDATE*	*YAMOUNT*
1	01/01/87	2500.00
2	01/01/87	3650.95
1	06/01/87	50000.00
2	06/01/87	49000.00

Note the use of the alias B→ in the following command.

```
. LIST ALL B→XIDNO, B→XCONAME, YDATE, YAMOUNT
```

Record#	*B->XIDNO*	*B->XCONAME*	*YDATE*	*YAMOUNT*
1	1	PRIME MOVER	01/01/87	2500.00
2	2	BIG COMPANY	01/01/87	3650.95
3	1	PRIME MOVER	06/01/87	50000.00
4	2	BIG COMPANY	06/01/87	49000.00

Since we have established the desired environment, we can now create a view from this environment.

```
. CREATE VIEW XY FROM ENVIRONMENT
XY.vue:
. LIST ALL OFF
```

YIDNO	*YDATE*	*YAMOUNT*
1	01/01/87	2500.00
2	01/01/87	3650.95
1	06/01/87	50000.00
2	06/01/87	49000.00

Notice that the view created from the environment has a problem. We cannot find any of the fields in X. We must make at least one of the fields in one of the database files inaccessible through the use of the Set Fields option in the MODIFY VIEW XY command.

```
. LIST ALL OFF
```

YIDNO	*YDATE*	*YAMOUNT*	*XIDNO*	*XCONAME*	*XADDRESS*
1	01/01/87	2500.00	1	PRIME MOVER	MAIN STREET, ANY CITY
2	01/01/87	3650.95	2	BIG COMPANY	MAPLE STREET, ANOTHER CITY
1	06/01/87	50000.00	1	PRIME MOVER	MAIN STREET, ANY CITY
2	06/01/87	49000.00	2	BIG COMPANY	MAPLE STREET, ANOTHER CITY

Notice that we have our linkage from Y to X, rather than from X to Y. If the linkage is from X to Y, then we will have one record displayed for each record in X and we will not see all the sales information recorded in Y. If we have the linkage from Y to X, then we will have one record displayed for each record in Y. As a result, we see all the sales information, but the information from X is duplicated. A slightly different listing of the data reveals that the company name and ID are not in order. This makes the data hard to read.

```
. LIST ALL XIDNO, XCONAME, YDATE, YAMOUNT
```

Record#	*XIDNO*	*XCONAME*	*YDATE*	*YAMOUNT*
1	1	PRIME MOVER	01/01/87	2500.00
2	2	BIG COMPANY	01/01/87	3650.95
3	1	PRIME MOVER	06/01/87	50000.00
4	2	BIG COMPANY	06/01/87	49000.00

If we now index Y in the field YIDNO and use this index when we access the view, the listing is much more readable.

```
. INDEX ON YIDNO TO YIDNO
. LIST ALL OFF XIDNO, XCONAME, YDATE, YAMOUNT
```

XIDNO	*XCONAME*	*YDATE*	*YAMOUNT*
1	PRIME MOVER	01/01/87	2500.00
1	PRIME MOVER	06/01/87	50000.00
2	BIG COMPANY	01/01/87	3650.95
2	BIG COMPANY	06/01/87	49000.00

2.11 THE SCREEN PAINTER

The screen painter is used to create an input form to facilitate entry of data. You can write your own program, manually create an FMT file, or use the screen painter to create the FMT file for you.

The screen painter is invoked by using the CREATE/MODIFY SCREEN command. Once the command has been executed, a menu bar will appear at the top of the screen, containing the following items: Set Up, Modify, Options, and Exit. For an explanation of these items, refer to the MODIFY SCREEN command earlier in this chapter.

```
Set Up                  Modify                  Options                 Exit 11:14:52 am

 Select Database File
 Create New Database File
 ------------------------
 Load Fields

MODIFY SCREEN | <C:> | SCREEN.SCR | Opt | 1/3 | |
   Position selection bar - ↑ ↓.  Select - ↵.  Leave menu - ←→. Blackboard - F10.
               Select a database file to use in defining a screen format.
```

The first step in creating an FMT file is to select Set Up from the menu bar. If you have already selected files with another procedure (like CREATE VIEW), the Set Up menu item will use these files; otherwise you should select the names of the database files that will be used in association with this FMT file. When individual fields are selected from the indicated database files, they are placed in the upper left-hand corner of the work area, which is called the blackboard. Both the name and the picture of each of these fields are placed on the blackboard. The names of the fields are treated by dBASE as ordinary text, and the pictures are treated as both pictures and placement indicators for the data from the database(s). You can add text, modify text, move text, and delete text. You can also modify the display characteristics of the data (as indicated by the picture), add a new field to the blackboard, delete a field from the blackboard, and move the picture to another location. Unfortunately, you cannot use the editor of your choice when using the screen painter. You are limited to the use of the Ashton-Tate editor (the default dBASE III Plus editor), as described in this chapter.

You can move from the menu bar to the blackboard or from the blackboard to the menu bar at any time by pressing F10. Note that pressing F1 does not display a menu of keystrokes on the screen.

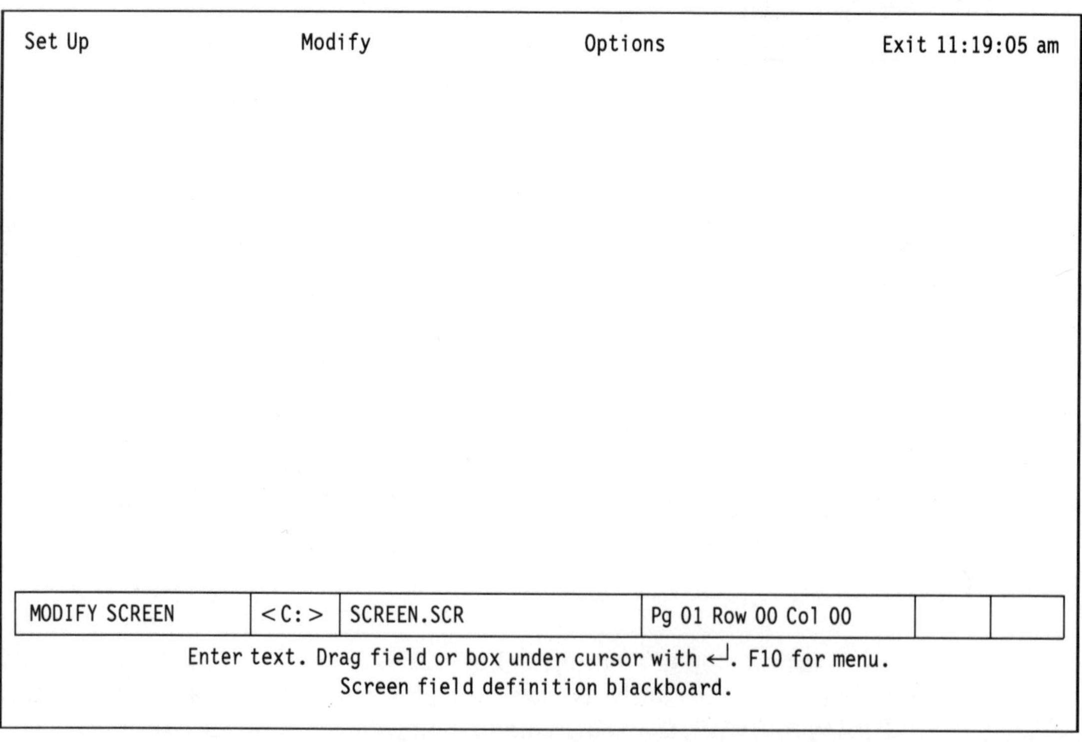

Table 2.28 contains a summary of text operations on the blackboard. Table 2.29 contains a summary of field operations on the blackboard.

TABLE 2.28

OPERATION	METHOD
Add a blank line	If necessary, press INS to enter insert mode, position the cursor, and press RETURN.
Add text	If desired, press INS to enter insert mode, position the cursor, and enter the text in the ordinary manner.
Delete a blank line	Place the cursor on the desired line and press ^Y.
Delete text	In order to delete the entire line, press ^Y. To delete a character, place the cursor on the character and press DEL, or place the cursor to the right of the character and press BACKSPACE.
Move text	Insert spaces or blank lines as appropriate.
Add a box	Select the type of box desired from the Options item in the menu bar, and then select the upper left-hand and the lower right-hand corners of the box. To select a corner, place the cursor at the desired location and press RETURN.

2.12 PROCEDURES

A procedure file is a collection of named subroutines. Each of the subroutines must start with a PROCEDURE statement that has the form:

PROCEDURE <procedure name>

A procedure file should be given the extension PRG. The subroutines in a procedure file are made available to dBASE through the use of the SET PROCEDURE TO <procedure name> statement in your application. The SET PROCEDURE statement is used to open the procedure file. Once open, all the subroutines in the file are available and can be executed with a simple statement of the form:

DO <subroutine name>

The major advantages of a procedure are derived from the fact that several subroutines are placed in one file. They are: (1) the use of a procedure file can speed up execution of your programs, and (2) you can reduce the number of files open at any one time. You may find the last feature handy if you try to open more than 15 files at any one time.

You will usually not need to close your procedure file, since an exit from your application system (QUIT) will automatically close it for you. Nevertheless, if you wish to close the procedure file, you can do it with the CLOSE PROCEDURE statement.

TABLE 2.29

OPERATION	METHOD
Add a field	When you first create the screen, you can use Set Up from the menu bar. After that, use Modify from the menu bar. Source is the name of the database to be used for this field, and Content is the name of the field to be used. Go to Content and press RETURN to see a list of field names. When you select a field, Type, Width, and Decimal are filled in for you. You can, of course, change the default values for these three entries.
Delete a field	In order to delete a field entirely from the blackboard, place the cursor on the picture and press ^U.
Move a field	There are two ways to move a field: You can insert blanks and lines in the ordinary manner, or you can reposition the field. To insert blanks and lines, press INS (if necessary) to enter insert mode, then press SPACEBAR or RETURN, as appropriate. In order to reposition the field, place the cursor on the picture, press RETURN, move the cursor to the position where you want the first character in the field, and then press RETURN again.
Change display characteristics	Move the cursor to the picture of the field to be changed and then select Modify from the menu bar to change the display characteristics. More display characteristics can be changed using Picture Function and Picture Template within Modify. See the @ . . SAY and the @ . . GET statements in this chapter for a description of the picture functions and templates. The allowable picture function characters are: A, R, and !. The allowable picture template characters are: A, L, X, #, 9, !, and certain insertion characters.
Select the action	Fields can be positioned on the screen either to be entered and edited, or to be displayed. In order to select the desired mode, place the cursor on the picture, press F10 to move to the menu bar, select Modify from the menu bar, place the highlight on Action, and press RETURN to change the action mode. The two action modes are Edit/GET and Display/SAY.

2.13 PARAMETERS, RANGES, AND DEFAULTS

The parameters that can be SET either on or off, or to a value, are presented in Table 2.30. If an asterisk (*) appears next to the name of the parameter, it cannot be included in the CONFIG.DB file. If a plus sign (+) appears next to the name of the parameter, then it can be included in the CONFIG.DB file, but cannot be used interactively or in a dBASE III Plus program.

TABLE 2.30

PARAMETER	RANGE	DEFAULT	
ALTERNATE		OFF	
BELL		ON	
+BUCKET	1–31		
CARRY		OFF	
CATALOG		OFF	
CENTURY		OFF	
COLOR		Determined by hardware	
+COMMAND		None	
CONFIRM		OFF	
CONSOLE		OFF	
* DATE		AMERICAN	
DEBUG		OFF	
DECIMALS	0–14	2	
DEFAULT		Directory when dBASE III Plus was executed	
DELETED		OFF	
DELIMITER		OFF and colon (:)	
DEVICE		SCREEN	
* DOHISTORY		OFF	
ECHO		OFF	
ESCAPE		ON	
EXACT		OFF	
* FIELDS		OFF	
* FILTER		All records in database	
* FIXED		OFF	
* FORMAT		Standard dBASE display	
FUNCTION	2–10	F1 = help;	F6 = disp status;
		F2 = assist;	F7 = display memory;

PARAMETER	RANGE	DEFAULT
		F3 = list; F8 = display;
		F4 = dir; F9 = append;
		F5 = disp structure; F10 = edit;
		NOTE: When the default value of a function key is to be entered in the CONFIG.DB file, the format for the <keyword> is F<integer>.
+GETS	35–1023	128
HEADING		ON
HELP		ON
HISTORY	0–16,000	ON/20
INTENSITY		ON
MARGIN	1–254	0
+MAXMEM	256–720	256
MEMOWIDTH	0–max memory	50
MENU		ON
* MESSAGE		SPACE(79)
+MVARSIZ	1–31K	6000
* ORDER	0–7	1
PATH		Current directory
PRINT		OFF
* PRINTER		LPT1
+PROMPT		Period (.)
PROCEDURE		No procedure file
* RELATION		No relation
SAFETY		ON
SCOREBOARD		ON
STATUS		ON
STEP		OFF

PARAMETER	RANGE	DEFAULT
STEP		OFF
TALK		ON
+TEDIT		dBASE III Plus editor
* TITLE		ON
TYPEAHEAD	0–32,000	20
UNIQUE		OFF
VIEW		No active view
WP		dBASE III Plus editor

2.14 NAMES

Names of memory variables and database fields are limited to 10 characters. The specific characters that you can use are letters (uppercase or lowercase, with no distinction made between cases), numbers, and the underline (_). Names must start with a letter. In most cases, I prefer to include a small number of letters (usually less than or equal to three) from the name of the database as part of the name of each field in the database. For example, if the name of the database is EMPLOYEE, and I wish to include a field in this database for salary, I will make the name of the field EMPSALARY. This naming technique always identifies the name of the database that the field is in and helps me visually distinguish between database field names and names of memory variables, both of which make debugging easier. In many cases, when I wish to specifically indicate a memory variable, I will prefix the variable with the letters MEM. In this case, a memory variable for salary will be MEMSALARY.

Although, dBASE III Plus recognizes file and program names that consist of more than 8 characters, I recommend that you use names with no more than 8 characters in them. If you use a true compiler for dBASE III Plus, you will need to link the compiled code and some linkers do not recognize DOS file names with more than 8 characters. I also recommend that you use all the dBASE III Plus file name defaults and never provide extensions of your own. For example, when you use a database file name

When you choose a name for a database file, do not use any of the letters A through J, or M. A through J are reserved for the 10 areas and M is reserved for memory variables. M is used only in those cases when you have a database field and a memory variable with exactly the same name. If you have a database field and a memory variable named, for example, EMPNAME, then there are situations when you will need to distinguish between the field and the memory variable. EMPNAME will be treated as a field name by dBASE unless you prefix the name with the three characters M->. Then you can use EMPNAME as the name of the field and M-> EMPNAME as the name of the memory variable. If you have a good naming strategy, as described previously, then you will not need to use the M-> prefix.

```
Options          Groups          Columns          Locate          Exit 11:09:21 am

 Page title
 Page width (positions)       80
 Left margin                   8
 Right margin                  0
 Lines per page               58
 Double space report         No
 Page eject before printing  Yes
 Page eject after printing   No
 Plain page                  No

CURSOR   <--  -->   | Delete char:    Del | Insert column:   ^N | Insert:     Ins
  Char:  <-    ->   | Delete word:     ^T | Report format:   F1 | Zoom in:   ^PgDn
  Word:  Home End   | Delete column:   ^U | Abandon:        Esc | Zoom out:  ^PgUp

MODIFY REPORT       | <C:> | REPORT.FRM           | Opt | 1/9 |     |
           Position selection bar - ↑ ↓.  Select - ↵.  Leave menu - ←→.
      Enter up to four lines of text to be displayed at the top of each report page.
```

2.15 MENUS

dBASE III Plus has a number of menu-driven features, including CREATE/MODIFY: FILE, REPORT, SCREEN, and VIEW. The figure on the preceding page shows the CREATE/MODIFY REPORT menu.

Whenever you see a menu bar at the top of the screen, use the left and right arrows to move between items in the menu bar and use up and down arrows to move around in menus that pop up when you highlight an item. In order to select an item from a pop-up menu, highlight it and press RETURN. In some cases, selection of an item causes a black arrowhead to be placed next to the item, indicating that it has been selected. In others, an action will occur immediately after the selection has taken place. If the action is to present an auxiliary menu on the screen, move about within the auxiliary menu, make your selections, and then return to the previous menu with the left or right arrow keys. Use ESC to abort selection in the current menu. If you press ESC at the highest level of a menu-driven system, you can abort execution of that system.

CHAPTER

3

Fundamental dBASE III Plus Programming Concepts

3.1 INTRODUCTION

There are five basic operations that must be included in every programming language and that you will need to know as the basis for programming. These are:

1. Input
2. Output
3. Assignment
4. Decision
5. Looping

Although each of these items is explained more fully elsewhere in this book, you might find it helpful to see all these grouped together in one place. It is often easier to understand the basic structure of a language when it is presented simply and concisely, rather than having to dig it out of a primer. The database operations are described elsewhere in this book.

3.2 OBTAINING INPUT FROM THE USER

In dBASE III Plus, there are four fundamental methods of obtaining input from the user. They use the statements: ACCEPT, INPUT, GET, or WAIT. Use the ACCEPT statement to obtain a string, since it requires no quotation marks around the string; use the INPUT to enter numbers; and use the @ . . SAY . . GET when full-screen editing is desired. The WAIT is used to obtain single keystroke information from the user. Examples are selections from application menus and simple Y(es) and N(o) answers. Full-screen edited input is most useful when you desire to:

1. Delimit the beginning and the end of the input field
2. Allow the correction of previous lines of input
3. Signal with the bell if nonnumeric data is placed in a numeric field, or
4. Display a document on the screen to be filled in

The ACCEPT and the INPUT place the prompt for the input on the next available line. When the GET is used, the programmer erases the screen and prompts for input in document form. The GET is always used in combination with the SAY in order to provide the appropriate prompt information. I personally use the

```
@ . . SAY . . GET
```

for all the data input and editing in application systems that I build, and I like to use the WAIT for all selections from menus and all Y(es) or N(o) answers. A simple statement of the form

```
WAIT "Continue with this operation Y/N?" TO ANSWER
```

will suffice. Not only is the user restricted to one keystroke, but the content of the memory variable ANSWER is always 1 character after the input operation. The WAIT statement also allows you to prompt and then pause for the input.

3.3 PRODUCING OUTPUT

Output may be sent either to the screen or to the printer. The "?" will send output to the next available line of the screen. If the screen is full, it will scroll. The "??" will send output to the same line as the most recent output from either the "?" or the "??". The @ . . SAY will produce output either to the screen or the printer. The output device is determined by the SET DEVICE TO statement. SET DEVICE TO PRINT will cause output to go to the printer, and SET DEVICE TO SCREEN will cause output to go to the screen. The default is the screen.

You can also send output to a file, but this feature is not as powerful as I would like it to be. Use SET ALTERNATE TO to establish a TXT file, and use SET ALTERNATE ON to cause much of the screen output to be copied to the file of your choice. When you have completed capturing the screen output, use SET ALTERNATE OFF or QUIT to close this file. Unfortunately, output from the @ . . SAY statements do not go to this alternate file, even if DEVICE is set to SCREEN. In dBASE II there was a way of sending output from @ . . SAY statements directly to a file, but there is, as yet, no way to do this in dBASE III Plus. The purpose of an alternate file is to make a record of the screen activity of a running program or of some interactive commands. You can use this file for debugging purposes or for a printed copy to be given to your client.

Reports can be produced in two ways: you can use programs that contain @ . . SAY statements (a procedural technique) or you can use the dBASE III Plus report writer feature (a descriptive technique). Choose between programs and the report writer or use them in combination in our application system.

3.4 ASSIGNMENT

It is possible to assign values to memory variables or to fields in the current record of the current database file. A memory variable is any storage location that is not a field in a database record. The operator for assignment to a memory variable is STORE or "=". The operator for assignment to a field in a database record is REPLACE. Examples are:

```
STORE "ABC" TO X
X = "ABC"
REPLACE EMPSALARY WITH 1.1 * EMPSALARY
```

3.5 DECISION: THE IF-THEN-ELSE

The IF-THEN-ELSE construct is provided in the following form:

```
IF expression
        <statements>
ELSE
        <statements>
ENDIF
```

and the IF-THEN is provided in the form:

```
IF expression
        <statements>
ENDIF
```

The IF expression, the ELSE, and the ENDIF must each be on lines by themselves, except possibly for the inclusion of the && symbol and a comment at the end of the line. There must be a separate ENDIF for each IF, and you can nest an IF statement within either the THEN clause or the ELSE clause of another IF. If you are working interactively and need to enter an IF statement, use the IIF function. This function allows you to emulate a simple IF, but you do not need to write your entry on several lines. Note that dBASE III Plus statements that require entry on more than one line (like the IF and the DO WHILE) cannot be entered interactively.

3.6 LOOPING

There is only one type of loop in dBASE III Plus. It is of the form:

```
DO WHILE expression
     <statements>
ENDDO
```

The DO WHILE expression and the ENDDO must be on lines by themselves, except possibly for the inclusion of the && symbol and a following comment. This satisfies the need for a condition-controlled loop. To create counter-controlled loops, use the following type of construct:

```
LOOPINDEX = 1
DO WHILE LOOPINDEX <= <value>
     <statements>
     LOOPINDEX = LOOPINDEX + 1
ENDDO
```

To skip all the statements in a loop from some point on, execute the statement LOOP. For example, if an error condition occurs in a loop and you wish to skip the remainder of the statements in the loop, but continue execution of the loop, use the following construct:

```
DO WHILE expression
     <statements group a>
     IF ERROR
          LOOP
     ENDIF
     <statements group b>
ENDDO
```

In this case, if ERROR is .T. (TRUE), then <statements group b> will not be executed, but the execution of the loop continues if the "expression" is .T. (TRUE). To leave a loop immediately but continue execution of the program at the statement immediately following the last statement of the loop (the ENDDO), use the EXIT statement.

```
DO WHILE expression
     <statements group a>
     IF ERROR
          EXIT
     ENDIF
     <statements group b>
ENDDO
<next statement>
```

During the execution of this loop, if ERROR is .T. (TRUE), then control passes to <next statement> when the EXIT statement is executed.

CHAPTER

4

Working with Database Files

4.1 THE STRATEGY

dBASE III Plus contains a wide variety of features. Some of them are useful and others are not. Before you do any significant programming in dBASE III Plus, it is a good idea to be able to answer each of the following:

1. What kind of file and program design works best for dBASE III Plus?
2. Which of the features of dBASE III Plus work correctly and which don't?
3. Which features of dBASE III Plus are fast and which are slow?
4. What programming aids are provided by the dBASE III Plus system?
5. How should the error messages be interpreted?

Each of these questions will be addressed in this book.

4.2 GOALS FOR APPLICATION DEVELOPMENT

If you are a professional, you know that users often understand their own systems better than analysts do, at least at the start, and the analyst often has a considerable amount to learn about the current system before being able to construct a successful application system. Even if you are a user yourself and you plan to build a system for your own use, you will find that your understanding of the system will evolve over a period of time. In order for the analyst to be able to incorporate his or her improved understanding of the actual and the desired system into the design of the new system, the design must be as general as the analyst can make it and the design of the system must facilitate changes, both during the development of the system and after the system becomes operational.

> **Goal Number 1:**
> The design of the application system must be flexible enough to accommodate practically any kind of changes.

Even though microcomputers are becoming faster, it is still true that microcomputers are relatively slow. Because of the relatively slow speed of microcomputers, it is necessary to avoid any practices that will cause application programs to run slowly. Operations that take several seconds should be avoided, whenever possible, by using faster techniques. It is sometimes necessary to use faster algorithms, to avoid the use of commands that are inherently slow, or to use a compiler.

> **Goal Number 2:**
> Features of dBASE III Plus that take several seconds to execute should be avoided when possible.

The application system should be as easy to use as you can make it. First of all, the user should be able to select appropriate functions from a menu, rather than be forced to use an instruction manual. In addition, complex operations should be nested so that a complex function selected from one menu will display another menu on the screen. Secondly, all the user instructions should be given in nontechnical terms. This does not mean that there should not be any documentation for the system, but rather that the first line of documentation should be the first menu itself.

> **Goal Number 3:**
> Make the application system as easy to use as possible.
> In particular, use menus that allow the selection of functions.

The application system should work correctly. Use modern analysis, design, programming, and debugging techniques when you build your system. Avoid the features of dBASE III Plus that are known to work incorrectly.

> **Goal Number 4:**
> The application system should work correctly. Use good analysis, design, programming, and debugging techniques and avoid the features of dBASE III Plus that do not work correctly.

An excellent source of modern analysis and design techniques that lead to a flexible design is a book by Tom DeMarco, titled *Structured Analysis and System Specifications*, Prentice-Hall, 1979. The following is a sketch of the techniques recommended in DeMarco's book, specially modified and simplified for use with dBASE III Plus.

4.3 USEFUL ANALYSIS AND DESIGN TECHNIQUES

The most fundamental aspect of analysis technique is to treat the data as the most important item under observation and to treat processes (programs) as data transformations. I like to start with an examination of the input and output documents, because all the data that is used in and produced by an application system must be directly or indirectly derivable from the inputs. You can use the outputs to verify that you have considered all the relevant inputs. If you have an output field that cannot be derived from your present set of inputs, then you know that you have missed something. Determine the objects being described on these documents. For example, an employee time card contains information about two distinct objects: the employee and the work hours. The determination of objects turns out to be important, because separation of information by object type leads to a highly flexible system.

In general, each object about which you gather data will appear (eventually) in the system as a separate record type. Each instance of an object type (in this case, each employee and each work time) will appear as a distinct record in a file, where all the records in one file have the same structure. Not only is it not a good idea to attempt to place more than one kind of record in a database file, but dBASE III Plus will not let you do this. There will be a file for employees and each record in this file will contain information for one employee. In addition, all the records in the employee file will have the same structure. There will also be a file for the work times (time cards). Since this is repeated information (there is one start and one stop time for each work period), this data should be stored in a time card file in the following manner:

> Each time card record will contain at least two fields. One field will link it to the appropriate employee record (probably through the employee number) and the other field will contain elapsed time information. This record, depending on the requirements of the system, may contain more than two fields. For example, if start and stop dates and times are required, then the record will contain at least five fields: one field for the employee number, one for each of the start and stop dates, and one for each of the start and stop times.

The first reason for placing repeating information (reoccurrences of the same type of information) in separate records, one record for each occurrence of the data, is access speed. Much of your access to data stored in a database will be based on the use of indexes. If you attempt to have all the repeating information in just one record, the use of indexes will be made difficult or impossible. For example, consider the situation where you wish to access a time card by a combination of employee number and date. If you have several fields for dates, then it just isn't possible to create an index for this situation.

The second reason is that it is difficult to know just how many different occurrences to place in one record. Should there be enough room for six start and stop times? Is twelve better? What if you need more than just twelve?

After the files have been determined in a manner similar to the one described above, consider the objects being described in each file (remember that each file should describe exactly one object). If the same object is being described in more than one file, consider combining these into a single file. Since you often want to find all the information for an object at one time, placing all the (nonrepeating) information in one file speeds up access to the data.

The next step is to determine the processes necessary to produce the desired outputs. To make the most flexible possible application system, try to make the processes as simple as possible (DeMarco calls such processes functional primitives). Then, if processes have to be changed, the scope of effect of such changes is usually limited to the processes to be changed and any process for which it provides data. Examine the data needed by each process. If the data is already in a file, fine. If the data cannot be found in an existing file, consider whether a file already in existence describes the same object (the missing data may be descriptive of an object already in a file). If so, simply add the new field to the appropriate existing record type. If there is no appropriate file in existence, that is, you need at least one more piece of data, but it is not reasonable to place it in any existing file, then you will need to create a new file containing the field(s) for the missing data.

The data file construction techniques described above lend themselves very well to programming in dBASE III Plus, since you can modify the structure of an existing file at any time and you can add indexes to a file at any time.

EXAMPLE OF FILE CONSTRUCTION

A client wants to produce a report indicating the number of hours each employee spends on assigned projects. As we analyze the situation, we discover that there are three object types: employees, projects, and time cards. Using the principles outlined above, we decide to create three files, one for each object type. Let us call the files EMPLOYEE, PROJECTS, and TIMECARDS. Further analysis indicates that the records in these files will need at least the following fields.

EMPLOYEE : EMPLOYEENO, NAME, HOURLYRATE

PROJECTS : PROJECTID, MAXBUDGET

TIMECARDS: EMPLOYEENO, PROJECTID, DATE, ELAPSEDHRS

After further discussions with the client we discover that the firm also desires to keep track of the employee costs associated with each project. For this purpose, we need to add a new field to each PROJECTS record. The records in this file will then contain the fields:

PROJECTS : PROJECTID, MAXBUDGET, EMPCOST

We then discover that the client desires to give awards for the most productive employees. Since an employee may receive more than one award (repeating information) and since the client wishes to record each award (more repeating information) for future reference, we decide to create a new file for the awards with the record structure:

AWARDS : EMPLOYEENO, AWARDTYPE, DOLLARAMT,
AWARDDATE

These four files represent the state of the analyst's understanding up to a particular point in time. You must always assume that your understanding will evolve over a period of time and that your design will go through several revisions. Since each file describes just one type of object, the record type in each file consists of a unique identifier for the object and descriptive information for the object. For example, the EMPLOYEE record has EMPLOYEENO as the unique identifier and NAME and HOURLYRATE describe the employee. The object described by the TIMECARDS file is the number of hours worked by an employee on a particular project on a particular date, so the unique identifier consists of a combination of the three fields EMPLOYEENO, PROJECTID, and DATE.

Files (or more precisely, records in files) are logically related to each other in the following manner: if an employee with EMPLOYEENO = 1 has worked on a project with PROJECTID = P1, then the EMPLOYEE record with EMPLOYEENO = 1 provides the employee's name and hourly salary, the PROJECTS record with PROJECTID = P1 provides the budget information, and the TIMECARDS records with EMPLOYEENO = 1 and PROJECTID = P1 provide the time that this employee has worked on this project. If the specific start and stop times for work performed by employees are recorded in the TIMECARDS file and if the client desires the time worked on a specific day by this employee on this project, then this information will be available.

The example given above illustrates a number of points.

1. In a number of simple systems, the construction of the files can start with an examination of the input documents.
2. As the understanding of the analyst grows, the files that have been constructed from the input documents can be modified to more closely match what is desired by the client.
3. A good choice of file structure will make it easy to change the system when modifications are necessary.

The principles of good analysis and design will be continued in subsequent chapters in this book.

4.4 SPECIFYING THE DATABASE FILE(S)

There may only be one database file currently in use and a maximum of 10 database files may be open at any one time. To specify the database file currently in use, use the statement:

```
USE filename
```

If you wish to specify index files to be used with the current database file, use the statement:

```
USE filename INDEX index1, index2, . . .
```

You may specify a maximum of seven index files on any one USE statement and the first named index file is the primary or controlling index.

Warning:
Remember that there is a limitation of 15 open files at any one time. Database files, index files, and program files are counted in this limitation. In addition, the first index file is used whenever a FIND or a SEEK statement is used for direct access.

If you choose to have more than one database file open at one time, you must distinguish between them, and only one of them may be the current database file. When you open a database file for use, you must assign it to a work area. Each work area may have no more than one database file assigned to it, and there are a maximum of 10 work areas. The work areas are numbered 1 through 10. The following demonstrates how three database files might be opened for use:

```
SELECT 1
USE filea
SELECT 2
USE fileb INDEX X,Y,Z
SELECT 3
USE filec
```

The file that appears in the most recent USE statement is the one currently in use. In the above example, to now select filea as the one currently in use, execute the command

```
SELECT 1
```

When a USE statement is executed, information about the file structure and the indexes that you have named are obtained from your disk. When you place a SELECT and a USE statement together, you specify both the database file and the area that it should be placed in. When you use a subsequent SELECT statement without accompanying it with a USE statement, then the work area named after the word USE becomes the current work area, and no access is made to the disk. Each open database file (actually each work area) has a currency pointer associated with it. When you change the work area (you execute a SELECT statement without an accompanying USE), dBASE saves the currency pointer (the number of the current record) and moves to the new area. The database associated with the new work area becomes the current database file. When you move back to the old area, the currency pointer for the database file in this area is restored, so you can process records in this work area at the point that you left off.

4.5 CREATING DATABASE FILES

Database files are created through the use of the CREATE command. The user is prompted for the name, the type, and the size of each field. You may create an index of any type of field in a database file, except for a MEMO field. Nevertheless, it is a good idea to make a field numeric only if you expect that you might need to perform arithmetic with it. For example, if you have a field for a zip code, make it a character string, rather than a number, because you will not perform any arithmetic computations involving the zip code.

Hint:
When creating a database file, make those fields numeric only when you actually expect to use them in arithmetic operations.

To indicate that a field is a character string, enter C for the TYPE or strike the RETURN (since Character is the default type) and enter the desired length of the character string as the WIDTH. To indicate that a field is an integer, enter N as the TYPE and the max number of digits as the WIDTH. To indicate that a field is a real number (noninteger number), enter N as the TYPE, the total number of digits + 2 as the WIDTH, and the number of digits to the right of the decimal point as the value of DEC. The WIDTH of digits + 2 allows room for the decimal point and the sign in the field. To indicate that a field is a date, enter D as the type. To indicate that the field is a MEMO, enter M as the type. To indicate that the field is a logical (Boolean), enter L as the type. If you enter D, M, or L as the TYPE of the field, then the field width will automatically be entered for you.

Note:
When you specify the name of the database file, you should give a name such as EMPLOYEE without an extension. dBASE III Plus will assign the extension DBF, so the actual name of the database file, at the level of DOS, will be EMPLOYEE.DBF. In addition, always refer to this file in dBASE III Plus programs as EMPLOYEE, not as EMPLOYEE.DBF.

4.6 STORING DATA IN A DATABASE FILE

There are two major techniques for adding a new record to an existing file. Both of them add the new record to the end of the file. The two techniques are the APPEND and the APPEND BLANK, both of which automatically invoke the full-screen editing features of dBASE III Plus. You can also use the INSERT command, but I don't recommend it, since it can increase the amount of time necessary to enter a new record.

The APPEND is used when you wish to access the database fields directly. You can use either the default or a custom screen format with the APPEND. When you use the default screen format, the field names that you defined when you created the file are displayed on the screen, together with room for you to enter the data. If you use a custom screen format, you can provide labels to describe the data fields, rather than the names of the fields themselves. The APPEND is usually used in the interactive mode. In addition, the relative record number (the position of the record in the file) is displayed on the screen.

The APPEND BLANK creates a new blank record in the current database file. You can then use a format or PRG program of your choice to enter data into this new record using data entered from the keyboard, data available in open databases, and/or memory variables. The APPEND BLANK also facilitates the use of memory variables, rather than working directly with the database fields. You can enter the data first, examine the entry, and then decide whether or not to create a new record to hold the data in the database. With the APPEND BLANK, the programmer is responsible to gather the data input by the user and place it in the empty (blank) record. A sample piece of code to accomplish this is:

```
USE EMPLOYEE INDEX EMPNO
APPEND BLANK
CLEAR
@ 1, 1 SAY "EMPLOYEE NUMBER" GET EMPNO
@ 2, 1 SAY "DEPARTMENT"      GET DEPT
@ 2,30 SAY "TELEPHONE"       GET TEL
READ
```

Note:
For a further explanation of the coordinate system used in the @ statement, refer to Chapter 2.

In the above example, EMPNO, DEPT, and TEL are fields in the EMPLOYEE record. The @ . . SAY . . GET statements actually consist of two separate parts: a SAY and a GET. You can use code similar to that shown above, or you can use the following:

```
USE EMPLOYEE INDEX EMPNO
APPEND BLANK
CLEAR
@ 1, 1 SAY "EMPLOYEE NUMBER"
@ 1,16 GET EMPNO
@ 2, 1 SAY "DEPARTMENT"
@ 2,16 GET DEPT
@ 2,30 SAY "TELEPHONE"
@ 2,39 GET TEL
READ
```

In either case, the screen is erased, the input document is displayed on the screen, and the system enters full-screen editing mode for the purpose of input (this type of input is really equivalent to changing blank fields to data). In both the above examples, the index EMPNO is updated automatically.

4.7 INDEXES, DIRECT ACCESS, THE FIND, AND THE SEEK

An index is actually an additional file that you create and that is maintained for you by the dBASE III Plus system. The major purpose of an index file is to speed up access to a file by providing direct access to the records, using the data values in these records. To create an index, you use the INDEX ON statement (usually interactively). Once you have created the desired index, you can use it or ignore it. If you use it when you add new records to a file, change the data in the records, or delete records from a file, dBASE automatically updates the index for you. For example, assume that you wish to index the database file named EMPLOYEE on the field named EMPNO. In order to accomplish this, use the following code:

```
USE EMPLOYEE
INDEX ON EMPNO TO <index file name>
```

In the example in Section 4.6, we have used EMPNO as the name of the index file. This means that the name of the file (at the operating system level) is actually EMPNO.NDX. There is no confusion caused by naming the index the same as the field name, as far as dBASE is concerned.

Whenever you append a record to a database file, remember to supply all the names of the associated index files. Only the index files named by you in the most recent USE or SET statement for this file will be updated by the system. To name the index files in the USE statement, use the following technique, where A, B, and C are indexes (index files) for the database file X:

```
USE X INDEX A, B, C
      or
USE X
SET INDEX TO A, B, C
```

If you neglect to name an index file in a USE or SET statement and then you add, change, or delete a record, then that index file will not be updated, and access to data in the file using that index will be incorrect.

For the operation of appending a record to a database file, the order of the indexes in the USE statement is not important. The order of the indexes is only important when you are using the SEEK or the FIND, since the first index is the controlling one. Since you are limited to seven index names in the USE statement, you ought to restrict the total number of indexes on a single database file to seven if you can.

Hint:
Restrict the number of indexes on any one database file to seven.

The most fundamental use of an index is to perform direct access to a record. For example, suppose we wish to directly access the employee record with the value of EMPNO = "ABCDE". Remember that direct access is possible only on a field that has been indexed. It is necessary to specify both the database file to be used and the index to be used for the direct access. In this case, the position of the index to be used for the direct access is very important. In fact, it must be the first index in the list. For example, it is possible to specify this information in any of the following ways:

```
USE EMPLOYEE INDEX EMPNO
USE EMPLOYEE INDEX EMPNO,A
USE EMPLOYEE INDEX EMPNO,A,B
Etc.
```

as long as the name of the index to be used for direct access is the first in the list of specified indexes.

To perform the act of direct access, we use the SEEK statement. The FIND statement can also be used, but I do not recommend it, since you must use the macro expansion character (&) and a memory variable with the FIND. For example:

```
USE EMPLOYEE INDEX EMPNO
SEEK "ABCDE"
     or
FIND "ABCDE"
```

The result of the SEEK is reflected in the value of EOF( ) and in the value of FOUND( ). The value of EOF( ) is .T. (TRUE) and the value of FOUND( ) is .F. (FALSE), if the SEEK was unsuccessful. If the SEEK was successful, then the value of EOF( ) is .F. (FALSE), the value of FOUND( ) is .T. (TRUE), and the value of RECNO( ) is > 0 (it actually is the number of the record found). In addition, the record in the user buffer (the current record) is available for use if the SEEK was successful. It is not possible to use RECNO( ) as a way to judge whether or not a SEEK was successful, since RECNO( ) is not necessarily 0 when the SEEK fails.

To use the FIND statement with a character string variable, rather than with a character string constant (such as "ABCDE"), use the following technique:

```
CLEAR
STORE SPACE(5) TO MEMEMPNO
@ 5,1 SAY "ENTER THE EMPLOYEE NUMBER" GET ;
  MEMEMPNO
READ
USE EMPLOYEE INDEX EMPNO
FIND &MEMEMPNO
IF .NOT. FOUND( )
     ? "NO RECORD ON FILE FOR THIS EMPLOYEE NUMBER"
     WAIT
ELSE
     <other code goes here>
ENDIF
```

The same code using the SEEK statement is:

```
CLEAR
```

```
STORE SPACE(5) TO MEMEMPNO
@ 5,1 SAY "ENTER THE EMPLOYEE NUMBER" GET ;
  MEMEMPNO
READ
USE EMPLOYEE INDEX EMPNO
SEEK MEMEMPNO
IF .NOT. FOUND( )
     ? "NO RECORD ON FILE FOR THIS EMPLOYEE NUMBER"
     WAIT
ELSE
     <other code goes here>
ENDIF
```

Note:
If the FIND is used in conjunction with a memory variable (like MEMEMPNO above), the macro function (&) must immediately precede the memory variable name in the FIND statement. The & symbol should not be used with the SEEK statement.

The purpose of the WAIT in the above code is to freeze the screen. After a WAIT statement has been executed, the user must press a key to resume execution of the program. This ensures that the information displayed on the screen does not disappear before it can be read by the user. The & is the symbol for macro expansion. When the dBASE III Plus system encounters the &, it literally replaces the occurrence of the & and the name of the memory variable that follows it with the contents of the memory variable.

In the above code an assumption is made. The assumption is that the employee number entered will match an employee number in the file, where the size of the field in the database is 5. What if the employee numbers in the database file have length 6? Then the first employee number that starts with "ABCDE" in the database file (in index order) will be the one that is found. If the size of the field in the database is 6 and you wish to find only the record with the employee number "ABCDE" (the string ABCDE followed by exactly 1 space), a slightly different technique is required. The code to accomplish this is:

```
STORE SPACE(6) TO MEMEMPNO
CLEAR
@ 5,1 SAY "ENTER THE EMPLOYEE NUMBER" GET ;
  MEMEMPNO
```

```
READ
USE EMPLOYEE INDEX EMPNO
SEEK MEMEMPNO
IF .NOT. FOUND( )
      ? "NO RECORD ON FILE FOR THIS EMPLOYEE NUMBER"
      WAIT
ELSE
      <other code goes here>
ENDIF
```

The above code insures that the string in MEMEMPNO has length exactly equal to 6, so, if all the EMPNOs have length 6, then an exact match must take place.

4.8 SEQUENTIAL ACCESS

Sequential access to a database file may be started either at the beginning of the file or may follow a previous direct access. The first allows sequential access to the entire file and the second allows sequential access from a point other than the beginning of the file. Both these methods are of value in appropriate circumstances. In either case, the dBASE III Plus statement that allows you to move sequentially to the next record of the current database file is the SKIP statement. An example of a sequential scan of a database file is:

```
USE EMPLOYEE
STORE 0 TO ROW
STORE 50 TO MAXLINES
SET DEVICE TO PRINT
DO WHILE .NOT. EOF( )
      STORE ROW+1 TO ROW
      IF ROW > MAXLINES
            EJECT
            STORE 1 TO ROW
      ENDIF
      @ ROW, 1 SAY EMPNO
      SKIP 1
ENDDO
EJECT
SET DEVICE TO SCREEN
RETURN
```

The USE statement opens the database file EMPLOYEE and makes the first record in the file, if any, the current record. If the file is empty, EOF( ) is set to .T. (TRUE); otherwise EOF( ) is set to .F. (FALSE). If EOF( ) is TRUE, the loop is entered. The purpose of the SKIP statement is to make the next record in the database file the current record (the currency pointer is advanced to the next record). If the SKIP statement is not included, the loop will be executed an infinite number of times, using the first record for each iteration of the loop. Note also the inclusion of output control: the employee number (EMPNO) of each record in the database file will be printed and each page of output will contain a maximum of fifty lines. Note also that a page advance is performed using the EJECT statement. The purpose of the EJECT statement is to insure that the print head is moved back to its initial (leftmost) position and that the page is advanced at the end of the report. The records in the database file are accessed in the order in which they physically reside in the file. To access the records in order by employee number (it is assumed that the file has been indexed on EMPNO), use the following code, where the only difference between the previous code and the next example is the use of the INDEX.

```
USE EMPLOYEE INDEX EMPNO
STORE 0 TO ROW
STORE 50 TO MAXLINES
SET DEVICE TO PRINT
DO WHILE .NOT. EOF( )
      STORE ROW+1 TO ROW
      IF ROW > MAXLINES
             EJECT
             STORE 1 TO ROW
      ENDIF
      @ ROW, 1 SAY EMPNO
      SKIP 1
ENDDO
EJECT
SET DEVICE TO SCREEN
RETURN
```

As another example, let's assume that we have a database file named SALARY that contains the salary history for each employee and that each record has the following fields: SALEMPNO, SALDATE, and SALSALARY, where SALEMPNO is the name of the field in the file that contains the employee number, SALDATE is the effective date of the salary, and SALSALARY is the salary amount. Assume that this file has been indexed on SALEMPNO and let SALEMPNO be the name of the index file created by the statement:

```
INDEX ON SALEMPNO TO SALEMPNO
```

If we wish to access only those records for employee number "123456", use the following code:

```
USE SALARY INDEX SALEMPNO
SEEK "123456"
IF .NOT. FOUND( )
      ? "NO SALARY RECORDS FOR THIS EMPLOYEE NUMBER"
      WAIT
ELSE
      DO WHILE .NOT. EOF( ) .AND. SALEMPNO = "123456"
                  .
                  .
                  .
            SKIP 1
      ENDDO
ENDIF
RETURN
```

CHAPTER

5

Programming Hints and Notes on Style and Problems

5.1 CONSTRUCTING MENUS

It is strongly suggested that all application systems be menu driven, that is, that the user be presented with a menu from which he or she may select operations appropriate to his or her needs. This reduces the amount of documentation necessary and makes the system much easier to use. The use of a menu entails four distinct functions: the display of the menu itself, obtaining an indicator of the selected function from the user, the execution of the function itself, and the return to the menu. I prefer to embed all these functions in a loop that will be executed until the user decides to exit from the module in which the menu is contained. Exit implies a return to the calling routine or an exit from the application system, as appropriate. The sequence of operations is as follows:

1. Display the menu
2. Obtain the indicator of the selected function
3. Perform the operation indicated by the selection indicator, and
4. Loop to display the menu again

An outline of the code to accomplish this is:

```
SET TALK OFF
DO WHILE .T.
    CLEAR
    SET DEVICE TO SCREEN
    @  1, 1 SAY "MAIN SELECTION MENU"
    @  2, 1 SAY "______________________"
    @  3, 5 SAY     "A. EXIT"
    @  4, 5 SAY     "B. EMPLOYEE RECORD, ENTER"
    @  5, 5 SAY     "C. EMPLOYEE RECORD, CHANGE"
    @  6, 5 SAY     "D. PROJECT RECORD, ENTER"
    @  7, 5 SAY     "E. PROJECT RECORD, CHANGE"
    @  8, 5 SAY     "F. TIME CARD       , ENTER"
    @  9, 5 SAY     "G. TIME CARD       , CHANGE"
    @ 10, 5 SAY     "H. PRINT REPORT"
    WAIT "ENTER A SELECTION CODE" TO CODE
    DO CASE
        CASE CODE = "A"
            ? "NORMAL TERMINATION OF PROJECT ",;
              "REPORTING SYSTEM"
            QUIT
```

```
            CASE CODE = "B"
                DO EMPENTER
            CASE CODE = "C"
                DO EMPCHANGE
            CASE CODE = "D"
                DO PROJENTER
            CASE CODE = "E"
                DO PROJCHANGE
            CASE CODE = "F"
                DO TCENTER
            CASE CODE = "G"
                TO TCCHANGE
            CASE CODE = "H"
                DO PRINTREP
            OTHERWISE
                ? "ILLEGAL SELECTION CODE: PLEASE ",;
                  "REENTER"
                WAIT
        ENDCASE
        CLEAR ALL
    ENDDO
```

An explanation of each of the features in the above code is:

SET TALK OFF:	Inhibits display on the screen of results of program operations
QUIT:	Exit from dBASE III Plus and return to the operating system
DO X:	Obtain the dBASE III Plus program located in the MS/PC DOS file with name = X.PRG and execute it
CLEAR ALL:	Release all memory locations and close all database files

5.2 NAME SELECTION

The choice of names for procedures, files, fields in record, and memory variables is, of course, up to the individual programmer. Nevertheless, a reasonable and uniform technique for naming may save the programmer considerable debugging time. I recommend the following:

1. Name files so that the contents of the file are clear. For example, name the file for employees EMPLOYEE, not something like X27A4. In addition, you may make the names of files longer than the names allowed by most operating systems. For example, MS/PC DOS allows file names 8 characters in length. If the name that you select, when you create a file, is longer than 8, the first 8 characters are used for the actual name of the file. But you may still refer, in your programs, to the file by its longer name. For example, say that you created a database file with the name SERVICECENTER. The name of the file at the level of the operating system is SERVICEC.DBF, but you may always refer to it in dBASE III Plus programs as SERVICECENTER. Similar comments apply to the names of programs. If you are using a compiler and linking the compiled modules, you may find that the use of names that are longer than 8 characters may cause problems for the linker. As a result, if there is any chance that you will use a compiler for your dBASE III Plus programs, I strongly recommend that you restrict all file names used in your programs to 8 characters or less.
2. The names of memory variables and the names of fields in database records are limited to 10 characters. Again, I recommend that you always choose meaningful names. In addition, it is useful to distinguish between names of fields in database records and memory variables. One suggested technique is to prefix the names of fields in database records with the first two or three letters of the database file name and to prefix the names of memory variables with the three letters "MEM". For example, a field in the database file EMPLOYEE and a memory variable may both contain salary information. Name them EMPSALARY and MEMSALARY, respectively. You will then be able to distinguish which names refer to memory variables, which refer to fields in database records, and which database file the fields are in. I am not recommending that you become a slave to this naming procedure, but that you use it to your best advantage. For example, you may wish to accumulate the total salary for display at the end of a report. Since you have used MEMSALARY in your program to contain the salary of an individual employee, you may wish to store the accumulated total in the memory location named TOTSALARY, rather than something like MEMTSALARY.

3. If you name fields in database records in the manner described in the previous item, you may then assign names to index files in a reasonable manner. Choose as the name of an index the same name as the field. For example, if EMPLOYEE is the name of the database file and EMPLASTNAM is a field in the record, then:

   ```
   INDEX ON EMPLASTNAM TO EMPLASTN
   ```

   insures that you will always be able to remember which file and which field in the record that the index is associated with. Since it is the programmer's responsibility to inform dBASE III Plus of the index files associated with a database file (through the USE or SET statements), this technique can be quite helpful. dBASE III Plus does not keep track of the database with which an index is associated. If you create two database files with a field name in common and index one of these files on the common name, it is your responsibility to make sure that the index file is used only for the one database with which it should be associated. dBASE III Plus does not check that you are using the correct indexes with a database. If you make a mistake and use an index with the incorrect database file, then you may end up with a badly structured index file and incorrect access to both database files.

4. Use the default naming convention. A procedure might have the name CASHPURC.PRG at the level of the operating system, but, when you wish to invoke the procedure with this name, do not include the ".PRG." For example, invoke the procedure with the statement:

   ```
   DO CASHPURC
   ```

   When referring to the name of a database file, use EMPLOYEE rather than EMPLOYEE.DBF. Similarly, when referring to the name of an index file, use EMPSALAR rather than EMPSALAR.NDX.

5. When using more than one database file, there is a possibility that the dBASE III Plus system will not be able to distinguish between fields in the two files. For example, if a field is named SALARY in both the databases, the system does not know to which file you are referring. To solve this problem, use A- > SALARY and B- > SALARY to indicate, respectively, the SALARY field in the current record of the database in work areas 1 and 2.

5.3 USING THE CLEAR ALL: CLOSING DATABASE FILES, CONTROL OF OVERLAYS, AND MODULARITY

5.3.1 CLOSING DATABASE FILES

Each database file has associated with it information that reflects the current number of records in the file. Let's call this information the header. Data that you append to a file actually is stored in a temporary buffer and then transferred to the database file either when the buffer is full or when you close the file. Sometimes the header is updated when you enter the data, sometimes when the data is transferred, and sometimes when the database file is closed. If you exit from dBASE III Plus without properly closing the database file, then you may cause two distinct types of problems.

Problem 1—There may be data (records) in the temporary buffer not yet transferred to the database file.

Problem 2—The header may not have been updated and the number of records actually in the database file is greater than the count of data records reflected in the header.

These problems might occur from abnormal program termination due, for example, to static electricity, to removal of the disks from the drives without execution of the QUIT statement, etc. One way to insure that database files are properly closed (the records in the buffer are transferred to the database file and the header is properly updated) is to execute the QUIT statement to exit from the dBASE III Plus system. In addition, execution of the CLEAR ALL or the CLOSE DATABASES statement properly closes all database files currently open.

Note:
In order to close just one database at a time, make the desired work area the current one and execute the USE statement without any parameters.

One advantage of the CLEAR ALL and CLOSE DATABASES statements is that you are not forced to exit from the dBASE III Plus system as with the QUIT statement. One disadvantage of the CLEAR ALL statement is that all the memory variables are deallocated. If you wish to close all the database files but keep the memory variables, use the

CLOSE DATABASES statement. I personally prefer to execute the CLEAR ALL statement each time execution of a menu item is completed. See, for example, the code for the menu in Section 5.1, Constructing Menus.

Even though dBASE III Plus makes every effort to match the header with the data in the file, there may be some cases when the header will not reflect the correct number of records in the database file. In this case, try closing the database in question, using the CLEAR ALL, CLOSE DATABASES, or the QUIT statement.

It is sometimes possible to recover from Problem 1. If you remove the disks from the system but do not power-off and you have not disturbed the contents of main memory, then simply reinsert the disks into their proper places and resume processing. If you power-off or in any other way disturb the contents of main memory, you will not be able to recover the records in the buffer that have not yet been transferred to the database file.

In dBASE III Plus, if you have Problem 2 and the CLEAR ALL, CLOSE DATABASES, and QUIT commands do not help, you will simply have to enter the data again. Having to re-enter data can be a considerable chore, so I recommend that you make backups of your files on a regular basis.

5.3.2 CONTROL OF OVERLAYS AND MODULARITY

Consider the following sequence of statements in dBASE III Plus:

```
DO A
DO B
DO C
```

When each of these statements is executed, the code from the files A.PRG, B.PRG, and C.PRG, respectively, is brought into main memory and executed. Public memory variables retain their values, except for those referenced in RELEASE statements, and form a type of common data area. In this manner, values may be "passed" from A to B to C. This technique (the use of global variables) may lead to problems. One possible problem is that the overlays may destroy the integrity of the memory variables. Another problem is that you may lose control of the meaning and use of the memory variables; you might be using a memory variable to mean one thing in one module and another thing in another module. To overcome this problem, I recommend that you design your code so that it is not necessary to pass values from A to B, from B to C, etc. You may then replace the above code with the following:

```
DO A
CLEAR ALL
DO B
CLEAR ALL
DO C
CLEAR ALL
```

Note:
In the above description of global variables, we are not discussing the passing of parameters to subroutines called from a higher level program. We are discussing the passing of values from one routine to another at the same level, using a common data area.

There should be no problems with overlays, when this technique (using the CLEAR ALL after the execution of a routine) is used. In addition, this technique tends to limit the effect of global variables (the memory variables) and so promotes modularity.

5.4 HINTS AND TECHNIQUES

This section is a collection of hints and techniques that will help you "program around" certain problems that occur because of application design decisions or because of problems with dBASE III Plus commands. As such, it has not been structured with any particular central theme but is presented here as a miscellaneous collection of hints and techniques. I suspect that the reader will find it useful to browse through this material to gain a feel for the types of problems that occur when using dBASE III Plus, and then to refer to this section for specific help by using either the table of contents or the index to this book, when programming or design problems arise.

5.4.1 PROGRAMMING FOR SPEED

Because of the speed limitations associated with microcomputers, it is always important to avoid use of operations that might cause a program to run too slowly. Some principles to be applied are:

1. Avoid use of statements that unnecessarily access the disks or that create new files. In particular, avoid COUNT FOR, JOIN, RESTORE, SAVE, SORT, TOTAL and do not create an index in a program unless it is truly necessary. In addition, see if you can place all your USE statements outside of loops and specify files used inside of loops through the SELECT statement. Each time you execute a USE statement, the system obtains the definition of the data file and all the index files specified in the USE statement from the disk. The SELECT statement allows you to use database files and indexes that were opened previous to (and are therefore outside of) a loop. Avoid the use of the macro function (&) inside of a loop. It can slow down the execution of your program by as much as 30%. In addition, some compilers do not allow the use of the macro function in any of your programs.
2. Avoid use of statements that sequentially scan files, when direct access will do. In particular, use the SEEK (or FIND) statements where appropriate. In addition, avoid use of the COUNT . . FOR statement on large files, when possible.
3. Avoid INSERTing records into large files, since all the records from the point of insertion to the end of the file have to be physically moved.

5.4.2 AUTO GENERATION OF UNIQUE ID'S

As a matter of style, I prefer to have the application system generate unique ID's rather than require the user to input them. Clearly, this does not apply to ID's such as social security numbers but does apply to ID's arbitrarily assigned by an organization. This certainly applies to all the situations in which the user assigns a unique ID only for the purpose of distinguishing between records in a database file and the user is free to assign any ID that he or she chooses. In this case, I recommend storing either the last used ID or the ID to be used next (choose which is more convenient for you) in a database file in order to avoid use of the SAVE and RESTORE statements. In addition, if you make this field a number, then it is easy to increment. In dBASE III Plus, you may index on a numeric field and may then use that numeric field index in either the SEEK or the FIND commands.

If you elect to store system generated ID's as character strings, you will probably store the ID last used (or to be used next) as a number in one database and store the actual ID as a character string. This implies that the number stored in one database file must then be converted to a character string using the STR function. There is the potential of a problem with correct function of the SEEK or FIND statement, when the character string is created from a number using the STR function.

EXAMPLE:

If the data is typed as a character string, say of size 4, and you enter an integer, then the number is left-justified. If you enter the number 1 in the field and then press RETURN, then the data is stored as "1   ", that is, as a 1 followed by three blanks. If you enter the data into the same field with a statement of the form

```
REPLACE <field name> WITH STR(1,4)
```

then the data is left-justified and the stored data is "   1", that is, three blanks followed by a 1. You must make sure that your entry techniques will store the data in the same format.

Hint:
Don't use techniques that will store the same data in a file using two different storage techniques.

5.4.3 FREEZING THE SCREEN

It is occasionally necessary to display messages on the screen for consumption by the user. In the case of prompts for input, the message will stay on the screen at least until input is accomplished. In the case where no input is expected from the user, but the programmer wishes to present the user with a message, it is advisable to force the user to enter some kind of input. The technique that I recommend is demonstrated by the following code:

```
? "NO RECORD ON FILE FOR THE GIVEN ID."
WAIT
```

or

```
@ 5,1 SAY "NO RECORD ON FILE FOR THE GIVEN ID."
WAIT
```

The message NO RECORD ON FILE FOR THE GIVEN ID remains on the screen at least until one of the keys on the keyboard is depressed. The WAIT statement causes the execution of the program to pause until you press a key and also prompts the user for input.

5.4.4 A REINDEXING PROGRAM

During the operation of a system, situations sometimes occur that cause an index file to disagree with the corresponding database file. An example is where records have been appended to a database file and static electricity has caused system failure before the appropriate files have been properly updated. An example of a dBASE III Plus error message that indicates this situation is RECORD IS OUT OF RANGE. In this case, it is advisable to reindex the file in question. One technique to accomplish this is to have a program that will recreate all the indexes used in the system. In addition, reindexing a large file might decrease processing time after a large number of records have been appended to the file. An example of such a program is:

```
* PROGRAM TO REINDEX ALL THE FILES IN THE SYSTEM
SET SAFETY OFF
USE A
INDEX ON A1 TO A1
INDEX ON A2 TO A2
USE B
INDEX ON B1 TO B1
INDEX ON B2 TO B2
INDEX ON B3 TO B3
RETURN
```

5.4.5 A FILE EMPTY PROGRAM

After you finish debugging an application system, you will want to empty out all the database files and may also want to initialize some of these files before delivery to a client. In addition, you may wish to empty out files and initialize some of them before addition of a new module, while you are debugging the system. It is recommended that you create a program that will perform these operations for you and which will recreate the index files. An example of such a program follows:

```
SET SAFETY OFF
```

```
USE A
  ZAP
  INDEX ON A1 TO A1
  INDEX ON A2 TO A2
USE B
  ZAP
  INDEX ON B1 TO B1
  INDEX ON B2 TO B2
  INDEX ON B3 TO B3
USE C
  ZAP
  APPEND BLANK
  REPLACE CEMPNO WITH 1000
RETURN
```

5.4.6 DELETING RECORDS AND SPACE RECOVERY

It is occasionally necessary to delete records from existing database files, either because of new system installation or because the user no longer desires to have old records on the production disk. If you PACK a file with indexes currently in use, the PACK will be immediately followed by an automatic reindex for all active index files for the database file. If you PACK a file, the space previously occupied by records in the database file is recovered at the operating system level, at the time that the database is properly closed.

5.4.7 MULTIPLE DISKS

In those situations where you find it desirable to have your programs (procedures) on one disk and have your data files on another disk, merely prefix your file names with the name of the disk (disk drive and directory) when referring to them in the programs. For example, assume that your programs are on disk A and that your data files are on disk B. When you create your database file, give it the name B:EMPLOYEE, and refer to it by exactly that name in your programs. You can use the same technique for indexes. When you create your index file, use the code:

```
USE B:EMPLOYEE
INDEX ON EMPNO TO B:EMPNO
```

to insure that the index file will also reside on disk B.

If all your programs and data files are on the same drive and directory, you can use the SET DEFAULT TO statement instead of the technique described above.

5.4.8 TESTING FOR END OF FILE

You will want to test for the end of the file whenever you perform a sequential search of the database. The sequential search may be performed either with or without an associated index file. In the case of no index file, the search is in physical record order. In the case of an associated index file, the search is in index file order. The end of file test works correctly for both the database file and the associated index files, whether the database file is empty or not. To test for end of file, you can use EOF( ) if the search is in a forward direction (toward higher record numbers) and you can use BOF( ) if the search is in the backward direction (toward lower record numbers).

5.4.9 USING THE GET . . PICTURE WITH A NUMBER

If you wish to enter a real number in the interactive mode, using full-screen editing, you can accomplish this using the

```
@ . . SAY . . GET . . PICTURE
```

statement. For example, if we wish to enter a number with the PICTURE "99.99", then we can use code similar to the following:

```
CLEAR
STORE 0 TO HEIGHT
@ 1,1 SAY "ENTER THE HEIGHT" GET HEIGHT PICTURE;
  "99.99"
```

The STORE statement is used to initialize the value of the memory variable named HEIGHT before it appears in the @ . . SAY statement. If you enter a number such as 5.1, then, after you enter the 5 and the decimal point, dBASE III Plus automatically aligns the decimal point that you entered with the decimal point in the displayed field.

In the above explanation of the @ . . SAY . . GET . . PICTURE, the numeric memory variable was initialized with zero (0). If you initialize the variable with spaces, then the GET statement works quite differently. For example, assume that the code is:

```
STORE SPACE(5) TO HEIGHT
```

```
@ 1,1 SAY "ENTER THE HEIGHT" GET HEIGHT PICTURE ;
  "99.99"
```

In this case, HEIGHT will be a character string that will contain a number in the indicated format and there will be some problems entering the data. If you enter a 5 in the leading position and then attempt to enter a decimal point in the second position (actually in any position), a tone will be sounded and the keystroke will be ignored.

Hint:
Never use spaces to initialize a numeric field to be used in a GET . . PICTURE statement.

5.4.10 INPUT CHARACTER STRINGS WITHOUT QUOTATION MARKS

In addition to full-screen editing, there are two major techniques that you may use to enter character strings: the ACCEPT and the INPUT statements. The major advantage of using the ACCEPT statement over the INPUT statement, when you want to enter a string, is that quotation marks around the string are not needed (indeed, they must not be entered). Of course, you may use full-screen editing (the @ . . SAY . . GET) as an alternative to both the ACCEPT and the INPUT statements. For the syntax of the ACCEPT and INPUT statements, see Chapter 2. In most cases, the use of full-screen editing is preferred over the use of either the INPUT or the ACCEPT statement.

EXAMPLE 1:

```
ACCEPT "ENTER THE NAME OF THE EMPLOYEE:" TO ;
  MEMNAME
```

EXAMPLE 2:

```
CLEAR
STORE SPACE(3) TO MEMNAME
@ 1,1 SAY "ENTER THE NAME OF THE EMPLOYEE" GET ;
  MEMNAME
READ
```

5.4.11 INTERFACING WITH THE OUTSIDE WORLD

It is often important either to input data produced by or output data for use by other software systems. To input data from an ASCII, DIF, SYLK, or WKS file prepared by another system, use the APPEND FROM statement. To input data from a PFS file, use the IMPORT statement. To output data to an ASCII, DIF, SYLK, or WKS file use the COPY TO statement. To output data to a PFS file, use the EXPORT statement. Whenever you use the APPEND FROM or the COPY TO statements, you can specify the type of file format to be used. When you are working with ASCII files, you can specify the format either as DELIMITED or as SDF. DELIMITED refers to files of the BASIC type, that is, character strings are delimited (often by quotation marks) and the individual fields are separated by commas. SDF refers to files of the FORTRAN type, that is, the data is arranged in columnar fashion, without quotation marks and without field separators. If you refer to an ASCII file by the name TEMP, dBASE III Plus will use the full name TEMP.TXT. If you specify the full name, for example, TEST.XXX, then dBASE III Plus will use the full name as given. For more information of the APPEND FROM and the COPY TO statements, see Chapter 2.

Warning:
When you use a COPY statement, the new file replaces an existing file of the same name.

5.4.12 AVOID THE USE OF CERTAIN INTERACTIVE STATEMENTS IN A PROGRAM

Some of the commands (statements) available in dBASE III Plus are really designed for interactive use. Two examples are the DISPLAY and the LOCATE statements. Avoid using these statements within a program. For example, instead of using the DISPLAY statement, use the @ . . SAY. To list several records, place the @ . . SAY in a loop. Also, instead of using the LOCATE on an unindexed file, use the SEEK on an indexed file.

5.4.13 MULTIPLE LINE STATEMENTS

All the dBASE III Plus statements can be used in programs, although you may choose to avoid doing so for reasons of speed, accuracy, programming style, and so on. Some of the statements can be used only in programs, that is, they cannot be used interactively; these are the statements that require more than one line. An example is the IF-THEN-ELSE. At least five lines are required for this type of statement. The IF-THEN requires a minimum of three lines and the DO-WHILE requires at least three lines. The IIF function can be used to emulate an IF-THEN-ELSE or an IF-THEN in the interactive mode.

5.4.14 USING THE CASE STATEMENT TO SIMPLIFY NESTED IF'S

It is not unusual to have nested IF's, even if you carefully adhere to the techniques of modern structured programming. For example, if you have the following code:

```
IF X = "A"
        DO A
ELSE
IF X = "B"
        DO B
ELSE
IF X = "C"
        DO C
ELSE
        DO E
ENDIF
ENDIF
ENDIF
```

you may wish to use the CASE statement, which has the form:

```
DO CASE
        CASE X = "A"
                DO A
        CASE X = "B"
                DO B
        CASE X = "C"
                DO C
        CASE X = "D"
                DO D
        OTHERWISE
                DO E
ENDCASE
```

Hint:
Use the CASE statement instead of nested IF's, where appropriate. In general, it will make your code easier to debug and maintain.

Note that you may physically nest CASE statements in a single program and you may also logically nest CASE statements. For example, in the above code, the program A may contain a CASE statement.

5.4.15 USING THE EJECT TO INITIALIZE THE PRINT HEAD

When you print the last line of a report on the printer, the print head usually remains in the column just to the right of the last character printed. On some printers, even if you perform a manual form feed, the print head will remain in the same position, forcing you to shut the printer power off and then turn it back on again in order to position the print head at column 1 for the next report. To avoid this problem, always insert the EJECT statement after the last output statement in the program.

Hint:
Always end a report with an EJECT statement.

5.4.16 SENDING SPECIAL CHARACTERS TO THE PRINTER

Some printers may be reconfigured by special codes sent to it from the microcomputer. For example, when you power up your printer, it is often initialized to a standard print font: 6 lines per inch vertical and 10 characters per inch horizontal. You may wish to dynamically reconfigure your printer to an alternate print font, 8 lines per inch, and/or 12 characters per inch. The CHR function is used for this purpose. To change the printer configuration at the beginning of a report, I recommend that you use code of the type:

```
SET DEVICE TO PRINT
@ 0,0 SAY CHR(some decimal number)
```

To change the printer configuration at the end of a report, I recommend that you use code of the type:

```
@ 51,0 SAY CHR(some decimal number)
```

where it is assumed that you are printing a maximum of 50 lines per page of the report. The choice of "some decimal character" and the number of special characters is dependent upon the type of printer. To send a string containing more than one code to the printer, use something like the following:

```
@ 0,0 SAY CHR(27) + "A6"
```

5.4.17 TECHNIQUES FOR MODIFYING THE STRUCTURE OF A DATABASE FILE

During the analysis, design, and construction of an application system, one often discovers data elements that have not yet been included. As previously mentioned in Section 4.3, Useful Analysis and Design Techniques, it is helpful to organize the various files so that each file describes exactly one type of object and each record in a file describes exactly one instance (occurrence) of the object. For example, the EMPLOYEE file used in previous examples has these properties. In addition, note that all the fields in a record in the EMPLOYEE file have the property that they directly describe attributes of a specific employee. If you discover that you need to include an employee attribute not yet contained in the records in the EMPLOYEE file, you may add a new field to the existing record (file) definition at any time. You may either insert the new field before an existing field definition or you may append it to the end of the record definition. All modifications are started by the following commands. It is recommended that you perform all modifications in the interactive mode.

```
USE EMPLOYEE
MODIFY STRUCTURE
```

When you modify the structure of an existing database file, the current contents are saved for you in a backup file and are copied to the new database file from the backup file after the modifications have been completed.

Warning:
The restoration of the data records from the backup file does not always take place as expected. Refer to the MODIFY STRUCTURE command in Chapter 2 for more information on this subject.

The backup file is given the extension of BAK and remains on your disk, even after the database has been given a new structure and the data has been copied by dBASE into your new file. In case of error, you can use this backup file to recover your data or the previous database structure. Just rename the file so that it has an extension of DBF.

Remember that you are limited to a maximum of 128 fields in a record. In the event that you attempt to insert a field into a record definition that already contains 128 fields, you will receive a warning message. If you already have 128 fields in a record definition, you will need to delete one of the field definitions before you will be allowed to insert a new one. If you must have more than 128 fields in a record, the recommended technique is to break the record into two or more parts, contained, respectively, in two or more database files, and link the records together. To link the records together, merely give them the same key values and access the database files for the required information using the appropriate key values. You may also link records together by relative record number. (See also SET RELATION in Chapter 2.) Many of the full-screen editing features are available when modifying the definition of a database record.

5.4.18 DOCUMENT DISPLAY AND FULL-SCREEN EDITING

Although it is possible to enter records with the default APPEND function and to edit them with the default EDIT function, it is recommended that you do not use these features in your completed application system. Two major reasons for this are:

1. The names used for the fields in the database records will probably not be meaningful to the end user, and
2. When the user has completed the entry of a record, the user is prompted for entry of another record, even if there are no more records to be entered. If the user is editing a record and there is another record in the database, the user must specifically inform dBASE III Plus that no more records are to be edited.

To provide a better means of control for record entry, use the APPEND BLANK in combination with the appropriate SAY's, GET's, and READ's. This allows the programmer to place a document on the screen to facilitate entry of the data. By REPLACING selected fields in the empty record before presentation of the document on the screen, the programmer may also create a partially filled in document, which is useful in controlling redundancy and in controlling system generated values. To edit an existing record, SEEK or FIND the appropriate record and display it on the screen as a document. This technique is similar to the one used for document entry, except that the current values of the database record fields are displayed on the screen available for change. When you display a record on the screen in document form, you usually use a combination of SAY's and GET's. The SAY's allow you to label fields with programmer selected names and allow the display of the contents of selected fields without allowing them to be changed. The GETs (in combination with the READ) will display the current contents of the fields in the record and allow them to be changed. If the APPEND BLANK precedes the record display, then the current field content is blank, facilitating data entry. If a SEEK or FIND precedes the record display, the current field content was obtained from the database file, facilitating data modification.

Whenever you use full-screen editing, make sure that you do not attempt to either display (SAY) or enter (GET) any information on the first line of the screen (actually row/line 0 in a program). Part of this line is reversed by dBASE III Plus to print messages of various types on the screen. In particular, this line is used by dBASE III Plus to indicate when dBASE is in INSERT mode. INSERT mode is a toggle that is turned on/off by striking either ^V (CTRL V) or the INS key. Remember also that the row and column numbers used in your programs will be one less than the actual row and column printed. For example:

```
@ 1,2 SAY "ABC"
```

will print the output on row 2 and column 3 of the output device.

5.4.19 SPECIAL END PROCESSING ROUTINES

If you find that you always wish to perform an operating system function or execute either a COM or an EXE file upon exit from a dBASE III Plus application system, you may accomplish this using the dBASE III Plus RUN statement. Insert the RUN statement in your dBASE III Plus program at the appropriate point. See Chapter 2 for a discussion of the RUN statement.

Warning:
In order to use the RUN statement, you will need COMMANDS.CMD on your disk and you may need as much as 256K of additional main memory.

5.4.20 COMPOUND INDEXES (CONCATENATING FIELDS)

You may wish to create an index that allows you to access data that is (logically) sorted in a complex manner. For example, you may wish to logically organize your data so that it can be accessed in order by city within state. One technique is to physically sort the data. If you need to access the data in this form rather infrequently, this may be an acceptable solution to the problem, but in the case where access is frequent, the sort operation will be both inconvenient and time consuming. dBASE III Plus allows you to access data in a database file using only one index at a time (the first one in the INDEX list in the current USE statement—the controlling or primary index), but you can form the index in a manner that simulates nesting of indexes. In this case, create the index in the following manner:

```
USE EMPLOYEE
INDEX ON EMPSTATE+EMPCITY TO EMPSTATCITY
```

This will create an index that allows access to the records in the EMPLOYEE database file in order of EMPCITY within EMPSTATE. This index can be used sequentially to access the records in a manner that simulates a sort and can still be used in direct access using the SEEK or the FIND. In the case of the SEEK or the FIND, a special word of caution is required. The length of the value required for this index is now the length of EMPSTATE plus the length of EMPCITY. For example, assume that EMPSTATE has length 2 and that EMPCITY has length 15. If you attempt to SEEK or FIND a record in EMPLOYEE using this index and you use code of the form:

```
USE EMPLOYEE INDEX EMPSTATCIT
SEEK MEMKEY
```

then the length of MEMKEY should equal the length of EMPSTATE plus the length of EMPCITY. If, for illustrative purposes, you are using a one-letter code "C" for the state of California, then MEMKEY = "C SACRAMENTO   " would be correct, but MEMKEY = "CSACRAMENTO   ", with no space between C and SACRAMENTO, would be incorrect.

5.4.21 SPECIAL NOTES ON DEBUGGING

Every programmer eventually encounters the situation where a program should work but doesn't, and the programmer cannot figure out why. dBASE III Plus has features for debugging such programs. The way that I prefer to use them is as follows. For the program to be debugged, use your editor to remove any SET TALK OFF statements and replace any SET DEVICE TO PRINT with SET DEVICE TO SCREEN statements. Turn your printer on. Enter dBASE III Plus and wait for the dBASE III Plus prompt (the "."). At this point, enter the following code:

```
SET TALK ON
SET PRINT ON
SET ECHO ON
SET DEBUG ON
```

then execute your program (module) with a DO statement. I also recommend that you use wide paper in your printer if possible, so that statements continued on more than one line will not be chopped off at about 80 columns. The output to the printer will include:

1. Each statement executed.
2. The contents of memory locations after each store operation.

All the output from the "@" statements goes to the screen. If you forget to replace the SET DEVICE TO PRINT with SET DEVICE TO SCREEN statements, you will have a number of pages of output with one line per page. Having this type of output go to the screen does not seem to affect most debugging procedures. To stop the execution of the program, press ESC (or the equivalent on your system). After you press ESC, the output from dBASE III Plus may still be directed to the printer. If you SET TALK, PRINT, ECHO, and DEBUG off, you will regain control of output and may proceed as usual with your debugging procedure.

After you press ESC, dBASE will ask you if you wish to C(ancel), S(uspend), or I(gnore). If you choose S(uspend), you can examine the contents of the memory variables and the status of dBASE, aiding in debugging. In addition, you can RESUME execution of your program from the point of interruption.

5.4.22 EMERGENCY EXIT FROM A PROGRAM

To effect a quick exit from a program, strike the ESCAPE key or its equivalent. This is useful when caught in an infinite loop or if you observe that a program is behaving improperly. Since you have interrupted the updating of database and index files, there is a (remote) possibility of file problems. I have not noted any errors caused by the use of the ESCAPE key, but you might find some. If you find that update of the database file has not been completed, you may need to reindex the database files to guarantee that the index files match the associated database files. There may also be records in a buffer that have not been transferred to the database file. In addition, the number of records in the database file may not match the count of records in the header for the database file, so you may need to apply an appropriate technique to make the count in the header agree with the actual number of records in the database file. A CLEAR ALL, a CLOSE DATABASES, or a QUIT may work in this case.

5.4.23 USING AN ALTERNATE FILE TO PRESERVE OUTPUT

It is possible to cause a copy of whatever is sent to the screen to also go to a file. The two-step process is given by the following:

```
SET ALTERNATE TO filename
SET ALTERNATE ON
```

After the SET ALTERNATE ON statement is executed, all output to the screen is copied to the specified file. If you CLOSE ALTERNATE or if you QUIT, then the alternate file is closed. When you SET ALTERNATE ON for the first time in a program, you will destroy the contents of any file of the same name. Subsequent use of SET ALTERNATE OFF and SET ALTERNATE ON will append output to the alternate file, until either a CLOSE ALTERNATE, a SET ALTERNATE TO another file name, or a QUIT is executed. Alternate files are useful when showing a client what a screen display will look like, etc. Note that full-screen editing features move the cursor both backward and forward on the screen, and that there is no good way to show this action in an ALTERNATE file. As a result, none of the operations from full-screen editing show up in an alternate file. In many cases, output to the alternate file will need to be edited before it is in a form suitable to show to a client.

5.4.24 SYSTEM LIMITATIONS: DISASTERS AND HINTS

A. Number of fields in a record = 128.
   The maximum number of fields in a record is 128. You may need a record that has more than 128 fields in it. The recommended approach is to construct more than one database file, where they all can logically be linked together by key values, to simulate a record with more than 128 fields. For example, suppose that you have a need for an employee record with 380 fields. We will need three database files for this purpose. Make employee number one of the fields in each type of database record. Then distribute the remaining 379 required fields among the three database files as needed. This technique will cause the processing to take longer than if all the fields were to fit into one database file, but in this case it is unavoidable.

B. Number of characters per record = 4000.
If you have need for more space in a record than 4000 characters, you will need to use a technique similar to that used in the case where you need more than 128 fields in a record.

C. Number of records in a database file = 1,000,000,000.
I cannot imagine an application on a microcomputer that would require more than one billion records in a database file. If too many records in a database causes either speed or reliability problems, or if you start to run out of room on your disk, you might wish to identify old records (the ones that are no longer in use) and either to delete (physically remove) them or to transfer them to another file. This file may be another database file or a text file.

D. Accuracy of numeric fields = 15.9 digits.
This is usually not a problem for most business or scientific computations. If you need more than 15.9 digits of accuracy, you either will have to perform your own multiple precision arithmetic, or you must live with this limitation.

E. Largest number = 1*10**99.
No problem for most applications.

F. Smallest number = 1*10**−307.
No problem for most applications.

G. Number of memory variables = 256.
Total number of bytes for memory variables = 6000, by default, but can be changed in the CONFIG.DB file. In most situations, 256 memory variables and 6000 bytes should be enough. If you try to use more than 256 memory variables at one time, you will be informed of the problem by the message

```
OUT OF MEMORY VARIABLE SLOTS
```

The recommended technique for overcoming this problem is to do one or more of the following:

a. Construct your program in a modular fashion and use the RELEASE statement to free the memory variables no longer needed in the program. If you have used all 256 memory variables and you RELEASE 10 of them, you will have 10 more to use.

b. Use the CLEAR ALL statement after each major program module (for example, in the CASE statement in the menus). The CLEAR ALL statement releases all the memory variables.

c. In some instances you may wish to store data in a field in a database record rather than in a memory variable. The database fields are available in addition to the maximum number of memory variables.

H. Number of characters per command line = 254, and
Number of characters per character string = 254.
If all goes well, dBASE III Plus will not let you create a command line or a character string longer than 254 characters. If you find some way to circumvent this protective feature, you will probably meet with disaster.

I. Number of characters in index key = 100.
It is difficult to conceive of a single indexed field that will exceed 100 characters, but a concatenated index might. Two possibilities to overcome this problem are either to decrease the number of fields used in the concatenated key or decrease the size of one or more of the fields used in the index. Sometimes you will not need all the characters in the index field that appear in the corresponding data field. For example, if you have reserved 25 characters in the database record for the last name, you might choose to use only the first 15 characters of the last name in the index. An example is:

```
INDEX ON SUBSTR(LASTNAME,1,15)+FIRSTNAME TO NAME
```

J. Number of pending GETS.
The default is 128, but this can be changed in the CONFIG.DB file.

K. Number of files open at one time = 15.
Be cautious here. You may not have more than 15 files of all types open at any one time. This includes database files, index files, memo files, format files, alternate files, and program files. dBASE requires an additional five files, so make use of the

```
FILES = 20
```

statement in your CONFIG.SYS file.

L. Number of database files open at one time = 10.
If there is a memo field in your database file, then the database file and the memo file are both counted. Thus, if you have five open database files and if each of these database files has an associated memo file, then you will not be able to open an additional database file.

M. Number of open index files for a single database file = 7.
You might be tempted to associate more than seven index files with

a database file, using only seven at a time. In general this technique will increase your processing time, so it isn't worth it.

Warning:
Never have more than seven index files associated with a single database file.

N. Number of open format files for a single database file = 1.
O. Number of characters in a MEMO field = the capacity of your word processor. The capacity of the Ashton-Tate editor is 5000 bytes.
P. Number of characters in a date field = 8.
Q. Number of characters in a logical field = 1.

5.4.25 ARRAYS

Arrays can be created and used in two ways. You can use the features supplied in the option called *dBASE Tools for C: The Programmer's Library*, or you can simulate arrays. *dBASE Tools for C* are covered in a later chapter.

You can simulate arrays through the use of memory variables and the macro expansion feature. For example, consider the character string NUM that has a number left-justified in it. If, for example, NUM = 1, then A&NUM is A1. You may then use A&NUM where you would use A(NUM) and A1 where you would use A(1). The problems with this technique are:

1. You are limited to 256 memory variables at any one time
2. NUM must be a character string that contains a number, and
3. The number in NUM must be left-justified in the string

In order to left-justify a number in a character string, use code similar to the following:

```
K = LTRIM(STR(MYNUM,4))
```

where MYNUM is the numeric variable.

5.4.26 DATE VARIABLES

Variables (both memory variables and database fields) can have type DATE. An object of type date always takes 8 bytes of storage. When you create a database with a field to type date, then a width of size 8 is automatically assigned to it by the dBASE III Plus system.

When you wish to display the contents of a date variable on the screen or on the printer, the form is MM/DD/YY or DD/MM/YY. The default form is MM/DD/YY. To print a date in the form DD/MM/YY, use the @ . . SAY command with the E format function.

A number of functions are available for the direct manipulation of date variables. They are:

CDOW	Name of day of week
CMONTH	Name of month
CTOD	Convert character string to date
DAY	Number of day of month
DOW	Number of day of week
DTOC	Convert date to a character string
MONTH	Number of month
YEAR	Number of year (four-digit number)

In addition to these functions, arithmetic using date variables is possible. When a date variable is used in arithmetic, it is converted by the system to an integer. The arithmetic operation is performed and the result, if possible, is then converted back to a date variable. In the following examples, we will consider each date of the form 01/01/87 to be a variable or a constant of type date.

1. 01/01/87 + 1 produces the date 01/02/87. In this example, the date 01/01/87 is converted to an integer, the number 1 is added to the integer, and then the integer is converted back to a date.
2. 01/30/87 − 01/01/87 produces the integer 29. Each date is converted to an integer and then the integer on the right is subtracted from the integer on the left.
3. 01/31/87 − 1 produces the date 01/30/87.

The CTOD function does not verify the range of the day and month entries, so strange conversions can take place.

1. CTOD("01/40/87") produces the date 02/09/87.
2. CTOD("13/01/87") produces the date 01/01/88.

If you have a variable of type date, you will not be allowed to enter nonnumeric characters. In addition, the day and month fields of the date that you enter are checked for the correct range. If the range is incorrect, you will receive the error message

```
INVALID DATE
```

It will then be necessary for you to re-enter the date.

If you need to print the date so that all the digits of the year are displayed, just SET CENTURY ON.

If you index on a date field by itself, the index will be in the correct date order. If you index on a combination of a character string field and a date field, the records will not be in the correct date order unless you take additional steps. In addition, you will need to convert the date field to a character string.

EXAMPLE:

If A and B are fields in the current database, and if B is a date, then code of the following type

```
INDEX ON A+B TO C
```

produces an error, since you cannot concatenate a string and a date. If you use the following code to create the index

```
INDEX ON A+DTOC(B) TO C
```

then you will get records that are in string order, not in date order. For example, if two records have the values

A	*B*
SMITH	01/01/87
SMITH	12/01/86

and we index in A+DTOC(B), then the records appear in the order shown above, with the earlier date after the later date. In other words, the records are listed in the order

```
SMITH      01/01/87
SMITH      12/01/86
```

because, as strings,

```
"SMITH      01/01/87"
```

and

```
"SMITH      12/01/86"
```

is the correct order.

In order to correct this problem, that is, in order to create an index that will allow access in correct date order, use code of the following type:

```
INDEX ON A+STR(YEAR(B)*10000+MONTH(B)*100+DAY(B),6)
```

Note:
The technique for converting a dBASE II program, that is, one that does not use variables and fields of type date, to dBASE III Plus is not a complicated process, so you may wish to do so if you have such programs to convert. If you are about to write programs in dBASE III Plus that use dates, I strongly recommend that you use date variables and fields, rather than try to use strings for dates. The reason for the recommendation is that programming is greatly simplified.

Converting from "String" Dates to dBASE III Plus Dates

1. Examine each database file in your application. For every field that is a string date, change it to a field of type date. Some of your databases may have had two representations for the same date: one for display and one for indexing (MM/DD/YY and YYMMDD formats). You can delete the one with the YYMMDD format. When you make the modification to the database structure using the MODIFY STRUCTURE command, data in the string fields of the form MM/DD/YY are changed for you to dates.
2. Carefully examine all input using the "string" dates. Instead of initializing a date field with space(8), initialize it with CTOD(" / / "). Completely eliminate all manual verification for the correct format of the date being input. When you use CTOD(" / / ") to initialize an object of type date, make sure that you do not try to compare this empty date with any other dates, or the comparisons will not work correctly. For example, it is not meaningful to ask if

   ```
   CTOD(" / / ") < DATE ( )
   ```

   or if

   ```
   CTOD(" / / ") >= DATE( ).
   ```

3. Carefully examine all output using the "string" dates. If the "string" date was concatenated to other strings for output, you will now need to change the date to a character string.

EXAMPLE:

```
@ 3,25 SAY "DATE PRINTED: "+DTOC(MEMDATE)
```

4. The use of special routines to convert a "string" date to an integer (a Julian date), add or subtract an integer, and then convert the integer back to a "string" date can be eliminated. Instead, just add the integer to or subtract it directly from the variable or field of type date. Look at all the other conversions and computations using "string" dates and make the appropriate changes.
5. If "string" dates were used as part of an index, use the DTOC function to convert the date to the correct form. For example, use

   ```
   INDEX ON NAME+DTOC(THISDATE)
   ```

   rather than

   ```
   INDEX ON NAME+THISDATE.
   ```

CHAPTER

6

An Illustrative Example

6.1 INTRODUCTION

The purpose of this chapter is to demonstrate a number of the techniques discussed in Chapters 1 through 5. You will see an example system, how files are designed for this system, and how the dBASE III Plus programming language is used. The system used in this chapter is an easy one to understand.

6.2 THE ORIGINAL PROBLEM

A small company does most of their sales over the telephone, and, at the present time, all their information about current inventory is displayed on a large board. The sales staff examines this board each time they receive a request over the telephone. It is critical that the sales staff know the exact quantity on hand, since customers for this company always want fast delivery of their products. If a customer places an order and it is not delivered quickly, then the customer will not place another order with this company. The sales staff has been given instructions not to accept an order unless the product is in stock, feeling that it is better to turn a customer away than to promise an order that cannot be delivered on time.

As sales have increased, it has become clear that the information on the board is not keeping up with actual sales. When sales were slower, it was possible to update the board within 10 minutes after each sale, and the information was sufficiently up to date. Now that sales have increased, it just takes too much time to update the board, and a number of customers have received their shipments after the promised date. As a result, these customers have emphatically stated that they will not do business with this company again.

The sales manager has decided to automate the big board so that it will reflect changes in inventory right at the time of the sale. We have been called in to build this system.

6.3 THE ANALYSIS AND DESIGN

It is clear from the beginning that a small computer will be sufficient for the task, and that we need a single, integrated collection of files. We want all the sales personnel to use the same files, so that a sale made by one of them is immediately reflected in the current inventory. The decision has been made to use a small network of PC compatible machines, where the server has a 30M hard disk. Because there will be several people using the same data files, dBASE III Plus, with its local area network features, was selected. It is planned that each of the sales personnel will have either a microcomputer or a terminal connected to the server. The choice of hardware is preliminary. Since dBASE III Plus runs a wide variety of PC compatible computers, we can delay actual selection of the computers until later in the project. The plan is to build and test the telephone ordering system using the server and one additional microcomputer. Additional microcomputers and terminals will be added at a later date.

Since the central feature of the system is the inventory, we start first with an examination of the needs of that file. In addition to an item number, description, and current cost, we need to be able to differentiate between quantity on hand and quantity available for sale. Actually, there are several categories of items in inventory. They are:

1. Available for sale
2. On hand, but promised to a customer, and
3. Returned by a customer, but not yet examined

When an item is returned by a customer, it must be examined by someone to determine if it can be resold. Some returned items cannot be resold, since they are returned in poor condition.

It is now time to start the design of the files. We start first with the inventory file. We do not know at this point if we have the final (needed) database structure, since we are just starting the analysis and design of the system. It is expected that our understanding of the system will evolve over a period of time, possibly requiring changes in our database structure. The structure for the inventory database is:

```
Structure for database  :   C:INVENTOR.dbf
Number of data records:     0
Date of last update     :   06/01/87
```

Field	*Field Name*	*Type*	*Width*	*Dec*	*Description*
1	INVID	Character	6		Inventory identifier
2	INVDESCRIP	Character	35		Description
3	INVQFORSAL	Numeric	5		Quantity for sale
4	INVQPRMSD	Numeric	5		Quantity promised
5	INVQRET	Numeric	5		Quantity returned
** Total **			57		

We will also need a file for the customers and another file for the orders that they place. The structure for the customer database is:

Structure for database : C:CUSTOMER.dbf
Number of data records: 0
Date of last update : 06/01/87

Field	*Field Name*	*Type*	*Width*	*Dec*	*Description*
1	CUSID	Character	5		Customer identifier
2	CUSCOMPANY	Character	20		Company name
3	CUSSTREET	Character	15		Street
4	CUSCITY	Character	15		City
5	CUSSTATE	Character	2		State
6	CUSZIP	Character	10		Zip code
7	CUSTEL	Character	13		Telephone number
8	CUSCONTACT	Character	30		Name of contact person
** Total **			111		

The two database files for the order are ORDERS.DBF and ITEMS.DBF.

Structure for database : C:ORDERS.dbf
Number of data records: 0
Date of last update : 06/01/87

Field	*Field Name*	*Type*	*Width*	*Dec*	*Description*
1	ORDNUMBER	Character	7		Order number
2	ORDCUSID	Character	5		Customer identifier
3	ORDDATE	Date	8		Date ordered
** Total **			21		

Structure for database : C:ITEMS.dbf
Number of data records: 2
Date of last update : 10/07/86

Field	*Field Name*	*Type*	*Width*	*Dec*	*Description*
1	ITORDNUMB	Character	7		Order number
2	ITINVID	Character	6		Inventory identifier
3	ITQTYORD	Numeric	5		Quantity ordered
4	ITPROMDATE	Date	8		Date promised
5	ITSHIPDATE	Date	8		Date shipped
** Total **			35		

Notice that the order information has been split into two database files: ORDERS and ITEMS. The ORDERS file contains the nonrepeating order information, and the ITEMS file contains the repeating order information. The items that are associated with a specific order can be found through the use of the order number.

All four database files use identifiers. The company has decided to use as their own inventory identifiers, the identifiers that are already in use by their suppliers, but they intend to generate their own identifiers for both customers and orders. Since it is neither efficient nor reliable for the sales personnel to manually generate identifiers for new customers or for orders, we desire that the application system generate them automatically. This requires a new database file that we will call MISC, short for miscellaneous. The structure of this database file is:

Structure for database : C:MISC.dbf
Number of data records: 0
Date of last update : 10/02/86

Field	*Field Name*	*Type*	*Width*	*Dec*	*Description*
1	MISCUSID	Numeric	5		Next customer ID
2	MISORDID	Numeric	7		Next order number
** Total **			13		

The identifiers are stored in the MISC database as numbers, since we expect to perform arithmetic with them. In particular, we will increment these numbers as needed. The database file named MISC (for miscellaneous) contains bits and pieces of data that do not reasonably fit in any other database file.

Note:
The initial version of the database files can be constructed independently of any programs that use them. We expect to use these files to store inventory information, display this information on the screen, and produce simple printed reports concerning the status of the inventory. In addition, we will need the customer information for shipping and billing purposes.

Step 1:
Make an initial determination of the files from the system inputs, outputs, and processes. The final files will be obtained from modifying and adding to your original guess.

The next step in the process of developing the application is to build a system of menus. These menus become a blueprint for the development of the system, indicating what processes are necessary for the system. The main menu for the system is given in the program named SALES.PRG:

```
* SALES.PRG
* MAIN MENU FOR THE TELEPHONE ORDERING SYSTEM
SET TALK OFF
SET SAFETY OFF
SET STATUS OFF
DO WHILE .T.
   CLEAR
   SET DEVICE TO SCREEN
   @  5, 5 SAY "TELEPHONE ORDERING SYSTEM"
   @  6, 5 SAY "-------------------------"
   @  7,10 SAY "A. EXIT FROM THE SYSTEM"
   @  8,10 SAY "B. CUSTOMERS"
   @  9,10 SAY "C. INVENTORY"
   @ 10,10 SAY "D. ORDERS"
   @ 11,10 SAY "E. SHIPPING"
   @ 12,10 SAY "F. BILLING"
   @ 13,10 SAY "G. REPORTS"
   @ 14,10 SAY "H. SYSTEM MAINTENANCE"
   WAIT "ENTER A SELECTION CODE:" TO CODE
   CODE = UPPER(CODE)
   DO CASE
      CASE CODE = "A"
         ? "NORMAL TERMINATION OF THE SYSTEM"
         QUIT
```

```
        CASE CODE = "B"
           DO CUSTOMER
        CASE CODE = "C"
           DO INVENTOR
        CASE CODE = "D"
           DO ORDERS
        CASE CODE = "E"
           DO SHIPPING
        CASE CODE = "F"
           DO BILLING
        CASE CODE = "G"
           DO REPORTS
        CASE CODE = "H"
           DO MAINT
        OTHERWISE
           ? "ILLEGAL SELECTION CODE"
           WAIT
     ENDCASE
     CLEAR ALL
ENDDO
************ END OF PROGRAM ************
```

Notes on SALES.PRG:
SET TALK OFF is used to hide information concerning the execution of the programs in the application system from the user. SET SAFETY OFF allows certain database operations (such as INDEX ON) to take place without a warning message to the user. SET STATUS OFF is used to hide the status bar from the user. The UPPER function is used to convert the selection code to uppercase. Note also the use of the WAIT to obtain a selection code. The CLEAR ALL at the end of the loop will close all the database files and release all the memory variables. This controls global variables and insures a modular design.

Note that building the main menu first, then building the secondary menus (if any), and then writing the other programs is essentially a top-down approach to design and implementation.

Each of the subsystems for the telephone ordering application system will now be presented.

The programs for the customer subsystem are:

```
* CUSTOMERS.PRG

SELECT A

USE CUSTOMER INDEX CUSID

SELECT B

USE MISC

DO WHILE .T.

   CLEAR

   @  5, 5 SAY "CUSTOMER SUBSYSTEM"

   @  6, 5 SAY "------------------"

   @  7,10 SAY "A. RETURN TO THE MAIN MENU"

   @  8,10 SAY "B. ENTER NEW CUSTOMER RECORD"

   @  9,10 SAY "C. MODIFY A  CUSTOMER RECORD"

   @ 10,10 SAY "D. VIEW   A CUSTOMER RECORD"

   WAIT "ENTER A SELECTION CODE:" TO CODE1

   CODE1 = UPPER(CODE1)

   DO CASE

      CASE CODE1 = "A"

         RETURN

      CASE CODE1 = "B"

         DO CUSTENT

            CASE CODE1 = "C"

         DO CUSTMOD
```

```
        CASE CODE1 = "D"
            DO CUSTVIEW
    ENDCASE
ENDDO
************ END OF PROGRAM ************
```

Notes on CUSTOMERS.PRG:
Since we will use only two different database files in this subsystem, it seems appropriate to open them when we enter the subsystem and then use them as needed. Note that there is no CLEAR ALL at the end of the loop; otherwise we will close these two databases before we wish to. They will be closed when we exit from the subsystem and return to the main menu.

```
* CUSTENT.PRG
* ENTER A RECORD FOR A NEW CUSTOMER
DO WHILE .T.
   CLEAR
   @  5, 5 SAY "A. RETURN TO THE PREVIOUS MENU"
   @  6, 5 SAY "B. ENTER A NEW CUSTOMER RECORD"
   WAIT "ENTER A SELECTION CODE:" TO CODE2
   CODE2 = UPPER(CODE2)
   DO CASE
      CASE CODE2 = "A"
         RETURN
      CASE CODE2 = "B"
         CLEAR
         SELECT B
         MEMCUSID = MISCUSID
```

```
        REPLACE MISCUSID WITH MISCUSID + 1
        SELECT A
        APPEND BLANK
        REPLACE CUSID WITH STR(MEMCUSID,5)
        DO CUSTFSE
   OTHERWISE
      ? "ILLEGAL SELECTION CODE"
      WAIT
   ENDCASE
ENDDO
************ END OF PROGRAM ************
```

Notes on CUSTENT.PRG:
The program CUSTFSE is used both to enter and to modify a record in the CUSTOMER database file. If you use one program to accomplish both tasks, then you will simplify your programming task. The autogeneration of customer identifier also guarantees that you cannot use the same identifier more than once.

```
* CUSTFSE.PRG
* PROGRAM TO ENTER OR MODIFY A CUSTOMER RECORD
CLEAR
@  1,25 SAY "ENTER OR MODIFY A CUSTOMER RECORD"
@  2,25 SAY "---------------------------------"
@  4, 1 SAY "CUSTOMER NUMBER: "+CUSID
@  6, 1 SAY "COMPANY NAME" GET CUSCOMPANY
@  8, 1 SAY "ADDRESS"
@  9, 5 SAY "STREET" GET CUSSTREET
@ 10, 5 SAY "CITY  " GET CUSCITY
@ 11, 5 SAY "STATE " GET CUSSTATE
@ 12, 5 SAY "ZIP   " GET CUSZIP
```

```
@ 14, 1 SAY "TELEPHONE" GET CUSTEL
@ 16, 1 SAY "CONTACT PERSON" GET CUSCONTACT
READ
RETURN
************ END OF PROGRAM ************

* CUSTMOD.PRG
DO WHILE .T.
   CLEAR
   @ 5, 5 SAY "A. RETURN TO THE CUSTOMER MENU"
   @ 6, 5 SAY "B. MODIFY A CUSTOMER RECORD"
   WAIT "ENTER A SELECTION CODE:" TO CODE3
   CODE3 = UPPER(CODE3)
   DO CASE
      CASE CODE3 = "A"
         RETURN
      CASE CODE3 = "B"
         CLEAR
         STORE 0 TO MEMCUSID
         @ 5,1 SAY  ;
          "ENTER THE ID OF THE CUSTOMER RECORD TO BE CHANGED:" ;
          GET MEMCUSID
         READ
         SELECT A
         SEEK STR(MEMCUSID,5)
         IF .NOT. FOUND()
                 @ 7,0 SAY "THIS CUSTOMER NUMBER NOT ON FILE"
            WAIT
```

```
         ELSE
            DO CUSTFSE
         ENDIF
      OTHERWISE
         ? "ILLEGAL SELECTION CODE"
         WAIT
   ENDCASE
ENDDO
************ END OF PROGRAM ************

* CUSTVIEW.PRG
* DISPLAY A CUSTOMER RECORD ON THE SCREEN
DO WHILE .T.
   CLEAR
   @ 5, 5 SAY "A. RETURN TO THE CUSTOMER MENU"
   @ 6, 5 SAY "B. VIEW A CUSTOMER RECORD"
   WAIT "ENTER A SELECTION CODE:" TO CODE3
   CODE3 = UPPER(CODE3)
   DO CASE
      CASE CODE3 = "A"
         RETURN
      CASE CODE3 = "B"
         CLEAR
         STORE 0 TO MEMCUSID
         @ 5,1 SAY  ;
          "ENTER THE ID OF THE CUSTOMER RECORD TO BE VIEWED:" ;
          GET MEMCUSID
         READ
         SELECT A
```

```
            SEEK STR(MEMCUSID,5)
            IF .NOT. FOUND()
               @ 7,0 SAY "THIS CUSTOMER NUMBER NOT ON FILE"
               WAIT
            ELSE
               DO CUSTDISP
            ENDIF
         OTHERWISE
            ? "ILLEGAL SELECTION CODE"
            WAIT
   ENDCASE
ENDDO
************ END OF PROGRAM ************
```

Notes on CUSTVIEW.PRG:
This program does not use CUSTFSE.PRG, because we do not wish to make any changes in this program. We merely wish to display a record on the screen. Instead of using CUSTFSE.PRG, we use CUSTDISP.PRG. Note also the use of the semicolon (;) as a continuation character in this program.

```
* CUSTDISP.PRG
* PROGRAM TO DISPLAY A CUSTOMER RECORD
CLEAR
@  1,25 SAY "DISPLAY A CUSTOMER RECORD"
@  2,25 SAY "-------------------------"
@  4, 1 SAY "CUSTOMER NUMBER: "+CUSID
@  6, 1 SAY "COMPANY NAME: " + CUSCOMPANY
@  8, 1 SAY "ADDRESS"
@  9, 5 SAY "STREET: " + CUSSTREET
```

```
@ 10, 5 SAY "CITY   : " + CUSCITY
@ 11, 5 SAY "STATE : " + CUSSTATE
@ 12, 5 SAY "ZIP    : " + CUSZIP
@ 14, 1 SAY "TELEPHONE: " + CUSTEL
@ 16, 1 SAY "CONTACT PERSON: " + CUSCONTACT
@ 20,0 SAY ""
WAIT
RETURN
************ END OF PROGRAM ************
```

The only index that we have used so far is on the customer identifier in the CUSTOMER database file (an index on the field named CUSID). This index was chosen because we expect to access records in the customer database file by the customer identifier.

> **Step 2:**
> Indexes are chosen so as to facilitate access to files that we have already constructed.

As your system grows, you will find that it is hard to keep track of the indexes that you have created for each of your database files, so it seems to be a good idea to record them somewhere. If you place the information about indexes in a program, you can use it not only to record the information, but also to reindex your files in case of error. The index information that we will use for all the programs in this sample system will be stored in a program named INDEXES.PRG. As you build your system, you will probably add indexes to this file as you discover the need for them.

```
* INDEXES.PRG
SET TALK ON
SET ECHO ON
SET SAFETY OFF
```

```
USE CUSTOMER
   INDEX ON CUSID TO CUSID
USE INVENTOR
   INDEX ON INVID TO INVID
USE ITEMS
   INDEX ON ITORDNUMB+ITINVID TO ITNUMINV
USE ORDERS
   INDEX ON ORDNUMBER TO ORDNUMBER
   INDEX ON ORDCUSID  TO ORDCUSID
SET ECHO OFF
SET TALK OFF
RETURN
************ END OF PROGRAM ************
```

> **Step 3:**
> Record your choice of indexes for each file in a program. It will be a record of indexes and may be used to reindex files in the event of errors.

> **Step 4:**
> As your understanding of the data requirements of the system grows, you will find yourself adding data elements to existing files and also adding new database files.

As you develop your application system, you will start with the menus, because they allow you to develop your system in a top-down manner. I recommend that you next write the programs that allow you to enter data into files. Once you have written these programs, write the programs that modify data, and finally write the programs that report the data. This recommendation is a rough guide to the order of program development, but it works because:

1. You need to have data in the files before you can modify it or report it, and
2. In many cases, the routines that you use to enter the data can also be used to modify the data.

You may wish to write all the programs for one subsystem before you move on to another one. In the telephone ordering system used as the example in this chapter, the CUSTOMER subsystem was developed first. As a result, programs for the CUSTOMER subsystem were written in the following order:

1. CUSTENTER—Enter a new customer record
2. CUSTFSE—The subroutine to perform full-screen entry of the customer record
3. CUSTMOD—Modify an existing customer record
4. CUSTVIEW—Display an existing customer record, and
5. CUSTDISP—The actual display routine

> **Step 5:**
> After you have written the menus for your system, write the programs that enter, modify, and display data, in that order. This will facilitate the testing of your programs.

The next subsystem to be developed is inventory. Like the CUSTOMER subsystem, there will be programs to enter, modify, and view inventory data. The programs in the INVENTORY subsystem are similar to the programs in the CUSTOMER subsystem, since they each have functions for the entry, modification, and display of records. If you have the same type of similarities in your application system, you can take advantage of the similarities by writing the programs first for one subsystem, and then modifying these programs for another subsystem. The programs for the inventory subsystem are now given.

```
* INVENTOR.PRG

SELECT E

USE INVENTOR INDEX INVID

DO WHILE .T.

   CLEAR
```

```
   @  5, 5 SAY "INVENTORY SUBSYSTEM"
   @  6, 5 SAY "-------------------"
   @  7,10 SAY "A. RETURN TO THE MAIN MENU"
   @  8,10 SAY "B. ENTER NEW INVENTORY RECORD"
   @  9,10 SAY "C. MODIFY AN INVENTORY RECORD"
   @ 10,10 SAY "D. VIEW   AN INVENTORY RECORD"
   WAIT "ENTER A SELECTION CODE:" TO CODE1
   CODE1 = UPPER(CODE1)
   DO CASE
      CASE CODE1 = "A"
         RETURN
      CASE CODE1 = "B"
         DO INVENT
      CASE CODE1 = "C"
         DO INVMOD
      CASE CODE1 = "D"
         DO INVVIEW
   ENDCASE
ENDDO
************ END OF PROGRAM ************

* INVENT.PRG
* ENTER A RECORD FOR A NEW INVENTORY ITEM
DO WHILE .T.
   CLEAR
   @  5, 5 SAY "A. RETURN TO THE INVENTORY MENU"
   @  6, 5 SAY "B. ENTER A NEW INVENTORY RECORD"
   WAIT "ENTER A SELECTION CODE:" TO CODE2
   CODE2 = UPPER(CODE2)
```

```
    DO CASE
       CASE CODE2 = "A"
          RETURN
       CASE CODE2 = "B"
          CLEAR
          MEMINVID = SPACE(6)
          @ 1,1 SAY "ENTER THE NEW INVENTORY NUMBER" ;
            GET MEMINVID
          READ
          SEEK MEMINVID
          IF FOUND()
             ? "THIS INVENTORY NUMBER IS ALREADY IN USE"
             WAIT
             LOOP
          ELSE
             APPEND BLANK
             REPLACE INVID WITH MEMINVID
             DO INVFSE
          ENDIF
    OTHERWISE
       ? "ILLEGAL SELECTION CODE"
       WAIT
    ENDCASE
ENDDO
************ END OF PROGRAM ************
```

Notes on INVENTOR.PRG:
Since the user generates the inventory item identifier when a new item is entered into the database, it is necessary to verify that the item number is not already in use.

```
* INVFSE.PRG
* PROGRAM TO ENTER OR MODIFY AN INVENTORY RECORD
CLEAR
@  1,25 SAY "ENTER OR MODIFY AN INVENTORY RECORD"
@  2,25 SAY "-----------------------------------"
@  4, 1 SAY "INVENTORY NUMBER: "+INVID
@  6, 1 SAY "DESCRIPTION: " GET INVDESCRIP
@  8, 5 SAY "QUANTITY FOR SALE" GET INVQFORSAL
@ 10, 5 SAY "QUANTITY PROMISED" GET INVQPRMSD
@ 12, 5 SAY "QUANTITY RETURNED" GET INVQRET
READ
RETURN
************ END OF PROGRAM ************

* INVMOD.PRG
DO WHILE .T.
   CLEAR
   @ 5, 5 SAY "A. RETURN TO THE INVENTORY MENU"
   @ 6, 5 SAY "B. MODIFY AN INVENTORY RECORD"
   WAIT "ENTER A SELECTION CODE:" TO CODE3
   CODE3 = UPPER(CODE3)
   DO CASE
      CASE CODE3 = "A"
         RETURN
      CASE CODE3 = "B"
         CLEAR
         MEMINVID = SPACE(6)
         @ 5,1 SAY  ;
          "ENTER THE ID OF THE INVENTORY RECORD TO BE CHANGED:" ;
```

```
         GET MEMINVID
        READ
        SEEK MEMINVID
        IF .NOT. FOUND()
           @ 7,0 SAY "THIS INVENTORY NUMBER NOT ON FILE"
           WAIT
        ELSE
           DO INVFSE
        ENDIF
     OTHERWISE
        ? "ILLEGAL SELECTION CODE"
        WAIT
   ENDCASE
ENDDO
************ END OF PROGRAM ************


* INVVIEW.PRG
* DISPLAY AN INVENTORY RECORD ON THE SCREEN
DO WHILE .T.
   CLEAR
   @ 5, 5 SAY "A. RETURN TO THE INVENTORY MENU"
   @ 6, 5 SAY "B. VIEW AN INVENTORY RECORD"
   WAIT "ENTER A SELECTION CODE:" TO CODE3
   CODE3 = UPPER(CODE3)
   DO CASE
      CASE CODE3 = "A"
         RETURN
      CASE CODE3 = "B"
```

```
         CLEAR
         MEMINVID = SPACE(6)
         @ 5,1 SAY  ;
          "ENTER THE ID OF THE INVENTORY RECORD TO BE VIEWED:"  ;
          GET MEMINVID
         READ
         SEEK MEMINVID
         IF .NOT. FOUND()
            @ 7,0 SAY "THIS INVENTORY NUMBER NOT ON FILE"
            WAIT
         ELSE
            DO INVDISP
         ENDIF
      OTHERWISE
         ? "ILLEGAL SELECTION CODE"
         WAIT
   ENDCASE
ENDDO
************ END OF PROGRAM ************



* INVDISP.PRG
* PROGRAM TO DISPLAY AN INVENTORY RECORD
CLEAR
@  1,25 SAY "DISPLAY A INVENTORY RECORD"
@  2,25 SAY "--------------------------"
@  4, 1 SAY "INVENTORY NUMBER: "+INVID
@  6, 1 SAY "DESCRIPTION: "+INVDESCRIP
```

```
@  8, 5 SAY "QUANTITY FOR SALE: " + STR(INVQFORSAL,5)
@ 10, 5 SAY "QUANTITY PROMISED: " + STR(INVQPRMSD,5)
@ 12, 5 SAY "QUANTITY RETURNED: " + STR(INVQRET,5)
@ 20,0 SAY ""
WAIT
RETURN
************ END OF PROGRAM ************
```

Notes on INVDISP:
Rather than use two @ . . SAY statements to display a label and an amount, just one @ . . SAY statement is used. As a result of this choice, it is necessary to convert the number to a character string, since the @ . . SAY statement can display only one value.

The next subsystem is the one to process orders. Again, we see a marked similarity to the CUSTOMER and to the INVENTORY subsystems.

```
* ORDERS.PRG
DO WHILE .T.
   CLEAR
   @  5, 5 SAY "ORDERING SUBSYSTEM"
   @  6, 5 SAY "------------------"
   @  7,10 SAY "A. RETURN TO THE MAIN MENU"
   @  8,10 SAY "B. EXAMINE INVENTORY"
   @  9,10 SAY "C. ENTER AN ORDER"
   @ 10,10 SAY "D. MODIFY AN ORDER"
   @ 11,10 SAY "E. DISPLAY AN ORDER"
   WAIT "ENTER A SELECTION CODE:" TO CODE1
   CODE1 = UPPER(CODE1)
   DO CASE
```

```
        CASE CODE1 = "A"
           RETURN
        CASE CODE1 = "B"
           SELECT E
           USE INVENTOR INDEX INVID
           DO INVVIEW
        CASE CODE1 = "C"
           DO ORDENT
        CASE CODE1 = "D"
           DO ORDMOD
        CASE CODE1 = "E"
           DO ORDVIEW
   ENDCASE
   CLEAR ALL
ENDDO
************ END OF PROGRAM ************
```

Notes on ORDERS.PRG:

As a convenience, the program INVVIEW.PRG (used to view an inventory record) has been included in this subsystem. The inclusion of INVVIEW.PRG in the ORDERs subsystem requires that we add a USE statement just before the program is called. When INVVIEW.PRG is called from the inventory subsystem, the appropriate database and index are established within the driver (menu) for that subsystem, not within the program itself. When we wish to use the program in another place in the application system, we must place the appropriate USE statement in the calling routine.

```
* ORDENT.PRG
* ENTER AN ORDER
SELECT A
```

```
USE CUSTOMER INDEX CUSID
SELECT B
USE MISC
SELECT C
USE ORDERS INDEX ORDNUMBE, ORDCUSID
SELECT D
USE ITEMS INDEX ITNUMINV
SELECT E
USE INVENTOR INDEX INVID
DO WHILE .T.
   CLEAR
   @  5, 5 SAY "A. RETURN TO THE ORDER MENU"
   @  6, 5 SAY "B. ENTER A NEW ORDER RECORD"
   WAIT "ENTER A SELECTION CODE:" TO CODE2
   CODE2 = UPPER(CODE2)
   DO CASE
      CASE CODE2 = "A"
         RETURN
      CASE CODE2 = "B"
         CLEAR
         * GET CUSTOMER INFORMATION
         CLEAR
         MEMCUSID = 0
         @ 1,25 SAY "IF CUSTOMER NUMBER NOT ON FILE, ENTER 0"
         @ 2,25 SAY "---------------------------------------"
         @ 5,1 SAY "ENTER THE CUSTOMER ID" GET MEMCUSID
         READ
         IF MEMCUSID = 0
```

```
      SELECT B
      DO CUSTENT
      IF TYPE("MEMCUSID") = "C"
         MEMCUSID = VAL(MEMCUSID)
      ENDIF
      IF MEMCUSID = 0
         LOOP
      ENDIF  && DIDN'T GET A CUSTOMER ID
   ELSE
      SELECT A
      SEEK STR(MEMCUSID,5)
      IF .NOT. FOUND()
         ? "NO RECORD ON FILE FOR THIS CUSTOMER NUMBER"
         WAIT
         LOOP
      ELSE
         @ 7,1 SAY "COMPANY NAME="+A->CUSCOMPANY
         @ 9,0 SAY ""
         WAIT "IS THIS CORRECT (Y/N)? " TO ANSWER
         IF UPPER(ANSWER) <> "Y"
            LOOP
         ENDIF
      ENDIF
   ENDIF
   * GET ORDER
   SELECT B
   MEMORDID = MISORDID + 1
   REPLACE MISORDID WITH MEMORDID
```

```
SELECT C  && THE ORDER HEADER FILE
APPEND BLANK
REPLACE ORDNUMBER WITH STR(MEMORDID,7), ORDCUSID WITH;
   STR(MEMCUSID,5), ORDDATE WITH DATE()
DO ORDFSE
* GET ITEM INFORMATION
AGAIN = .T.
DO WHILE AGAIN
   CLEAR
   MEMINVID = SPACE(6)
   @ 5,1 SAY ;
    "ENTER THE INVENTORY ID - RETURN TO ABORT" ;
      GET MEMINVID
   READ
   IF MEMINVID = SPACE(6)
      AGAIN = .F.
      LOOP
   ENDIF
   SELECT E
   SEEK MEMINVID
   IF .NOT. FOUND()
      ? "THIS NUMBER NOT ON FILE"
      LOOP
   ENDIF
   @ 10,1 SAY "DESCRIPTION: " + INVDESCRIP
   @ 12,0 SAY ""
   WAIT "IS THIS THE CORRECT ITEM (Y/N):" TO ANSWER
   IF UPPER(ANSWER) <> "Y"
```

```
            LOOP
         ENDIF
         @ 12,0 CLEAR
         MEMQORD = 0
         MAXORD = INVQFORSAL
         @ 12,1 SAY "QUANTITY FOR SALE: "+STR(INVQFORSAL,5)
         @ 13,1 SAY "QUANTITY RETURNED: "+STR(INVQRET,5)
         @ 15,0 SAY "QUANTITY ORDERED" GET MEMQORD ;
           RANGE 0,MAXORD
         READ
         IF MEMQORD <> 0
              REPLACE INVQFORSAL WITH INVQFORSAL-MEMQORD, ;
               INVQPRMSD WITH INVQPRMSD+MEMQORD
           SELECT D
           APPEND BLANK
           MEMDATE = DATE() + 7
           @ 17,1 SAY "DATE PROMISED" GET MEMDATE
           READ
           REPLACE ITORDNUMB WITH STR(MEMORDID,7), ;
             ITINVID WITH MEMINVID, ITQTYORD WITH ;
             MEMQORD, ITPROMDATE WITH MEMDATE
          ENDIF
       ENDDO
    OTHERWISE
       ? "ILLEGAL SELECTION CODE"
       WAIT
    ENDCASE
ENDDO
************ END OF PROGRAM ************
```

Notes on ORDENT.PRG:

This program uses all the database files. As a result, aliases are used to access data in fields not in the current work area. The double ampersand symbol (&&) is used to start a comment on the same line as, but after, an executable statement. An @ . . SAY " " (where " " is used to indicate the NULL string) can be used to position the cursor on the screen. Especially note the use of the RANGE clause in the statement starting with @ 15,0. This clause is used to validate the entry of the data. It must be between zero (0) and the quantity available for sale. The total quantity of an item in inventory is the sum of the quantity promised, the quantity available for sale, and the quantity returned.

```
* ORDFSE.PRG

* ENTER AN ORDER HEADER

CLEAR

@ 1,25 SAY "ENTER OR CHANGE AN ORDER"

@ 2,25 SAY "------------------------"

@ 4, 1 SAY "ORDER NUMBER: "+ORDNUMBER

@ 6, 1 SAY "COMPANY ID: "+ ORDCUSID

@ 7, 1 SAY "COMPANY NAME: " + A->CUSCOMPANY

@ 9, 1 SAY "ORDER DATE" GET ORDDATE

READ

RETURN

************ END OF PROGRAM ************
```

```
* ORDMOD.PRG

* ENTER AN ORDER

SELECT A

USE CUSTOMER INDEX CUSID

SELECT B

USE MISC

SELECT C
```

```
USE ORDERS INDEX ORDNUMBE, ORDCUSID
SELECT D
USE ITEMS INDEX ITNUMINV
SELECT E
USE INVENTOR INDEX INVID
DO WHILE .T.
   CLEAR
   @  5, 5 SAY "A. RETURN TO THE ORDER MENU"
   @  6, 5 SAY "B. MODIFY AN ORDER RECORD"
   WAIT "ENTER A SELECTION CODE:" TO CODE2
   CODE2 = UPPER(CODE2)
   DO CASE
      CASE CODE2 = "A"
         RETURN
      CASE CODE2 = "B"
         CLEAR
         * GET ORDER INFORMATION
         CLEAR
         MEMORDID = 0
         @ 5,1 SAY "ENTER THE ORDER ID - 0 TO ABORT" GET MEMORDID
         READ
         IF MEMORDID = 0
            LOOP
         ELSE
            SELECT C
            MEMORDID = STR(MEMORDID,7)
            SEEK MEMORDID
            IF .NOT. FOUND()
```

```
      ? "NO RECORD ON FILE FOR THIS ORDER NUMBER"
      WAIT
      LOOP
   ELSE
      MEMCUSID = ORDCUSID
      SELECT A
      SEEK MEMCUSID
      IF FOUND()
         MEMNAME = CUSCOMPANY
      ELSE
         MEMNAME = SPACE(20)
      ENDIF
      CLEAR
      @ 1,1 SAY "ORDER NUMBER: " + MEMORDID
      @ 2,1 SAY "COMPANY NAME: " + A->CUSCOMPANY
      @ 3,1 SAY "ORDER DATE  : " + DTOC(C->ORDDATE)
      @ 5,0 SAY ""
      WAIT "IS THIS THE CORRECT ORDER (Y/N)? " TO ANSWER
      IF UPPER(ANSWER) <> "Y"
         LOOP
      ENDIF
   ENDIF
ENDIF
* GET ORDER
SELECT C  && THE ORDER HEADER FILE
DO ORDFSE
* GET ITEM INFORMATION
DO WHILE .T.
```

```
CLEAR
MEMINVID = SPACE(6)
@ 5,1 SAY ;
 "ENTER THE INVENTORY ID - RETURN TO ABORT" ;
   GET MEMINVID
READ
IF MEMINVID = SPACE(6)
   EXIT
ENDIF
SELECT D
MEMKEY = MEMORDID+MEMINVID
SEEK MEMKEY
IF .NOT. FOUND()
   ? "ITEM NOT ON FILE FOR THIS ORDER"
   WAIT
   LOOP
ENDIF
SELECT E
SEEK MEMINVID
IF FOUND()
   @ 7,1 SAY "DESCRIPTION: " + INVDESCRIP
ENDIF
@ 9,0 SAY ""
WAIT "IS THIS THE CORRECT ITEM (Y/N):" TO ANSWER
IF UPPER(ANSWER) <> "Y"
   LOOP
ENDIF
@ 9,0 CLEAR
```

```
            MEMQORD = D->ITQTYORD
            MEMNEWQORD = MEMQORD
            MAXORD = INVQFORSAL
            @ 12,1 SAY "QUANTITY FOR SALE: "+STR(INVQFORSAL,5)
            @ 13,1 SAY "QUANTITY RETURNED: "+STR(INVQRET,5)
            @ 15,0 SAY "QUANTITY ORDERED" GET MEMNEWQORD ;
              RANGE 0,MAXORD
            READ
            MEMDIFORD = MEMQORD-MEMNEWQORD
            IF MEMDIFORD <> 0
                 REPLACE INVQFORSAL WITH INVQFORSAL+MEMDIFORD, ;
                INVQPRMSD WITH INVQPRMSD-MEMDIFORD
            ENDIF
            SELECT D
            MEMDATE = ITPROMDATE
            @ 17,1 SAY "DATE PROMISED" GET MEMDATE
            READ
            REPLACE ITQTYORD WITH MEMNEWQORD, ITPROMDATE ;
              WITH MEMDATE
         ENDDO
      OTHERWISE
         ? "ILLEGAL SELECTION CODE"
         WAIT
   ENDCASE
ENDDO
************ END OF PROGRAM ************


* ORDVIEW.PRG
```

```
* DISPLAY AN ORDER ON THE SCREEN
SELECT A
USE CUSTOMER INDEX CUSID
SELECT C
USE ORDERS INDEX ORDNUMBE
SELECT D
USE ITEMS INDEX ITNUMINV
SELECT E
USE INVENTOR INDEX INVID
DO WHILE .T.
   CLEAR
   @ 5,1 SAY "A. RETURN TO THE ORDER MENU"
   @ 6,1 SAY "B. DISPLAY AN ORDER"
   WAIT "ENTER A SELECTION CODE:" TO CODE2
   CODE2 = UPPER(CODE2)
   DO CASE
      CASE CODE2 = "A"
         RETURN
      CASE CODE2 = "B"
         CLEAR
         STORE 0 TO MEMORDNUMB
         @ 5,1 SAY "ENTER THE NUMBER OF THE ORDER - 0 TO ABORT";
            GET MEMORDNUMB
         READ
         IF MEMORDNUMB = 0
            LOOP
         ENDIF
         MEMORDNUMB = STR(MEMORDNUMB,7)
```

```
SELECT C
SEEK MEMORDNUMB
IF .NOT. FOUND()
   ? "NO ORDER ON FILE FOR THIS NUMBER"
   WAIT
   LOOP
ENDIF
CLEAR
@ 1, 1 SAY "ORDER NUMBER: " + MEMORDNUMB
@ 3, 1 SAY "CUSTOMER NUMBER: " + ORDCUSID
SELECT A
SEEK C->ORDCUSID
@ 3,35 SAY "NAME: "
IF FOUND()
   @ 3,41 SAY CUSCOMPANY
ENDIF
@ 4, 1 SAY REPLICATE("-",79)
@ 5, 1 SAY "ITEM #"
@ 5,10 SAY "DESCRIPTION"
@ 5,47 SAY "Q ORD"
@ 5,55 SAY "PROMISED"
@ 5,65 SAY "SHIPPED"
@ 6, 1 SAY REPLICATE("-",6)
@ 6,10 SAY REPLICATE("-",35)
@ 6,47 SAY REPLICATE("-",5)
@ 6,55 SAY REPLICATE("-",8)
@ 6,65 SAY REPLICATE("-",8)
ROW = 6
```

```
          SELECT D
          SEEK MEMORDNUMB
          DO WHILE .NOT. EOF() .AND. MEMORDNUMB = ITORDNUMB
             ROW = ROW + 1
             IF ROW > 22
                WAIT
                @ 7,0 CLEAR
                ROW = 7
             ENDIF
             SELECT E
             SEEK D->ITINVID
             @ ROW, 1 SAY D->ITINVID
             IF FOUND()
                @ ROW,10 SAY E->INVDESCRIP
             ENDIF
             @ ROW,47 SAY D->ITQTYORD
             @ ROW,55 SAY D->ITPROMDATE
             @ ROW,65 SAY D->ITSHIPDATE
             SELECT D
             SKIP 1
          ENDDO
          WAIT
       OTHERWISE
          ? "ILLEGAL SELECTION CODE"
          WAIT
    ENDCASE
ENDDO
************ END OF PROGRAM ************
```

Notes on ORDVIEW.PRG:

The REPLICATE function is used here to display a line of dashes in the column headers.

Once again, the SHIPPING subsystem that is listed next has a marked similarity to previous subsystems.

```
* SHIPPING.PRG
SELECT A
USE CUSTOMER INDEX CUSID
SELECT C
USE ORDERS INDEX ORDNUMBER
SELECT D
USE ITEMS INDEX ITNUMINV
SELECT E
USE INVENTORY INDEX INVID
DO WHILE .T.
   CLEAR
   @ 5, 5 SAY "ENTER OR CHANGE A SHIPPING DATE"
   @ 6, 5 SAY "-------------------------------"
   @ 7,10 SAY "A. RETURN TO MAIN MENU"
   @ 8,10 SAY "B. ENTER/CHANGE A SHIPPING DATE"
   WAIT "ENTER A SELECTION CODE:" TO CODE1
   CODE1 = UPPER(CODE1)
   DO CASE
      CASE CODE1 = "A"
         RETURN
      CASE CODE1 = "B"
         MEMORDNUMB = 0
```

```
CLEAR
@ 5,1 SAY "ENTER THE ORDER NUMBER" GET MEMORDNUMB ;
  PICTURE "9999999"
READ
SELECT C
MEMKEY = STR(MEMORDNUMB,7)
SEEK MEMKEY
IF .NOT. FOUND()
   @ 7,0 SAY "THIS ORDER NUMBER NOT FOUND"
   WAIT
   LOOP
ENDIF
MEMCUSID = ORDCUSID
MEMORDDATE = ORDDATE
SELECT A
SEEK MEMCUSID
IF FOUND()
   MEMCOMPANY = CUSCOMPANY
ELSE
   MEMCOMPANY = SPACE(20)
ENDIF
CLEAR
@ 1,1 SAY "ORDER NUMBER: " + MEMKEY
@ 3,1 SAY "COMPANY NAME: " + MEMCOMPANY
@ 5,1 SAY "ORDER   DATE: " + DTOC(MEMORDDATE)
WAIT "IS THIS THE CORRECT ORDER (Y/N):" TO ANSWER
IF UPPER(ANSWER) <> "Y"
   LOOP
```

```
ENDIF
@ 8,1 SAY ""
WAIT "CHANGE ALL ITEMS (Y/N):" TO ANSWER
IF UPPER(ANSWER) = "Y"
   * PROCESS ALL ITEMS IN THIS ORDER
   MEMDATE = CTOD("  /  /  ")
   @ 10,1 SAY "ENTER THE SHIPPING DATE" GET MEMDATE
   READ
   SELECT D
   SEEK MEMKEY
   DO WHILE .NOT. EOF() .AND. ITORDNUMB = MEMKEY
      REPLACE NEXT 1 ITSHIPDATE WITH MEMDATE
      SKIP 1
   ENDDO
ELSE
   * PROCESS INDIVIDUALLY
   DO WHILE .T.
      @ 8,0 CLEAR
      MEMINVID = SPACE(6)
      @ 8,1 SAY "ITEM NUMBER - RETURN TO ABORT" GET ;
         MEMINVID
      READ
      IF MEMINVID = SPACE(6)
         EXIT
      ENDIF
      SELECT E
      SEEK MEMINVID
      IF .NOT. FOUND()
```

```
        ANSWER = SPACE(1)
        @ 10,1 SAY ;
         "ITEM NOT FOUND IN INVENTORY-CHANGE ANYWAY (Y/N)" ;
            GET ANSWER
        READ
        IF UPPER(ANSWER) <> "Y"
           LOOP
        ENDIF
     ELSE
        @ 12,1 SAY "DESCRIPTION: "+INVDESCRIP
        ANSWER = SPACE(1)
        @ 13,1 SAY "IS THIS THE CORRECT ITEM (Y/N)" ;
        GET ANSWER
        READ
        IF UPPER(ANSWER) <> "Y"
           LOOP
        ENDIF
     ENDIF
     SELECT D
     SEEK MEMKEY+MEMINVID
     IF .NOT. FOUND()
        @ 15,1 SAY "THIS ITEM NOT IN THIS ORDER"
        WAIT
        LOOP
     ENDIF
     @ 15,1 SAY "SHIPPING DATE" GET ITSHIPDATE
     READ
  ENDDO
```

```
        ENDIF
      OTHERWISE
        ? "ILLEGAL SELECTION CODE"
        WAIT
   ENDCASE
ENDDO
************ END OF PROGRAM ************
```

Notes on SHIPPING.PRG:
The SHIPPING subsystem, at the current time, just allows you to change the shipping date. In an operational system, one would expect that you could record and change other information, such as the quantity shipped, in addition to the date shipped. This is an example of how a system evolves. You write your programs to perform the operations that you currently know about, and then you modify or add to both programs and data when you learn more about the desired system.

The REPORTS subsystem differs from the previous subsystems in that it is not designed to enter or modify records. Its sole purpose is to print reports. The grouping of reports in one subsystem has both advantages and disadvantages. One of the main advantages is that all the reports are grouped together in one place, making it easy to see which reports the system can print. It is also easy to add new reports anytime that you want. Just add a function to the menu in the report subsystem, enter the call to the function, and write the code for the program. The major disadvantage is that the user may need to exit from one subsystem and subsequently enter another in order to print related reports. The REPORTS subsystem is listed next.

```
* REPORTS.PRG
SELECT A
USE CUSTOMER INDEX CUSID
SELECT C
USE ORDERS INDEX ORDNUMBER
```

```
SELECT D
USE ITEMS INDEX ITNUMINV
SELECT E
USE INVENTOR INDEX INVID
DO WHILE .T.
   CLEAR
   @  5, 5 SAY "REPORT SUBSYSTEM"
   @  6, 5 SAY "----------------"
   @  7,10 SAY "A. RETURN TO MAIN MENU"
   @  8,10 SAY "B. LIST LATE SHIPMENTS"
   @  9,10 SAY "C. LIST RETURNS"
   WAIT "ENTER A SELECTION CODE:" TO CODE1
   CODE1 = UPPER(CODE1)
   DO CASE
      CASE CODE1 = "A"
         RETURN
      CASE CODE1 = "B"
         DO LATESHIP
      CASE CODE1 = "C"
         ? "NOT IMPLEMENTED YET"
         WAIT
   ENDCASE
ENDDO
************ END OF PROGRAM ************
```

Notes on REPORTS.PRG:
In an operational system, there would be more reports.

```
* LATESHIP.PRG
* LIST ORDER ITEMS NOT SHIPPED ON TIME
CLEAR
ANSWER = SPACE(1)
@ 1,1 SAY "PRINT THE LATE SHIPMENT REPORT (Y/N):" GET ANSWER
READ
IF UPPER(ANSWER) <> "Y"
        RETURN
ENDIF
MAXLINES = 50
PAGENO = 1
SET DEVICE TO PRINT
@ 0,0 SAY CHR(15)
DO LATEHEAD
ROW = 6
SELECT D
GOTO TOP
DO WHILE .NOT. EOF()
        IF DAY(ITSHIPDATE) <> 0
                SKIP 1
                LOOP
        ENDIF
        ROW = ROW + 1
        IF ROW > MAXLINES
                EJECT
                PAGENO = PAGENO + 1
                DO LATEHEAD
                ROW = 7
```

```
ENDIF
MEMORDNUMB = ITORDNUMB
MEMINVID = ITINVID
SELECT C
SEEK MEMORDNUMB
IF .NOT. FOUND()
        ? "CAN NOT FIND ORDER NO: "+MEMORDNUMB
        WAIT
        SELECT D
        SKIP 1
        LOOP
ENDIF
MEMCUSID = ORDCUSID
SELECT A
SEEK MEMCUSID
IF FOUND()
        MEMCOMPANY = CUSCOMPANY
ELSE
        MEMCOMPANY = SPACE(20)
ENDIF
SELECT E
SEEK MEMINVID
IF FOUND()
        MEMDESCRIP = INVDESCRIP
ELSE
        MEMDESCRIP = SPACE(35)
ENDIF
SELECT D
```

```
        @ ROW, 1 SAY D->ITORDNUMB
        @ ROW, 9 SAY    MEMCOMPANY
        @ ROW,30 SAY D->ITINVID
        @ ROW,38 SAY    MEMDESCRIP
        @ ROW,74 SAY D->ITPROMDATE
        @ ROW,83 SAY D->ITQTYORD
        SKIP 1
ENDDO
@ 55,0 SAY CHR(18)
EJECT
SET DEVICE TO SCREEN
RETURN
************ END OF PROGRAM ************
```

Notes on LATESHIP.PRG:

The purpose of this program is to print a report showing all the items whose delivery was promised by today's date but have not yet been shipped. All the formatting and output statements are included in the program (rather than use the report writer) to illustrate how reports are printed from a program. LATEHEAD.PRG is the name of the file that contains the code to print headings for each page of the report. The

@ . . SAY CHR(15)

statement is used to place the printer in compressed print mode and

@ . . SAY CHR(18)

is used to return the printer to normal print mode. Note also the use of the EJECT statement at the end of the report, followed by the SET DEVICE TO SCREEN. Remember to change back to screen output mode after each report. If you forget to do this, the menus that should be displayed on the screen might be sent to the printer instead.

```
* LATEHEAD.PRG
@ 1,33 SAY "ITEMS NOT SHIPPED REPORT"
@ 2,33 SAY "DATE PRINTED:"
@ 2,46 SAY DATE()
@ 2,60 SAY "PAGE NO:"
@ 2,68 SAY PAGENO PICTURE "999"
@ 4,74 SAY "DATE     QTY"
@ 5,1 SAY "ORD NO  COMPANY NAME         ITEM NO DESCRIPTION"
@ 5,74 SAY "PROMISED ORDERED"
@ 6,1 SAY "------- ------------------- ------- ------------------"
@ 6,56 SAY "----------------- -------- -------"
RETURN
************ END OF PROGRAM ************
```

The programs in the maintenance subsystem allow the user to reindex the files and to delete records. I recommend that your application system have a special maintenance subsystem, one that is similar to the one given here. It should contain both the reindexing program and the record deletion program. You may add to this subsystem any maintenance functions that you feel your system should have. Since INDEXES.PRG was listed previously in this chapter, it is not repeated here.

```
* MAINT.PRG
DO WHILE .T.
   CLEAR
   @ 5, 5 SAY "MAINTENANCE MENU"
   @ 6, 5 SAY "----------------"
   @ 7,10 SAY "A. RETURN TO MAIN MENU"
   @ 8,10 SAY "B. REINDEX THE FILES"
```

```
   @ 9,10 SAY "C. DELETE RECORDS"
   WAIT "ENTER A SELECTION CODE:" TO CODE2
   CODE2 = UPPER(CODE2)
   DO CASE
      CASE CODE2 = "A"
         RETURN
      CASE CODE2 = "B"
         DO INDEXES
      CASE CODE2 = "C"
         DO DELETE
      OTHERWISE
         ? "ILLEGAL SELECTION CODE"
         WAIT
    ENDCASE
ENDDO
************ END OF PROGRAM ************


* DELETE.PRG
* DELETE RECORDS FROM FILES
SELECT A
USE CUSTOMER INDEX CUSID
SELECT C
USE ORDERS INDEX ORDNUMBER
SELECT D
USE ITEMS INDEX ITNUMINV
SELECT E
USE INVENTOR INDEX INVID
DELCUS = .F.
```

```
DELORD = .F.
DELIT  = .F.
DELINV = .F.
DO WHILE .T.
   CLEAR
   @  5, 5 SAY "DELETIONS"
   @  6, 5 SAY "---------"
   @  7,10 SAY "A. REFORMAT FILES AND RETURN TO MAIN MENU"
   @  8,10 SAY "B. CUSTOMERS"
   @  9,10 SAY "C. ORDERS"
   @ 10,10 SAY "D. ITEMS FROM AN ORDER"
   @ 11,10 SAY "E. INVENTORY"
   WAIT "ENTER A SELECTION CODE:" TO CODE1
   CODE1 = UPPER(CODE1)
   DO CASE
      CASE CODE1 = "A"
         ? "THIS PROCESS MAY BE TIME CONSUMING"
         * PACK AND REINDEX
         IF DELCUS
            SELECT A
            SET INDEX TO
            PACK
            INDEX ON CUSID TO CUSID
         ENDIF
         IF DELORD
            SELECT C
            SET INDEX TO
            PACK
```

```
        INDEX ON ORDNUMBER TO ORDNUMBER
        INDEX ON ORDCUSID  TO ORDCUSID
    ENDIF
    IF DELIT
        SELECT D
        SET INDEX TO
        PACK
        INDEX ON ITORDNUMB+ITINVID TO ITNUMINV
    ENDIF
    IF DELINV
        SELECT E
        SET INDEX TO
        PACK
        INDEX ON INVID TO INVID
    ENDIF
    RETURN
CASE CODE1 = "B"
    * CUSTOMERS AND ALL ASSOCIATED ORDERS
    DO WHILE .T.
        CLEAR
        MEMCUSID = 0
        @ 5,1 SAY ;
            "ENTER THE ID OF THE CUSTOMER - 0 TO ABORT" ;
            GET MEMCUSID PICTURE "99999"
        READ
        IF MEMCUSID = 0
            EXIT
        ENDIF
```

```
MEMKEY = STR(MEMCUSID,5)
SELECT A
SEEK MEMKEY
IF .NOT. FOUND()
   @ 7,0 SAY "THIS ID NOT ON FILE"
   WAIT
   LOOP
ENDIF
DELCUS = .T.
DELETE NEXT 1
SELECT C
SET INDEX TO ORDCUSID
SEEK MEMKEY
DO WHILE .NOT. EOF() .AND. ORDCUSID = MEMKEY
   MEMORDNUMB = ORDNUMBER
   DELETE NEXT 1
   DELORD = .T.
   SELECT D
   SEEK MEMORDNUMB
   DO WHILE .NOT. EOF() .AND. ITORDNUMB = MEMORDNUMB
      DELETE NEXT 1
      DELIT = .T.
      SKIP 1
   ENDDO
   SELECT C
   SKIP 1
ENDDO
SELECT A
```

```
    ENDDO
    SELECT C
    SET INDEX TO ORDNUMBER
CASE CODE1 = "C"
    * ORDERS AND ALL ASSOCIATED ITEMS
    DO WHILE .T.
       CLEAR
       MEMORDID = 0
       @ 5,1 SAY ;
         "ENTER THE ID OF THE ORDER - 0 TO ABORT" ;
         GET MEMORDID PICTURE "9999999"
       READ
       IF MEMORDID = 0
          EXIT
       ENDIF
       MEMKEY = STR(MEMORDID,7)
       SELECT C
       SEEK MEMKEY
       IF .NOT. FOUND()
          @ 7,0 SAY "THIS ID NOT ON FILE"
          WAIT
          LOOP
       ENDIF
       DELORD = .T.
       DELETE NEXT 1
       MEMORDNUMB = ORDNUMBER
       SELECT D
       SEEK MEMORDNUMB
```

```
            DO WHILE .NOT. EOF() .AND. ITORDNUMB = MEMORDNUMB
               DELETE NEXT 1
               DELIT = .T.
               SKIP 1
            ENDDO
         ENDDO
      CASE CODE1 = "D"
         * ITEMS FROM AN ORDER
         DO WHILE .T.
            MEMORDNUMB = 0
            MEMINVID = SPACE(6)
            CLEAR
            @ 5,1 SAY ;
               "ORDER NUMBER - 0 TO ABORT" ;
               GET MEMORDNUMB PICTURE "9999999"
            @ 6,1 SAY "ITEM  NUMBER" GET MEMINVID
            READ
            IF MEMORDNUMB = 0
               EXIT
            ENDIF
            MEMORDNUMB = STR(MEMORDNUMB,7)
            SELECT C
            SEEK MEMORDNUMB
            IF .NOT. FOUND()
               ? "ORDER NOT ON FILE"
               WAIT
               LOOP
```

```
ENDIF
MEMCUSID = ORDCUSID
SELECT A
SEEK MEMCUSID
IF .NOT. FOUND()
   ? "NO CUSTOMER RECORD ON FILE FOR THIS ORDER"
   WAIT
   LOOP
ENDIF
MEMCOMPANY = CUSCOMPANY
SELECT D
SEEK MEMORDNUMB+MEMINVID
IF .NOT. FOUND()
   ? "THIS ITEM NOT ON FILE FOR THIS ORDER"
   WAIT
   LOOP
ENDIF
MEMINVID = ITINVID
SELECT E
SEEK MEMINVID
IF FOUND()
   MEMDESCRIP = INVDESCRIP
ELSE
   MEMDESCRIP = SPACE(35)
ENDIF
@ 8,1 SAY "COMPANY:"+MEMCOMPANY
@ 9,1 SAY "ITEM   :"+MEMDESCRIP
```

```
         WAIT "DELETE THIS ITEM (Y/N):" TO ANSWER
         IF UPPER(ANSWER) = "Y"
            DELIT = .T.
            SELECT D
            DELETE NEXT 1
         ELSE
            ? "ITEM WILL NOT BE DELETED"
            WAIT
         ENDIF
      ENDDO
   CASE CODE1 = "E"
      * INVENTORY AND ALL ASSOCIATED ITEMS
      DO WHILE .T.
         CLEAR
         MEMINVID = SPACE(6)
         @ 5,1 SAY ;
           "ENTER THE INVENTORY ITEM ID - RETURN TO ABORT" ;
           GET MEMINVID
         READ
         IF MEMINVID = SPACE(6)
            EXIT
         ENDIF
         SELECT E
         SEEK MEMINVID
         IF .NOT. FOUND()
            ? "THIS ITEM NOT ON FILE"
            WAIT
         ENDIF
```

```
            @ 8,1 SAY "DESCRIPTION: "+INVDESCRIP
            WAIT "DELETE THIS INVENTORY ITEM (Y/N):" TO ANSWER
            IF UPPER(ANSWER) <> "Y"
               ? "WILL NOT DELETE THIS ITEM"
               LOOP
            ENDIF
            DELETE NEXT 1
            DELINV = .T.
            SELECT D
            DELETE ALL FOR ITINVID = MEMINVID
            DELIT = .T.
         ENDDO
   ENDCASE
ENDDO
************ END OF PROGRAM ************
```

Notes on DELETE.PRG:
Because packing and reindexing can take a considerable amount of time in dBASE III Plus, care is taken to pack and reindex only those database files from which records have actually been deleted. In some cases, deletion of a record from one file requires the deletion of one or more records from other files. Two different techniques for the deletion of records are shown in this program:

1. The first is a SEEK for the desired record(s), followed by a DELETE NEXT 1 and a sequential search for more records, and
2. The second is a DELETE ALL FOR <condition>.

In general, I expect that the SEEK followed by a sequential search will be the more efficient of the two techniques for large database files in which a relatively small percentage of records will be deleted (the normal case), and that a DELETE ALL FOR will be more efficient in small database files and in those where the percentage of records to be deleted is large.

The above system is shown after it has been constructed and debugged, but you will probably develop your application systems one step at a time. In particular, you will probably find that you add database files and indexes to the program INDEXES.PRG several times during the development process. You may also find that you need to add additional indexes to programs that you have already written.

> **Step 6:**
> Add additional indexes to your database files as it becomes clear that they are necessary.

Once you have completed the application system, you will want to clear out all the database files before you deliver it to your client. For this purpose, I recommend that you write a small program, one that is a modification of the INDEXES.PRG program. This program is also handy for debugging purposes, since you can use it to initialize the system before you enter new data. This type of program is shown in FILEEMPT.PRG.

```
* FILEEMPT.PRG

* INITIALIZE THE SYSTEM

USE CUSTOMER

   ZAP

   INDEX ON CUSID TO CUSID

USE MISC

   ZAP

   APPEND BLANK

   REPLACE MISCUSID WITH 1, MISORDID WITH 1

USE ORDERS

   ZAP

   INDEX ON ORDNUMBER TO ORDNUMBER

   INDEX ON ORDCUSID  TO ORDCUSID

USE ITEMS

   ZAP
```

```
   INDEX ON ITORDNUMB+ITINVID TO ITNUMINV
USE INVENTOR
   ZAP
   INDEX ON INVID TO INVID
RETURN
************ END OF PROGRAM ************
```

Notes on FILEEMPT.PRG:
This program empties out all the databases and reindexes them. In addition, a record is added to the MISC database file to initialize it. This record contains the values to be used for autogeneration of customer and order identifiers.

Step 7:
Include a program in your system to clear out and initialize all the database files.

The last of the programs listed in the system given above is used to delete records from your database files. I like to place all the deletion routines in one program, because deletions and the associated packs and reindexing are relatively slow. Placing all these routines in one program tends to insure that deletions are performed as a group, rather than one record at a time, and this speeds up the deletion process. I always write this program last, so that I know exactly what records are in the system, what the indexes are, and how the records will be used. If records have dates associated with them, you might want to include the ability to delete old records by date.

Step 8:
Include a program in your system to delete old or undesirable records.

As you build a system, you will probably find that you have added or deleted files, fields, and indexes in various programs. Verify that no program that enters data includes an index that is never used, and also verify that the indexes in your mainline programs match those listed in INDEXES.PRG and FILEEMPT.PRG. Also verify there are no unused fields in your database files.

> **Step 9:**
> After completion of your system, bring it up to date by verifying that additions or deletions of indexes, database files, and fields have been accounted for in all appropriate programs.

A last note on the system:
Not all the functions listed in the menus have been included in this sample system. In addition, you probably can think of a number of functions (and reports) that you would like to see in this system. The data files have been constructed using fairly advanced techniques, techniques that essentially guarantee that you can utilize the data in a wide variety of situations without making substantial changes to the basic structure of the files. Nevertheless, you may find that files designed using these techniques are rather slow for certain operations. A modification of the technique that I like is to duplicate certain data elements. For example, when the report of items promised but not yet shipped is printed, there is a considerable amount of access to secondary files (like the CUSTOMER file). If you include the name of the company in each item record, it will not be necessary to access the CUSTOMER file for each item listed in the report. The disadvantages of duplicating data in this manner are:

1. The maintenance of the duplicated data must be managed by the system, or inconsistencies might occur, and
2. The amount of storage for the file may increase substantially.

Nevertheless, you might choose to carefully duplicate certain data in order to increase the speed of certain procedures in your system.

> **Step 10:**
> It may be necessary to duplicate data so as to facilitate report production. This type of redundancy should always be performed by the system itself, in order to control system integrity.

CHAPTER

7

Advanced Design Principles

7.1 REASONS FOR DESIGN PRINCIPLES

We are interested in good design principles for three major reasons:

1. To help us to quickly build systems that work efficiently
2. To allow us to modify systems during construction, and
3. To allow us to modify systems after they have been in use for some time.

7.2 THE DESIGN PRINCIPLES

7.2.1 WHERE TO START

7.2.1.1 Discover the Nature of the Problem to be Solved

Most of the time, when you construct a new system using dBASE III Plus you will be converting from a manual (paper work) system to an automated one (one that uses a computer). Even if you are converting from another computerized system, most of the principles are the same. In this section, we will look at some of the more modern design principles and adapt them especially for use with dBASE III Plus.

I think of analysis as attempting to determine the nature of the current system (the current method of doing business) and of determining what is wrong with it. Design is the determination of a solution to problems with the current system. If there is no current system, that is, if the system to be designed will be an entirely new one, then design changes from "what do we have to do to fix the problem" to "what do we want to do here." In order to understand what is wrong with the current system, we must understand the nature of the current system. There are two parts to an existing system:

1. The problem to be solved by the system
2. The manner in which the system attempts to solve the problem.

> In order to understand a system, we must understand both the nature of the problem that it is attempting to solve and the manner in which it attempts to solve it.

> One task of analysis is to determine how the current system falls short of meeting the needs of the users. In order to do this, you will need to determine both the problem to be solved by having a system in the first place and the manner in which the system attempts to solve that problem. You will then be able to determine the manner in which the current system falls short of what is desired.

7.2.1.2 Examine the Inputs, Outputs, and Processes

The first step in the analysis of an existing system is to examine all the paper work associated with it. Examine both the input documents and the output documents for data elements. Also examine what the people or the computer do with the data. The processing of the raw data, either by people or by the computer, can often give valuable insights into the entire process of converting raw data into information.

We examine how people (or computers) use the data in order to determine the nature of the problem that they are trying to solve. At this point, we are interested in what they wish to do, not how they actually do it. Since people almost always think in terms of how they do their job, it is necessary to convert what they say into a different form. For example, consider this situation:

EXAMPLE:

A clerk must produce the payroll for all the employees in the company. When you talk to her about her job, she gives the following information.

> "I go to the main office and collect all the time cards for the employees. Then I compute the number of hours worked during the week for each employee. From John, I get a list that has the name of each hourly employee and his or her hourly pay rate. I carefully examine the number of hours for each employee to make sure that only authorized employees have submitted time cards with more than 40 hours per week. Then I fill out the pay checks and record the amount paid."

It is clear from the above that we must be able to separate "what" must be done from "how" it is done. We must also be able to fill in the missing details for the payroll computation. The following is a description of "what" must be done to produce a payroll, with many of the missing details filled in.

For each hourly employee
Verify the number of hours

For each salaried employee
Determine amount to be paid

Then, for each employee
Compute the gross earnings
Compute all deductions
Compute taxes and withholding
Compute net pay
Update quarterly and year-to-date totals

In this manner, we strip the *nature of the problem to be solved* away from *how someone has chosen to solve the problem.* This does not mean that we ignore or discard the manner in which the problem is currently being solved. Rather, we wish to understand the nature of the problem before we attempt to build a system in dBASE III Plus to solve it. At each step we ask the question "How do you do your job?" Then we analyze the responses to determine "What is the actual problem that you are trying to solve?".

Analysis rule 1:
Ask people how they do their job. Then separate the "how" from the "what," in order to increase your understanding of the real nature of the problem to be solved.

At this point, you have obtained a list of all the input documents, all the reports (output documents), and all the things that people (or machines) do. At least all that you currently know about. There will always be gaps in your knowledge at this stage.

Analysis rule 2:
Your understanding of a system will evolve over a period of time.

7.2.1.3 A First Attempt at Files

The next step in our understanding of the current system is to examine the nature of the stored data, or the files. From discussions with the clients (users), you may discover what data is currently being kept on file. Compare the data items (sometimes called fields) in these records with the data items on the input documents and the output documents. It is clear that all the data used by processes must come either directly or indirectly from the input documents and that all the data used for reports must come (directly or indirectly) from these files. Our task now is to discover the true nature of the data. We now wish to understand "what" the data really is, not just "how" it is currently used and stored.

> **Analysis rule 3:**
> Understand what the data is, not just how it is currently stored.

The technique that I prefer, in an attempt to understand the nature of the data, is to start with the input documents. There is great organizational knowledge manifested in the standard working documents of an organization. Consider, as an example, a sales receipt of the following form:

SALES RECEIPT

RECEIPT NUMBER: DATE:
NAME:
STREET:
CITY:
STATE: ZIP:

TYPE OF SALE
CASH: CHARGE: ACCOUNT NUMBER:

ITEMS SOLD

ITEM NUMBER	DESCRIPTION	QUANTITY	COST	TOTAL

DIAGRAM 7.1

This input document has two main parts, the fields at the top and the tabular arrangement at the bottom. The fields at the top allow the clerk to enter specific information exactly once on the form and there is room at the bottom for each item sold. The major difference between the two parts of the form is that the information at the top can (and need) be entered only once. The information at the bottom may be repeated. We will call the information entered in the top part the HEADER and the information entered in the bottom part the ITEMs. The organization has placed each of the indicated fields into the SALES RECEIPT, because it considers it appropriate to do so. Use this kind of information as a starting point in your analysis of the data.

Analysis rule 4:
Look for input documents that have both a HEADER and ITEMs. They will help you understand how the organization views the relationship between certain types of raw data items.

For now, we will think of the SALES RECORDs as being stored in a file in the imaginary collection of files that we are building. We will construct this imaginary collection of files for our own use, so that we can better understand the nature of the data that we are working with. We continue in this manner, building data files for each of the input documents that we have encountered so far in our analysis.

Assume that we have discovered the following files: INVENTORY, SALES, and CHARGE ACCOUNTS. The main input document for the SALES file is the SALES RECEIPT. The organization uses this document to update the INVENTORY FILE and, if the sale is a charge, to update the CHARGE ACCOUNTS FILE. We are not specifically interested here in precisely how the organization currently stores this data. We are interested in constructing an imaginary collection of files in order to better understand the data that we are working with. The major rule that we now impose is that HEADERs and ITEMs will always be separated into different files and that each file will contain exactly one type of record. For example, there will be a file for all SALES HEADERs, and there will be another file for all SALES ITEMs, no matter which SALES RECEIPT they originally came from. In fact, whenever we find a document that has both HEADER and ITEMs (the items are the repeating information), we will separate the document and store it in two files. In each case, we will need to record which ITEMs are associated with which HEADERs, in order to make the stored data useful. The process of breaking up a document into two parts and storing the data in two files (one for the header and one for the items) is often called normalization. When we break up the document in this manner, we are changing a single record that contains repeating information into a collection of records that do not contain repeating information. This new collection of records is easier and faster to work with, and it is just what we need for dBASE III Plus.

A record in the SALES HEADER (at this point in our analysis) file will have the fields:

RECEIPT NUMBER
DATE
NAME
STREET
CITY
STATE
ZIP
TYPE OF SALE
ACCOUNT NUMBER

and a record in the SALES ITEM file will have the fields:

RECEIPT NUMBER
ITEM NUMBER
DESCRIPTION
QUANTITY
COST
TOTAL

Analysis rule 5:
Every file will contain exactly one type of record, that is, each of the records in any one file will look just like any other record in that file, expect for the actual data that it contains.

Analysis rule 6:
Whenever we have input documents that contain a HEADER and ITEMs, or any type of repeating information, we will store the HEADER in one file and store the ITEMs in another file.

Further investigation reveals that the INVENTORY file contains the following fields:

ITEM NUMBER
DESCRIPTION
COST TO ORGANIZATION
RETAIL COST
QUANTITY ON HAND
REORDER POINT
REORDER AMOUNT

and that the CHARGE ACCOUNTS file contains the following fields:

ACCOUNT NUMBER
NAME
STREET
CITY
STATE
ZIP
TOTAL AMOUNT DUE
CURRENT AMOUNT DUE
AMOUNT DUE OVER 30 DAYS
AMOUNT DUE OVER 60 DAYS
AMOUNT DUE OVER 90 DAYS

We observe that some of the data appears in more than one file. In particular, the fields NAME, STREET, CITY, STATE, ZIP, and ACCOUNT NUMBER appear both in the SALES HEADER file and in the CHARGE file.

ACCOUNT NUMBER appears in the CHARGE ACCOUNTS file, because it identifies the specific account (it is the key of the CHARGE ACCOUNTS file). The ACCOUNT NUMBER appears in the SALES HEADER file in order to identify the associated CHARGE ACCOUNTS file record. It is clear that we cannot remove it from either file. Note the role that the ACCOUNT NUMBER plays in each of the files. In the CHARGE ACCOUNTS file, ACCOUNT NUMBER is the key or major identifier. In the SALES HEADER file, it provides information for us to link the SALES RECEIPT to the correct CHARGE ACCOUNTS file record. It is necessary that it appears in both these files. But what about the fields NAME, STREET, CITY, STATE, and ZIP? Must they appear in *both* files? The answer is no. We can remove these fields from the SALES HEADER file records, and obtain them when we need them from the CHARGE ACCOUNTS file record. Remember that we are now performing analysis. We are trying to understand the data that we are working with, so we remove any extraneous fields from our files.

> **Analysis rule 7:**
> Group fields into records so that each record describes just one type of object (like a charge account record, a sale, or a sale item).

> **Analysis rule 8:**
> If the same field appears in more than one file (type of record), determine where it most appropriately belongs. Make sure that it appears in that file. In all other files where it appears, determine if it must appear there for linking purposes. If so, leave it there. If it does not *have* to appear there, entirely remove it from that file.

7.2.1.4 A Refinement of the Files

Applying Analysis rule 8, we remove the fields NAME, STREET, CITY, STATE, and ZIP from the SALES HEADER file records and the new SALES HEADER file records will contain only the fields:

RECEIPT NUMBER

DATE

TYPE OF SALE

ACCOUNT NUMBER

We apply this rule to the SALES ITEM file records and remove the DESCRIPTION and COST fields, since they are available in the corresponding INVENTORY file record:

RECEIPT NUMBER

ITEM NUMBER

QUANTITY

TOTAL

At this point, we might examine the SALES ITEM file to see if there are any more fields that should be removed. Since TOTAL can always be computed from the COST (available from the INVENTORY file) and the QUANTITY, it is not absolutely necessary that we retain this field in the SALES ITEM record. The TOTAL field in the SALES ITEM records may, in the end, not even be something that we wish to store. At this point we just don't know, so we remove it from the SALES ITEM file records. The new SALES ITEM file has the fields:

RECEIPT NUMBER

ITEM NUMBER

QUANTITY

Analysis rule 9:
If a field can be computed from other fields already in the collection of files, then remove it. (It can always be put back in later, if we decide that we really do want it.)

We are now close to a "bare bones" collection of files. We have a minimal number of files and a minimal number of fields in each file. This helps us to understand the data itself:

7.2.1.5 Indicating Linkages

The next step is to indicate how the data will be used. In our system, we may wish to perform the following operations:

1. Enter records.
2. Change records.
3. Delete (remove) records.
4. Produce bills for the customers.

Therefore, we will need to directly access CHARGE ACCOUNTS records by account number, INVENTORY records by ITEM NUMBER, SALES HEADERs by receipt number, and SALES ITEMs by a combination of receipt number and item number. In addition, we will need to link SALE HEADERs to the corresponding SALE ITEMs and SALE ITEMs to the appropriate INVENTORY records. We will see later that all these access and linkages will determine what index files are necessary in our final files, so it is important to record them as we discover them.

> **Analysis rule 10:**
> As you discover the need for access to your files, record this information.

I personally like to record the necessary accesses with the following type of diagram:

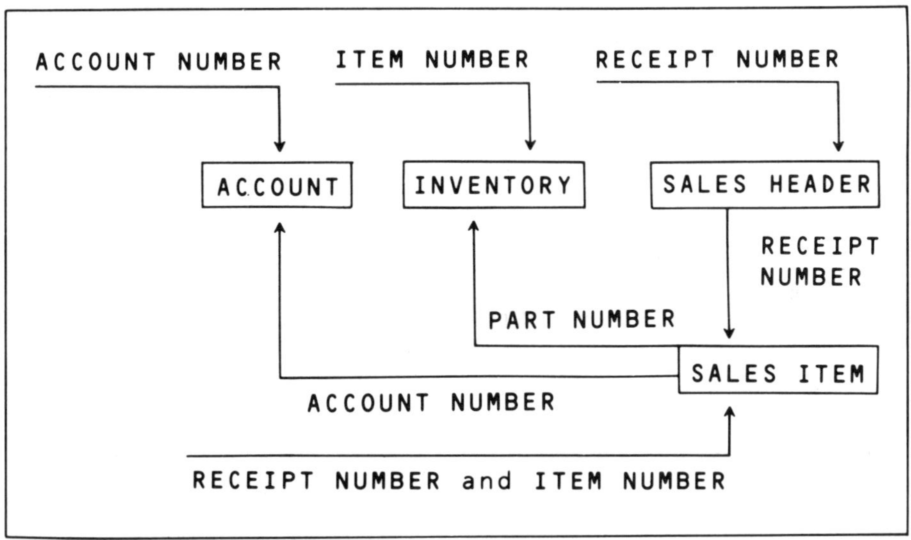

DIAGRAM 7.2

In the above diagram, rectangular boxes represent the files that we have constructed so far and each arrow represents a type of access to a file. Each arrow is labeled with the name of a field. If we wish to access the INVENTORY file and obtain a record with a specific ITEM NUMBER, then we show this in the following manner:

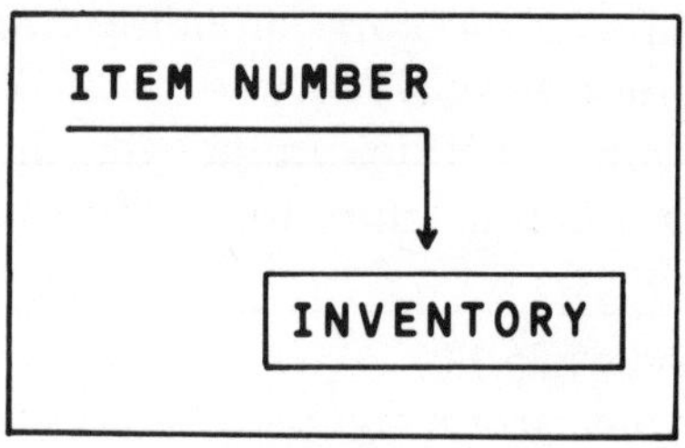

DIAGRAM 7.3

In a later place, we will see that this means that it will be necessary to index the INVENTORY file on the field ITEM NUMBER.

7.2.1.6 Additions to the Current Files

As our knowledge of the system evolves, and it most assuredly will, we may discover more input documents. This may lead to the need for more files or for more fields in existing files. It may also lead to the need for more accesses, as represented by the access arrows. Even an examination of output documents (reports) could tell us that we need more files, fields, and/or access arrows. But we must be careful here. No matter what we add to our (imaginary) file structure (the files together with the arrows), we must make sure that our files are as clean and as simple as possible. We wish to increase our understanding of the data items and how they are related to each other, not confuse things with a messy diagram.

Whenever we wish to add new fields to our collection of files, we follow these simple rules:

1. Determine the type of object that the field describes
2. See if there is a file that describes that same object
3. If the field in question is already in the file, no further action is necessary
4. If the field is not already in the file, add it to the file
5. If there is no file that describes the same object, add a new file and put the field in it (with any necessary key), and
6. Add new linkages as necessary

Consider our simple SALES/INVENTORY system as developed in this chapter. Suppose that we discover the need to have a credit limit for each of our accounts. Surely this is account information so we try to add it to the CHARGE ACCOUNTS file records. It does not already exist in the file, so we add it to each of the records in that file. In the case where we wish to record individual payments for each account, we first determine that this is account information. But, since there may be a number of payments for each account, this is really repeating account information. As demonstrated above, we do not add this information directly to the CHARGE ACCOUNTS file. Rather, we create a new file for the payments and link it to the CHARGE ACCOUNTS file. If we wish to find all payments associated with a specific account, we will need the linkage shown by the following:

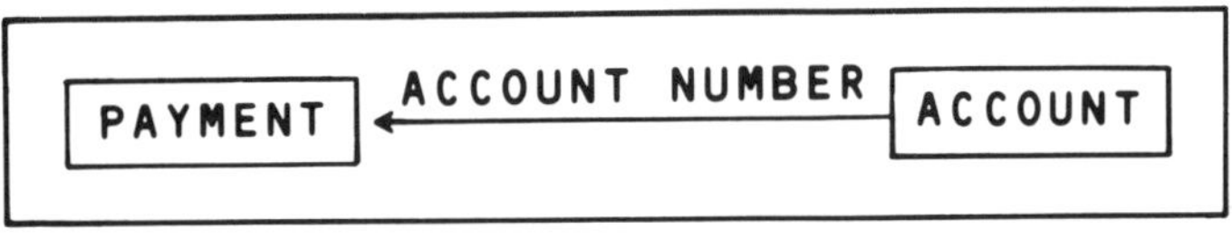

DIAGRAM 7.4

and the fields in the PAYMENT file will be:

ACCOUNT NUMBER

AMOUNT PAID

DATE PAID

CHECK NUMBER

7.2.2 EXAMINATION OF THE FILES FOR OTHER PROBLEMS

7.2.2.1 Problems Caused by Data Redundancy

Redundancy, or the duplication of data, might be useful or it might cause trouble. Most of the trouble caused by redundancy shows up in maintenance of the files. In particular, it may be difficult to add, delete, or modify records in files if there is data redundancy. We will examine some of the problems caused by data redundancy in this section. Let us examine a relatively simple situation first.

EXAMPLE:

A company wishes to maintain a record for each employee. The specific information to be stored is last name, first name, current address, name of spouse, date hired, the department where employed, and the name of the manager of the department. If the data for each employee is placed all in one record, that is, there is one record for each employee and there are no other records in the system, then the record will have the following structure:

EMPLOYEE FILE FIELD NAMES
EMPNO (EMPLOYEE NUMBER)
LAST NAME
FIRST NAME
ADDRESS
SPOUSE
DATE
DEPARTMENT
MANAGER

EMPLOYEE FILE

EMPNO	LAST NAME	FIRST NAME	ADDRESS	SPOUSE	DATE	DEPARTMENT	MANAGER
25	Able	Mary	Elm	John	1984	Research	A. Jones
37	Green	Tom	Maple	Jane	1985	Accounting	S. Smith
15	Black	John	Main	Sally	1982	Research	A. Jones
20	Brown	Nancy	Oak	Bill	1983	Research	A. Jones
	. . .	. . .	. . .	. . .	. . .	. . .	. . .

DIAGRAM 7.5

This file has problems with maintenance. If you wish to record the name of a manager for a new department, you will have to wait until there is at least one employee in the department. If there is only one employee in a department and that employee leaves that department, then the name of the manager of the department will also be removed from the file. If the manager of the department is changed, then every occurrence of the name in the MANAGER field must be changed. Finally, we must always be concerned that all the occurrences of a MANAGER name in a file are spelled the same.

All the problems mentioned above are directly related to the inclusion of the MANAGER field in the employee record file. In fact, the employee file, as it is currently structured, contains information about two different types of objects: employees and managers. If we separate the two types of information into two different files, we obtain the following:

New Employee File	*Department File*
EMPNO	DEPARTMENT
LAST NAME	MANAGER
FIRST NAME	
ADDRESS	
SPOUSE	
DATE	
DEPARTMENT	

and the data now looks like:

NEW EMPLOYEE FILE

EMPNO	LAST NAME	FIRST NAME	ADDRESS	SPOUSE	DATE	DEPARTMENT
25	Able	Mary	Elm	John	1984	Research
37	Green	Tom	Maple	Jane	1985	Accounting
15	Black	John	Main	Sally	1982	Research
20	Brown	Nancy	Oak	Bill	1983	Research
	. . .	. . .	. . .	. . .	. . .	. . .

DIAGRAM 7.6

DEPARTMENT FILE

DEPARTMENT	MANAGER
Research	A. Jones
Accounting	S. Smith

DIAGRAM 7.7

Now the only duplicated data is in the DEPARTMENT field. This kind of duplication is normally considered to be acceptable, since it is necessary to link employees to the departments in which they work. The kind of problems with file maintenance that we encountered in this example are not unusual. Since file maintenance is always important, we need some general techniques both to determine problems and to fix the problems.

One method to determine problems is to use DEPENDENCY DIAGRAMs. A dependency diagram shows which fields in a file (or collection of files) are determined by which other fields. We say that a field named B is determined by a field named A, if A and B are fields in the same record and, knowing the value of A, you can then uniquely determine the value of B. In this case, we also say that B is dependent upon A. In the example given Diagram 7.5, each of the following is dependent upon or determined by EMPNO: LAST NAME, FIRST NAME, ADDRESS, SPOUSE, DATE, DEPARTMENT, and MANAGER. In addition, MANAGER is determined by DEPARTMENT, since, if you know the department, then you can determine the manager. In the example in Diagram 7.5, if you know that the DEPARTMENT is Research, then you can search through the file for a record with the value "Research" in the DEPARTMENT field. Once such a record is obtained, the MANAGER field in the same record gives you the name of the manager of the Research department. A dependency diagram for the original EMPLOYEE file is:

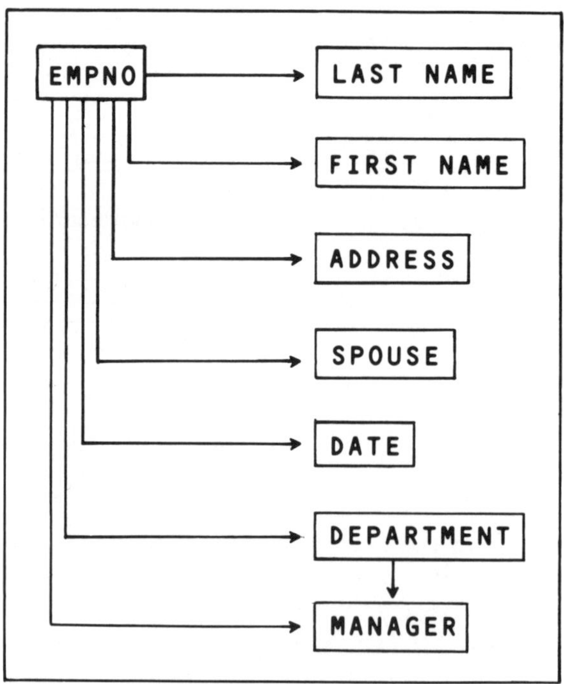

DIAGRAM 7.8

After the decomposition, the two dependency diagrams are:

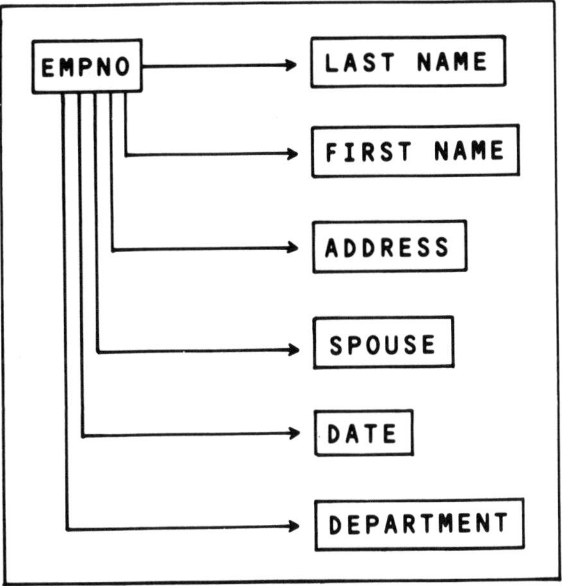

DIAGRAM 7.9

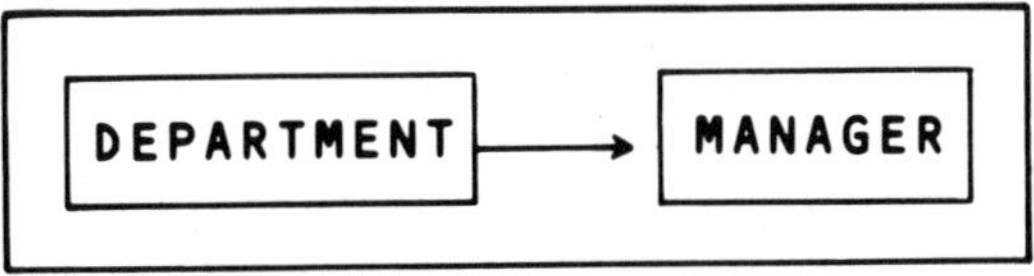

DIAGRAM 7.10

In Diagram 7.8 we can clearly see that all the fields in the record are dependent upon the key, EMPNO. We can also see that MANAGER is dependent upon DEPARTMENT.

In general, there are good dependencies and bad dependencies. In the following, a field or a minimal combination of fields is called a KEY, if it can be used to uniquely distinguish one record in a file from any other.

1. If a record has only one choice for a key and if that key has exactly one field in it, then a good dependency is when a nonkey field, that is, one that is not the key, is dependent upon the key.
2. If a record has only one choice for a key and if that key has more than one field in it, then a good dependency is when a nonkey field, that is, one that is not part of the key, is dependent upon the entire key, but not dependent upon any subpart of the key.
3. If a record has a choice of more than one key, then a good dependency is when a nonkey field, that is, one that is not part of any choice for a key, is dependent upon each choice of the key, but not dependent upon any subpart of any choice of a key.

Any other dependency is considered to be a bad dependency. Note that the two major kinds of bad dependencies are (1) a nonkey field is dependent upon another nonkey field and (2) a nonkey field is dependent upon part of a key. There are other kinds of bad dependencies but they are much more complex and are not easily determined by dependency diagrams.

When we break up a file into two or more files, in order to remove any bad dependencies, we call this process FILE DECOMPOSITION. The following provides examples of bad dependencies and the decompositions that remove these bad dependencies. Remember: Bad dependencies will lead to problems with maintenance of files.

EXAMPLE 1: A DEPENDENCY BETWEEN NONKEY FIELDS (ONE KEY)

See the employee record system above.

EXAMPLE 2: A DEPENDENCY BETWEEN NONKEY FIELDS (TWO KEYS)

Let's use the same file as used in Example 1, but let's add a field for the social security number (SSN). In this case, both the employee number (EMPNO) and the social security number (SSN) could be used as keys. The dependency diagram that we start with is:

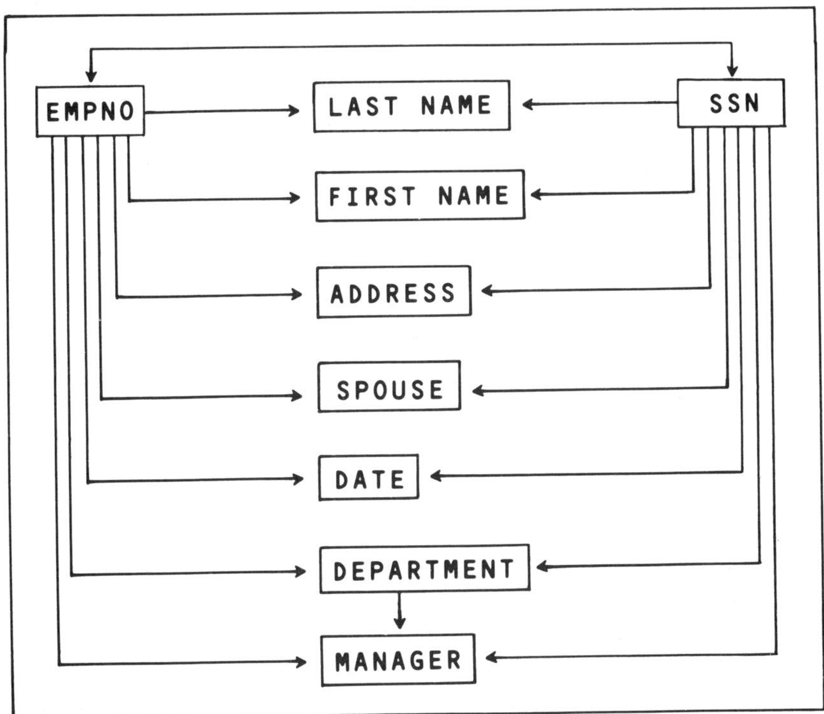

DIAGRAM 7.11

This example is almost the same as Example 1 above, except that there are two keys. Note that *either* EMPNO *or* SSN could be chosen for the key here. We will decompose this diagram in a manner similar to the decomposition used in Example 1 and obtain the following two diagrams:

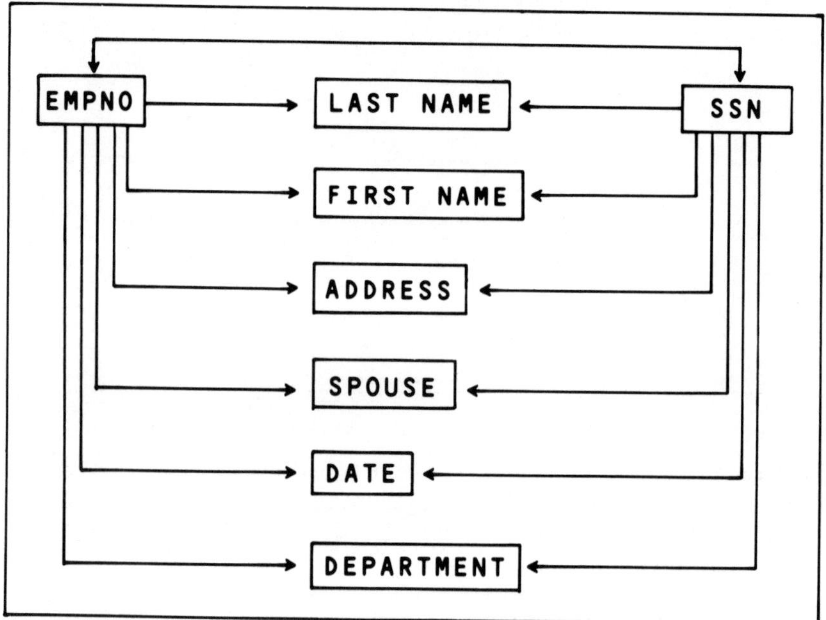

DIAGRAM 7.12

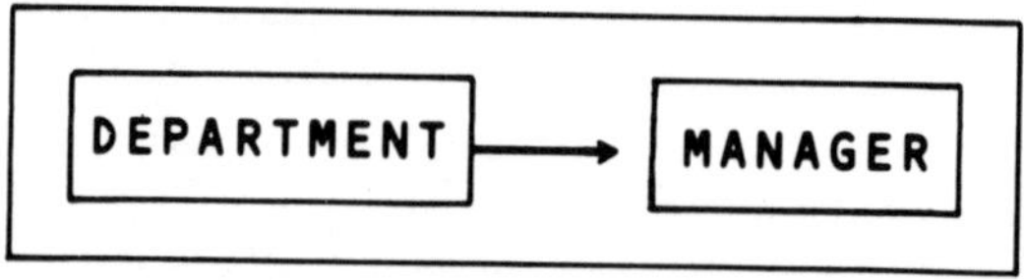

DIAGRAM 7.13

This decomposition would lead to two files. The first file would have the fields: EMPNO, SSN, LAST NAME, FIRST NAME, ADDRESS, SPOUSE, DATE, and DEPARTMENT. The second file would have the fields DEPARTMENT and MANAGER.

EXAMPLE 3: DEPENDENCY UPON PART OF THE KEY

In this example, we consider inventory records. The fields that we wish to store in our records are PARTNO (part number), DESCRIPTION, ITEM WEIGHT, SUPPLIERNO (supplier number), SUPPLIERNAME, ADDRESS, and QOH (quantity on hand). If we store all these fields in one record, then the dependency diagram is:

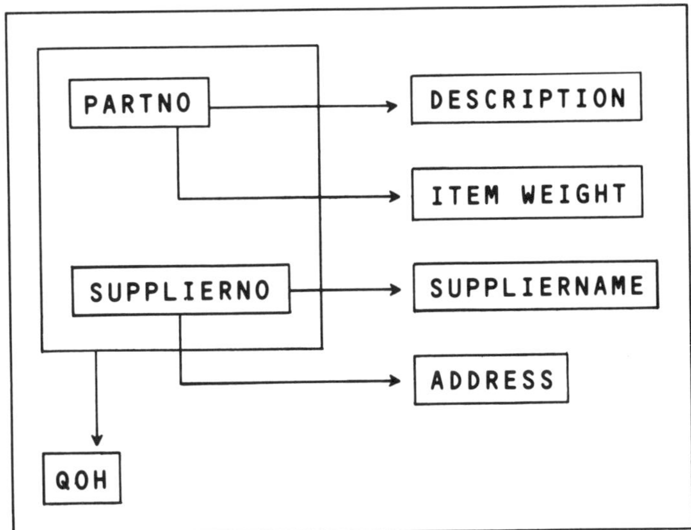

DIAGRAM 7.14

We actually have three types of information in this record: part, supplier, and quantity. The part information consists of PARTNO, DESCRIPTION, and ITEM WEIGHT. The supplier information consists of SUPPLIERNO, SUPPLIERNAME, and ADDRESS. The quantity information consists of PARTNO, SUPPLIERNO, and QOH, where QOH depends, in this example, upon both PARTNO and SUPPLIERNO. In this manner, we can keep track of the quantity on hand from each supplier. The key for the whole record is the combination of PARTNO and SUPPLIERNO, since, if we know these two values, we can determine all the other field values. Note that DESCRIPTION and ITEM WEIGHT are each dependent only upon PARTNO and that SUPPLIERNAME and ADDRESS are each dependent only upon SUPPLIERNO. An example of the duplication that you would obtain with this type of file is given by the following:

PARTNO	DESCRIPTION	ITEM WEIGHT	SUPPLIERNO	SUPPLIERNAME	ADDRESS	QOH
P1	COMPUTER	55	S1	OFFICE MACH.	NEW YORK	5
P1	COMPUTER	55	S2	BUSINESS SUP.	CHICAGO	3
P2	PRINTER	35	S1	OFFICE MACH.	NEW YORK	2
P2	PRINTER	35	S2	BUSINESS SUP.	CHICAGO	4
.	.	.	.	.	.	.
.	.	.	.	.	.	.
.	.	.	.	.	.	.

DIAGRAM 7.15

In Diagram 7.15 we see that both part and supplier information must be duplicated. In particular, DESCRIPTION and ITEM WEIGHT is the duplicated part information, and SUPPLIERNAME and ADDRESS is the duplicated supplier information. If we wish to remove this unnecessary duplication, we will need to decompose the original file into a number of new files. To accomplish this, we make use of the dependency diagram given in Diagram 7.14. The key for the original record is the combination of PARTNO and SUPPLIERNO. Since DESCRIPTION and ITEM WEIGHT are dependent only upon PARTNO, we place PARTNO, DESCRIPTION, and ITEM WEIGHT in one file. Similarly, we place SUPPLIERNO, SUPPLIERNAME, and ADDRESS in another file. Since QOH depends upon both PARTNO and SUPPLIERNO, we place PARTNO, SUPPLIERNO and QOH in a third file. At this point, we have the following (decomposed) dependency diagrams:

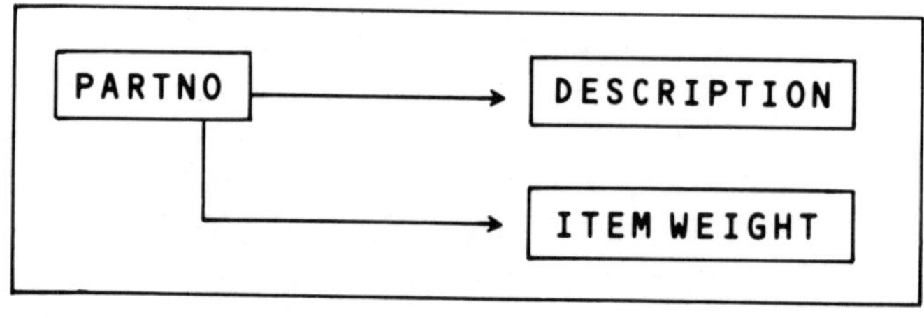

DIAGRAM 7.16 (A)

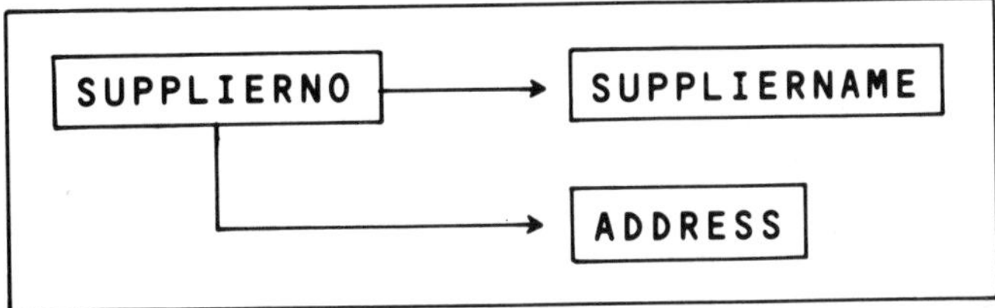

DIAGRAM 7.16 (B)

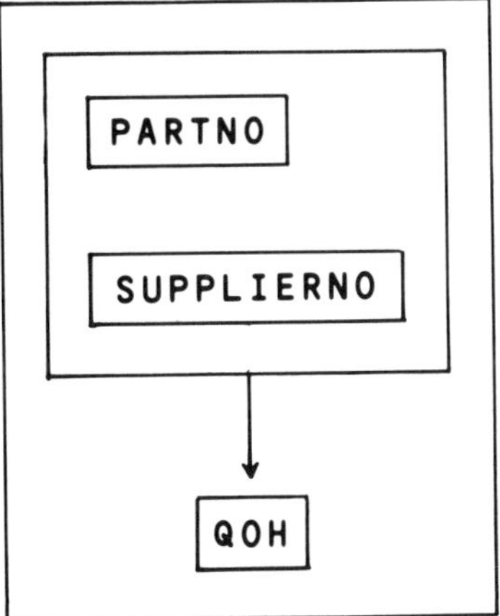

DIAGRAM 7.16 (C)

Each of the separate diagrams (7.16: A, B, and C) would correspond to separate dBASE III Plus files. The key of the first is PARTNO, the key of the second is SUPPLIERNO, and the key of the third is the combination of PARTNO and SUPPLIERNO. The date given in Diagram 7.15 would now appear as shown in Diagram 7.17.

When we create the dBASE III Plus files to match our dependency diagrams, we do not use a KEY in the sense of the dependency diagrams. We always use index files to facilitate the accesses needed. The term KEY, as used in the discussions of dependency diagrams, is employed to help us identify the type of data that we are working with. In this example, we were able to identify three distinct types of data (part, supplier, and quantity). This helped us to construct the final choice of files. Only after the files have been chosen do we consider the index files.

PARTNO	DESCRIPTION	ITEM WEIGHT
P1	COMPUTER	55
P2	PRINTER	35
.	.	.
.	.	.
.	.	.

DIAGRAM 7.17 (A)

SUPPLIERNO	SUPPLIERNAME	ADDRESS
S1	OFFICE MACH.	NEW YORK
S2	BUSINESS SUP.	CHICAGO
.	.	.
.	.	.
.	.	.

DIAGRAM 7.17 (B)

PARTNO	SUPPLIERNO	QOH
P1	S1	5
P1	S2	3
P2	S1	2
P2	S2	4
.	.	.
.	.	.
.	.	.

DIAGRAM 7.17 (C)

7.2.2.2 Over-decomposition

Whenever we construct files, there is a danger of over-decomposition. To over-decompose is to break up a file into too many pieces. For example, consider an employee file that contains SSN, NAME, and ADDRESS. Even if the only dependencies in the file are of NAME and ADDRESS upon SSN, we might still decompose the file into two files, each having SSN as the key. Then the first file would have the fields SSN and NAME, and the second file would have the fields SSN and ADDRESS. What, if anything, have we gained and what have we lost?

This type of decomposition *never* gains us anything and is always expensive in terms of time. Over-decomposition has no advantages and, if we wish to determine both the name and the address from the social security number, then it is quite time-consuming. The general rule to avoid over-decomposition is: If two files have exactly the same key, and if the combination of the two files introduces no bad dependencies, then the two files *must* be combined.

7.2.3 DATA CLUSTERING: A SPEED TECHNIQUE

In previous sections in this chapter, we have seen how to construct a collection of data and index files that will give us the greatest degree of flexibility. Using files constructed in this manner, we will be able to access all the data, we will be able to easily add (or delete) both fields and records (files), and we will easily be able to add (or delete) indexes as needed. This type of file system also helps us see the real nature of the data that we are working with, since it is as simple as we can make it. At this point, our collection of files has little or no redundancy. The lack of redundancy will simplify file maintenance, but it will probably make certain types of processing slow.

To understand this problem, let us look at a collection of files constructed in the manner described earlier in this chapter.

EXAMPLE:

A personnel department keeps records on all their employees, present and past. The type of information maintained by this department includes each of the following data items:

EMPLOYEE File
1. Name
2. Address
3. Social security number

DEPARTMENT File
1. Department name
2. Department number

WORK HISTORY File
1. Social security number
2. Department number
3. Date started work in department
4. Date terminated work in department

These three files really have no unnecessary duplication, since both the social security number and the department number are necessary for identification purposes in the WORK HISTORY file (in fact, the combination of these two fields constitutes the key for this file). These three files satisfy all the rules previously given in this chapter for the construction of a good file system, but there may still be some speed problems.

If we wish to print a report that shows, for a single department, a list of all the employees that have ever worked in that department, in order by starting date, we will probably perform the following steps:

1. Obtain the number of the department
2. Find all the records in the WORK HISTORY file for this department (access the records in date order or sort to put in the proper date order), and
3. For each record selected from the WORK HISTORY file, print the employee name and the starting data

In order to perform Step 3, we will need the name of the employee for each record selected. The records that we are looking at are in the WORK HISTORY file, but the employee names are in the EMPLOYEE file. Thus, for each record selected from the WORK HISTORY file, we will have to make a separate access to the EMPLOYEE file. If we are working with large files, it might take 1 second to find each required name. If the number of employees that has worked in a specific department is 1000, then the amount of time required to print this simple report is at least 1000 seconds, or almost 17 minutes.

Note that just about all the time required for the report came from accessing the EMPLOYEE file to obtain the names of the employees. If, whenever we enter a new record into the WORK HISTORY file, we take the name of the employee from the EMPLOYEE file and copy it into the WORK HISTORY file record, we will save about 17 minutes each time the above mentioned report is produced.

What have we really done in the above example? We have a process that can be performed with our current collection of files (and indexes), but it is too slow. We decide to speed up this process by carefully duplicating selected information. By doing so, we break some of the rules presented earlier in this chapter, since we have a field in the new EMPLOYEE WORK file that is dependent only upon part of the key: the key consists of the combination of SOCIAL SECURITY NUMBER and DEPARTMENT NUMBER, but the EMPLOYEE NAME is dependent only upon part of the key, the SOCIAL SECURITY NUMBER.

The *careful* duplication of fields in order to speed up selected processes is called DATA CLUSTERING. Since data clustering forces us to break some of the rules that we have set for ourselves, we must now examine the consequences of doing so. The duplication of the employee name in the WORK HISTORY file will:

1. Take extra space, and
2. Make name changes more difficult.

In general, because data clustering forces us to change our collection of files and to put them into a form in which file maintenance is more difficult, we must carefully decide if we wish to use data clustering.

I recommend the following approach to file design:

1. First design the files so that they are in the best form.
2. Determine from the prospective users (the clients) which operations will be performed frequently.
3. Use data clustering and the other speed techniques introduced in this book to speed up those processes that you know will be so time-consuming that the users cannot live with them.
4. As the users gain familiarity with the system that you have constructed for them and as the size of each of the files grows, more speed problems may appear. Make the appropriate modifications to speed up the system.

7.2.4 CHOOSING INDEXES

Once you have chosen a structure for your files in dBASE III Plus, you can easily choose indexes. The indexes can be chosen either at the time that you create the files, or they can be added at a later time. dBASE III Plus allows you to add or delete an index at any time. The basic technique is as follows:

1. Look at your diagrams and determine how access is to be made.
2. For each access, determine the field or combination of fields to be used for the access.
3. If the field required for one access constitutes the leading substring of the combination of fields needed for another access, then delete the first access from the list.

EXAMPLE:

One access is based on a customer ID and another access is based on the combination of the customer ID and the date. The first access can be disregarded, since the second one (the one using the combination) can serve for both of the accesses.

4. For each field or combination of fields in the access list, create an index. If only one field is used, create the index using a statement of the form:

```
INDEX ON A TO A
```

where A is the name of the field. If a combination of fields is to be used, create the index using a statement of the form:

```
INDEX ON B+C TO <index file name>
```

where we assume that both B and C are character strings. If either B or C is not a character string, use the appropriate dBASE III Plus functions to convert one or both of them to character strings in the INDEX statement. You can continue to store the actual data in the database file in any form that you wish. In the example used above, where the index is to be on a combination of the customer ID and the date, the INDEX statement might look like:

```
INDEX ON ORDCUSID+DTOC(ORDDATE) TO ORDCDATE
```

CHAPTER

8

Local Area Networks

8.1 INTRODUCTION

In most environments, a *local area network* (LAN) is merely a collection of microcomputers that are linked together via communication lines and that share data and programs in a predetermined manner. One of the microcomputers, or micros (possibly two or more) is usually designated as the *server* and has a hard disk that is used to store the data and the programs that are used by a variety of users in the organization. All the micros in the LAN other than the server are often called *workstations*. In many cases, a special communications board is inserted in each micro in the network and the combination of this additional hardware and special communication software form the basis of the network.

The designation of one of the micros as the server allows a number of users to access the data and programs stored on the server's hard disk, and the LAN handles most of the problems with multiple access requests. If two requests for access to programs or data are received at the same time, then the LAN decides which request to honor first and stores the other request to be honored later.

The use of a LAN can dramatically increase the usefulness of organizational data, because it makes the data simultaneously available to a wide variety of users. This situation dictates that access to the data (and the programs) must be carefully controlled. Members of the organization whose jobs require access to the data should be able to access it without undue delay. All others should be denied access to the data unless they have special permission. Since several micros are linked to the server, it may not be possible to provide physical security for the data. For example, it may not be possible to place all the computers in the network in a locked room. It is therefore necessary to provide a measure of security through some other means. Another problem that arises is associated with multiple users of databases. If two people are using a database file at the same time, and one of the users closes the file as a result of a CLOSE DATABASES, a USE, or a QUIT statement, then the database file must appear closed to the first user but still appear open to the other user. As a result of these problems caused by the existence of multiple users of the same database files, dBASE III Plus must provide special software to handle these situations.

The number of LANs on the market is growing quite rapidly. Today's standard LANs may be joined by several others in the near future, so you should check the current list of LAN hardware and software supported by dBASE III Plus before you purchase a LAN system. At the time of the writing of this book, dBASE III Plus supports the following processors:

Intel 8086

Intel 8088

Intel 80286

The required operating system is PC DOS 3.1 or higher, or its equivalent. The network systems supported are:

1. NOVELL Advanced Network/86, version 1.01 and higher, using the NETWARE Server Board
2. IBM PC Network Program, version 1.0 and higher, using the Network Adapter Card
3. 3COM 3 +

There is also a requirement for the amount of main memory (RAM) in the server and in each workstation, together with a requirement for a floppy disk drive at each workstation. In addition, you may need to adjust the number of files and buffers for each network.

8.2 AN OVERVIEW OF THE dBASE III PLUS NETWORK SYSTEM

The system can be broken down into three main parts: ADMINISTRATOR, ACCESS, and PROTECT. ADMINISTRATOR is an extended (network) version of the single-user dBASE III Plus system and is run on the server; ACCESS is a program that is run at each workstation and interacts with ADMINISTRATOR; and PROTECT is a utility program that is used to protect access to the database files. No user can make direct access to dBASE III on the server. Access is provided as a result of the user's communicating with the ACCESS program at the workstation and as a result of ACCESS's communicating with ADMINISTRATOR on the server. The use of PROTECT as a part of your LAN is optional, so you can use the database system in an open environment if you wish. If you wish to protect access to your data, you can use this option and all access from that point on will be protected.

8.3 THE PROTECT PROGRAM

PROTECT allows you to associate an access privilege with each user and establish access levels with files. If the user has an access privilege at least as powerful as the one required by a file, then access is granted. There are eight levels of access privileges, numbered 1 through 8. The power of the access privilege is related to the number, with the lower numbers indicating a more powerful access privilege.

The file access types are Read, Extend, Update, and Delete, and an access level can be assigned to a file for each of these types of access. If the access privilege number of a user is less than or equal to the number required for access, then the user is granted access. In addition to access levels for four different types of access, it is also possible to assign an access type for each field in a database. The access types for fields are: Full, Read only, and None. Notice that numbers are not used to describe access privileges to fields. Access privileges are assigned for DBF files and their associated index files only. DBT files cannot be protected in this manner.

When the PROTECT program is used, the database files are encrypted and can be accessed only through ADMINISTRATOR. Encryption is automatically performed when you specify the access privileges and save the privilege information. When the database is encrypted, an encrypted copy is created and the encrypted version of the database is given an extension of CRP. It is a good idea to save a copy of the empty, unencrypted database file for future reference. You will need to delete the original DBF file yourself from your work disk and then rename the CRP file so that it has a DBF extension. You do not need to take any action to encrypt the index files. All maintenance of the index files is performed for you by dBASE.

8.4 ACCESS PRIVILEGES AND GROUP MEMBERSHIP

Access privileges are given to the user each time he or she logs on to the system. As part of the log-in procedure, the user must provide a group name, a user name, and a password. Access to a database file is determined by group membership. If a user is a member of a group that has access to a file, then the type of access associated with the group is granted to the user. If a user is a member of more than one group, he or she can specify which group to use at log-in time and therefore select the files and the access privileges to be used during the current session.

When PROTECT is used, a security file named DBSYSTEM.DB is created or modified. This file is maintained in encrypted form. Each of the records in this file contains a group name, a user name, a password, and the associated access level. When a user successfully logs on, the access privilege information (the profile) is obtained from this file. If DBSYSTEM.DB is not available when the user logs on, then none of the encrypted files can be used.

8.5 USING THE PROTECT PROGRAM

To run PROTECT, enter the command PROTECT followed by a RETURN at the DOS level. Each time that you use PROTECT, you will need to enter a password. This protects the system from unauthorized use of the PROTECT program. When PROTECT is used for the first time, you will need to enter the (new) password twice, ensuring that it is entered correctly. Every time that you subsequently use PROTECT, you will need to enter the password only once. When you have successfully envoked PROTECT and entered the correct password, a menu bar is placed on the screen. The items in the menu bar are: Users, Files, and Exit (see figure on p. 314).

The Users menu item is used to create, change, or delete a user profile. The profile consists of a log-in name, a group name, an account name, and an access level. The log-in name, the group name, and the password are used to verify access rights at log-in time. The user (or account) name is not used in the verification procedure. It is included in the profile almost as a comment, so that the person responsible for setting up the profiles can tell who has been granted which access privileges. In order to save the current selection entered with the Users menu item on the screen, you must store the information using the Store User Profile option in this menu. Then, when you select the Exit menu item and save the changes, the information entered through the Users menu item is actually stored in a file. Individual user access information (a profile) is stored in the DBCONFIG.DB filc.

The Files menu item is used to associate a group name and access levels with a file and to set the access level and privileges for each field. More than one file can be associated with a group and more than one group can be associated with a file. You can create a new group record or change existing information. In order to save the current selection

```
Users                          Files                         Exit 02:29:14 pm
 Login name
 Password
 Group name
 Account name
 Access level          1
 Store user profile
 Delete user from group

 PROTECT | <C:> |  | Opt | 1/7 |  | Caps
        Position selection bar - ↑ ↓.  Select - ↵.  Leave menu - ←→.
                    Enter the login name for this user.
```

entered with the Files menu item on the screen, you must store the information using the Store File Privileges option in this menu. Then, when you select the Exit menu item and save the changes, the information entered through the Files menu item is actually stored in a file. Group access information is stored right with the database file itself.

Your LAN system may allow you to specify access privileges for files. As a result, you might use PROTECT to specify an access privilege that is even more restrictive than that which is allowed by the LAN.

Note:
PROTECT can store profiles for no more than 10 database files at a time. If you wish to assign profiles to more than 10 database files, save the current profiles and then continue. Remember that access decreases as the level increases, that is, number 1 has the highest privilege and number 8 has the lowest.

EXAMPLE:

Select the Files item from the menu bar and assign number 6 as the delete privilege level. Then all the users in this group with an access level less than or equal to 6 will have deletion privileges, but those with an access level greater than 6 will not have this privilege.

Once you have established the group access level for each of the types of file access (Read, Update, Extend, and Delete), you can then establish an access level for each field. Again, if the access level for a member of the group is less than or equal to the field access level, then access to the fields is granted. Once access to the field has been obtained, the Field Privileges (Full, Read only, and None) determine what the user can do with the field. For the group as a whole, there is at most one field privilege associated with a field. This restriction applies to each member of the group. If you wish to allow access to a field so that one user has one field privilege and another user has a different privilege, then they must belong to different groups.

8.6 ACCESSING THE DATABASE FILES

As long as there can be more than one simultaneous user of a database file, it must be possible to control access so that two or more users are not trying to change the same record at the same time. In addition, there must be some way to make sure that the indexes correctly match the database file. If access is not correctly controlled, the system "locks up" and is said to be deadlocked.

In dBASE III Plus one of two access modes is assigned to a file when it is opened: exclusive mode or shared mode. If a file is opened in exclusive mode, only one user at a time can access the database. Exclusive mode guarantees that there will be no problems with simultaneous use of the database, because it does not allow it. On the other hand, allowing access to just one user at a time may not be what you want from a LAN. Shared access allows simultaneous use of the database by more than one user, but there must be some way to control this access. It may be necessary to switch from shared mode to exclusive mode, temporarily gaining exclusive access to the database file or to one specific record in the database, and then switching back to shared mode. A temporary switch to exclusive access is called "locking the database" or "locking the record," as appropriate.

Note:
A file cannot be shared unless it is in a directory that has been designated to store shared files. Shared directories are created by the installation program named

INSTALL.BAT or ADMINISTRATOR DISK #1

Even if a file is contained in a directory for shared files, you can open it in either shared or exclusive mode. A file that is not stored in a directory for shared files can only be opened in exclusive mode. The default mode for opening any database file is exclusive access. In order to open a file in shared mode, use the

```
SET EXCLUSIVE OFF
```

statement before the file is opened. Files that are already open are not affected by the use of the SET EXCLUSIVE statement. You can open some of the files that you need in one mode and then open more in the other mode. Index and memo files are always opened in the same mode as the associated database file.

Note:
Make sure to SET EXCLUSIVE OFF for shared files in your application system.

8.7 ACCESS MODES AND NETWORK PROGRAMMING

Some of the dBASE III Plus statements change the current access mode and some can be used only if a particular mode is in effect. This information is given in the following three lists:

Statements That Change the Access Mode to Shared
CHANGE
EDIT
The ASSISTANT

Statements That Require Exclusive Access As the Current Mode
INSERT
MODIFY STRUCTURE
PACK
REINDEX
ZAP

Statements That Cause a Shared File to Be Locked

APPEND	COUNT	REPLACE ALL
AVERAGE	DELETE ALL	SORT
BROWSE	INDEX	SUM
COPY	JOIN	TOTAL
COPY STRUCTURE	RECALL ALL	UPDATE

Note:
Each of the statements in this list actually use all the records in the file. If dBASE attempts to lock the file for you and it is currently being accessed by another user, then the attempt to lock the file will fail and an error will occur. It is possible to trap the error and try again. When each of these commands has been completed, the database is automatically unlocked for you.

If you would like to lock a shared file in preparation for a statement that requires exclusive access, you can explicitly lock it yourself after it has been opened. After you have completed the desired operation, you can later release or unlock the file. If you need exclusive access to just one record at a time, you can lock just the one record, perform the desired operations, and then unlock it. In general, record locking is more desirable than file locking, since it is less restrictive.

dBASE does not always handle potential deadlocks in an elegant manner. Rather, in many cases, the programmer is responsible to make sure that a deadlock cannot happen. A deadlock can possibly occur in a number of situations. Some of these situations and comments on how to avoid or recover from a deadlock are:

1. When a user attempts to lock a file or record already locked by another user: The FLOCK, RLOCK, and LOCK functions are used to avoid this problem.
2. When two users have each opened a database for exclusive access, they each want to open another file for exclusive access, and the file that each one is waiting to open has already been locked (opened for exclusive access) by the other user, then each user might wait indefinitely: The program must count how long a user has waited for the file. If you wait beyond the accepted time, release all currently locked records and files (so that someone else can continue) and then either give up or retry the entire process.
3. When two or more users access a database file at the same time for sequential access: This can be handled by the correct use of the

RLOCK or the LOCK functions. Just lock each record one at a time, as needed, and then release it.

4. When a needed file is not available for an extended period of time (because it is locked): Either wait for the file to become available or abort the operation.

A deadlock is often a situation where two programs (or users) are each waiting for a database (or other resource) controlled by the other. Neither program (or user) can proceed, since each is waiting for the other. A deadlock can also occur in dBASE III Plus (in the network environment) if two or more users attempt to access a database file in a manner other than the approved one, for example, if two users attempt sequential access to a database file and at least one of them does not lock records before appending, changing, or deleting records.

Two functions are provided by dBASE to help avoid a deadlock. The function FLOCK can be used to lock a file and the function RLOCK can be used to lock a record. The LOCK function is an alternative to RLOCK, and is completely equivalent to RLOCK. If the file or record is already locked, then the function returns the value .F. (FALSE), indicating that the attempt to lock failed. If the file or record is not locked when the function is invoked, then the file or record is locked and the function returns the value .T. (TRUE), indicating that the attempt to lock succeeded. These functions are used as follows:

1. First open the desired files in shared mode, and
2. Then attempt to lock the desired records or files by using the appropriate function.

You can release a lock by using the UNLOCK statement, by locking another file or record, or by closing the database. Note that you cannot lock more than one record or one file through the use of the FLOCK or RLOCK functions at any one time. If you need to work with more than one file at a time and both of them must be locked, then open them in exclusive access mode (open with EXCLUSIVE set ON).

If you are interactively editing a record (a procedure that I do not recommend in the LAN environment), you must lock it before you can update or change it. Use the toggle ^O (CTRL-O) to lock and then unlock a record. If you move away from a locked record or you terminate editing, the record is automatically unlocked for you.

Warning:
In a program in the LAN environment, never use an expression of the form

IF FLOCK( ) = .T.

Rather, use an expression of the form

IF FLOCK( )

This caution applies to all three of the lock functions.

Note that you must lock a record in a shared environment before you can change it. In particular, you must use FLOCK to lock the file or use RLOCK to lock the record before you use an @ . . GET . . READ or a REPLACE statement.

8.8 NETWORK COMMANDS AND FUNCTIONS

TABLE 8.1 Network Commands

CATEGORY	COMMAND	DESCRIPTION
Control	SET ENCRYPTION	Turn Encryption mode on or off
	SET EXCLUSIVE	Determine the access mode
	UNLOCK	Release locks
	USE EXCLUSIVE	Open a file in exclusive mode
Editing	EDIT	Modify record content
	CHANGE	Modify record content
Output	SET PRINTER	Select output device
Programming	RETRY	Exit from the current program and re-enter it
Security	LOGOUT	Log the current user off the system
Status	DISPLAY STATUS	Display program and environment status
	DISPLAY USERS	Display a list of current workstations
	LIST STATUS	Display program and environment status

8.8.1 THE COMMANDS

Note that some of the commands (statements) used in the LAN environment are extensions of statements that are used in the single-user environment.

**CHANGE [<scope>][FIELDS <list of field names>]
[FOR/WHILE <condition>]**

See Chapter 2 for a description of this command. In the LAN environment, file status (whether the file is locked or unlocked) and access rights are also displayed. Use ˆO (CTRL-O) to lock and unlock a record from the keyboard in interactive mode.

**EDIT [<scope>][FIELDS <list of field names>]
[FOR/WHILE <condition>]**

The EDIT command is equivalent to the CHANGE command.

DISPLAY STATUS [TO PRINT]

See Chapter 2 for a description of this command. In the LAN environment, the current status of SET ENCRYPTION and SET EXCLUSIVE are also given. When the information for the currently open database files is given, locked records and files are also indicated (see figure on the next page).

DISPLAY USERS

Display the names of the workstations currently running under dBASE in network mode.

LIST STATUS [TO PRINT]

See Chapter 2 for a description of this command. In the LAN environment, the current status of SET ENCRYPTION and SET EXCLUSIVE are also given. When the information for the currently open database files is given, locked records and files are also indicated (see figure on the next page).

LOGOUT

Close all open database and associated files, log out the current user, clear the screen, display the log-in menu on the screen, and wait for input of the group name, user name, and password. You can use this command to force a user to log off the system. You can use this statement in a program to control the number of times that a user

```
Currently Selected Database:
Select area:  1, Database in Use: C:\BOOK\CHARGES.dbf    Alias: CHARGES
          Lock:

File search path:
Default disk drive: C:
Print destination:  PRN:
Margin =     0
Current work area =    1

ALTERNATE - OFF   DELETED    - OFF   EXCLUSIVE - ON    PRINT      - OFF
BELL      - ON    DELIMITERS - OFF   FIELDS    - OFF   SAFETY     - ON
CARRY     - OFF   DEVICE     - SCRN  FIXED     - OFF   SCOREBOARD - ON
CATALOG   - OFF   DOHISTORY  - OFF   HEADING   - ON    STATUS     - OFF
CENTURY   - OFF   ECHO       - OFF   HELP      - ON    STEP       - OFF
CONFIRM   - OFF   ENCRYPTION - ON    HISTORY   - ON    TALK       - ON
CONSOLE   - ON    ESCAPE     - ON    INTENSITY - ON    TITLE      - ON
DEBUG     - OFF   EXACT      - OFF   MENU      - ON    UNIQUE     - OFF

Programmable function keys:
F2  - assist;
F3  - list;
F4  - dir;
F5  - display structure;
F6  - display status;
F7  - display memory;
F8  - display;
F9  - append;
F10 - MODIFY COMMAND
```

attempts to log on. For example, you can count the number of attempted log-ins and log the user off after the maximum allowable number of attempts (see figure on p. 322).

RETRY

See Chapter 2 for a description of this command. This statement can be of particular use in the LAN environment, because you may be attempting to access a file or record that has been locked by another user. If an error occurs when you attempt to access the file or record, an ON ERROR statement can call a routine that examines the situation, waits as appropriate, retries a designated number of times, and then aborts.

```
dBASE ADMINISTRATOR Login

Enter group name
Enter your name
Enter password
```

EXAMPLE:

```
* RECOVER.PRG
* EXECUTE AS A RESULT OF AN ERROR CONDITION
IF ERROR( ) = 158
      TIMER = 1
      DO WHILE TIMER < 100
            TIMER = TIMER + 1
      ENDDO
      * TIMES IS A GLOBAL VARIABLE THAT COUNTS THE
      * NUMBER OF RETRIES. IT IS INITIALIZED IN
      * THE CALLING ROUTINE.
      TIMES = TIMES + 1
      IF TIMES < 10
            RETRY
      ELSE
            ? "FILE IS LOCKED"
            <error processing here>
      ENDIF
ELSE
      <other processing goes here>
ENDIF
```

SET

When used in the LAN environment, the OPTIONS menu of the SET command includes entries for both ENCRYPTION and EXCLUSIVE (see figure on the next page).

SET ENCRYPTION ON/OFF DEFAULT: ON

If ENCRYPTION is ON, then database files created as a result of the COPY, JOIN, SORT, or TOTAL are encrypted. Files that have been encrypted are available to any authorized user, that is, a user who

```
Options    Screen    Keys    Disk    Files    Margin    Decimals    03:37:55 pm

 Alternate     OFF
 Bell          ON
 Carry         OFF
 Catalog
 Century       OFF
 Confirm       OFF
 Deleted       OFF
 Delimiters    OFF
 Device        SCREEN
 Dohistory     OFF
 Encryption    ON
 Escape        ON
 Exact         OFF
 Exclusive     ON
 Fields        OFF
 Fixed         OFF
 Heading       ON
 Help          ON

 Set          |<C:>|              |Opt |1/27      |     |Caps
     Position selection bar - ↑ ↓.  Change - ↵.  Leave menu - ←→. Exit - Esc.
                    Specify the dBASE III environment options.
```

provides valid information at log-in. Access to a database file encrypted in this manner follows the same rules as any other database file. The access control assigned to this type of file is the same as the access control assigned to the source database. If you have access to an encrypted file, you can set ENCRYPTION OFF and produce a copy of the file that is not encrypted.

Note:
You can COPY to a nondatabase file (a file with an extension other than DBF) only if ENCRYPTION is OFF.

SET EXCLUSIVE ON/OFF DEFAULT: ON

This command is used to establish the access mode (exclusive or shared) for database files that are opened during the current session. Changing the value of EXCLUSIVE does not affect the access mode of a file that is already open. Set EXCLUSIVE to ON to open a file in exclusive mode (not shared) and OFF to open a file in shared mode.

Note:
In a single-user environment, EXCLUSIVE is always ON, even if you attempt to set it OFF.

SET PRINTER TO [<device name>]

Use this statement to redirect output to a local printer (one connected directly to your own workstation). You can select LPT1, LPT2, LPT3, PRN, COM1, or COM2 as the <device name>. To empty the print queue and select the default printer, use the statement without the option. The default printer is the shared network printer.

EXAMPLES:

```
SET PRINTER TO LPT1
SET PRINTER TO
```

SET PRINTER TO [\\SPOOLER]

Use this statement when you desire to redirect printer output to the Novell network printer. To empty the print queue and select the default printer, use the statement without the option. The default printer is the shared network printer.

EXAMPLES:

```
SET PRINTER TO \\SPOOLER
SET PRINTER TO
```

SET PRINTER TO [\\<workstation name>\ <printer name> = <device name>]

Use this statement to redirect printer output to an IBM network printer. The <workstation name> is the name that the network has assigned to the workstation, <printer name> is the name of the network printer, and <device name> is LPT1, LPT2, or LPT3. To empty the print queue and select the default printer, use the statement without the option. The default printer is the shared network printer.

EXAMPLES:

```
SET PRINTER TO \\WKSTN1\PRINTER=LPT1
SET PRINTER TO
```

UNLOCK [ALL]

Use UNLOCK to unlock the current file or record lock in the current area. Use the ALL option to unlock all locks in all areas.

USE [<database file name>] [INDEX <list of index names>] EXCLUSIVE [ALIAS <alias name>]

See Chapter 2 for specific information on the USE statement. The appearance of EXCLUSIVE in the statement indicates that the database file and its associated index files should be opened in exclusive access mode.

Note:
If the named file is already open, it is closed and reopened in EXCLUSIVE access mode.

8.8.2 THE FUNCTIONS

ACCESS( ) RETURN TYPE: NUMERIC

Return the integer that identifies the access privilege of the user. Once you have obtained this integer, you can use it to determine additional or replacement privileges. For example, if a user's privilege level is 5, then, for some files, you can prohibit access even

TABLE 8.2 Network Functions

CATEGORY	FUNCTION	DESCRIPTION
Access Rights	ACCESS	Return the access level of user that logged in last
Error	ERROR	Return the code for the most recent error
	MESSAGE	Return an error message
Lock	FLOCK	Attempt to lock the current file
	LOCK	Attempt to lock the current record
	RLOCK	Same function as LOCK

though the required privilege is 5 or higher. Typical code might be

```
IF ACCESS( ) = 5 .AND. <additional conditions>
      <prohibit access>
ELSE
      <allow access>
ENDIF
```

You can also use this function to establish access privileges in a nonstandard manner. Instead of associating a user group and a file, it is possible to assign an access privilege to each individual user and then always perform the test for access privileges in the application programs. If you use this technique, you are effectively assigning an access level of 8 to the files and then checking the access privileges of each user yourself instead of letting dBASE check the access privileges.

Note:
In a single-user environment, ACCESS always returns the value zero (0).

ERROR( ) RETURN TYPE: NUMERIC

See Chapter 2 for a description of this function. See also the entry for the RETRY statement earlier in this chapter for an example of its usage.

FLOCK( ) RETURN TYPE: LOGICAL

Use this function to lock the current database file. If the attempt to lock the file is successful, then the value .T. (TRUE) is returned. If the file is already locked, the attempt is unsuccessful and the value .F. (FALSE) is returned. After the user has completed the desired operation, the file should be UNLOCKed as soon as possible. The FLOCK function should only be used when access to the entire database file is required; otherwise RLOCK or LOCK should be used. In particular, if you can perform your operations on a record-by-record basis, then do not use FLOCK. If it is necessary to lock a file using the FLOCK function, you will probably want to do it under program control rather than interactively, so as not to deny access to qualified users.

EXAMPLE:

```
SELECT A            && THE FILE IS CURRENTLY SHARED
IF FLOCK( )
     SORT TO NEWA ON AFIELD
ENDIF
UNLOCK
```

MESSAGE( ) RETURN TYPE: CHARACTER

See the description of the MESSAGE function in Chapter 2.

LOCK( ) RETURN TYPE: LOGICAL

Use this function to lock the current record in the current database file. If the attempt to lock the record is successful, then the value .T. (TRUE) is returned. If the record is already locked, the attempt is unsuccessful and the value .F. (FALSE) is returned. After the user has completed the desired operation, the record should be UNLOCKed as soon as possible. Use LOCK or RLOCK, rather than FLOCK, whenever the records are accessed individually. In particular, use one of these functions when a file is being updated interactively. More than one user can interactively and simultaneously update a database file, if each user locks records only as needed.

RLOCK( ) RETURN TYPE: LOGICAL

This function is equivalent in all ways to LOCK.

CHAPTER

9

C Tools: The Programmer's Library

9.1 INTRODUCTION

As users put pressure on Ashton-Tate to provide more features in dBASE III Plus, expect to see new releases or versions of this product. Since the production of new versions requires a considerable expenditure of time and money, alternative approaches need to be found. An alternative to new versions is economically desirable if it allows users to upgrade their original version of dBASE III Plus themselves with the new features, thereby saving Ashton-Tate both time and money. After a reasonable amount of time, Ashton-Tate will probably incorporate many of these new features in a new version of dBASE III Plus. The technique of having users performing their own updates allows Ashton-Tate to reduce the total number of new versions that they release and to increase the amount of time between releases.

Since dBASE III Plus is written in the C language, the alternative approach adopted by Ashton-Tate is to provide additional routines that can be added to the C library on your computer. You can then include these routines in your copy of dBASE III Plus when you link the C programs together. Ashton-Tate provides a compiled version of dBASE III Plus (an OBJ file) for this purpose. Since you can place in your library any C routine that matches the dBASE III Plus interface specifications, you can even write your own routines to be added to dBASE.

The two products of this type that have been distributed by Ashton-Tate (for an additional fee) are called *dBASE Tools for C: The Programmer's Library* and *The Graphics Library*. A supplementary disk containing some additions to and replacements for items in the The Programmer's Library (the Incentive Disk) is also available. The Programmers Library is discussed in this chapter and The Graphics Library is discussed in Chapter 10.

Not all the C compilers on the market can be used to compile the C routines that you have created yourself. The compilers that can currently be used are:

1. Lattice C, version 2.15 (large model)
2. Lattice C, version 3.0 (large model)
3. Microsoft C, version 3.0 (large model)
4. Aztec C Prime (small model)

In addition, not all the C routines will work with all the compilers. See the README and README.TOO files on the distribution disks for compatibility information.

The Programmer's Library distribution disks come organized by directories. Important information (README files) may be found in the root directory of the disk and information and files appropriate to a specific compiler may come in individual directories.

9.2 INSTALLING THE PROGRAMMER'S LIBRARY

1. Install dBASE on your hard disk (drive C).
2. Copy the files from A:\DBDIR\ to drive C.
3. Select the type of compiler that you will use and copy all the files from the appropriate directory on the distribution disk. For example, if you will use the Lattice C compiler, version 2.15, copy the files from A:\LC2\ to drive C. Use \AZ\ for the Aztec compiler; \L2\ for Lattice version 2.15; \LC3\ for Lattice version 3.0; and \MS\ for the Microsoft compiler. Note especially that the files DCTMISC.LIB and each of

   AZ_CATCH.LIB
   L2_CATCH.LIB
   L3_CATCH.LIB
   MS_CATCH.LIB

   are compiler specific.
4. Copy the files from A:\SOURCE\ to drive C.
5. Make sure that your C compiler is installed on your hard disk in the expected manner. For example, if you are using Lattice C, version 2.15, the instructions that come with the compiler instruct you to install certain files in the directory \LC\ and certain files in the directory \LC\C\. The examples of compiler commands supplied by Ashton-Tate for The Programmer's Library assume that you have followed the Lattice instructions.

9.3 GETTING READY TO USE C TOOLS

Before you run dBASE III Plus, run the program DCT1.EXE, provided on the distribution disk. If you do not have an EXE version of this program, you can make one by compiling and linking the appropriate programs. The instructions are either in the manual that accompanied The Programmer's Library, or they are in a README file on the disk. Note that some of the versions of DCT1 may not allow the use of the Microsoft linker. For example, if you are using Lattice C, version 2.15, Ashton-Tate assumes that you are using the Phoenix PLINK86 linker, not the Microsoft linker. DCT1 installs The Programmer's Library and also reserves room in memory for arrays through the use of an optional parameter. The syntax of the DCT1 command is:

```
DCT1 [<space in kilobytes>]
```

If the parameter is not used, then the default value is 10K bytes when the Aztec C compiler is used and 16K bytes when the Lattice and Microsoft compilers are used.

Note:
If you do not expect to use any arrays, use a parameter of zero (0).

After you have run DCT1.EXE, run dBASE and then interactively or under program control enter the command

```
LOAD CFUNC
```

Note that CFUNC.BIN is a file provided on the distribution disk. It provides the interface between dBASE III Plus and the C programs. The interface is not the cleanest I have seen, but it does work. In general, CFUNC is a function that accepts a character string as its only parameter, calls the desired C routine, and then passes the appropriate parameters to this routine. The character string passed to CFUNC will contain the name of the C function to be executed, together with its required parameters. Before a C function can be executed, it is necessary to initialize both the dBASE III Plus variables used as parameters to send data to the C function and the variables used to receive data returned by the function.

When initializing numeric return variables, initialize them with a value (probably zero) that will establish the correct decimal precision (number of places to the right of the decimal). This sets the precision for display purposes, not for storage. Numeric data is always returned with a precision of 15.9. A character string return variable must be initialized (using the SPACE function) to the correct size, that is, to a size greater than or equal to the size of the string to be returned. You may wish to initialize six (6) different return variables, one for each type of data that can be returned. The interface between dBASE III Plus can use no more than six return variables, one variable for each type of data to be returned. Note also that a C function can return only one value at a time.

Ashton-Tate recommends, for documentation purposes and to match their programming convention, that you initialize these six specific memory (return) variables with data similar to the following:

```
C_C_RESULT = SPACE(35), for a character string
C_N_RESULT = 0.0000, with the correct number of digits to
             the right of the decimal point
C_L_RESULT = .T., for a logical value
C_D_RESULT = CTOD("01/01/84"), for a date
C_STATUS   = 0, for a status code, and
C_ERROR    = 0, for an error code
```

Once you have initialized your return variables, you must also inform the interface of your choice of name and type for each return variable. You must supply the name (address) and data type of each variable. The description of each of these six dBASE memory variables is passed to the interface in the following manner:

```
CALL CFUNC WITH "SETDVAR <data type>"
CALL CFUNC WITH <the name of the memory variable>
```

with the function calls entered in precisely the given order. In addition, each of the memory variables must be declared public and initialized before use in the second CFUNC call. Do this for each of the return variables that you expect to use. If you are using functions that return only numbers and character strings, then you need to define only two return variables. It is necessary to define only one return variable of each data type, since a C function can return only one value and since the functions are used just one at a time. In the above function calls, the allowable <data type>'s are single letters as shown in Table 9.1:

TABLE 9.1

DATA TYPE	MEANING
C	Character string
D	Date
E	Error (an integer)
L	Logical
N	Numeric
S	Status (an integer)

EXAMPLE:

```
PUBLIC C_N_RESULT
C_N_RESULT = 0.000
CALL CFUNC WITH "SETDVAR N"
CALL CFUNC WITH C_N_RESULT
```

I recommend that you create a PRG file that contains all your PUBLIC, CALL, and initialization statements. You might also want to include the LOAD CFUNC statement in this file. A sample PRG file for this purpose is:

```
* CFUNC.PRG
* EXECUTE THE STATEMENTS FOR THE INTERFACE
LOAD CFUNC.BIN
PUBLIC C_N_RESULT, C_C_RESULT, C_ERROR, ;
  C_STATUS
C_N_RESULT=0.00
C_C_RESULT=SPACE(35)
C_ERROR=0
C_STATUS=0
CALL CFUNC WITH "SETDVAR N"
CALL CFUNC WITH C_N_RESULT
CALL CFUNC WITH "SETDVAR E"
CALL CFUNC WITH C_ERROR
CALL CFUNC WITH "SETDVAR S"
CALL CFUNC WITH C_STATUS
CALL CFUNC WITH "SETDVAR C"
CALL CFUNC WITH C_C_RESULT
```

Warning:
Because the interface between dBASE III Plus and the C library uses a fixed address scheme, there are some potential problems when numbers and character strings are returned from C routines. In general, dBASE changes the memory location (address) of a variable whenever you change its type or its size. For example, if AX is a character string variable of length 6 and you assign a string of length 7 to it, then a new location in memory is used to hold the string of length 7. Since you establish the address of a return variable with the statement

```
CALL CFUNC WITH "SETDVAR <type>"
```

the interface always expects the return variable to be located at the given address. If you cause a change in address of the variable, the interface will no longer work properly. There are two possible solutions to this problem:

1. Never change a return value within a dBASE III program, or
2. Call the function, change the variable, use the variable, and then call the initialization sequence again to re-establish a correct interface. This is done by executing two statements of the form:

   ```
   CALL CFUNC WITH "SETDVAR <data type>"
   CALL CFUNC WITH <the name of the memory variable>
   ```

   where you might wish to use the same name for the variable that you originally did.

Note:
If you run DCT1, LOAD CFUNC, create arrays, and then exit from dBASE, the interface and the arrays remain in memory. As a result, if you do not disturb the interface, you can re-enter dBASE, LOAD CFUNC, and the arrays will still be recognized. In particular, STARRAY will give the name, size, and count of each of the arrays in existence during the previous usage of dBASE.

9.4 GENERAL SYNTAX OF THE TOOLS

All the tools are called with the following syntax:

```
CALL CFUNC WITH "<command>"
```

where <command> is a character string constant or variable that contains both the name of the C function and the required parameters. The name of the function is separated from the first parameter by a space and each of the other parameters is separated from the preceding parameter by a comma (,). Note that <command> must be delimited and that it can be delimited in the usual manner (by an apostrophe, quotation marks, or square brackets). The parameters can be memory variables, constants, or expressions, as allowed by the syntax of the individual functions.

Note that the CALL statement does not pass a value back in the manner that function calls or procedure calls do in C. Rather, a value is passed back to the interface buffer using the addresses that you established in the CALL . . SETDVAR statements, selecting the appropriate address by the type of the return value. If you have chosen C_N_RESULT as the name of the return variable (interface variable) and the function passes back a number, then C_N_RESULT does not appear in an assignment statement and does not appear in the parameter list, but will contain the value after the function has executed.

Square brackets "[ ]" are used in this chapter to indicate optional entries in the command string.

9.5 dBASE III PLUS SUPPLEMENTARY ROUTINES

A number of small dBASE III Plus programs are supplied with The Programmer's Library. They are designed to simplify the interface between dBASE III Plus and the C routines. They are valuable both as programs and as examples of how to call the C routines from dBASE III Plus programs. These routines can be found in the DBDIR directory of your distribution disk(s). In many cases, the simplification takes the following form: Instead of entering a CALL statement, a DO statement is used. The DO statement invokes the appropriate dBASE III Plus routine which in turn invokes the desired CALL . . CFUNC statement(s).

9.6 USER WRITTEN C FUNCTIONS

You can write your own functions to supplement the C functions provided in The Programmer's Library. In order to do this, a number of steps must be followed:

1. Write and compile the new function.
2. An entry must be made in DCT1.C to specify how the <command> should be parsed by the SETUP routine.
3. An entry must be made in DCT1.C to record the name of the new function, and
4. Compile and link DCT1.C.

Unfortunately, Ashton-Tate has not supplied any utilities to simplify the task of adding routines to The Programmer's Library—specifically to simplify Steps 2 and 3 above. Refer to The Programmer's Library documentation and sample programs on the distribution disk(s) for the specifics on the four items listed above.

9.7 THE FUNCTIONS IN THE PROGRAMMER'S LIBRARY

TABLE 9.2 C TOOLS

CATEGORY	NAME	DESCRIPTION
Array	ARAND	Fill an array with random numbers
	ARESTORE	Retrieve an array from a disk file
	ASAVE	Store an array in a disk
	COUNT	Count the number of entries in an array
	CRARRAY	Create an array
	DUMPARRAY	Dump contents of array to screen
	FDUMPARRAY	Dump contents of array to a file
	FRARRAY	Free (erase) an array
	GETARRAY	Extract a value from an array
	GETSIZE	Get the size of an array
	PUTARRAY	Store a value in an array
	RNARRAY	Rename an array
	STARRAY	Report status of arrays
Financial	AMORT	Amortization of a loan
	FV	Future value
	IRR	Internal rate of return
	MIRR	Modified internal rate of return
	NPV	Net present value
	PMT	Calculate loan payments
	PV	Present value
	SF	Calculate sinking fund amount
Help	HELP	List names of functions in the library
	MEMSTAT	Get memory status (Lattice only)
Interface	SETDVAR	Declare return variable

CATEGORY	NAME	DESCRIPTION
	SETBELL	Set error bell
	SETERR	Set error flag
	SOUND	Generate a tone
Input/Output	CLRWINDOW	Clear a window on the screen
	PUTWINDOW	Draw a window on the screen
Mathematical	MAX	Find the largest value
	MIN	Find the smallest value
	RAND	Generate a random number
	RANGE	Calculate the range
Memory	PEEK	Examine the contents of a memory location
	POKE	Store a value in a memory location
Comparison	EQN	Count for equal
	GEN	Count for greater than or equal
	GTN	Count for greater than
	LEN	Count for less than or equal
	LTN	Count for less than
Security	GETPASS	Get a password
Statistical	CHI	Chi-square distribution
	CORR	Correlation of two arrays
	COVAR	Covariance of two arrays
	CV	Coefficient of variance
	DIST	Frequency distribution
	KURT	Compute sample kurtosis
	MEAN	Calculate the mean
	MEDIAN	Calculate the median
	NSK	Normal scores
	ROS	Sort the contents of an array

CATEGORY	NAME	DESCRIPTION
	SKEW	Calculate skewedness (asymmetry)
	STDEV	Standard deviation
	VAR	Covariance of two arrays
Trigonometric	ACOS	Arccosine
	ASIN	Arcsine
	ATAN	Arctangent
	COS	Cosine
	SIN	Sine
	TAN	Tangent

MULTIDIMENSIONAL ARRAYS: In the examples used below, it will be assumed that the arrays are one-dimensional, unless specified otherwise. You can have up to 10 dimensions in an array.

ARRAY INDEXES: The first index in an array is zero (0). If the array is one-dimensional, then <index> is an offset. If the array is multidimensional, then <index> is an array expression. An array expression has the form

<number>x<number>x . . . x<number>

where <number> is the offset within the individual dimension. All the index values of arrays start at zero (0), so the array expressions start at 0x0 for a two-dimensional array, and so forth.

USE OF OFFSETS: In the following syntactical descriptions, an offset is an integer that indicates the distance from the first element in an array. An offset of zero (0) indicates the first position in the array. In general, an offset of n indicates the n+1 position in the array. The term offset may also be used with a multidimensional array. For example, if an array expression of 2x5 is used, then the offset is computed as follows:

offset = 2 * LENGTH OF A ROW + 5

RATES: When an interest rate is used as a parameter for a function, it is always a decimal fraction. For example, if the interest rate for a period is 1.5%, then the rate is entered as .015, that is, as a decimal fraction.

USE OF THE SIZE PARAMETER: A number of functions in The Programmer's Library allow the optional use of the <size> parameter. When arrays are created, they are statically allocated, that is, the size of the array is determined when it is created, and the entire array is initialized. If the array is numeric, then each element of the array is initialized to zero (0). When a statistical function is used to process data stored in an array, it will, by default, use all the data in the array, including any data that is the result of the initialization process. As a result, you can easily get incorrect results by using too many observations. The function COUNT can be used to determine the index of the last value that you have stored in an array (it actually returns this index value plus 1) and you can then instruct the statistical function to examine and use only some of the values in the array (from index 0 through <size> − 1).

C_STATUS AND C_ERROR: Most of the routines in The Programmer's Library set C_STATUS to −1 in the event of an error, even if this assignment is not specifically mentioned in the description of the functions. When C_STATUS is set to −1, a value is also assigned to C_ERROR, reflecting the type of error that occurred. The routines in The Programmer's Library assign values to C_STATUS and C_ERROR only when an error has occurred. As a result, you will need to reset these variables to 0 yourself, after you have handled the error.

REFERENCE TO AN ARRAY NAME: When an array name is used as a parameter in a function, the array must already be in existence and have the correct size and shape.

PARAMETERS: In a number of cases, neither variables nor functions can be used as parameters. For example, consider the CRARRAY function. It might be nice to use the size of one array to determine the size of another. Code of the form

```
CALL CFUNC WITH;
  "CRARRAY NEWARRAY,GETSIZE(MYARRAY),N"
```

cannot be used, since the functions return values to specific memory variables (like C_N_RESULT). In this case, even code of the form

```
CALL CFUNC WITH "GETSIZE MYARRAY"
CALL CFUNC WITH "CRARRAY NEWARRAY,C_N_RESULT,N"
```

and code of the form

```
CALL CFUNC WITH "GETSIZE MYARRAY"
X = C_N_RESULT
CALL CFUNC WITH "CRARRAY NEWARRAY,X,N"
```

also fails. You will need to use a constant, not a variable, for the size of the new array as a parameter in the CRARRAY function.

The Syntax of Each of the Functions in the Programmer's Library

ACOS — *Arccosine*

SYNTAX: CALL CFUNC WITH "ACOS<n>"
where <n> is a decimal number.

DESCRIPTION: Find the angle in radians whose cosine is n.

RETURN VALUE: A number between 0 and PI is returned to C_N_RESULT.

EXAMPLE:

```
. CALL CFUNC WITH "ACOS 0"
. ? C_N_RESULT
     1.57
```

AMORT — *Amortization of a loan*

SYNTAX: CALL CFUNC WITH "<principle>, <rate>, <# of periods>, <# of payments>"
where principle and rate are real numbers, and periods and payments are integers. <principle> is the original amount due, <rate> is the interest rate for each payment period, <periods> is the number of pay periods from the beginning of the loan, and <payments> is the number of payments to be made.

DESCRIPTION: Calculate the amount of the loan principal remaining after the specified payments are made.

RETURN VALUE: A decimal number is returned to C_N_RESULT.

EXAMPLE:

```
* COMPUTE THE REMAINING PRINCIPLE FOR
* AN INITIAL LOAN OF $40,000, WITH AN INTEREST
* RATE OF 12% PER YEAR (OR 1% PER MONTH), FOR A
* PERIOD OF 30 YEARS (OR 360 MONTHS), AFTER
* PAYMENTS HAVE BEEN MADE FOR 20 YEARS
CALL CFUNC WITH "AMORT 40000, .01, 360, 240"
      2867.7934
```

ARAND — *Fill an array with random numbers*

SYNTAX: CALL CFUNC WITH "ARAND <array name> [, <factor>, <start>, <end>]"
where <factor> is used as a multiplier for each number, <start> is an offset from the beginning of the array, and <end> is an offset from the beginning of the array.

DESCRIPTION: Generate random numbers, multiply each random number by <factor>, and place these values, one at a time, in the named array. The values are inserted starting at the position indicated by <start>, through the position indicated by <end>.

RETURN VALUE: None.

Notes:
This function can be used to initialize an array to zeros (0), simply by choosing zero (0) for the <factor>. Some of the functions, including GETARRAY and NSK cannot use or access the data in the array, until at least one data element is inserted into the array using the PUTARRAY function.

EXAMPLE:

```
* CREATE AN ARRAY OF NUMBERS OF SIZE 100 AND FILL IT
* WITH RANDOM NUMBERS BETWEEN 0 AND 100
CALL CFUNC WITH "CRARRAY MYARRAY,100,N"
```

```
CALL CFUNC WITH "ARAND    MYARRAY,100"
```

ARESTORE — *Retrieve an array from a disk file*

SYNTAX: CALL CFUNC WITH "ARESTORE <array name>, <file name> [,<start> [, <end>]]"
where <start> and <end> are array offsets.

DESCRIPTION: Read the values stored in the given file and place them in the array. If <start> and <end> are used, the first value in the file is placed in the position indicated by <start>, with the remaining values being placed, one at a time, in subsequent positions. The process continues until the end of the array is encountered or until no more data values remain to be copied.

RETURN VALUE: The actual number of elements copied from the file is returned to C_N_RESULT.

Notes:
If <end> is not specified, then an offset equivalent to the last position in the array is assumed. It is also assumed that <file name> was created through the use of the ASAVE function.

EXAMPLE:

```
. CALL CFUNC WITH "ASAVE MYARRAY,MYFILE.ARY"
      <process here>
. CALL CFUNC WITH "ARESTORE MYARRAY,MYFILE.ARY"
. ? C_N_RESULT
      10.0
```

ASAVE — *Store an array in a disk file*

SYNTAX: CALL CFUNC WITH "ASAVE <array name>, <file name> [,<start>[,<end>]]"
where <start> and <end> are array offsets.

DESCRIPTION: The elements of the array, starting at the position indicated by <start>, are saved in the file. The process continues until either the

	element in the position indicated by <end> is copied to the file, or until the end of the array is reached.
RETURN VALUE:	A count of the number of elements saved is returned to C_N_RESULT.

Notes:
If <end> is not specified, then an offset equivalent to the last position in the array is assumed. If <end> indicates a position past the end of the array, then the process stops when the end of the array is encountered. The numbers are stored to six decimal places of accuracy.

EXAMPLE:

```
. CALL CFUNC WITH "ASAVE MYARRAY,MYFILE.ARY"
. ? C_N_RESULT
      10.0
```

ASIN — *Arcsine*

SYNTAX:	CALL CFUNC WITH "ASIN <n>"
DESCRIPTION:	Find the angle in radians whose sine is n.
RETURN VALUE:	A number between −PI/2 and PI/2 is returned to C_N_RESULT.

EXAMPLE:

```
. CALL CFUNC WITH "ASIN 0"
. ? C_N_RESULT
           0.00
```

ATAN — *Arctangent*

SYNTAX:	CALL CFUNC WITH "ATAN <n>"
DESCRIPTION:	Find the angle in radians whose tangent is n.
RETURN VALUE:	A number between −PI/2 and PI/2 is returned to C_N_RESULT.

EXAMPLE:

```
. CALL CFUNC WITH "ATAN 1"
. ? C_N_RESULT
           0.79
```

CHI — *Chi-square distribution*

SYNTAX: CALL CFUNC WITH "CHI <array with expected values>, <array with observed values>[,<n>]"
where n indicates the size of the arrays.

DESCRIPTION: Compute the chi-square value using the following formula

$$\sum_{i=0}^{n-1} ((\text{expected}[i] - \text{observed}[i])\hat{\ }2)/\text{expected}[1]$$

RETURN VALUE: A decimal number is returned to C_N_RESULT.

EXAMPLE:

```
. CALL CFUNC WITH "CHI MYEXP,MYOBS,100"
? C_N_RESULT
      318.68
```

CLRWINDOW — *Clear a window on the screen*

SYNTAX: CALL CFUNC WITH "CLRWINDOW <x1>, <y1>, <x2>, <y2> [, <clear flag>]"
where <x1> and <y1> are the coordinates of the upper left-hand corner of the rectangle and <x2> and <y2> are the coordinates of the lower right-hand corner. <clear flag> is an integer.

DESCRIPTION: Clear a rectangle or just the border of a rectangle on the screen.

RETURN VALUE: None.

Notes:

If <clear flag> is zero (0) or omitted, then both the border and the interior of the rectangle are cleared. If <clear flag> is nonzero, then only the border is cleared. The same numbering scheme is used for this function as is used in normal dBASE III. In particular, the coordinates of the point in the upper left-hand corner of the screen are <0,0> and the coordinates of the point in the lower right-hand corner of the screen are <23,79>.

EXAMPLE:

```
. * TO CLEAR THE ENTIRE SCREEN
. CALL CFUNC WITH "CLRWINDOW 0,0,23,79"
      <or>
. CALL CFUNC WITH "CLRWINDOW 0,0,24,79"
```

CORR — *Correlation of two arrays*

SYNTAX: CALL CFUNC WITH "CORR <array name 1>, <array name 2>"

DESCRIPTION: Calculate the correlation of the data, pairing the data by index numbers in their respective arrays. For example, if X and Y are the names of the two arrays, X[1] is paired with Y[1], X[2] is paired with Y[2], and so forth. Note that the two arrays must have the same size.

RETURN VALUE: The correlation is returned to C_N_RESULT.

EXAMPLE:

```
. CALL CFUNC WITH "CORR MYARRAY1,MYARRAY2"
. ? C_N_RESULT
          -0.0799
```

COS — Cosine

SYNTAX: CALL CFUNC WITH "COS <angle>"

DESCRIPTION: Find the cosine of the <angle> expressed in radians.

RETURN VALUE: A decimal (real) number is returned to C_N_RESULT.

EXAMPLE:

```
. CALL CFUNC WITH "COS 0"
. ? C_N_RESULT
          1.00
```

COUNT — *Count the number of entries in an array*

SYNTAX: CALL CFUNC WITH "COUNT <array name>"

DESCRIPTION: When an array is created, the size of the array is specified and each of the elements in the array is set to zero (0). The functions that access the array need to know where in the array the actual data stops and where the values used for initialization begin. This function finds the highest position (largest index) plus 1 in the array in which data has been stored after the array has been created.

RETURN VALUE: The largest index plus 1 is returned to C_N_RESULT.

Notes:

Array index values start with 0, not 1. If data has been stored at index n, then COUNT will return the value n+1, even if index positions 0 through n still contain their default (initialization) values.

EXAMPLE:

```
CALL CFUNC WITH "CRARRAY GRADES,75,N"
CALL CFUNC WITH "COUNT GRADES"
? C_N_RESULT
      0.00
CALL CFUNC WITH "PUTARRAY GRADES,5,100"
CALL CFUNC WITH "COUNT GRADES"
? C_N_RESULT
    6.00
```

COVAR — *Covariance of two arrays*

SYNTAX: CALL CFUNC WITH "COVAR <array name 1>, <array name 2>"

DESCRIPTION: Compute the covariance of the elements in the two numeric arrays, using the corresponding elements in the arrays.

RETURN VALUE: The covariance is returned to C_N_RESULT.

EXAMPLE:

```
. CALL CFUNC WITH "COVAR MYARRAY"
. ? C_N_RESULT
        -0.0069
```

CRARRAY – *Create an array*

SYNTAX: CALL CFUNC WITH "CRARRAY
<array name>,<dimensions and sizes>,
<data type>"
where <dimensions and sizes> is used to specify both the number of dimensions in the array and the size of each dimension.

DESCRIPTION: Create an array with the given number of dimensions and of the appropriate size. The type of data that can be stored in the array is also stated. If the array is to be 1 – dimension, just enter the size of the array as the second parameter. If the array is to be multidimensional, then you must enter the size of each of the dimensions. In the case of a multidimensional array, specify the size of each dimension with the numeric values separated by the letter x.

RETURN VALUE: If the function was executed successfully, return the count of the elements in the array to C_N_RESULT.

Notes:

There are only two types of arrays: numeric and character string. If you wish to create an array of dates, you must simulate date values either with integers or with character strings. Character string arrays can store strings with a maximum length of 255 characters. Array names are limited to a maximum length of ten (10). The maximum size of an array is determined by the C compiler that you choose. Since the amount of room (free space) in main memory is affected by the number and the size of arrays, you should free the space used by arrays when they are no longer needed. Use the FRARRAY function to release the memory used by an array. Since ALL is a reserved work that is optionally used in conjunction with the function FRARRAY, you should not use ALL as the name of an array.

EXAMPLE 1:

```
. * CREATE AN ARRAY WITH OFFSETS FROM 0 TO 74, I.E.,
. * WITH C INDEXES FROM 0 TO 74
. CALL CFUNC WITH "CRARRAY GRADES,75,N"
```

EXAMPLE 2:

```
. * CREATE AN ARRAY WITH C INDEXES FROM 0 TO 11
. * AND FROM 0 TO 9
. CALL CFUNC WITH "CRARRAY RAIN,12×10,N"
```

CV – *Coefficient of variance*

SYNTAX: CALL CFUNC WITH "CV <array name> [, <size>]"

DESCRIPTION: Compute the coefficient of variance of the numbers in the named array. The array should be one-dimensional. If <size> is specified, then the first <size> elements in the array (from index 0 through index <size> – 1) are used in the computation. If <size> is not specified or the value of <size> is zero (0), then all the elements in the array (including the default initialization values, if any) are used.

RETURN VALUE: The numeric value of the coefficient is returned to C_N_RESULT.

Notes:

The coefficient of variance is computed using the following formula:

CV = SD/MEAN

EXAMPLE:

```
. CALL CFUNC WITH "CV GRADES,50"
. ? C_N_RESULT
        0.6209
```

DIST – *Frequency distribution*

SYNTAX: CALL CFUNC WITH "DIST <source>, <sorted>, <distinct>, <frequency> [, <size>]"

where <source> is the name of the original array, <sorted> is the array containing the same data in sorted order (lowest to highest), <distinct> is the array containing each value just once in sorted order, and <frequency> is

	the array that contains the number of times that each distinct value occurs in <source>.
DESCRIPTION:	The frequency of each distinct value in the array is computed. The distinct values are placed in one array, and the counts are placed in another array. It is up to the programmer to use and display the resultant data, perhaps using the routines in The Graphics Library.
RETURN VALUE:	The number of distinct values in <source>.

Notes:
If <size> is not given or has the value zero, then all the data in the array is used. Each of the arrays named in the statement must exist before the statement is executed.

EXAMPLE:

```
. CALL CFUNC WITH "DIST MYARRAY,MYS,MYD,MYF"
. ? C_N_RESULT
        89.00
```

DUMPARRAY — *Dump contents of array to screen*

SYNTAX:	CALL CFUNC WITH "DUMPARRAY <array name> [, <start> [, <end>]]" where <start> and <end> are array offsets.
DESCRIPTION:	Display the contents of an array on the screen in a preset format. If <start> is used, then it specifies the beginning index. If <start> is not used, then the beginning index is zero (0). If <end> is used and is less than or equal to the last index in the array, then it specifies the ending index. If <end> is not specified or is greater than the number of elements in the array, then elements from the starting position through the end of the array are displayed.
RETURN VALUE:	The COUNT value is returned to C_N_RESULT.

Notes:
This function is in the "quick and dirty" category and there are some problems with other screen displays like the status bar. In addition, the data is displayed in a linear fashion, not as an array. You might prefer to use the GETARRAY function to obtain the data and then display it yourself in a more controlled fashion.

EXAMPLE:

```
. CALL CFUNC WITH "DUMPARRAY MYARRAY"
     0 0.000848
     1 0.797827
     2 0.768187
     3 0.313723
     4 0.022157
     5 0.062071
     6 0.548537
     7 0.330650
     8 0.916024
     9 0.340738
```

EQN — *Count for equal*

SYNTAX: CALL CFUNC WITH "EQN <numeric value>, <array name> [, <size>]"

DESCRIPTION: Count the number of elements in the array that are equal to the given <numeric value>.

RETURN VALUE: The count of all elements in the specified range of the array that are equal to the given value is returned to C_N_RESULT.

Notes:
If the size option is used, then the scope is limited. If this option is not used, then the entire array is examined.

EXAMPLE:

```
. CALL CFUNC WITH "EQN .5,MYARRAY"
. ? C_N_RESULT
        10.00
```

FDUMPARRAY — *Dump contents of array to a file*

SYNTAX: CALL CFUNC WITH "FDUMPARRAY <array name>, <file name>, <start>, <end>"
where <start> and <end> are array offsets.

DESCRIPTION: Copy values and index positions from an array to a file. The values copied begin at the position indicated by <start> and stop at the position indicated by <end>.

RETURN VALUE: The number of elements copied to the file is returned to C_N_RESULT.

EXAMPLE:

```
. CALL CFUNC WITH "FDUMPARRAY MYARRAY,MYFILE.ARY,0,9"
. TYPE MYFILE.ARY
    0 0.000848
    1 0.797827
    2 0.768187
    3 0.313723
    4 0.022157
    5 0.062071
    6 0.548537
    7 0.330650
    8 0.916024
    9 0.340738
```

FRARRAY — *Free (erase) an array*

SYNTAX: CALL CFUNC WITH "FRARRAY <array name>/ALL"

DESCRIPTION: Erase the named array from memory and free the space.

RETURN VALUE: If the operation is successfully completed, then a nonnegative number is returned to C_N_RESULT. According to the Ashton-Tate documentation, if the operation was not successful, then the value −1 is supposed to be returned to C_STATUS. Unfortunately, I found that a positive number is returned to

C_STATUS in the event of an error. As a result, I recommend that you set C_ERROR to 0 before the operation and then check C_ERROR to see if it is greater than 0. If so, an error has occurred. Alternatively, you can change the code for this function and return −1 to C_STATUS in the event of an error.

Notes:
If ALL is used instead of the name of the array, then all the active arrays are erased and the spaces are freed.

Warning:
Failure to release an array from memory before you exit from dBASE III Plus can cause memory maintenance problems.

EXAMPLE:

```
. CALL CFUNC WITH "FRARRAY MYARRAY"
. ? C_N_RESULT
          50.00
```

FV — *Future value*

SYNTAX: CALL CFUNC WITH "FV <payment amount>, <interest rate>, <number of periods>" where the payment amount and the number of periods are integers, and the interest rate is a decimal fraction.

DESCRIPTION: Compute the future value, including all payments and interest earned.

RETURN VALUE: The future value is returned to C_N_RESULT.

EXAMPLE:

```
. * INVEST $1000 EACH MONTH FOR 12 MONTHS AT 1.5%
. * INTEREST PER MONTH
. CALL CFUNC WITH "FV 1000,.015,12"
. ? C_N_RESULT
          13041.21
```

GEN — *Count for greater than or equal*

SYNTAX: CALL CFUNC WITH "GEN <numeric value>, <array name> [, <size>]"

DESCRIPTION: Count the number of elements in the array that are greater than or equal to the given <numeric value>.

RETURN VALUE: The count of all elements in the specified range of the array that are less than or equal to the given value is returned to C_N_RESULT.

Notes:

If the size option is used, then the scope is limited. If this option is not used, then the entire array is examined.

EXAMPLE:

```
. CALL CFUNC WITH "GEN .5,MYARRAY"
. ? C_N_RESULT
          40.00
```

GETARRAY — *Extract a numeric value from an array*

SYNTAX: CALL CFUNC WITH "GETARRAY <array name>, <index>"
where <index> is an array expression indicating the location of the element in the array.

DESCRIPTION: Obtain a copy of the data in the indicated position.

RETURN VALUE: The value stored in the indicated position is returned to a variable of the appropriate type. If the value to be returned is numeric, then the value is returned to C_N_RESULT. If the value to be returned is a character string, then the value is returned to C_C_RESULT.

Notes:

I created an array and used ARAND to place random numbers in it. When I attempted to use GETARRAY to retrieve a value, it failed. I then placed a value in the array using PUTARRAY and the subsequent uses of GETARRAY worked, both for values placed in the array with ARAND and for those values placed in the array with PUTARRAY. It appears that you must insert at least one value in the array using PUTARRAY before you can use GETARRAY.

EXAMPLE:

```
. CALL CFUNC WITH "GETARRAY MYARRAY,2x3"
. ? C_N_RESULT
          3.00
```

GETPASS — *Get a password*

SYNTAX:	CALL CFUNC WITH "GETPASS"
DESCRIPTION:	Get a password from the user. A character string of length 8 is obtained.
RETURN VALUE:	The entry is returned as a character string to C_C_RESULT.

Notes:

Only alphanumeric characters are accepted. As each character is successfully entered, the # symbol is displayed on the screen. The deletion of the previous characters is accomplished by pressing BACKSPACE. The program should clear the screen or the entry area (possibly using a window) before this function is used. Once the password has been returned, your application program can test the C_C_RESULT for correctness.

EXAMPLE:

```
. CALL CFUNC WITH "GETPASS"
      <enter the password>
. ? C_C_RESULT
    MYPASS
```

GETSIZE — *Get the size of an array*

SYNTAX:	CALL CFUNC WITH "GETSIZE <array name>"
DESCRIPTION:	Count the number of positions in the array.

RETURN VALUE: A number (integer) reflecting the number of positions in the array is returned to C_N_RESULT.

EXAMPLE:

```
. CALL CFUNC WITH "CRARRAY MYARRAY,100,N"
. CALL CFUNC WITH "GETSIZE MYARRAY"
. ? C_N_RESULT
          100.00
. CALL CFUNC WITH "COUNT MYARRAY"
. ? C_N_RESULT
          0.00
```

GTN – *Count for greater than*

SYNTAX: CALL CFUNC WITH "GTN <numeric value>, <array name> [, <size>]"

DESCRIPTION: Count the number of elements in the array that are greater than the given <numeric value>.

RETURN VALUE: The count of all elements in the specified range of the array that are greater than the given value is returned to C_N_RESULT.

Notes:
If the size option is used, then the scope is limited. If this option is not used, then the entire array is examined.

EXAMPLE:

```
. CALL CFUNC WITH "GTN .5,MYARRAY"
. ? C_N_RESULT
          5.00
```

HELP – *List names of functions or give specific syntax*

SYNTAX: CALL CFUNC WITH "HELP [<function name>]"

DESCRIPTION: If no function name is used, then a list of the names of the functions in the C Tool's library is displayed. If the name of the function is

	provided, then a brief description of the function and its parameters are displayed.
RETURN VALUE:	None.

Notes:
When this function is used, a window is placed on the screen and the information is displayed within this window. You are prompted to press a key to continue. When the key is pressed, the window is removed from the screen and the previous screen display is restored.

EXAMPLES:

```
. CALL CFUNC WITH "HELP"
. CALL CFUNC WITH "HELP SETDVAR"
```

IRR — *Internal rate of return*

SYNTAX:	CALL CFUNC WITH "IRR <initial guess>, <array name>, <number of periods>" where <initial guess> is usually between 0 and 1.
DESCRIPTION:	Compute the rate of return that will result in a net present value of zero (0).
RETURN VALUE:	If successful, the internal rate of return is returned to C_N_RESULT; otherwise 0 is returned to C_N_RESULT and −1 is returned to C_STATUS.

Notes:
Enter income as positive values in the array and enter losses as negative numbers. Use index [0] to hold the initial investment.

EXAMPLE:

```
. CALL CFUNC WITH "IRR .5,MYARRAY,5"
. ? C_N_RESULT
         -0.0095
```

KURT — *Compute sample kurtosis*

SYNTAX: CALL CFUNC WITH "KURT <array name> [, <size>]"
where the array has been created with the NSK function and <size> is the index of the last array element to be used.

DESCRIPTION: Compute the sample kurtosis using the elements with index 0 through <size>.

RETURN VALUE: The sample kurtosis is returned to C_N_RESULT.

Notes:
If <size> is not given or has the value zero (0), then the entire array is used.

EXAMPLE:

```
. CALL CFUNC WITH "CRARRAY NEWARRAY"
. CALL CFUNC WITH "NSK MYARRAY,NEWARRAY"
. CALL CFUNC WITH "KURT NEWARRAY"
. ? C_N_RESULT
          -0.1887
```

LEN — *Count for less than or equal*

SYNTAX: CALL CFUNC WITH "LEN <numeric value>, <array name> [, <size>]"

DESCRIPTION: Count the number of elements in the array that are less than or equal to the given <numeric value>.

RETURN VALUE: The count of all elements in the specified range of the array that are less than or equal to the given value is returned to C_N_RESULT.

Notes:
If the size option is used, then the scope is limited. If this option is not used, then the entire array is examined.

EXAMPLE:

```
. CALL CFUNC WITH "LEN .5,MYARRAY"
. ? C_N_RESULT
        50.00
```

LTN — *Count for less than*

SYNTAX: CALL CFUNC WITH "LTN <numeric value>, <array name> [, <size>]"

DESCRIPTION: Count the number of elements in the array that are less than the given <numeric value>.

RETURN VALUE: The count of all elements in the specified range of the array that are less than the given value is returned to C_N_RESULT.

Notes:

If the size option is used, then the scope is limited. If this option is not used, then the entire array is examined.

EXAMPLE:

```
. CALL CFUNC WITH "LTN .5,MYARRAY"
. ? C_N_RESULT
        10.00
```

MAX — *Find the largest value*

SYNTAX: CALL CFUNC WITH "MAX <array name>, [, <size>]"

DESCRIPTION: Find the largest number in the array, searching the elements with index 0 through <size>.

RETURN VALUE: The largest number is returned to C_N_RESULT.

Notes:

If the size option is used, then the scope is limited. If this option is not used, then the entire array is examined.

EXAMPLE:

```
. CALL CFUNC WITH "MAX MYARRAY"
. ? C_N_RESULT
        3.0000
```

MEAN — *Calculate the mean*

SYNTAX: CALL CFUNC WITH "MEAN <array name> [, <size>]"

DESCRIPTION: Compute the mean as the sum of the values divided by the count.

RETURN VALUE: The mean value is returned to C_N_RESULT.

Notes:
If the size option is used, then the scope is limited. If this option is not used, then the entire array is examined.

EXAMPLE:

```
. CALL CFUNC WITH "MEAN MYARRAY,6"
. ? C_N_RESULT
        2.6667
```

MEDIAN — *Calculate the median*

SYNTAX: CALL CFUNC WITH "MEDIAN <array name> [, <size>]"

DESCRIPTION: Find or calculate the middle value in the array.

RETURN VALUE: The median value is returned to C_N_RESULT.

Notes:
If the size option is used, then the scope is limited. If this option is not used, then the entire array is examined.

EXAMPLE:

```
. CALL CFUNC WITH "MEDIAN MYARRAY,6"
. ? C_N_RESULT
        2.5000
```

MEMSTAT – *Get memory status (Lattice only)*

SYNTAX: CALL CFUNC WITH "MEMSTAT"

DESCRIPTION: Determine the amount of memory currently available for new arrays.

RETURN VALUE: An integer representing the amount of available memory is returned to C_N_RESULT.

Notes:

This function is available only for Lattice C.

EXAMPLE:

```
. CALL CFUNC WITH "MEMSTAT"
. ? C_N_RESULT
        13904.00
```

MIN – *Find the smallest value*

SYNTAX: CALL CFUNC WITH "MIN <array name> [, <size>]"

DESCRIPTION: Find and return the smallest value in the indicated array, using the appropriate scope.

RETURN VALUE: The smallest value in the array is returned to C_N_RESULT.

Notes:

If the size option is used, then the scope is limited. If this option is not used, then the entire array is examined.

EXAMPLE:

```
. CALL CFUNC WITH "MIN MYARRAY"
. ? C_N_RESULT
        0.0000
```

MIRR – *Modified internal rate of return*

SYNTAX: CALL CFUNC WITH "MIRR <estimate of interest on negative flows>, <estimate of interest on positive flows>, <array name>,

<number of periods>"

DESCRIPTION: Enter income as positive numbers and enter losses as negative numbers. Store the original investment in index [0] of the array as a negative number. MIRR does not rely on an initial guess, and so is more reliable than IRR.

RETURN VALUE: The modified internal rate of return is returned to C_N_RESULT. If the value cannot be determined, then −1 is returned to C_STATUS. If there is a mathematical error (such as a division by zero), then −2 is returned to C_STATUS.

EXAMPLE:

```
. CALL CFUNC WITH "MIRR .015,.01,MYARRAY,5"
. ? C_N_RESULT
          -0.1330
```

NPV — *Net present value*

SYNTAX: CALL CFUNC WITH "NPV <discount rate>, <array name>, <number of periods> where <discount rate> is a decimal fraction and is the constant rate for each period.

DESCRIPTION: Compute the net present value.

RETURN VALUE: The net present value is returned to C_N_RESULT.

Notes:
The <number of periods> must equal the count of data elements in the array.

EXAMPLE:

```
. CALL CFUNC WITH "NPV .015,MYARRAY,5"
. ? C_N_RESULT
          -588.42
```

NSK — *Normal scores*

SYNTAX: CALL CFUNC WITH "NSK <source array>, <destination array>[, <size>]"

DESCRIPTION: If SARRAY is the name of the source array and DARRAY is the name of the destination array, then the values placed in DARRAY are computed as follows:

DARRAY[i] = (SARRAY[i] – MEAN(SARRAY))/STDEV(SARRAY)

RETURN VALUE: The number of elements placed in the <destination> array is returned to C_N_RESULT.

Notes:

If the size option is used, then the scope is limited. If this option is not used, then the entire array is examined.

EXAMPLE:

```
. CALL CFUNC WITH "CRARRAY NEWARRAY"
. CALL CFUNC WITH "NSK MYARRAY,NEWARRAY"
. ? C_N_RESULT
          10.0000
```

PEEK — *Examine the contents of a memory location*

SYNTAX: CALL CFUNC WITH "PEEK <offset>, <segment>"
where <offset> and <segment> are decimal numbers.

DESCRIPTION: Returns a copy of the data stored at the given segment and offset.

RETURN VALUE: A number is returned to C_N_RESULT.

PMT — *Calculate loan payments*

SYNTAX: CALL CFUNC WITH "PMT <principle>, <rate of interest>, <number of periods>"
where principle is the remainder of the loan to

be paid off, rate is a decimal fraction representing the interest rate per period, and number of periods is an integer representing the number of periods until the loan is to be paid off.

DESCRIPTION: Calculate the constant payment to be made each period in order to completely pay off the loan.

RETURN VALUE: The constant value to be paid each period is returned to C_N_RESULT. Note that the final payment might be less than the constant monthly payment.

EXAMPLE:

```
. * LOAN OF $40,000.00 AT 9.5% INTEREST, MONTHLY
. * PAYMENTS FOR 30 YEARS
. CALL CFUNC WITH "PMT 40000,0079166,360"
. ? C_N_RESULT
        336.34
```

POKE — *Store a value in a memory location*

SYNTAX: CALL CFUNC WITH "POKE <decimal code>, <offset>, <segment>"

DESCRIPTION: Write the decimal number to the address indicated by <offset> and <segment>.

RETURN VALUE: None.

PUTARRAY — *Store a value in an array*

SYNTAX: CALL CFUNC WITH "PUTARRAY <array name>, <index> <value>"
where <value> is the value to be stored in the array.

DESCRIPTION: Store a value in the designated position in an array.

RETURN VALUE: If successful, the value of <index> is returned to C_N_RESULT.

EXAMPLE:

```
. CALL CFUNC WITH "PUTARRAY MYARRAY,0,1"
. ? C_N_RESULT
        0.00
```

PUTWINDOW — *Draw a window on the screen*

SYNTAX: CALL CFUNC WITH "PUTWINDOW <x1>, <y1>, <x2>, <y2>, [<clear code> [, <type>]]"
where <x1,y1> is the coordinate of the upper left-hand corner and <x2,y2> is the corner of the lower right-hand corner of the window.

DESCRIPTION: Draw a window on the screen using the indicated coordinates. If <clear code> is not zero (0), then the interior of the window will be filled with blanks. If <type> is zero (0), then the window will be drawn using single lines. If <type> is not zero (0), then the border of the window will be drawn using double lines.

RETURN VALUE: None.

EXAMPLE:

```
. * PUT A WINDOW WITH CORNERS <3,1> AND <5,8> ON
. * THE SCREEN
. CALL CFUNC WITH "PUTWINDOW 3,1,5,8"
```

PV — *Present value*

SYNTAX: CALL CFUNC WITH "PV <payment amount>, <interest rate>, <number of periods>"
where the payment amounts are constant and the interest rate is a decimal fraction.

DESCRIPTION: Compute and return the present value.

RETURN VALUE: Return the present value to C_N_RESULT.

EXAMPLE:

```
. * PAYMENT AMOUNT OF $336.34 AT 9.5% INTEREST,
. * WITH MONTHLY PAYMENTS FOR 30 YEARS
. CALL CFUNC WITH "PV 336.34,.0079166,360"
```

```
. ? C_N_RESULT
          40000.00
```

RAND – *Generate a random number*

SYNTAX: CALL CFUNC WITH "RAND [<seed value>]",
or
CALL CFUNC WITH "RAND <low>, <high>"

DESCRIPTION: If no parameters are used, RAND generates a random number greater than or equal to 0 and less than 1, using the system clock as a seed value. If a seed value is used, then the initial value returned is determined by the seed and the value generated is greater than or equal to 0 and less than 1. If the <low> and <high> parameters are used, then an integer greater than or equal to <low> and less than or equal to <high> is generated.

RETURN VALUE: A random number is returned to C_N_RESULT.

Notes:
<low> must be a positive integer and <high> must be less than 32767. If a seed value is used, it must be positive and less than 2147438647.

EXAMPLE:

```
I = 1
DO WHILE I <= 5
   CALL CFUNC WITH "RAND 10,100"
   CALL CFUNC WITH "PUTARRAY MYARRAY,"+STR(I,1)+","+;
     STR(C_N_RESULT,3)
I = I + 1
ENDDO
```

RANGE – *Calculate the range*

SYNTAX: CALL CFUNC WITH "RANGE <array name> [, <size>]"

DESCRIPTION: Compute the difference between the highest and the lowest values in the array.
RETURN VALUE: The difference is returned to C_N_RESULT.

Notes:
If the size option is used, then the scope is limited. If this option is not used, then the entire array is examined.

EXAMPLE:

```
. CALL CFUNC WITH "RANGE MYARRAY"
. ? C_N_RESULT
        94.00
```

RNARRAY – *Rename an array*

SYNTAX: CALL CFUNC WITH "RNARRAY <old array name>, <new array name>"
DESCRIPTION: Change the name of an array.
RETURN VALUE: None.

EXAMPLE:

```
. CALL CFUNC WITH "RNARRAY MYARRAY,NEWARRAY"
```

ROS – *Sort the contents of an array*

SYNTAX: CALL CFUNC WITH "ROS <source array>, <destination array>"
DESCRIPTION: Sort the data in the source array in ascending order and place the results in the destination array. The destination array can be the same as the source array.
RETURN VALUE: The actual number of items sorted and placed in the destination array is returned to C_N_RESULT.

Notes:
The destination array must already be in existence before ROS is executed. If necessary, use CRARRAY to create the destination array. ROS works only with numeric arrays.

EXAMPLE:

```
. CALL CFUNC WITH "CRARRAY MYSARRAY,5,N"
. CALL CFUNC WITH "ROS MYARRAY,MYSARRAY"
. ? C_N_RESULT
        5.00
```

SETBELL — *Set error bell* *DEFAULT: ON with SETERR ON*

SYNTAX: CALL CFUNC WITH "SETBELL <flag>" where <flag> is an integer.

DESCRIPTION: If an error occurs, sound the bell and display an error message. If <flag> is zero (0), turn the bell off. If <flag> is not zero (0), turn the bell on.

RETURN VALUE: None.

EXAMPLE:

```
. * TO TURN THE BELL OFF
. CALL CFUNC WITH "SETBELL 0"
```

SETDVAR — *Declare return variable*

SYNTAX: CALL CFUNC WITH "SETDVAR <variable type>" where the <return type> can be any of the following: N(umeric), C(haracter string), L(ogical), D(ate), E(rror), or S(tatus).

DESCRIPTION: Declare a return variable to be used in conjunction with C routines.

RETURN VALUE: The value −1 is returned to C_STATUS if <variable type> is not valid.

Notes:
The valid <variable type>s are N, C, L, D, E, and S. When the SETDVAR function is used, it must be immediately followed by a second CALL CFUNC statement that supplies the name of the return variable. Note in the following example that the name of the return variable is not delimited.

EXAMPLE:

```
PUBLIC MYSTRING
MYSTRING = SPACE(35)
CALL CFUNC WITH "SETDVAR C"
CALL CFUNC WITH MYSTRING
```

SETERR — *Set error flag* *DEFAULT: ON*

SYNTAX: CALL CFUNC WITH "SETERR <integer>" where <integer> is nonnegative.

DESCRIPTION: If <integer> is positive and an error occurs, then an error message is displayed, execution of the program will temporarily halt, and the user is prompted to press a key (similar to the dBASE III Plus WAIT statement). If <integer> has the value zero (0) and an error occurs, then no message is displayed and the program is not interrupted. In this case, the error code is stored in C_ERROR.

RETURN VALUE: This function does not return a value, but error codes will be returned to C_ERROR if SETERR has been set off (<integer> has the value 0) and an error occurs.

Notes:

After each operation, the program can test the value of C_ERROR to see if an error has occurred. If an error does occur, the program can perform its own error trapping.

EXAMPLE:

```
. * TO SET ERROR REPORTING MODE OFF
. CALL CFUNC WITH "SETERR 0"
```

SF — *Calculate sinking fund amount*

SYNTAX: CALL CFUNC WITH "SF <total amount>, <interest rate>, <number of periods>" where <total amount> is the amount to be accumulated and <interest rate> is a decimal fraction representing the rate for each period.

DESCRIPTION: Compute the constant deposit amount required to accumulate the <total amount> at the end of the periods.

RETURN VALUE: The amount of the constant deposit is returned to C_N_RESULT.

Notes:
The final deposit amount may not exactly equal the other deposit amounts.

EXAMPLE:

```
. * CALCULATE THE 12 REQUIRED DEPOSIT AMOUNTS IN
. * ORDER TO ACHIEVE $2500 AT THE END OF A YEAR, WHERE
. * THE INTEREST RATE IS 1% PER MONTH.
. CALL CFUNC WITH "SF 2500,.01,12"
. ? C_N_RESULT
         197.12
```

SIN — *Sine*

SYNTAX: CALL CFUNC WITH "SIN <angle>"

DESCRIPTION: Find the sine of the <angle> expressed in radians.

RETURN VALUE: A decimal (real) number is returned to C_N_RESULT.

EXAMPLE:

```
. CALL CFUNC WITH "SIN 0"
. ? C_N_RESULT
         0.00
```

SKEW — *Calculate skewedness (asymmetry)*

SYNTAX: CALL CFUNC WITH "SKEW <array name> [, <size>]"

DESCRIPTION: Calculate the sample skewedness or asymmetry of the data in the array.

RETURN VALUE: The sample skewedness is returned to C_N_RESULT.

Notes:
If the size option is used, then the scope is limited. If this option is not used, then the entire array is examined.

EXAMPLE:

```
. CALL CFUNC WITH "SKEW MYARRAY"
. ? C_N_RESULT
        0.2942
```

SOUND — *Generate a tone*

SYNTAX: CALL CFUNC WITH "SOUND <frequency>, <duration>"
where <frequency> is the frequency of the tone in MHz, and <duration> is the length of the tone.

DESCRIPTION: Generate a tone. The units used to measure the length of the tone are approximately 18.2 units (tics) per second. The duration is a multiple of this clock unit and must be between 0 and 65535.

RETURN VALUE: None.

EXAMPLE:

```
. * GENERATE A TONE FOR APPROXIMATELY 1/2 SECONDS
. CALL CFUNC WITH "SOUND 400,9"
```

STARRAY — *Report status of arrays*

SYNTAX: CALL CFUNC WITH "STARRAY"
where the function takes no parameters.

DESCRIPTION: Display a report showing the status of each array. Include array name, type, count (number of elements stored in the array), the actual size of the array, and the number of arrays that may still be created. The maximum number of arrays at any one time is 10.

RETURN VALUE: If successful, the number of arrays is returned to C_N_RESULT, otherwise −1 is returned.

EXAMPLE:

```
. CALL CFUNC WITH "STARRAY"
```

STDEV — *Standard deviation*

SYNTAX: CALL CFUNC WITH "STDEV <array name> [, <size>]"

DESCRIPTION: Calculate the standard deviation of the data in the array.

RETURN VALUE: The value of the standard deviation is returned to C_N_RESULT.

Notes:
If the size option is used, then the scope is limited. If this option is not used, then the entire array is examined.

EXAMPLE:

```
. CALL CFUNC WITH "STDEV MYARRAY"
. ? C_N_RESULT
        32.0736
```

TAN — *Tangent*

SYNTAX: CALL CFUNC WITH "TAN <angle>"

DESCRIPTION: Find the tangent of the <angle> expressed in radians.

RETURN VALUE: A decimal (real) number is returned to C_N_RESULT.

EXAMPLE:

```
. CALL CFUNC WITH "TAN .79"
. ? C_N_RESULT
        1.01
```

VAR — *Variance*

SYNTAX: CALL CFUNC WITH "VAR <array name> [, <size>]"

DESCRIPTION: Compute the variance of the data in the array.

RETURN VALUE: The variance is returned to C_N_RESULT.

Notes:
If the size option is used, then the scope is limited. If this option is not used, then the entire array is examined.

EXAMPLE:

```
. CALL CFUNC WITH "VAR MYARRAY"
. ? C_N_RESULT
        1028.7136
```

CHAPTER

10

C Tools: The Graphics Library

10.1 INTRODUCTION

The general topic of C Tools has been introduced in Chapter 9. Please refer to Section 9.1 in Chapter 9 for an introduction to the use of C routines in conjunction with dBASE III Plus. In addition to the mathematical, statistical, and financial functions introduced in Chapter 9, you can also purchase a library of graphics routines written in the C language. This product is called *dBASE Tools for C—The Graphics Library* and provides a graphics capability for dBASE III Plus. If you wish to write your own graphics programs in C and include them as a part of your dBASE III Plus system, refer to Section 9.6 in Chapter 9 of this book and the Ashton-Tate documentation for The Programmer's Library.

You will need a minimum of 512K bytes of main memory and a graphics card (adapter) to use The Graphics Library with dBASE III Plus. The supported graphics cards are:

1. IBM Color Graphics (CGA)
2. IBM Enhanced Graphics (EGA), and
3. Hercules monochrome

Those cards that are compatible with any of the above are also supported. Your computer has two modes: text and graphics. In text mode, the C routines use just two colors: black and white. In graphics mode, the number of colors depends on your particular graphics adapter. Table 10.1 shows the characteristics of several graphics adapters:

TABLE 10.1

TYPE OF ADAPTER	RESOLUTION		COLORS
CGA	Medium res	(320 × 200)	4
EGA	Very high res	(640 × 350)	16
	Mono graphics	(640 × 350)	2
	High res	(640 × 200)	16
	Medium res	(320 × 200)	16
Hercules	Mono graphics	(720 × 348)	2

The printers that are supported at the current time are the Epson FX and MX printers, and the IBM Graphics Printer. True compatibles are also supported.

The functions in The Graphics Library can be used either interactively or in programs, but have some different properties in these two modes. When the graphics commands are entered interactively, the graphs should be produced in monochrome (nongraphics) mode. Once the screen is placed in graphics mode, you will not see a copy of your input commands on the screen.

10.2 INSTALLING THE GRAPHICS LIBRARY

1. Install dBASE on your hard disk (drive C).
2. Copy all the files from the distribution disk to drive C, using the DOS COPY command:

```
COPY A:*.* C:
```

10.3 GETTING READY TO USE THE GRAPHICS C TOOLS

Before you run dBASE III Plus, run the program DCTGRAF.EXE provided on your distribution disk. Once you have entered dBASE III Plus, execute the command

```
LOAD GFUNC
```

Note that GFUNC.BIN is a file provided on your distribution disk. It provides the interface between dBASE III and the C programs. GFUNC is a program that accepts a character string as its only parameter, calls the desired C routine, and then passes the appropriate parameters to this C routine. The character string passed to GFUNC will contain the name of the C function to be executed, together with the required parameters. Before a C function can be executed, it is necessary to initialize both the dBASE III Plus variables used as parameters to send data to the C functions and the variables used to receive data returned by the functions. For a discussion of the return variables, see Section 9.3 of Chapter 9. The program DCTGRAF.PRG provided on your distribution disk contains the code necessary to LOAD GFUNC and to initialize the return variables. It also indicates how to tell dBASE which type of graphics to use (CGA, EGA, or Hercules monochrome). A listing of the DCTGRAF.PRG program now follows:

```
* DCTGRAF.PRG for initializing The Graphics Library
LOAD GFUNC
```

```
PUBLIC C_N_RESULT, C_C_RESULT, C_STATUS, C_ERROR
C_N_RESULT = 0.00
C_C_RESULT = SPACE(10)
C_STATUS = 0
C_ERROR = 0
CALL GFUNC WITH "SETDVAR N"
CALL GFUNC WITH C_N_RESULT
CALL GFUNC WITH "SETDVAR C"
CALL GFUNC WITH C_C_RESULT
CALL GFUNC WITH "SETDVAR S"
CALL GFUNC WITH C_STATUS
CALL GFUNC WITH "SETDVAR E"
CALL GFUNC WITH C_ERROR
* Set random number generator seed based on system clock
PUBLIC SEED
TEMP = TIME( )
SEED = VAL(SUBSTR(TEMP,7,2))*10000+VAL(SUBSTR;
            (TEMP,4,2))*100 + VAL(SUBSTR(TEMP,1,2))
CALL GFUNC WITH "RAND " + STR(SEED,6,0)
RELEASE TEMP
* The next line simplifies the interactive entry of
*    a function call.
SET FUNCTION 6 TO 'CALL GFUNC WITH " '
* The following line is for IBM medium resolution (CGA)
CALL GFUNC WITH "INITGR CGA, 1, 1, 1"
* The following line is an alternative to the above and
*    is used for the Hercules card
* CALL GFUNC WITH "INITGR HERC, 0, 0, 1"
```

10.4 GENERAL SYNTAX OF THE TOOLS

All the functions in The Graphics Library are called with the following syntax:

```
CALL GFUNC WITH "<command>"
```

where <command> is a character string constant or variable that contains the name of the C function and the required parameters. The name of the function is separated from the first parameter by a space and each of the other parameters is separated from the preceding parameter by a comma (,). Note that <command> must be delimited and that it can be delimited in the usual manner (by an apostrophe, quotation marks, or square brackets). The parameters can be memory variables, constants, or expressions, as allowed by the syntax of the individual functions.

Note that the CALL statement does not pass a value back in the manner that function calls or procedure calls do in C. Rather, a value is passed back to the interface buffer using the addresses that you established in the CALL . . SETDVAR statements, selecting the appropriate address by the type of the return value. If you have chosen C_N_RESULT as the name of the return variable (interface variable) and the function passes back a number, then C_N_RESULT does not appear in an assignment statement and does not appear in the parameter list, but will contain the value after the function has executed.

Square brackets "[ ]" are used in this chapter to indicate optional entries in the command string.

10.5 dBASE III PLUS SUPPLEMENTARY ROUTINES

A number of small dBASE III Plus programs are supplied with The Graphics Library. They are designed to simplify the interface between dBASE III Plus and the C routines. They are valuable both as programs and as examples of how to call the C routines from dBASE III Plus programs. These routines can be found in the main directory of your distribution disk. In many cases, the simplification takes the following form: Instead of entering a CALL statement, a DO statement is used. The DO statement invokes the appropriate dBASE III Plus routine which in turn invokes the desired CALL . . GFUNC statement(s).

10.6 THE FUNCTIONS IN THE GRAPHICS LIBRARY

TABLE 10.2 C Tools

CATEGORY	NAME	DESCRIPTION
Array	ARESTORE	Retrieve an array from a disk file
	ASAVE	Store an array in a disk file
	COUNT	Count entries in array

CATEGORY	NAME	DESCRIPTION
	CRARRAY	Create an array
	DUMPARRAY	Dump contents of array to screen
	FRARRAY	Free (erase) an array
	GETARRAY	Extract a value from an array
	PUTARRAY	Store a value in an array
	STARRAY	Report status of arrays
Graphs (Color)	BARCHART	Barchart
	CAKECHART	Cake graph
	HLC	High-low-close graph
	LINECHART	Draw a line graph
	MPCHART	Marked-points graph
	PIECHART	Pie graph
	SBARCHART	Stacked bar graph
	XYCHART	XY graph
Graphs (Mono)	MONOBAR	Monochrome bar graph
	MONOHLC	Monochrome high-low-close graph
	MONOMP	Monochrome marked points graph
	MONOSBAR	Monochrome stacked bar graph
	MONOXY	Monochrome XY graph
Graphs (Primitive)	ARC	Draw an arc
	BOX	Draw a box
	CIRCLE	Draw a circle
	DOT	Draw a dot
	LINE	Draw a line
	POLYGON	Draw a polygon
Help	HELP	List names of functions in the Library
Interface	SETDVAR	Declare return
	SETERR	Set error flag

CATEGORY	NAME	DESCRIPTION
Input/Output	GPRINT	Copy the screen contents to printer
	WAIT	Pause and wait for input
Mathematical	RAND	Generate a random number
Mode	ENDGR	Exit from graphics mode
	INITGR	Enter graphics mode
Parameters	SETBAR	Change bar graph characters
	SETCOLOR	Change the color
	SETSTYLE	Set line type
Screen manipulation	GRESTORE	Retrieve a graphics screen from a disk file
	GSAVE	Store a graphics screen in a disk file
Text & labels	GXTEXT	Display a horizontal string
	GYTEXT	Display a vertical string
	SETLEGEND	Set coordinates for legend
	SETXLAB	Toggle x-axis label on or off, or select a label
	SETYLAB	Toggle y-axis label on or off

Graphics Mode

When you are in Graphics mode (as a result of entering CALL . . INITGR), pressing keys at the keyboard does not cause an echo of the entry. As a result, you cannot see what you have just typed in, so you might wish to call the high-level graphics functions from a program. The high-level graphics functions are the functions that draw on the screen but which are not primitive. The high-level graphics functions always require that the current mode be the Graphics mode.

Working with Color

The SETCOLOR function allows you to enter a variety of numbers to designate the current color, but only three of them are valid. The valid numbers are 1, 2, and 3. These numbers indicate the foreground color to be used for objects drawn on the screen. The background color cannot be set using this function. In order to choose a palette of colors, a background color, and the current graphing color, use the INITGR function. See the SETCOLOR and the INITGR functions for more information.

When graphs are produced using data in four arrays, only three distinct colors are used. The user must distinguish between the parts of the graph that use the same color by labels, data, and/or position in the graph.

Use of the Fill Parameter

Several of the graphics functions allow you to draw an outline of the object or to draw a solid object (a filled outline). This is indicated by the use of the <fill> option as one of the parameters of the function. If the option is not used or if the value of <fill> is zero (0), then the outline of the graph is drawn. If a nonzero value is supplied for <fill>, then the outline is drawn and the figure is filled with the current color.

Use of the Size Parameter

See the discussion of the fill parameter in Section 9.7 of Chapter 9.

Options

Some of the functions allow you to enter the name of exactly one array or you can enter between one and four array names. If only one name is allowed, the notation

<array name>

will be used. If you can enter between one and four names, then the notation

<1-4 array names>

will be used.

Titles for the graph, the x-axis, and the y-axis are also optional. If one of these options is not used, then you must still use the comma (,) as a separator to indicate the missing parameter.

Another common parameter is the mode in which leave the screen after the graph has been plotted and the screen is cleared. If this parameter is not given or is zero, then the graph will remain on the screen (a pause) until RETURN is pressed. *after RETURN has been entered, the screen will clear and change to monochrome mode. If this parameter has the value 1, then the screen will remain in graphics mode and there will be no pause.

The Number of Data Points

The number of points to be plotted must be less than or equal to the smallest number of available points in all the arrays used in the function call. For example, if you are graphing data from four arrays, then the value of this parameter is the smallest number of points in all four arrays.

The Syntax of Each of the Functions in The Graphics Library

ARC – *Draw an arc*

SYNTAX:	CALL GFUNC WITH "ARC <x>, <y>, <r>, <s>, <e> [, <fill>] where <x,y> are the coordinates of a point, <r> is the radius of a circle, <s> is the angle in degrees of the starting point, <e> is the angle in degrees of the ending point, and <fill> indicates whether or not the arc is to be filled.
DESCRIPTION:	Draw a circular arc with center at <x,y> and radius <r>, with the given starting and ending angles.
RETURN VALUE:	None.

Notes:
If <fill> is 0 or omitted, then the arc is drawn in outline form. If <fill> is not zero, then the arc is filled with the current color.

EXAMPLE:

```
CALL GFUNC WITH "INITGR"
CALL GFUNC WITH "SETCOLOR 3"
CALL GFUNC WITH "ARC 160,100,100,45,90,1"
CALL GFUNC WITH "WAIT"
CALL GFUNC WITH "ENDGR"
```

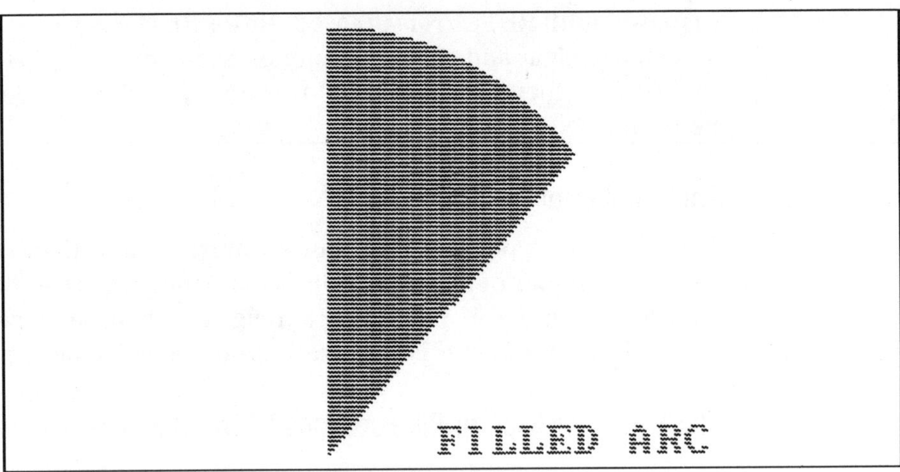

ARESTORE – *Retrieve an array from a disk file*

SYNTAX: CALL GFUNC WITH "ARESTORE <array name>, <file name> [, <start> [, <end>]]"
where <start> and <end> are array offsets.

DESCRIPTION: Read the values stored in the given file and place them in the array. If <start> and <end> are used, the first value in the file is placed in the position indicated by <start>, with the remaining values being placed, one at a time, in subsequent positions. The process continues until the end of the array is encountered or until no more data values remain to be copied.

RETURN VALUE: The actual number of elements copied from the file is returned to C_N_RESULT.

Notes:

If <end> is not specified, then an offset equivalent to the last position in the array is assumed. It is also assumed that <file name> was created through the use of the ASAVE function.

Warning:

The array <array name> must have already been created through the use of CRARRAY before this function is used or you will receive the error message:

ARRAY NAME INVALID

EXAMPLE:

```
. CALL GFUNC WITH "ASAVE MYARRAY,MYFILE.ARY"
      <process here>
. CALL GFUNC WITH "ARESTORE MYARRAY,MYFILE.ARY"
. ? C_N_RESULT
         10.0
```

ASAVE — *Store an array in a disk file*

SYNTAX: CALL GFUNC WITH "ASAVE <array name>, <file name> [, <start> [, <end>]]" where <start> and <end> are array offsets.

DESCRIPTION: The elements of the array, starting at the position indicated by <start>, are saved in the file. The process continues until either the element in the position indicated by <end> is copied to the file, or until the end of the array is reached.

RETURN VALUE: A count of the number of elements saved is returned to C_N_RESULT.

Notes:

If <end> is not specified, then an offset equivalent to the last position in the array is assumed. If <end> indicates a position past the end of the array, then the process stops when the end of the array is encountered. The numbers are stored to six decimal places of accuracy.

EXAMPLE:

```
. CALL GFUNC WITH "ASAVE MYARRAY,MYFILE.ARY"
. ? C_N_RESULT
         10.0
```

BARCHART — *Barchart*

SYNTAX: CALL GFUNC WITH "BARCHART <1-4 arrays>, <number of points> [, <graph title>, <x-axis title>, <y-axis title>] [, <screen mode after graphing>]"

DESCRIPTION: Display a color bar graph.

RETURN VALUE: None.

Notes:
Use MONOBAR for a monochrome bar graph.

EXAMPLE:

CALL GFUNC WITH "BARCHART MY1,MY2,MY3,5"
CALL GFUNC WITH "WAIT"
CALL GFUNC WITH "ENDGR"

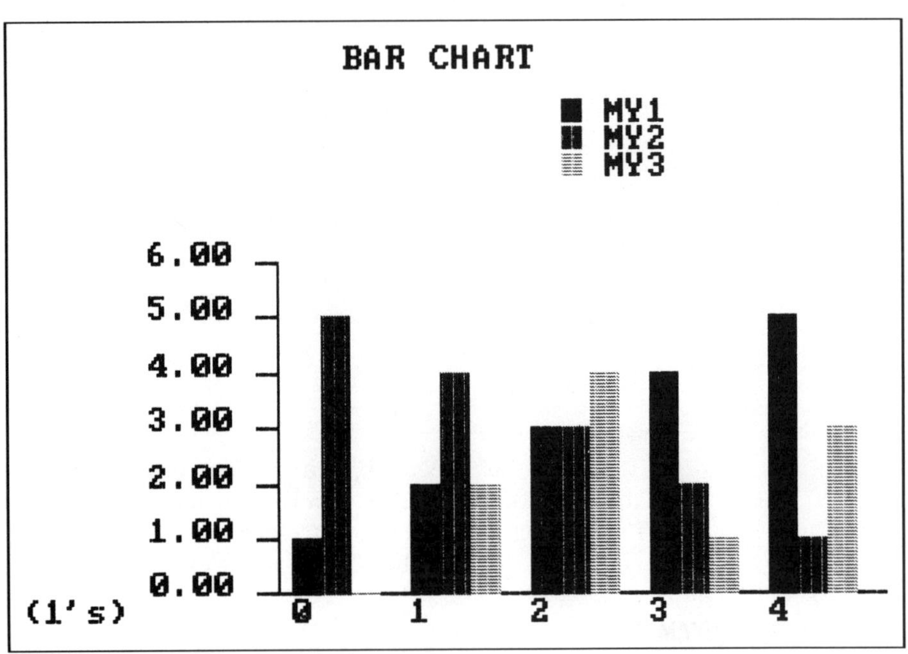

BOX — *Draw a box*

SYNTAX: CALL GFUNC WITH "BOX <x>, <y>, <horizontal>, <vertical>, [<fill>]" where <x,y> is the coordinate of the upper left-hand corner of the box, <horizontal> is the horizontal measurement of the box, and <vertical> is the vertical measurement of the box.

DESCRIPTION: Draw a box in the current color. The point

	<x,y> is the origin of the box, <horizontal> is a measurement from this point to the right, and <vertical> is a measurement from this point downward.
RETURN VALUE:	None.

EXAMPLE:

```
CALL GFUNC WITH "INITGR"
CALL GFUNC WITH "SETCOLOR 3"
CALL GFUNC WITH "BOX 50, 100, 25, 50, 1"
CALL GFUNC WITH "WAIT"
CALL GFUNC WITH "ENDGR"
```

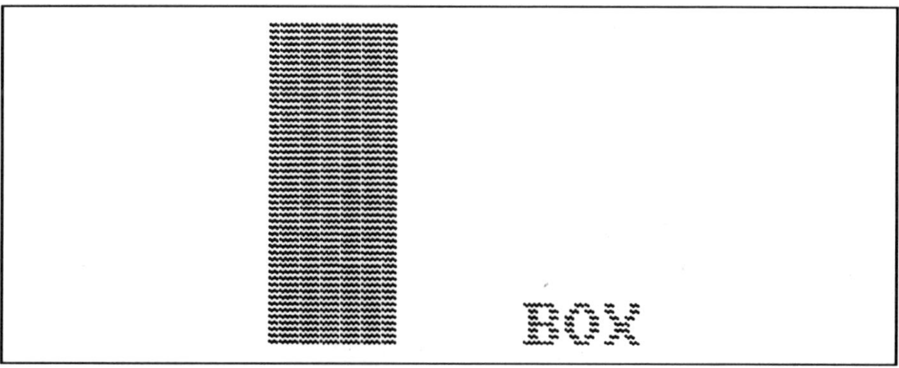

CAKECHART — *Cake graph*

SYNTAX:	CALL GFUNC WITH "CAKECHART <array name>, <number of points>, <graph title> [, <screen mode after graphing>]"
DESCRIPTION:	Represent the data as pieces of a cake, that is, as proportional pieces of a square.
RETURN VALUE:	None.

Notes:

All the data must have the same sign (nonnegative or nonpositive).

EXAMPLE:

CALL GFUNC WITH "CAKECHART MY2,5,CAKE CHART,1"
CALL GFUNC WITH "WAIT"
CALL GFUNC WITH "ENDGR"

CAKE

5
(35.71%)

4
(28.57%)

3
(21.43%)

2 (14.29%)

CIRCLE – *Draw a circle* (see figure on the next page)

SYNTAX:	CALL GFUNC WITH "CIRCLE <x>, <y>, <radius>"
DESCRIPTION:	Draw a circle in the current color with center at <x,y> and radius of <radius>.
RETURN VALUE:	None.

EXAMPLE:

CALL GFUNC WITH "INITGR"
CALL GFUNC WITH "SETCOLOR 3"
CALL GFUNC WITH "CIRCLE 50,100,25"
CALL GFUNC WITH "CIRCLE 75,125,50"
CALL GFUNC WITH "WAIT"
CALL GFUNC WITH "ENDGR"

COUNT – *Count entries in array*

SYNTAX:	CALL GFUNC WITH "COUNT <array name>"
DESCRIPTION:	When an array is created, the size of the array is specified and each of the elements in the

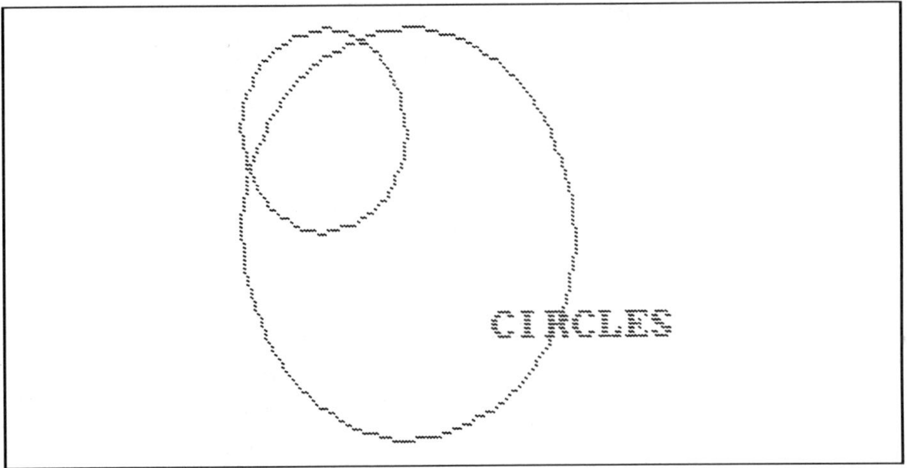

array is set to zero (0). The functions that access the array need to know where in the array the actual data stops and where the values used for initialization begin. This function finds the highest position (largest index) plus 1 in the array in which data has been stored after the array has been created.

RETURN VALUE: The largest index plus 1 is returned to C_N_RESULT.

Notes:

Array index values start with 0, not 1. If data has been stored at index n, then COUNT will return the value n+1, even if index positions 0 through n still contain their default (initialization) values.

EXAMPLE:

```
CALL GFUNC WITH "CRARRAY GRADES,75,N"
CALL GFUNC WITH "COUNT GRADES"
? C_N_RESULT
        0.00
CALL GFUNC WITH "PUTARRAY GRADES,5,100"
CALL GFUNC WITH "COUNT GRADES"
? C_N_RESULT
        6.00
```

CRARRAY — *Create an array*

SYNTAX: CALL GFUNC WITH "CRARRAY <array name>, <dimensions and sizes>, <data type>"
where <dimensions and sizes> is used to specify both the number of dimensions in the array and the size of each dimension.

DESCRIPTION: Create an array with the given number of dimensions and of the appropriate size. The type of data that can be stored in the array is also stated. If the array is to be 1 – dimension, just enter the size of the array as the second parameter. If the array is to be multidimensional, then you must enter the size of each of the dimensions. In the case of a multidimensional array, specify the size of each dimension with the numeric values separated by the letter x.

RETURN VALUE: If the function was executed successfully, return the count of the elements in the array to C_N_RESULT.

Notes:

There are only two types of arrays: numeric and character string. If you wish to create an array of dates, you must simulate date values either with integers or with character strings. Character string arrays can store strings with a maximum length of 255 characters. Array names are limited to a maximum length of ten (10). The maximum size of an array is determined by the C compiler that you choose. Since the amount of room (free space) in main memory is affected by the number and the size of arrays, you should free the space used by arrays when they are no longer needed. Use the FRARRAY function to release the memory used by an array. Since ALL is a reserved work that is optionally used in conjunction with the function FRARRAY, you should not use ALL as the name of an array.

EXAMPLE 1:

```
. * CREATE AN ARRAY WITH OFFSETS FROM 0 TO 74, I.E.,
. * WITH C INDEXES FROM 0 TO 74
. CALL GFUNC WITH "CRARRAY GRADES,75,N"
```

EXAMPLE 2:

```
. * CREATE AN ARRAY WITH C INDEXES FROM 0 TO 11
. * AND FROM 0 TO 9
. CALL GFUNC WITH "CRARRAY RAIN,12x10,N"
```

DOT — *Draw a dot* (see figure on p. 390)

SYNTAX: CALL GFUNC WITH "DOT <x>, <y>"

DESCRIPTION: Draw a dot on the screen using the current color.

RETURN VALUE: None.

EXAMPLE:

```
SET TALK OFF
CALL GFUNC WITH "INITGR"
CALL GFUNC WITH "SETCOLOR 3"
ROW = 0
COLUMN = 0
DO WHILE ROW <= 100 .AND. COLUMN <= 100
    CALL GFUNC WITH "DOT "+STR(110+ROW)+","+STR;
      (50+COLUMN)
    CALL GFUNC WITH "DOT "+STR(110+ROW)+",";
      +STR(150-COLUMN)
    ROW=ROW+1
    COLUMN=COLUMN+1
ENDDO
CALL GFUNC WITH "WAIT"
CALL GFUNC WITH "ENDGR"
```

Warning:
Programs with the DOT function will not work if TALK is ON.

DUMPARRAY — *Dump contents of array to screen*

SYNTAX: CALL GFUNC WITH "DUMPARRAY <array name> [, <start> [, <end>]]"
where <start> and <end> are array offsets.

DESCRIPTION: Display the contents of an array on the screen in a preset format. If <start> is used, then it specifies the beginning index. If <start> is not

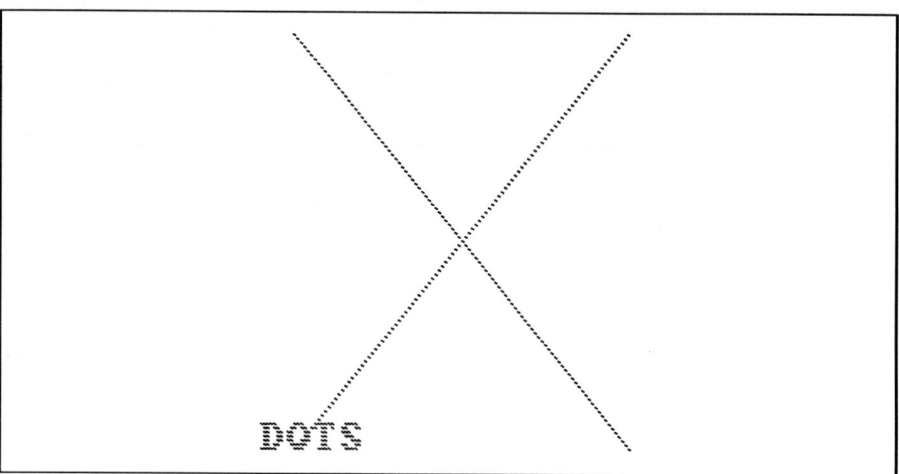

used, then the beginning index is zero (0). If <end> is used and is less than or equal to the last index in the array, then it specifies the ending index. If <end> is not specified or is greater than the number of elements in the array, then elements from the starting position through the end of the array are displayed.

RETURN VALUE: The COUNT value is returned to C_N_RESULT.

Notes:
This function is in the "quick and dirty" category and there are some problems with other screen displays like the status bar. In addition, the data is displayed in a linear fashion, not as an array. You might prefer to use the GETARRAY function to obtain the data and then display it yourself in a more controlled fashion.

EXAMPLE:

```
. CALL GFUNC WITH "DUMPARRAY MYARRAY"
     0 0.000848
     1 0.797827
     2 0.768187
     3 0.313723
     4 0.022157
```

```
5 0.062071
6 0.548537
7 0.330650
8 0.916024
9 0.340738
```

ENDGR — *Exit from graphics mode*

SYNTAX: CALL GFUNC WITH "ENDGR"
DESCRIPTION: Leave graphics mode and change to text mode.
RETURN VALUE: None.

EXAMPLE:

```
CALL GFUNC WITH "BARCHART MY1,MY2,MY3,5"
CALL GFUNC WITH "WAIT"
CALL GFUNC WITH "ENDGR"
```

FRARRAY — *Free (erase) an array*

SYNTAX: CALL GFUNC WITH "FRARRAY <array name>/ALL"
DESCRIPTION: Erase the named array from memory and free the space.
RETURN VALUE: If the operation is successfully completed, then a nonnegative number is returned to C_N_RESULT. According to the Ashton-Tate documentation, if the operation was not successful, then the value −1 is supposed to be returned to C_STATUS. Unfortunately, I found that a positive number is returned to C_STATUS in the event of an error. As a result, I recommend that you set C_ERROR to 0 before the operation and then check C_ERROR to see if it is greater than 0. If so, an error has occurred. Alternatively, you can change the code for this function and return −1 to C_STATUS in the event of an error.

Notes:
If ALL is used instead of the name of the array, then all the active arrays are erased and the spaces are freed.

Warning:
Failure to release an array from memory before you exit from dBASE III Plus can cause memory maintenance problems.

EXAMPLE:

```
. CALL GFUNC WITH "FRARRAY MYARRAY"
. ? C_N_RESULT
        50.00
```

GETARRAY — *Extract a value from an array*

SYNTAX:	CALL GFUNC WITH "GETARRAY <array name>, <index>" where <index> is an array expression indicating the location of the element in the array.
DESCRIPTION:	Obtain a copy of the data in the indicated position.
RETURN VALUE:	The value stored in the indicated position is returned to a variable of the appropriate type. If the value to be returned is numeric, then the value is returned to C_N_RESULT. If the value to be returned is a character string, then the value is returned to C_C_RESULT.

Notes:
I created an array and used ARAND to place random numbers in it. When I attempted to use GETARRAY to retrieve a value, it failed. I then placed a value in the array using PUTARRAY and the subsequent uses of GETARRAY worked, both for values placed in the array with ARAND and for those values placed in the array with PUTARRAY. It appears that you must insert at least one value in the array using PUTARRAY before you can use GETARRAY.

EXAMPLE:

```
. CALL GFUNC WITH "GETARRAY MYARRAY,2x3"
. ? C_N_RESULT
        3.00
```

GPRINT — *Copy the screen contents to the printer*

SYNTAX: CALL GFUNC WITH "GPRINT [<type of printer>]"
where the printer types are 0 for Epson FX or MX, and 1 for the IBM Graphics Printer.

DESCRIPTION: Send a copy of the screen to the printer.

RETURN VALUE: None.

Notes:
The graph is printed sideways, that is, down the paper instead of across.

Warning:
Before you print a graphics screen, make sure that your printer is set up to print properly. You may need to change the line spacing before the screen dump. See the EXAMPLE below.

EXAMPLE:

```
* SET PRINTER FOR GRAPHICS
SET DEVICE TO PRINT
@ 0,0 SAY CHR(27)+CHR(65)+CHR(7)+CHR(27)+CHR(50)
SET DEVICE TO SCREEN
* CONTINUE WITH THE REMAINDER OF THE PROGRAM
CALL GFUNC WITH "INITGR"
CALL GFUNC WITH "SETCOLOR 3"
CALL GFUNC WITH "CIRCLE 50,100,25"
CALL GFUNC WITH "CIRCLE 75,125,50"
CALL GFUNC WITH "GPRINT"
CALL GFUNC WITH "ENDGR"
```

GRESTORE — *Retrieve a graphics screen from a disk file*

SYNTAX: CALL GFUNC WITH "GRESTORE <disk file name>"

DESCRIPTION: Get a screen image and display it on the screen.
RETURN VALUE: None.

Notes:
The content of the file must have been correctly created by a previous call to GSAVE. When the image is displayed on the screen, the current graphics device must be the same as the device in effect when the screen was drawn and saved.

EXAMPLE:

```
CALL GFUNC WITH "INITGR"
CALL GFUNC WITH "GRESTORE MYPIC.PIC"
CALL GFUNC WITH "WAIT"
CALL GFUNC WITH "ENDGR"
```

GSAVE — *Store a graphics screen in a disk file*

SYNTAX: CALL GFUNC WITH "GSAVE <disk file name>"
DESCRIPTION: Place a copy of the screen in a disk file.
RETURN VALUE: None.

EXAMPLES:

```
CALL GFUNC WITH "BARCHART MY1,MY2,MY3,5,,,,1"
* LEAVE SCREEN IN GRAPHICS MODE BEFORE SCREEN SAVE
CALL GFUNC WITH "GSAVE MYPIC.PIC"
CALL GFUNC WITH "ENDGR"
```

GXTEXT — *Display a horizontal string*

SYNTAX: CALL GFUNC WITH "GXTEXT <text>, <x>, <y>, <color>"
DESCRIPTION: Add a character string in the indicated color to the screen at the indicated coordinates (at the point <x,y>). Display the string horizontally.
RETURN VALUE: None.

EXAMPLES:

CALL GFUNC WITH "BARCHART MY1,MY2,MY3,5,,,,1"
CALL GFUNC WITH "GXTEXT ANOTHER TITLE,0,190,3"
CALL GFUNC WITH "WAIT"
CALL GFUNC WITH "ENDGR"

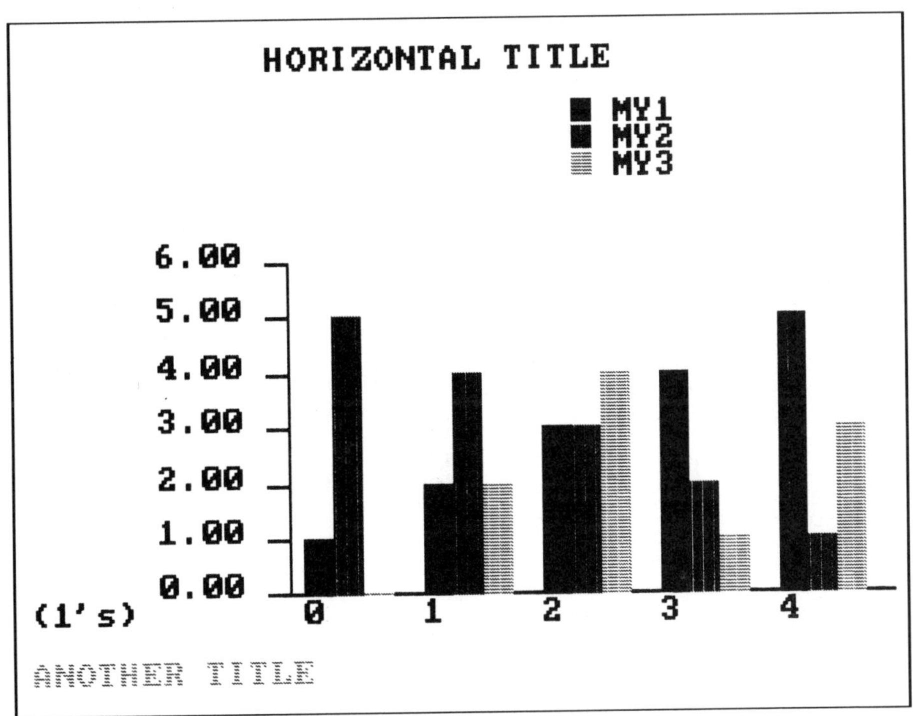

GYTEXT — *Display a vertical string*

SYNTAX: CALL GFUNC WITH "GYTEXT <text>, <x>, <y>, <color>"

DESCRIPTION: Add a character string in the indicated color to the screen at the indicated coordinates (at the point <x,y>). Display the string vertically.

RETURN VALUE: None.

EXAMPLES:

CALL GFUNC WITH "BARCHART MY1,MY2,MY3,5,,,,1"
CALL GFUNC WITH "GYTEXT ANOTHER TITLE,0,5,3"

CALL GFUNC WITH "WAIT"
CALL GFUNC WITH "ENDGR"

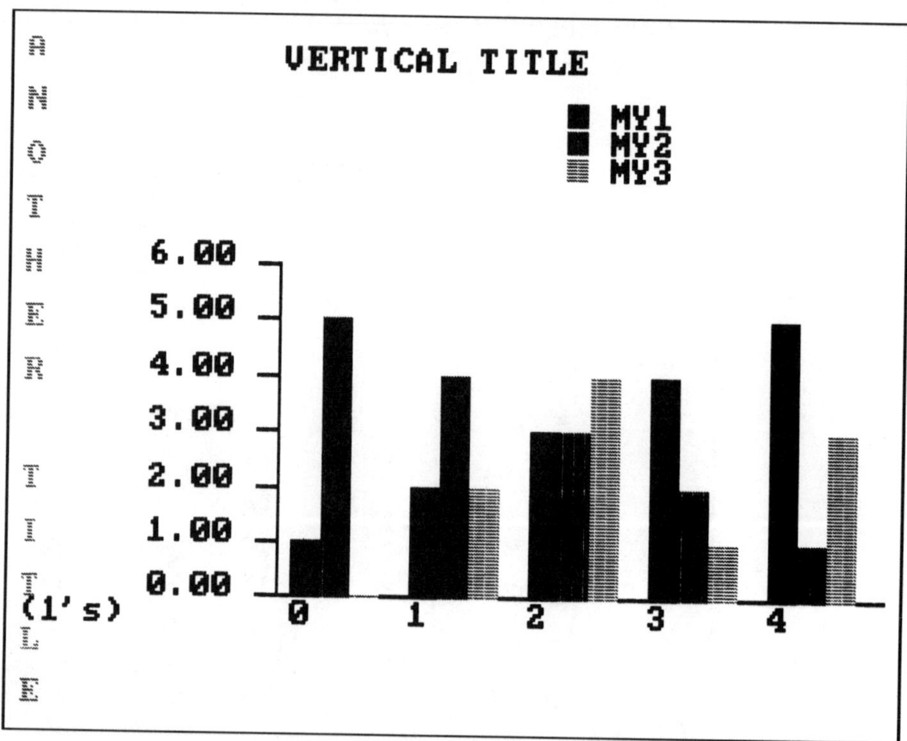

HELP — *List names of functions in the library*

SYNTAX: CALL GFUNC WITH "HELP [<function name>]"

DESCRIPTION: If no function name is used, then a list of the names of the functions in the C Tool's library is displayed. If the name of the function is provided, then a brief description of the function and its parameters are displayed.

RETURN VALUE: None.

Notes:

When this function is used, a window is placed on the screen and the information is displayed within this window. You are prompted to press a key to continue. When the key is pressed, the window is removed from the screen and the previous screen display is restored.

EXAMPLES:

```
. CALL GFUNC WITH "HELP"
. CALL GFUNC WITH "HELP SETDVAR"
```

ARC	ARESTORE	ASAVE	BARCHART	BOX	CAKECHART	CIRCLE
COUNT	CRARRAY	DOT	DUMPARRAY	ENDGR	FRARRAY	GETARRAY
GPRINT	GRESTORE	GSAVE	GXTEXT	GYTEXT	HELP	HLC
INITGR	LINE	LINECHART	MONOBAR	MONOHLC	MONOMP	MONOSBAR
MONOXY	MPCHART	PIECHART	POLYGON	PUTARRAY	RAND	SBARCHART
SETBAR	SETCOLOR	SETDVAR	SETERR	SETLEGEND	SETSTYLE	SETXLAB
SETYLAB	STARRAY	WAIT	XYCHART			

HLC — *High-low-close graph*

SYNTAX: CALL GFUNC WITH "HLC <array of highs>, <array of lows>, <array of closes>, <number of points> [, <graph title>, <x-axis title>, <y-axis title>] [, <screen mode after graphing>]"
where <array of highs> contains the high prices for each time period, <array of lows> contains the low prices for each time period, and < array of closes> contains the closing values for each time period.

DESCRIPTION: Display a high-low-close graph for stock.

RETURN VALUE: None.

EXAMPLES:

```
CALL GFUNC WITH "HLC HIGHS,LOWS,CLOSES,5"
CALL GFUNC WITH "WAIT"
CALL GFUNC WITH "ENDGR"
```

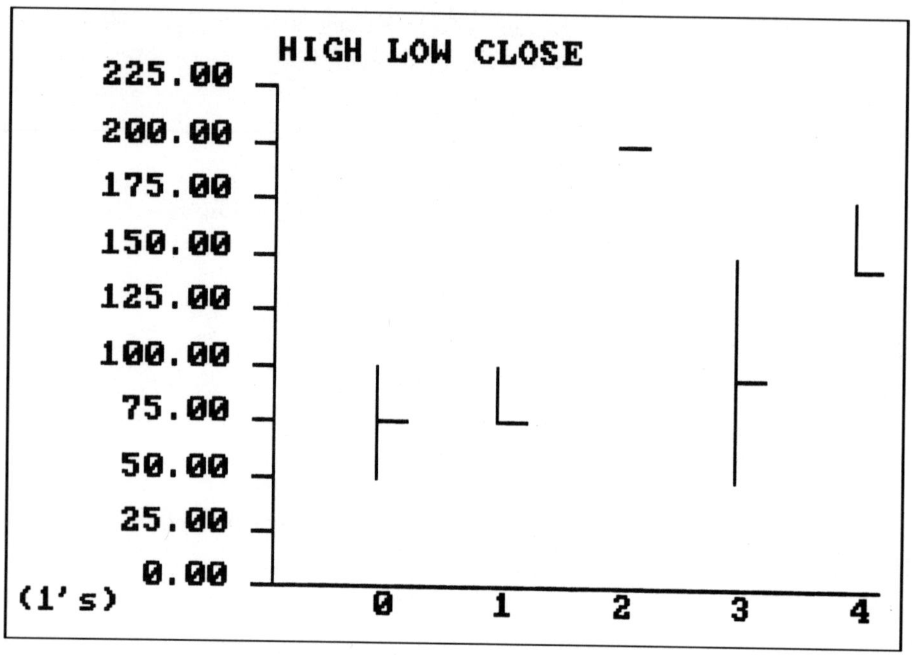

INITGR — *Enter graphics mode*

SYNTAX: CALL GFUNC WITH "INITGR [<type of display>, <background color>, <palette number>, <screen mode after graphing>]"

DESCRIPTION: Set the colors and then change to Graphics mode.

RETURN VALUE: None.

Notes:

The display types are CGA, EGA, and HERC. The colors and palettes for CGA in the display are given in Table 10.3.

TABLE 10.3

PALETTE	COLOR 1	COLOR 2	COLOR 3
0	Green	Red	Yellow
1	Cyan	Magenta	White

The background colors for both palettes are shown in Table 10.4.

If the function is used without any parameters, then the most recently used settings for palette and color are retained.

The INITGR function must be invoked before a low-level (primitive) graphics function is executed.

EXAMPLES:

```
CALL GFUNC WITH "INITGR CGA, 0, 1, 0"
CALL GFUNC WITH "SETCOLOR 2"
CALL GFUNC WITH "LINE 1,10,50,10"
CALL GFUNC WITH "WAIT"
CALL GFUNC WITH "ENDGR"
```

LINE — *Draw a line*

SYNTAX: CALL GFUNC WITH "LINE <x1>, <y1>, <x2>, <y2>"
where <x1,y1> and <x2,y2> are two points on the screen.

DESCRIPTION: Draw a line between the two given points.

RETURN VALUE: None.

TABLE 10.4

NUMBER	BACKGROUND COLOR
0	Black
1	Blue
2	Green
3	Light blue
4	Red
5	Magenta
6	Yellow
7	White
8	Grey

EXAMPLES:

CALL GFUNC WITH "INITGR"
CALL GFUNC WITH "SETCOLOR 3"
CALL GFUNC WITH "LINE 0,0,100,100"
CALL GFUNC WITH "LINE 100,100,0,100"
CALL GFUNC WITH "LINE 100,100,100,0"
CALL GFUNC WITH "WAIT"
CALL GFUNC WITH "ENDGR"

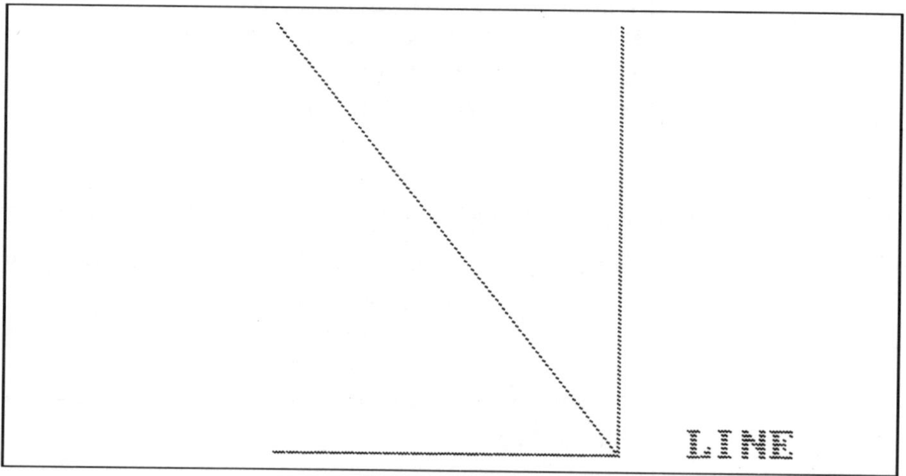

LINECHART – *Draw a line graph*

SYNTAX: CALL GFUNC WITH "LINECHART <1-4 array names>, <number of points> [, <graph title>, <x-axis title>, <y-axis title>] [, <screen mode after graphing>]"

DESCRIPTION: Draw a line graph using the data in up to four arrays.

RETURN VALUE: None.

Notes:
The line is drawn in the current color.

EXAMPLES:

CALL GFUNC WITH "LINECHART MY1,MY2,MY3,5"

```
CALL GFUNC WITH "WAIT"
CALL GFUNC WITH "ENDGR"
```

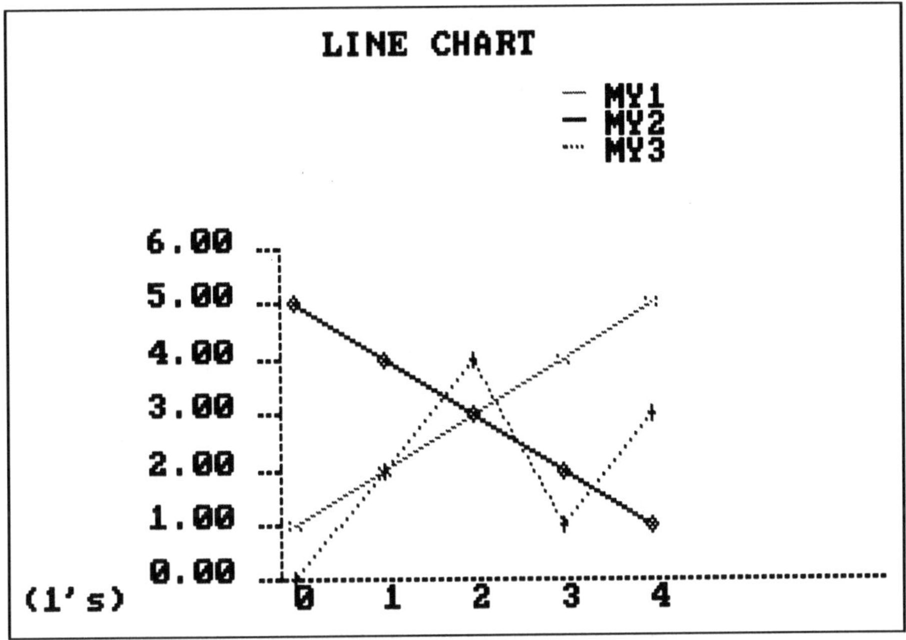

MONOBAR – *Monochrome bar graph*

SYNTAX: CALL GFUNC WITH "MONOBAR <1-4 arrays>, <number of points> [, <graph title>, <x-axis title>, <y-axis title>][, <screen mode after graphing>]"

DESCRIPTION: The monochrome version of BARCHART.

RETURN VALUE: None.

Notes:

Make sure that the screen is in Text mode before using this function.

EXAMPLES:

```
CALL GFUNC WITH "ENDGR"
CALL GFUNC WITH "MONOBAR MY1,MY2,MY3,5"
```

MONOHLC — *Monochrome high-low-close graph*

SYNTAX: CALL GFUNC WITH "MONOHLC <array of highs>, <array of lows>, <array of closes>, <number of points> [, <graph title>, <x-axis title>, <y-axis title>] [, <screen mode after graphing>]"
where <array of highs> contains the high prices for each time period, <array of lows> contains the low prices for each time period, and <array of closes> contains the closing values for each time period.

DESCRIPTION: The Monochrome version of HLC.

RETURN VALUE: None.

Notes:

Make sure that the screen is in Text mode before using this function.

EXAMPLES:

```
CALL GFUNC WITH "ENDGR"
CALL GFUNC WITH "MONOHLC HLCH,HLCL,HLCC,5"
```

MONOMP — *Monochrome marked-points graph*

SYNTAX: CALL GFUNC WITH "MONOMP <1-4 arrays>, <number of points> [, <graph title>, <x-axis title>, <y-axis title>][, <screen mode after graphing>]"

DESCRIPTION: The monochrome version of MPCHART.

RETURN VALUE: None.

Notes:

Make sure that the screen is in Text mode before using this function.

EXAMPLES:

```
CALL GFUNC WITH "ENDGR"
CALL GFUNC WITH "MONOMP MY1,MY2,MY3,5"
```

MONOSBAR — *Monochrome stacked bar graph*

SYNTAX: CALL GFUNC WITH "MONOSBAR <1-4 arrays>, <number of points> [, <graph title>, <x-axis title>, <y-axis title>][, <screen mode after graphing>]"

DESCRIPTION: The monochrome version of SBARCHART.

RETURN VALUE: None.

Notes:

Make sure that the screen is in Text mode before using this function.

EXAMPLES:

```
CALL GFUNC WITH "ENDGR"
CALL GFUNC WITH "MONOSBAR MY1,MY2,MY3,5"
```

MONOXY — *Monochrome XY graph*

SYNTAX: CALL GFUNC WITH "MONOXY <1-4 arrays>, <number of points>[, <graph title>, <x-axis title>, <y-axis title>] [, <screen mode after graphing>]"

DESCRIPTION: Monochrome version of XYCHART.

RETURN VALUE: None.

Notes:

Make sure that the screen is in Text mode before using this function.

EXAMPLES:

```
CALL GFUNC WITH "ENDGR"
CALL GFUNC WITH "MONOXY MY1,MY2,MY3,5"
```

MPCHART — *Marked-points graph*

SYNTAX: CALL GFUNC WITH "MPCHART <1-4 arrays>, <number of points> [<graph title>, <x-axis title>, <y-axis title>][, <screen mode after graphing>]"

DESCRIPTION: Display a marked-points graph (scattergram) of the data in up to four arrays.

RETURN VALUE: None.

EXAMPLES:

CALL GFUNC WITH "MPCHART MY1,MY2,MY3,5"
CALL GFUNC WITH "WAIT"
CALL GFUNC WITH "ENDGR"

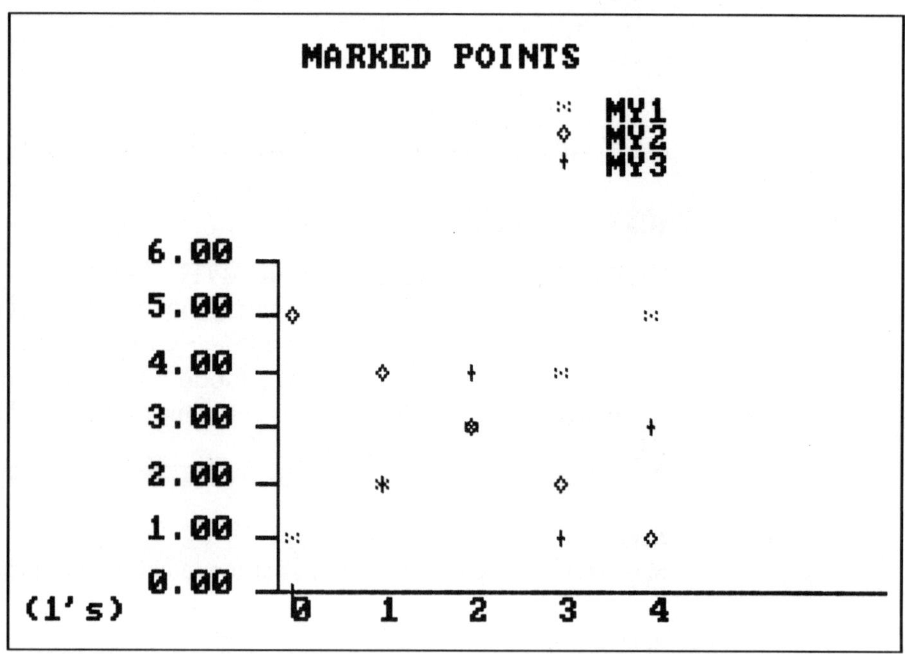

PIECHART – *Pie graph*

SYNTAX: CALL GFUNC WITH "PIECHART <array name>, <number of points>, <graph title>, [<screen mode after graphing>][, <s1>, <s2>, . . . , <sn>]"
where <s1>, <s2>, . . . , <sn> are the numbers of the slices to be exploded.

DESCRIPTION: The data from the array are represented as slices or wedges in a circle. The "exploded" slices are slightly offset from the origin of the circle.

RETURN VALUE: None.

Notes:
All the values in the array must be of the same sign, that is, they must all be nonnegative or all nonpositive. Slice numbers start with 0 (not 1) and represent the offset of the data in the array.

EXAMPLES:

```
CALL GFUNC WITH "PIECHART MY2,5,PIE CHART,1,0,2"
CALL GFUNC WITH "WAIT"
CALL GFUNC WITH "ENDGR"
```

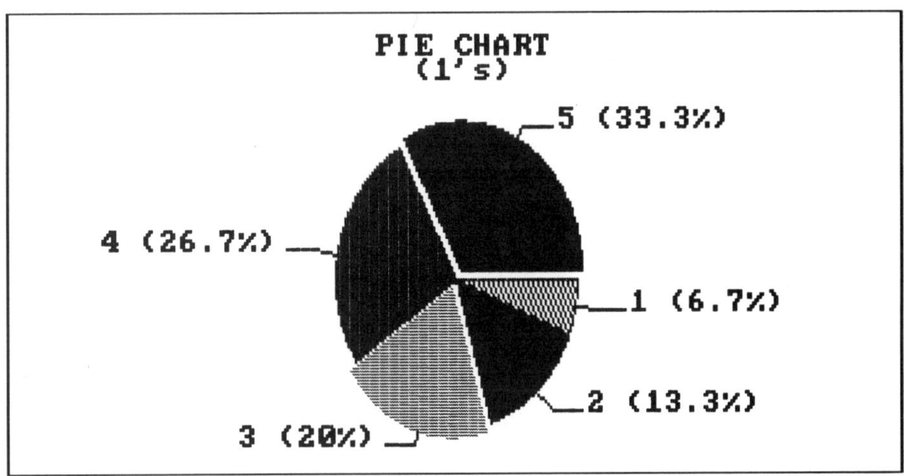

POLYGON — *Draw a polygon*

SYNTAX: CALL GFUNC WITH "POLYGON <array of x coordinates>, <array of y coordinates>, <number of sides>"
where <x[0],y[0]> are the coordinates of the first point, and so forth.

DESCRIPTION: Draw a polygon using the coordinates in the two arrays.

RETURN VALUE: None.

Notes:
<number of sides> is one more than the number of points to be used.

EXAMPLES:

```
CALL GFUNC WITH "INITGR"
CALL GFUNC WITH "SETCOLOR 3"
CALL GFUNC WITH "POLYGON POLYX, POLYY, 6"
CALL GFUNC WITH "WAIT"
CALL GFUNC WITH "ENDGR"
```

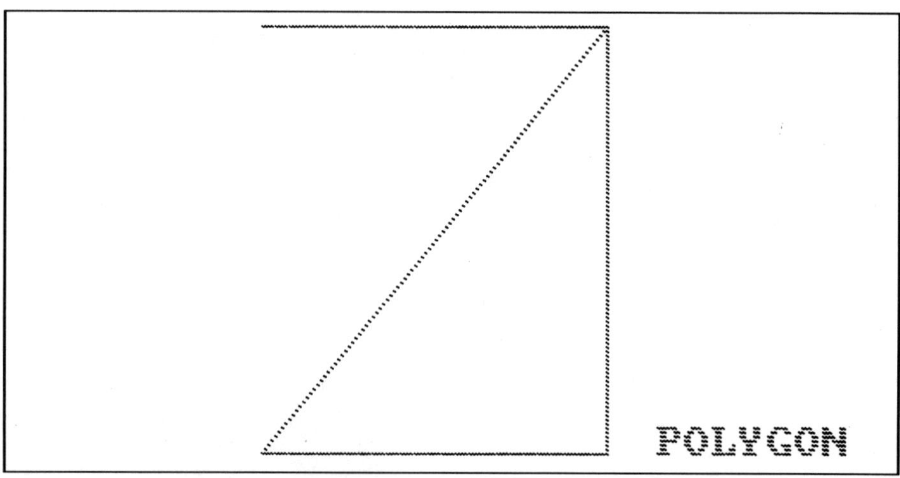

PUTARRAY – *Store a value in an array*

SYNTAX: CALL GFUNC WITH "PUTARRAY <array name>, <index>, <value>" where <value> is the value to be stored in the array.

DESCRIPTION: Store a value in the designated position in an array.

RETURN VALUE: If successful, the value of <index> is returned to C_N_RESULT.

EXAMPLES:

```
. CALL GFUNC WITH "PUTARRAY MYARRAY,0,1"
. ? C_N_RESULT
        0.00
```

RAND — *Generate a random number*

SYNTAX: CALL GFUNC WITH "RAND [<seed value>]", or CALL GFUNC WITH "RAND <low>, <high>"

DESCRIPTION: If no parameters are used, RAND generates a random number greater than or equal to 0 and less than 1, using the system clock as a seed value. If a seed value is used, then the initial value returned is determined by the seed and the value generated is greater than or equal to 0 and less than 1. If the <low> and <high> parameters are used, then an integer greater than or equal to <low> and less than or equal to <high> is generated.

RETURN VALUE: A random number is returned to C_N_RESULT.

Notes:
<low> must be a positive integer and <high> must be less than 32767. If a seed value is used, it must be positive and less than 2147438647.

EXAMPLE:

```
I = 1
DO WHILE I < =5
   CALL GFUNC WITH "RAND 10,100"
   CALL GFUNC WITH "PUTARRAY MYARRAY," + STR(I,1) + "," + ;
          STR(C_N_RESULT,3)
   I = I + 1
ENDDO
```

SBARCHART — *Stacked bar graph*

SYNTAX: CALL GFUNC WITH "SBARCHART <1-4 array names>, <number of points>, <graph title>, [<screen mode after graphing>]"

DESCRIPTION: Draw a stacked bar graph using the data in one to four arrays.
RETURN VALUE: None.

Notes:
All the data must be nonnegative.

EXAMPLES:

```
CALL GFUNC WITH "SBARCHART MY1,MY2,MY3,5"
CALL GFUNC WITH "WAIT"
CALL GFUNC WITH "ENDGR"
```

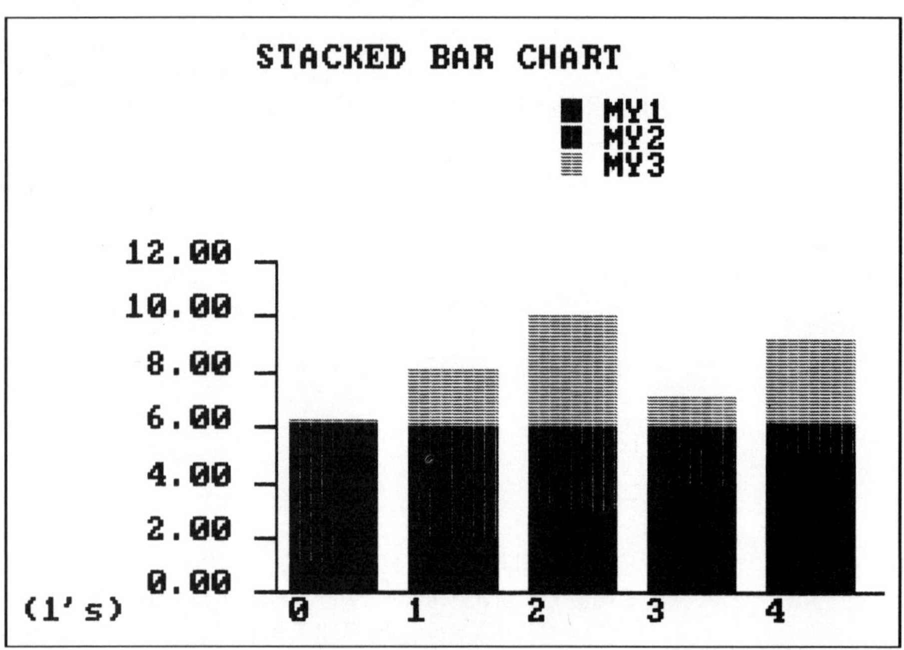

SETBAR – *Change bar graph characters*

SYNTAX: CALL GFUNC WITH "SETBAR [<character string>]"
where the <character string> can contain from 1 to 4 characters.
DESCRIPTION: Select the ASCII characters to be used for the monochrome version of the bar and stacked

bar graphs, one for each of the four possible bars in the graph.

RETURN VALUE: None.

Notes:

If the function is used without a parameter, then the system default characters are used. These default characters are identified by the decimal values: 219, 176, 178, and 177. In order to use a graphics character from the extended IBM character set, hold down ALT, enter the digits for the number while holding down ALT, and then release ALT.

EXAMPLES:

CALL GFUNC WITH "SETBAR *&#!"
CALL GFUNC WITH "ENDGR"
CALL GFUNC WITH "MONOBAR MY1,MY2,MY3,5"

```
                           SET BAR
                                        * MY1
                                        & MY2
                                        # MY3
   6.00

   5.00 | &                                           *
        | &                                           *
   4.00 | &         &          #          *           *
        | &         &          #          *           *
   3.00 | &         &         *&#         *           * #
        | &         &         *&#         *           * #
   2.00 | &        *&#        *&#        *&           * #
        | &        *&#        *&#        *&           * #
   1.00 |*&        *&#        *&#        *&#         *&#
        |*&        *&#        *&#        *&#         *&#
   0.00 |*&#       *&#        *&#        *&#         *&#
  (1's)  0          1          2          3           4
```

SETCOLOR — *Change the color*

SYNTAX: CALL GFUNC WITH "SETCOLOR <color number>"
where the possible numbers are 1, 2, or 3.

DESCRIPTION: Select the colors to be used for the low-level (primitive) graphics functions.

RETURN VALUE: None.

Notes:
This function is used to select a (another) color from the current palette while already in Graphics mode. See INITGR for the colors used with the CGA card.

EXAMPLES:

```
CALL GFUNC WITH "INITGR"
CALL GFUNC WITH "SETCOLOR 3"
CALL GFUNC WITH "LINE 0,0,100,100"
CALL GFUNC WITH "WAIT"
CALL GFUNC WITH "ENDGR"
```

SETDVAR – *Declare return variable*

SYNTAX: CALL GFUNC WITH "SETDVAR <variable type>"
where the <return type> can be any of the following: N(umeric), C(haracter string), E(rror), or S(tatus).

DESCRIPTION: Declare a return variable to be used in conjunction with C routines.

RETURN VALUE: The value −1 is returned to C_STATUS if <variable type> is not valid.

Notes:
The valid <variable type>s are N, C, E, and S. When the SETDVAR function is used, it must be immediately followed by a second CALL GFUNC statement that supplies the name of the return variable. Note in the following example that the name of the return variable is not delimited.

EXAMPLE:

```
PUBLIC MYSTRING
MYSTRING = SPACE(35)
CALL GFUNC WITH "SETDVAR C"
CALL GFUNC WITH MYSTRING
```

SETERR – *Set error flag*

SYNTAX:	CALL GFUNC WITH "SETERR <integer>" where <integer> is nonnegative.
DESCRIPTION:	If <integer> is positive and an error occurs, then an error message is displayed, execution of the program will temporarily halt, and the user is prompted to press a key (similar to the dBASE III Plus WAIT statement). If <integer> has the value zero (0) and an error occurs, then no message is displayed and the program is not interrupted. In this case, the error code is stored in C_ERROR.
RETURN VALUE:	This function does not return a value, but error codes will be returned to C_ERROR if SETERR has been set off (<integer> has the value 0) and an error occurs.

Notes:

After each operation, the program can test the value of C_ERROR to see if an error has occurred. If an error does occur, the program can perform its own error trapping.

EXAMPLE:

```
. * TO SET ERROR REPORTING MODE OFF
. CALL GFUNC WITH "SETERR 0"
```

SETLEGEND – *Set coordinates for legend* *DEFAULT: <16,150>*

SYNTAX:	CALL GFUNC WITH "SETLEGEND <x-coordinate>, <y-coordinate>" where <x,y> are the coordinates of the pivot point.
DESCRIPTION:	Indicate where the legend for a graph is to begin when it is displayed.
RETURN VALUE:	None.

Notes:

The default coordinates for the legend are <16,150>.

EXAMPLE:

CALL GFUNC WITH "SETLEGEND 16,100"

SETSTYLE – *Set line type* (see figure on the next page) *DEFAULT: 0 (SOLID)*

SYNTAX: CALL GFUNC WITH "SETSTYLE <style code>"
where <style code> is an integer between 0 and 2.

DESCRIPTION: Select the type of lines to be drawn by other functions.

RETURN VALUE: None.

Notes:

The styles are

0: Solid line
1: Dotted line
2: Dashed line

The default line type is solid.

EXAMPLE:

```
* SETSTYLE.PRG
CALL GFUNC WITH "INITGR"
CALL GFUNC WITH "SETCOLOR 1"
CALL GFUNC WITH "SETSTYLE 0"
CALL GFUNC WITH "LINE 0,0,100,0"
CALL GFUNC WITH "SETCOLOR 2"
CALL GFUNC WITH "SETSTYLE 1"
CALL GFUNC WITH "LINE 100,0,100,100"
CALL GFUNC WITH "SETCOLOR 3"
CALL GFUNC WITH "SETSTYLE 2"
CALL GFUNC WITH "LINE 100,100,0,100"
CALL GFUNC WITH "WAIT"
CALL GFUNC WITH "ENDGR"
```

SETXLAB – *Toggle x-axis label on or off, or select a label*

SYNTAX 1: CALL GFUNC WITH "SETXLAB <code>", or

SYNTAX 2: CALL GFUNC WITH "SETXLAB <array name>"

DESCRIPTION 1: Using SYNTAX 1, indicate whether or not the x-axis label should be displayed. If the value of <code> is 0, then the x-axis label will not be displayed. If the value of <code> is 1, then the label will be displayed. The default is to display the label.

DESCRIPTION 2: Using SYNTAX 2, select an array to be used for the x-axis labels.

RETURN VALUE: None.

Notes:

If SYNTAX 2 is used, then the array contains the text of the x-axis label for all graphs produced, until another call to SETXLAB. The number of elements in the array should match the number of plot points or bars in the graph.

EXAMPLES:

```
CALL GFUNC WITH "SETXLAB 0"
CALL GFUNC WITH "SETXLAB MONTHS"
```

SETYLAB — *Toggle y-axis label on or off*

SYNTAX: CALL GFUNC WITH "SETYLAB <code>"

DESCRIPTION: Indicate whether or not the x-axis label should be displayed. If the value of <code> is 0, then the x-axis label will not be displayed. If the

	value of <code> is 1, then the label will be displayed. The default is to display the label, using standard incrementation.
RETURN VALUE:	None.

EXAMPLES:

CALL GFUNC WITH "SETYLAB 0"
CALL GFUNC WITH "SETYLAB MONTHS"

STARRAY — *Report status of arrays*

SYNTAX:	CALL GFUNC WITH "STARRAY" where the function takes no parameters.
DESCRIPTION:	Display a report showing the status of each array. Include array name, type, count (number of elements stored in the array), the actual size of the array, and the number of arrays that may still be created. The maximum number of arrays at any one time is 10.
RETURN VALUE:	If successful, the number of arrays is returned to C_N_RESULT, otherwise −1 is returned.

EXAMPLE:

. CALL GFUNC WITH "STARRAY"

```
Array: MY1, Type: N, Size: 5, Count: 5
Array: MY2, Type: N, Size: 5, Count: 5
Array: MY3, Type: N, Size: 5, Count: 5
Array: POLYX, Type: N, Size: 5, Count: 5
Array: POLYY, Type: N, Size: 5, Count: 5
Array: HIGHS, Type: N, Size: 5, Count: 5
Array: LOWS, Type: N, Size: 5, Count: 5
Array: CLOSES, Type: N, Size: 5, Count: 5
There are 2 arrays (and 15232 bytes) available for use
```

WAIT – *Pause and wait for input*

SYNTAX: CALL GFUNC WITH "WAIT"
DESCRIPTION: Wait for RETURN to be pressed at the keyboard. Use this function to "freeze" the screen before continuing with execution of a program. No message is displayed on the screen, so graphs are not changed.
RETURN VALUE: None.

EXAMPLE:

```
CALL GFUNC WITH "INITGR"
CALL GFUNC WITH "SETCOLOR 3"
CALL GFUNC WITH "LINE 0,0,100,100"
CALL GFUNC WITH "WAIT"
CALL GFUNC WITH "ENDGR"
```

XYCHART – *XY graph* (see figure on p. 416)

SYNTAX: CALL GFUNC WITH "XYCHART <1-4 arrays>, <number of points> [, <graph title>, <x-axis title>, <y-axis title>][, <screen mode after graphing>]"
DESCRIPTION: Produce an XY graph of the data in up to four arrays.
RETURN VALUE: None.

EXAMPLE:

```
CALL GFUNC WITH "XYCHART MY1,MY2,MY3,5"
CALL GFUNC WITH "WAIT"
CALL GFUNC WITH "ENDGR"
```

10.7 ERRORS

In a number of situations, your graphics program will not produce any results and will freeze the screen. This usually happens as a result of a syntax error in a CALL statement. dBASE III Plus may not return an error message if parsing the CALL statement fails. A typical error of this type is leaving the final delimiter off at the end of the CALL statement. In order

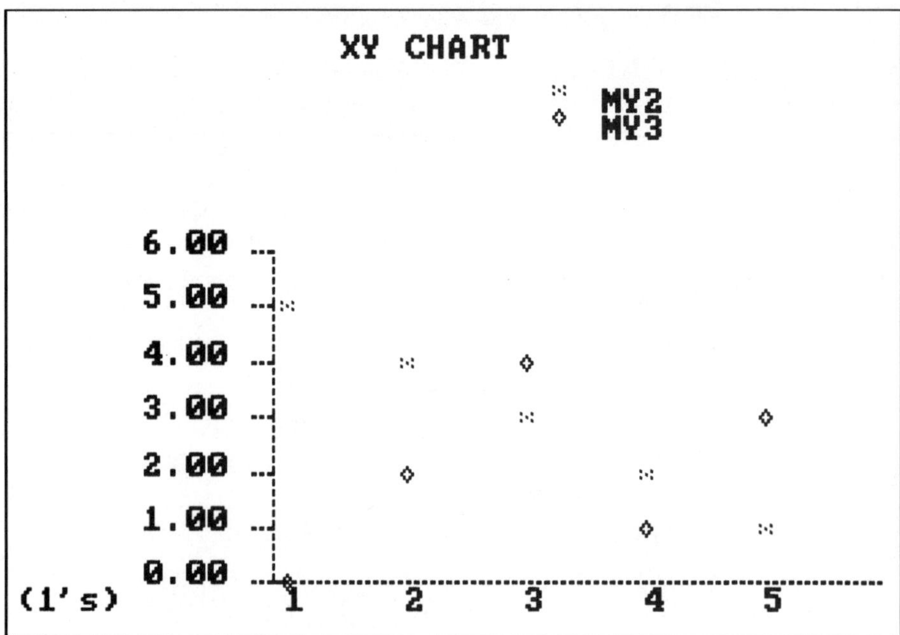

to recover from this type of error, press ESC to cancel the program and then enter the following statement

CALL GFUNC WITH "ENDGR"

to return to Text mode. When you are in Graphics mode, your entry will not show on the screen, and you might find entry of the statement difficult. When you are debugging your graphics programs, SET one of the function keys in your CONFIG.DB file to generate the appropriate statement

(CALL GFUNC WITH "ENDGR")

If you misspell the word WITH in the CALL statement, you may find that the entire system locks up. In this case, you will need to reboot the system (CTRL-ALT-DEL).

CHAPTER

11

Converting from dBASE II to dBASE III Plus

11.1 THE PROBLEM

dBASE III Plus has a number of features that do not exist in dBASE II, has some features that are different from those in dBASE II, and handles database files differently. In addition, the structure of the data and format files is different. If you try to run a dBASE II program using dBASE III Plus, you may get a syntax error. If you try to use a dBASE II data or format file using dBASE III Plus, you will get an error message similar to

```
NOT A dBASE III FILE
```

As a result, it is necessary to convert both files and programs before they can be used under dBASE III Plus.

11.2 CONVERTING FILES

The dBASE III Plus utility program called DCONVERT.EXE is used to convert files from the dBASE II format to the dBASE III Plus format. In order to convert database files, use the statement

```
DCONVERT *.DBF
```

at the level of the operating system. Similar statements are used to convert other types of files.

11.3 CONVERTING PROGRAMS

The DCONVERT.EXE program can be also used with programs, but you may wish to make the changes yourself. Making changes manually can be a bit tedious, but I think that you will derive a great deal of benefit from the manual changes, since DCONVERT does not alway convert the program in the manner that you would want it converted. In addition, DCONVERT makes no changes in the number of files that are open at any one time. Since dBASE II allows only two database files to be open at any one time and since dBASE III Plus allows you to have up to ten database files open at any one time, a considerable increase in efficiency can often be obtained by increasing the number of simultaneously open files, when the program is converted.

The steps that I use to convert a dBASE II program to a dBASE III Plus program are as follows:

1. Rename the file from <name>.CMD to <name>.PRG.

2. Replace each CLEAR with CLEAR ALL.
3. Replace each ERASE with CLEAR.
4. Replace each T with .T..
5. Replace each F with .F..
6. Replace each EOF with EOF( ).
7. Replace each # < > 0 with .NOT. EOF( ), after a FIND.
8. Replace each "FIND &" with SEEK.
9. Remove any extraneous macro-expansion symbols (&) and, if necessary, rewrite the code. In some cases, the & symbol dramatically slows down execution of a program.
10. Replace constant strings containing only blanks with the SPACE function and the correct parameter indicating the number of spaces.
11. Replace the ! function with the UPPER function.
12. Replace all $ functions with the SUBSTR function.
13. Replace each USING with PICTURE.
14. Replace SET FORMAT with SET DEVICE.
15. Replace # with RECNO( ), when it is used as a record number.
16. Replace * with DELETED( ), when it is used to indicate a deleted record.
17. Replace the code

    ```
    DELETE ALL
    PACK
    ```

    with

    ```
    ZAP
    ```

18. Examine each USING clause for the use of $ and * characters, and then replace them with their dBASE III Plus equivalent.
19. Rewrite some of your code to take advantage of the ROUND function in dBASE III Plus.
20. Insert colons as necessary in ACCEPT and WAIT statements in order to make the screen displays more readable.
21. If necessary, add the statement

    ```
    GOTO TOP
    ```

    after a COUNT.
22. If variables are created in subroutines (programs that are called by a DO statement), you will need to declare them as PUBLIC if you wish to pass data back to the calling routine using these variables.

23. Remove any code that obtained today's date from the user. Instead, get the date from the MS DOS system date. Any reference in a dBASE III Plus program to DATE( ) always uses this system date.
24. Change character string dates to variables and constants of type date. In general, this change will make your programs easier to read and modify. When dBASE III was first released, I thought that changing character string dates to objects of type data was too difficult to be worthwhile. Since then I have changed my mind. It really is easy to make the changes.

    Remember:
    If you make changes in your programs, make the corresponding changes in the database files. Happily, if you use the MODIFY STRUCTURE command to change your database file so that a character string field with data of the type MM/DD/YY is changed to a field of type date, then the data is converted for you. In this case, all the dates are converted for you and you do not have to re-enter them.

    If you have stored dates as integers (Julian dates), you may find that they will need to be converted to regular dates. In some cases, you may have duplicated date information (one field is a character string date and the other is an integral Julian date) and the Julian date can now be completely eliminated.
25. If your programs and files are on 5¼-inch disks that are not compatible with the IBM format, you can use a program like UNIFORM to read the disk files directly and transfer them to a disk of the IBM format. A program like UNIFORM is usually less expensive than obtaining a communications package and hard-wiring two computers together to transfer the files, is easier to use, and is faster.
26. Changing the way in which files are used is much more complicated than the preceding changes, since the changes may involve several lines, not just one.
    A. Examine how the files are used in the program. If you need to use more than two database files in a program, determine the required number of areas and assign each file to an area, near the beginning of the program. Make sure that each database file is opened no more than once (with the USE statement) in each program. Once the database files have been opened (at the

beginning of the program), you can choose to make one of them the current file with the SELECT statement.

B. Change any "P." and "S." prefixes to the appropriate ones. For example, field names prefixed by "P." might now be prefixed by A->.

C. Since you cannot directly reference names of fields associated with other areas (other than the current one), you may need to prefix a number of field names with an appropriate alias (like A->). If you reference a field that is not defined in your current area, then you will get a message like

VARIABLE NOT FOUND

Note that an alias cannot be used in a REPLACE statement for fields in the current area, but can be used for fields in other areas. As a result, always SELECT the correct area before executing a REPLACE statement.

11.4 FEATURES OF dBASE II THAT HAVE BEEN REPLACED IN dBASE III PLUS

dBASE II	*dBASE III Plus*
# (record number)	RECNO( )
* (deletion test)	DELETED( )
@( )	AT( )
$( )	SUBSTR( )
!( )	UPPER( )
CLEAR	CLEAR ALL
DELETE FILE	ERASE
ERASE	CLEAR
QUIT TO	RUN
SET COLON	SET DELIMITER
SET EJECT	Now incorporated in REPORT
SET HEADING	Now incorporated in REPORT
SET RAW	Now performed by TRIM
RANK( )	ASC( )
TEST	TYPE

11.5 FEATURES OF dBASE II THAT HAVE BEEN CHANGED IN dBASE III PLUS

Feature	*Change*
@ . . GET	Range option and PICTURE instead of USING
: in a name	_ in a name (change : to _)
APPEND	Can return to previous entry with PgUp
BROWSE	Can lock columns at left of screen plus the addition of the GOTO and the FIND
CHANGE	Now equivalent to the EDIT statement
CLEAR	Can be used to erase the screen, release all memory variables and files, release GETs, and release just the memory variables
DISPLAY	Column headings can be included with the listing of the data
DO . . WITH	Allows parameters to be passed
EDIT	Can use your choice of editor
F	Replaced by .F.
GOTO	Can use expressions as well as constants
HELP	On-screen syntax of functions and statements
MODIFY COMMAND	Can use your choice of editor
PRIMARY	Use an alias
REPORT	Can use full-screen editing and send output to a file
RETURN	New option [TO MASTER]
SECONDARY	Use an alias
SORT	New options
SET ESCAPE	Will ask you if you wish to abort execution of the program
T	Replaced by .T.
WAIT	Can use a prompt

11.6 FEATURES OF dBASE II WITH NO COUNTERPART IN dBASE III PLUS

READ NOUPDATE

REMARK
SET DATE ( )
SET SCREEN
UPDATE . . ADD

11.7 FEATURES OF dBASE III THAT ARE NOT IN dBASE II

** or ^
@ . . CLEAR
&&
ABS
Assignment using =
ASSIST
AVERAGE
BOF
Boxes on screen
CALL
Catalogs
CDOW
CLEAR TYPEAHEAD
CLOSE
CMONTH
COPY FILE
CREATE LABELS
CTOD
DAY
DBF function
Debugging, interactive
DIR
DISKSPACE
DOW

DTOC

ERROR

EXIT

EXP

FIELD function

FKLABEL

FKMAX

FOUND

GETENV

IIF

INKEY

ISALPHA

ISCOLOR

ISLOWER

ISUPPER

LOAD

LOG

LTRIM

LUPDATE function

MAX

Memo fields

MESSAGE

MIN

MOD

MODIFY LABELS

MONTH

NDX

ON KEY

ON ERROR

ON ESCAPE

OS

Parameters

PRIVATE variables

PROCEDURE

PUBLIC variables

Query

RANGE checking

READKEY

RECCOUNT

RECSIZE

REPLICATE

RESUME

RETRY

RIGHT

ROUND

RTRIM (same as trim)

RUN

Screen painter

SEEK

SET (used interactively)

SET CATALOG

SET CENTURY

SET COLOR

SET CONSOLE

SET DATE

SET DECIMALS

SET DELIMITERS

SET DEVICE

SET FILTER

SET FIXED

SET FUNCTION

SET HEADING

SET HELP
SET HISTORY
SET MARGIN
SET MEMOWIDTH
SET MENUS
SET ORDER TO
SET PATH
SET PROCEDURE
SET RELATION
SET SAFETY
SET SCOREBOARD
SET TYPEAHEAD
SET UNIQUE
SET VIEW
STUFF
SQRT
TIME
TRANSFORM
TYPE
VERSION
View
YEAR
ZAP

CHAPTER

12

Compilers — Speeding up dBASE III Plus

12.1 INTRODUCTION

Since dBASE III Plus is interpreted, execution of dBASE III programs can be slow. The obvious solution to this problem is to use a compiler. Unfortunately, the RUNTIME compiler provided by Ashton-Tate is difficult to use and provides only a marginal improvement in speed. In addition, the code produced by RUNTIME is not true machine code, and you will need to purchase a special program to execute this code. Because of Ashton-Tate's marketing policy, this program can only be used on one machine, so each of your clients will need to purchase their own copy. This amounts to paying a royalty to Ashton-Tate each time you compile a program and sell it to a client.

12.2 USING A TRUE COMPILER

Over the last year I have been using a true compiler from Nantucket, Inc., called Clipper. Not only is this product a true compiler, but some of the algorithms appear to work more efficiently than the corresponding dBASE III algorithms. Clipper, like dBASE III Plus, is written in C language, so it is possible to add new routines at any time. In addition, the interface between Clipper and the C library is much cleaner than it is in dBASE III Plus.

The major disadvantage of Clipper is that it is always behind the current release of dBASE III Plus. Each time that new features are added to dBASE III Plus, you must wait until there is a new release from Nantucket to upgrade Clipper. In addition, not all the features of dBASE III Plus will use the same syntax as used in Clipper. For example, Clipper introduced arrays before Ashton-Tate did. When Ashton-Tate added arrays through the use of The Programmer's Library, the syntax was different from that used by Clipper. I expect that Clipper will either change its syntax or allow an alternate syntax so that it can match Ashton-Tate.

Because some of the algorithms used by Clipper differ from those used in dBASE III Plus, you will sometimes find that programs that work in dBASE III Plus do not work the same way when compiled by Clipper. For example, I found that a program that sorted records in a database ran correctly under dBASE III Plus, but ran out of main memory when compiled by Clipper and then subsequently ran. By the way, this problem was handled by using a new index instead of sorting the data.

Since Clipper is a true compiler, the final product is a true machine language program and can be run without any additional software. As a result, Nantucket does not charge any royalties for multiple copies of your application systems and your clients can run your systems without any charges for software use. If you have a copy of dBASE III Plus and a copy of Clipper, you can produce executable code and your clients pay for this code, not for dBASE III Plus or for Clipper.

12.3 INSTRUCTIONS FOR USING CLIPPER

I recommend that you continue to use dBASE III Plus as you ordinarily do to create your files and programs. The debugging facilities in dBASE III Plus are quite reasonable, and compilation under Clipper and the subsequent linking can be quite time-consuming. If you have to compile and link your system each time that you wish to make a change and test it out, you will be quite frustrated. Once you have built, tested, and debugged your application system, compile it using Clipper or another true compiler. After the compilation, link the code and test it out again. You may find some errors under Clipper that did not occur in dBASE III Plus. When you compile your dBASE III Plus programs, you may also find some new syntax errors. For example, Clipper, unlike dBASE III Plus, requires that you have the same number of IFs as ENDIFs and the same number of DO . . WHILEs as ENDWHILEs.

When you compile a dBASE III Plus application, enter the MS DOS command

```
CLIPPER <name of program>  -l-n
```

where <name of program> is the name of the main menu (the driver) of your system without an extension (an extension of PRG is assumed), and −l and −n are parameters. Note that parameters must always appear as lowercase letters. The −n option is used to generate code that will execute faster, and the −l option is used to exclude line numbers, thereby reducing the size of the OBJ file. If you suspect that your code will not compile correctly, use the DOS command

```
CLIPPER <name of program>  -s
```

to suppress the generation of the OBJ file. The use of the −s parameter can also be put to good use when you make a change in a single program. Just compile the program that you have just changed (where <name of

program> is now the name of the program that was just changed) and see if the syntax is correct. When each of the changed programs compiles correctly, you can recompile the entire system. This technique may save you a considerable amount of time.

After the program has been compiled, link it using the DOS command

```
PLINK86 FILE <name of program>
```

where <name of program> is the same as the name used in the CLIPPER (compile) command and contains no extension name. You can use the Microsoft linker, but Nantucket strongly recommends that you use the PLINK86 linker (or a later version) provided at no additional cost as part of the Clipper system.

In addition to the features of Clipper listed above, there is also an overlay system. In the case of a large system, you can break it up into smaller pieces for more efficient memory management. I found that I was able to create a relatively large system without the use of overlays and it fit into main memory without any problems (I use 640K main memory and run about 150K in memory resident programs).

Since compiling and linking can be time-consuming, you may find the following BAT file helpful. It will compile your program and then link it for you if there were no compilation errors:

```
Clipper %1 –l–n
IF NOT ERRORLEVEL 1 Plink86 FI %1
```

When you run this BAT program, use the following command

```
CL <name of program>
```

and then press RETURN.

If you are using any of the extended Library functions in Clipper, change the linking command from

```
PLINK86 FILE <name of program>
```

to

```
PLINK86 FILE <name of program>,EXTENDA,EXTENDC, EXTENDB
```

where the OBJ files named <name of program> contain additional C routines. The names of the OBJ files in this PLINK86 command may change from time to time, so consult your Clipper documentation.

APPENDIX

Technical Specifications

A.1 SPECIFICATIONS

LARGEST NUMBER	10**99
MAXIMUM LENGTH OF A COMMAND	254 characters
MAXIMUM LENGTH OF AN INDEX ON STATEMENT	220 characters
MAXIMUM LENGTH OF AN INDEX KEY	100 characters
MAXIMUM NUMBER OF ACTIVE MEMORY VARIABLES	256
MAXIMUM NUMBER OF CHARACTERS IN A DATABASE	2 billion
MAXIMUM NUMBER OF CHARACTERS IN A FILE OR VARIABLE NAME	10
MAXIMUM NUMBER OF COLUMNS IN A LABEL	250
MAXIMUM NUMBER OF FIELDS IN A DATABASE	128
MAXIMUM NUMBER OF FIELDS IN A REPORT	24
MAXIMUM NUMBER OF LINES IN A REPORT HEADER	4
MAXIMUM NUMBER OF LOADed (bin) FILES	5
MAXIMUM NUMBER OF NESTED DOs	20
MAXIMUM NUMBER OF OPEN DATABASE FILES	10
MAXIMUM NUMBER OF OPEN FILES OF ALL TYPES	15
MAXIMUM NUMBER OF OPEN FORMAT FILES FOR EACH OPEN DATABASE FILE	1
MAXIMUM NUMBER OF OPEN INDEX FILES FOR EACH OPEN DATABASE FILE	7
MAXIMUM NUMBER OF PENDING GETs (DEFAULT = 128)	35 – 1,023
MAXIMUM NUMBER OF RECORDS IN A DATABASE	1 billion
MAXIMUM NUMBER OF SORT FIELDS	10
MAXIMUM SIZE OF A CHARACTER STRING	254 bytes
MAXIMUM SIZE OF A DATABASE RECORD	4,000 bytes
MAXIMUM SIZE OF A MEMO FIELD	Limited only by your editor
MAXIMUM SIZE OF A MEMO RECORD	512K bytes

MAXIMUM SIZE OF A NUMBER	19 bytes
MAXIMUM SIZE OF MEMORY VARIABLE AREA	6000 bytes, or as set in CONFIG.DB
MINIMUM NUMBER OF RECORDS FOR SORT TO WORK	2
NUMERIC ACCURACY	15.9
RESERVED NAMES (FOR ALIASES)	A-J and M
SIZE OF ALL DATE VARIABLES AND FIELDS	8 bytes
SIZE OF ALL LOGICAL VARIABLES AND FIELDS	1 byte
SIZE OF TYPEAHEAD BUFFER (DEFAULT = 20)	0-32,000
SMALLEST NUMBER	10**-307

A.2 COMMENTS ON SYSTEM LIMITATIONS

1. Number of Fields in a Record = 128.
   If you find that you need more than 128 fields in a record, just create another database and duplicate the primary key in the new database. The two databases can then be logically linked together through the use of the primary key values by using the SEEK statement to find the associated record in the second database file. You can link any number of database files together in this manner.
2. Maximum Length of an Index Key = 100.
   If you wish to create an index on a field or combination of fields that will have length greater than 100, you will need to concatenate fewer fields or use the substring function to limit the number of characters used. For example, if you have reserved 35 characters for the last name of a person, you probably need to use no more than 25 (possibly less) for an index value.
3. Number of Open Files of All Types = 15.
   This number (15) places a limitation on the number of index files as well as the number of database files that can be open at any one time. Note that this limitation includes not only your database, index, memo, format, and alternate files, but also your program (PRG) files. You will need to place a FILES=20 statement in your CONFIG.SYS file, since dBASE III Plus uses an additional five files.

APPENDIX

B

Error Messages

B.1 INTRODUCTION

The error messages in dBASE III Plus are often cryptic and can be misleading. In many cases, you will need to carefully examine the statements in error in order to determine the precise nature of the error.

The most common reasons for getting an error message are:

1. You have misspelled something.
2. You have run out of room on the disk.
3. You have used a valid dBASE III Plus statement, but dBASE III Plus itself has an error in it and cannot handle your statement properly.
4. You have exceeded the system limitations.
5. You have made a reference to a nonexistent memory variable, field, or file.

The HELP facility in dBASE III Plus is, for the most part, limited to the display of the correct syntax of the statement.

dBASE III Plus usually returns both an error message and an error number when an error occurs. Error numbers are not returned when the activity can only occur in an interactive environment. You can trap the errors that occur in your programs through the use of the ON ERROR statement, examine the error number using the ERROR( ) function, and then take an appropriate action. If you wish, you can take the easy way out and not trap any errors. In this case, your program will abort when an error occurs. In many cases, not trapping the error works quite well.

B.2 THE ERROR MESSAGES IN ALPHABETICAL ORDER

A DBF file in view is not in the current directory
A view operator cannot find the database file in the directory.

ALIAS name already in use [24]
You are attempting to open a file that is already open in another work area, or you are using an alias name as a file name.

ALIAS not found [13]
Undefined alias name or not in the range between A and J.

ALTERNATE could not be opened [72]
The alternate file named in the CONFIG.DB file cannot be opened. Either the name is invalid, or there is not enough room in the directory.

A Memo field cannot be selected
The Assistant will not let you reference a Memo field at the current time.

At least one file must be in use for this operation
You must select a database file before using the Options menu in CREATE/MODIFY VIEW.

Beginning of file encountered [38]
The currency pointer is just before the first record in the database file.

Cannot erase a file which is open [89]
You must close the database file before it can be deleted from the disk. Use CLOSE DATABASES or another appropriate command to close the database file.

Cannot have subgroups without groups
A REPORT subgroup must be a part of a group.

Cannot select requested database [17]
The work identifier area has been entered as a number not in the range between 1 and 10.

Cannot Write to Read only file [111]
You must use a utility program to change the status of the file from Read only to Read/Write before you can write to the file.

Command not recognized!
HELP does not recognize the keyword of the command. Either you have misspelled the keyword or the desired statement is not described in HELP.

CONTINUE without LOCATE [42]
You cannot CONTINUE unless there has been a previous LOCATE. If you have halted the execution of your program by pressing ESC and then selecting S (for suspend), you can continue with the execution of your program by entering RESUME and pressing RETURN.

Cyclic relation [44]
When database files are linked together using the SET RELATION statement, there cannot be a cycle in the chain. For example, if A is linked to B and B is linked to C, then C cannot, in turn, be linked back to A.

Database is encrypted [131]
Either you are accessing an encrypted database file in single-user mode or you do not have the appropriate access level.

Database is not indexed [26]
You must open an index file before you can use a FIND, SEEK, or an UPDATE statement.

Data catalog has not been established [122]
You cannot use a query clause (the ?) as part of a statement, before you open a catalog (use the SET CATALOG TO statement to open a catalog).

Data type mismatch [9]
You have attempted to perform an operation with the wrong data type. If necessary, convert the data to the correct type before performing the operation.

.DBT file cannot be opened [41]
When you opened a database file (DBF file), the associated memo file (DBT file) could not be found.

Disk full when writing file : <filename> [56]
You ran out of room on the disk. Before the disk gets full, delete unwanted records and PACK the file.

DOs nested too deep [103]
The maximum number of nested command files is 20. Examine your program structure and reduce the depth of the nesting.

Empty structure will not be saved
The database that you have just defined has no fields in it. It will not be saved on the disk.

End of file encountered [4]
Either the database or index file has a bad structure, or the SKIP statement has moved the currency pointer past the last record in the database. If your index file is bad, recreate the index. If your database file is bad, try using either the COPY or the APPEND to save as much of the file as you can.

End of file or error on keyboard input [51]
The file used to simulate keyboard input has been damaged. Such a file is established through the DOS Set Environment command.

Error in HELP system
The Help file for the Assistant (ASSIST.HLP) has been damaged. Get a new copy from your distribution disks.

Exceeding report print width
The column number exceeds the page width in the report specification.

Excess header lines lost
You cannot have more than four lines in the heading of a report created by CREATE/MODIFY REPORT.

Exclusive use on database is required [110]
You must SET EXCLUSIVE ON before you can carry out the desired operation.

******Execution error on + : Concatenated string too large [77]***
The result of the concatenation would be a string with length in excess of 254 characters.

*****Execution error on – : Concatenated string too large [76]**
The result of the concatenation would be a string with length in excess of 254 characters.

*****Execution error on ^ or ** : Negative base, fractional exponent [78]**
You cannot raise a negative number to a fractional power.

*****Execution error on CHR( ) : Out of range [57]**
The parameter in the CHR function must be an integer between 0 and 255.

*****Execution error on LOG( ) : Zero of negative [58]**
The parameter must be a positive number.

*****Execution error on NDX( ) : Invalid index number [87]**
The parameter (the index number) must be between 1 and 7.

*****Execution error on REPLICATE( ) : String too large [88]**
The string that you attempted to create would have length in excess of 254 characters.

*****Execution error on SPACE( ) : Negative [60]**
The parameter must be a nonnegative number.

*****Execution error on SPACE( ) : Too large [59]**
The string that you attempted to create would have length in excess of 254 characters.

*****Execution error on SQRT( ) : Negative [61]**
You cannot find the square root of a negative number.

*****Execution error on STORE : String too large [79]**
The string that you attempted to create would have length in excess of 254 characters.

*****Execution error on STR( ) : Out of range [63]**
The second parameter (the length) cannot exceed 19, or the third parameter (the number of places to the right of the decimal point) cannot exceed the length minus 2.

*****Execution error on STUFF( ) : String too large [102]**
The string that you attempted to create would have length in excess of 254 characters.

*****Execution error on SUBSTR( ) : Start point out of range [62]**
The value of the second parameter (the starting point) must be less than or equal to the length of the original string.

^^ Expected ON or OFF [73]
This parameter must be set either to ON or to OFF in the CONFIG.DB file.

Field name is already in use
A field name cannot be used more than once in a database file.

Field not found [48]
There is no field with this name in the database file.

Field type must be C, N, D, L, or M
The type of each field must be C(haracter), N(umeric), D(ate), L(ogical), or M(emo).

File already exists [7]
You cannot rename a file with a name that is already in use on the disk.

File does not exist [1]
No file of that name is in the indicated directory. Check the path and the spelling of the name.

File is already open [3]
You cannot open a database file that is already open in another work area.

File is in use by another [108]
The indicated file has either been locked or opened for exclusive use by another user.

File is not accessible [29]
Either the file name contains an invalid character or the directory is full.

File too large, some data may be lost
The dBASE III editor cannot handle files in excess of 5000 characters. Use an alternative editor (word processor).

File was not LOADed [91]
Either the LOAD operation failed, or you attempted to access a BIN file that has not been LOADed yet.

HELP text not found
The HELP.DBS file is not available.

Illegal character data length
The size of a character string field in a database file cannot exceed 254.

Illegal data length
The size of a character string field in a database file cannot exceed 254.

Illegal decimal length
The size of the integral part of a numeric field in a database file cannot exceed 15, and the number of places to the right of the decimal must be nonnegative and no greater than the total length minus 2.

Illegal field name
The name of the field contains an illegal character.

Illegal field type
The type of the field must be C, N, D, L, or M.

Illegal numeric data length
The size of a number cannot exceed 19 bytes.

Illegal value [46]
You must enter a number here.

Improper data type in subsubtotal expression
Neither a logical field nor a memo field can be used in a subsubtotal expression in the report writer.

Improper data type in subtotal expression
Neither a logical field nor a memo field can be used in a subtotal expression in the report writer.

Index damaged. REINDEX should be done before using data [114]
If an index file was partially created, that is, if the creation of an index file was interrupted, then the resultant index cannot be used. You must recreate the index before it can be used.

Index expression is too big (220 char maximum) [112]
The actual number of characters in the INDEX ON . . TO statement cannot exceed 220.

Index file does not match database [19]
This error *does not necessarily* indicate that you are using an index file that was created for another database file. Rather, it indicates that the key

expression in the index file does not match the list of fields in the database file. This might happen if you create a database file, create an index, and then change the structure of the database file.

Index interrupted. Index will be damaged if not completed [113]
If you interrupt the creation of an index file, then this message will be displayed.

Index is too big (100 char maximum) [23]
The key expression of an index must not exceed 100 characters.

Insert impossible
You cannot exceed the limitation of 24 fields in a report.

Insufficient dynamic memory for contents window
You have run out of main memory.

Insufficient memory [43]
You have run out of main memory.

Insufficient memory to display fields
You have run out of main memory.

Internal error: CMDSET( ): [66]
Your working copy of dBASE III Plus has been damaged. Get a new copy from your distribution disk.

Internal error: EVAL work area overflow [67]
You have used an expression that is too complex for dBASE III Plus to evaluate.

Internal error: Illegal opcode [68]
Your working copy of dBASE III Plus has been damaged. Get a new copy from your distribution disk.

Internal error: Unknown command code: [65]
Your working copy of dBASE III Plus has been damaged. Get a new copy from your distribution disk.

***** INTERRUPTED *****
A statement or program has been interrupted by pressing ESC.

Invalid data (press ESC) [81]
Your keyboard entry is incorrect. Press SPACEBAR to re-enter your data.

Invalid DIF Character [118]
There is an invalid character (possibly a control character) in your DIF file.

Invalid DIF File Header [115]
The file header for the DIF file is invalid or has been damaged.

Invalid DIF Type Indicator [117]
The data type indicator in the DIF file is invalid.

Invalid DOS SET option [99]
You are referencing an illegal DOS parameter.

Invalid function argument [11]
The data type of the parameter does not match the required data type.

Invalid function name [31]
No such function name in the Library.

Invalid index number [106]
The index number must be between 0 and 7.

Invalid operator [107]
The operator in an expression does not match the data types in the expression.

Invalid printer port [123]
The name of the device is not recognized by DOS.

Invalid printer redirection [124]
This network printer is not recognized by DOS.

Invalid SYLK File Dimension Bounds [120]
The data in the SYLK file is not within the specified bound.

Invalid SYLK File Format [121]
Either the SYLK file was not created correctly or it has been damaged.

Invalid SYLK File Header [119]
The file header for the SYLK file is invalid or has been damaged.

^— — — Keyword not found [86]
A statement in the CONFIG.DB file is incorrect.

Label contents cannot be Memo type
A memo field cannot be used to provide data in a label.

Label field invalid [54]
A file with an extension of LBL must be created with CREATE/MODIFY LABEL.

Line exceeds maximum of 254 characters [18]
A statement, line of a program, or line of a format file cannot exceed 254 characters in length.

Max number of fields already reached
You cannot have more than 128 fields in one database file.

Maximum record length exceeded [137]
You cannot have more than 4000 bytes in a record.

Memory Variable file is invalid [55]
The MEM file is invalid or has been damaged.

Mismatched DO WHILE and ENDDO [96]
An ENDDO with a matching DO WHILE was encountered.

No database is in USE. Enter file name: [52]
You have tried to access a database file and none is in use in the current work area.

No fields of the required type are present
The pull-down menu operation has failed because there are no fields on the indicated type in the current database file.

No fields to process [47]
The database has no numeric fields.

No find [14]
The previous FIND or SEEK has failed.

No PARAMETER statement found [93]
The PARAMETER statement is missing.

No room for heading
The heading cannot exceed the width of the page in the report.

Not a character expression [45]
A character string expression is required.

Not a dBASE database [15]
Either the dBASE DBF file is invalid or has been damaged. This can happen if you are trying to use a dBASE II DBF file with dBASE III Plus.

Not a Logical expression [37]
A logical expression is required here.

Not a numeric expression [27]
A numeric expression is required here.

Not a valid QUERY file [134]
Either the QUERY file is invalid or has been damaged. Separately examine the database files to verify that they are correct.

Not a valid VIEW file [127]
Either the VIEW file is invalid or has been damaged. Separately examine the database files to verify that they are correct.

Not enough disk space for SORT
You do not have enough room on your disk to perform the sort. There must be enough room for two additional files, each one having the same size as the original (source) file.

Not enough records to sort
You cannot sort a database with fewer than two records in it.

**** Not Found ** [82]**
The search failed to find a match.

Not readable
Unable to read the file.

Not suspended [101]
You can RESUME the execution of a program only if you selected the S(uspend) option when the program was interrupted.

Numeric overflow (data was lost) [39]
You have tried to REPLACE or TOTAL a field and the receiving database file was too small to hold the result.

Operation with Logical field invalid [90]
You cannot perform the desired operation on a logical field.

Operation with Memo field invalid [34]
You cannot perform the desired operation with a Memo field.

Out of memory variable memory [21]
You have run out of the memory reserved for memory variables. You can increase the size of this memory with the MVARSIZ parameter in the CONFIG.DB file.

Out of memory variable slots [22]
You cannot have more than 256 memory variables in use at any one time.

^– – – Out of range [75]
You have set a parameter in the CONFIG.DB file that has a value outside the allowable range.

Position is off screen [30]
When you access the screen with an @ . . SAY, the row must be between 0 and 24, and the column must be between 0 and 79.

Printer is not installed on port [126]
The SET PRINTER statement failed.

Printer is not ready [125]
Either the printer was not connected to your computer or it was shut off.

Record is in use by another[109]
The record is locked by another user.

Record is not in index [20]
You have referenced a record by number and that record number is not in the index file.

Record is not locked [130]
You must lock a record before you can update it (in the multiuser environment).

Record is out of range [5]
You have positioned the currency pointer past the last record in the database file.

Record not inserted [25]
The INSERT statement was cancelled, so the record was not inserted into the database file.

Records do not balance (program error)
Your working copy of dBASE III Plus has been damaged. Get a new copy from your distribution disk.

Report file invalid [50]
The FRM file was not created by CREATE/MODIFY COMMAND.

Structure invalid [33]
The structure of the database file used in the CREATE FROM statement is not valid.

Syntax error [10]
Your command can be identified by dBASE III Plus, but there is a spelling error in the command. This error message can be particularly perplexing, since it does not indicate the nature of the error, only the occurrence of one. A wide variety of errors can cause this message to be displayed. If this error occurs, be sure to enter S(uspend), not C(ancel), so that you can examine your memory variables.

Syntax error in contents expression
The entry for the LABEL was in error.

Syntax error in field expression
The entry for the REPORT was in error.

Syntax error in group expression
Error in the group expression for a REPORT.

Syntax error in subgroup expression
Error in the subgroup expression for a REPORT.

Table is full [105]
The maximum number of files that can be LOADed into memory is five.

The HELP file is not available
The HELP file ASSIST.HLP cannot be found.

There are no files of the type requested on this drive [53]
dBASE cannot find any files of the indicated type (extension).

This field must contain a valid dBASE expression
An invalid expression was entered in a QUERY or REPORT file.

This must be a valid dBASE expression
An invalid expression was entered in a LABEL line.

This string must not contain any semicolons
Titles and headings in a REPORT cannot contain a semicolon.

Too many characters in REPORT
You cannot specify more than 1440 bytes in the REPORT FORM parameters.

Too many files are open [6]
You cannot have more than 15 files of all types open at any one time. You must also have the statement FILES=20 in your CONFIG.SYS file.

Too many indexes [28]
No more than seven indexes can be referenced in a USE or SET INDEX statement.

Too many merge steps
Your working copy of dBASE III Plus has been damaged. Get a new copy from your distribution disk.

Too many sort key fields
You cannot sort on more than 10 fields at a time.

Total label width exceeds maximum allowable size
A LABEL cannot have a width of more than 250 columns.

^— — — Truncated [74]
A statement in CONFIG.DB is too long.

Two files must be in use in order to set a relation
It is necessary to select two files before you attempt to relate them.

Unable to load COMMAND.COM [92]
Cannot find COMMAND.COM on the default (root) directory.

Unable to Lock [129]
Cannot lock the record at the current time.

Unable to Skip [128]
Cannot SKIP to a record. It is currently locked by another user.

Unassigned file no [2]
Your working copy of dBASE III Plus has been damaged. Get a new copy from your distribution disk.

Unauthorized access level [133]
You do not have sufficient access privileges to access the file.

Unauthorized log-in [132]
Your attempt to log on to the multiuser system failed three times.

Unbalanced parentheses [8]
The number of left and right parentheses does not match.

Unknown function key [104]
The name or number of the function key does not exist.

Unknown SCEDIT( ) return code:
Your working copy of dBASE III Plus has been damaged. Get a new copy from your distribution disk.

*** **Unrecognized command verb [16]**
dBASE III Plus is unable to determine the command. Check the spelling.

Unrecognized phrase/keyword in command [36]
Cannot recognize the keyword in a command. Check the spelling and try again.

Unsupported path given [136]
Illegal path name.

Unterminated string [35]
The right-hand delimiter is missing from the string.

Valid only in programs [95]
Certain keywords can be used only in a program. They cannot be used interactively. They are:

1. CASE
2. DO CASE
3. DO WHILE
4. ELSE
5. ENDCASE
6. ENDDO
7. ENDIF
8. ENDTEXT
9. IF
10. LOOP
11. OTHERWISE
12. SUSPEND
13. TEXT

Variable not found [12]
No memory variable of that name in the current or indicated work area. Check the spelling of the name.

** **WARNING** ** **Data will probably be lost. Confirm (Y/N) [70]**
You tried to save a file, the disk was full, and you aborted the operation.

**** WARNING ** Report form empty**
No fields have been defined in the REPORT.

Wrong number of parameters [94]
The number of parameters in the DO . . WITH statement does not match the number of parameters in the PARAMETERS statement in the procedure.

B.3 THE ERROR MESSAGES IN NUMERICAL ORDER

A DBF file in view is not in the current directory

A Memo field cannot be selected

At least one file must be in use for this operation

Cannot have subgroups without groups

Command not recognized!

Empty structure will not be saved

Error in HELP system

Exceeding report print width

Excess header lines lost

Field name is already in use

Field type must be C, N, D, L, or M

File too large, some data may be lost

HELP text not found

Illegal character data length

Illegal data length

Illegal decimal length

Illegal field name

Illegal field type

Illegal numeric data length

Improper data type in subsubtotal expression

Improper data type in subtotal expression

Insert impossible

Insufficient dynamic memory for contents window
Insufficient memory to display fields
*** INTERRUPTED ***
Label contents cannot be Memo type
Max number of fields already reached
No fields of the required type are present
No room for heading
Not enough disk space for SORT
Not enough records to sort
Not readable
Records do not balance (program error)
Syntax error in contents expression
Syntax error in field expression
Syntax error in group expression
Syntax error in subgroup expression
The HELP file is not available
This field must contain a valid dBASE expression
This must be a valid dBASE expression
This string must not contain any semicolons
Too many characters in REPORT
Too many merge steps
Too many sort key fields
Total label width exceeds maximum allowable size
Two files must be in use in order to set a relation
Unknown SCEDIT( ) return code:
** WARNING ** Report form empty

[1] File does not exist
[2] Unassigned file no
[3] File is already open
[4] End of file encountered
[5] Record is out of range

[6] Too many files are open
[7] File already exists
[8] Unbalanced parentheses
[9] Data type mismatch
[10] Syntax error
[11] Invalid function argument
[12] Variable not found
[13] ALIAS not found
[14] No find
[15] Not a dBASE database
[16] *** Unrecognized command verb
[17] Cannot select requested database
[18] Line exceeds maximum of 254 characters
[19] Index file does not match database
[20] Record is not in index
[21] Out of memory variable memory
[22] Out of memory variable slots
[23] Index is too big (100 char maximum)
[24] ALIAS name already in use
[25] Record not inserted
[26] Database is not indexed
[27] Not a numeric expression
[28] Too many indexes
[29] File is not accessible
[30] Position is off screen
[31] Invalid function name
[33] Structure invalid
[34] Operation with Memo field invalid
[35] Unterminated string
[36] Unrecognized phrase/keyword in command
[37] Not a Logical expression

[38] Beginning of file encountered
[39] Numeric overflow (data was lost)
[41] .DBT file cannot be opened
[42] CONTINUE without LOCATE
[43] Insufficient memory
[44] Cyclic relation
[45] Not a character expression
[46] Illegal value
[47] No fields to process
[48] Field not found
[50] Report file invalid
[51] End of file or error on keyboard input
[52] No database is in USE. Enter file name:
[53] There are no files of the type requested on this drive
[54] Label field invalid
[55] Memory Variable file is invalid
[56] Disk full when writing file : <filename>
[57] ***Execution error on CHR( ) : Out of range
[58] ***Execution error on LOG( ) : Zero of negative
[59] ***Execution error on SPACE( ) : Too large
[60] ***Execution error on SPACE( ) : Negative
[61] ***Execution error on SQRT( ) : Negative
[62] ***Execution error on SUBSTR( ) : Start point out of range
[63] ***Execution error on STR( ) : Out of range
[65] Internal error: Unknown command code:
[66] Internal error: CMDSET( ):
[67] Internal error: EVAL work area overflow
[68] Internal error: Illegal opcode
[70] ** WARNING ** Data will probably be lost. Confirm (Y/N)
[72] ALTERNATE could not be opened
[73] ^^ Expected ON or OFF

[74] ^— — — Truncated

[75] ^— — — Out of range

[76] ***Execution error on – : Concatenated string too large

[77] ***Execution error on + : Concatenated string too large

[78] ***Execution error on ^ or ** : Negative base, fractional exponent

[79] ***Execution error on STORE : String too large

[81] Invalid date (press ESC)

[82] ** Not Found **

[86] ^— — — Keyword not found

[87] ***Execution error on NDX( ) : Invalid index number

[88] ***Execution error on REPLICATE( ) : String too large

[89] Cannot erase a file which is open

[90] Operation with Logical field invalid

[91] File was not LOADed

[92] Unable to load COMMAND.COM

[93] No PARAMETER statement found

[94] Wrong number of parameters

[95] Valid only in programs

[96] Mismatched DO WHILE and ENDDO

[99] Invalid DOS SET option

[101] Not suspended

[102] ***Execution error on STUFF( ) : String too large

[103] DOs nested too deep

[104] Unknown function key

[105] Table is full

[106] Invalid index number

[107] Invalid operator

[108] File is in use by another

[109] Record is in use by another

[110] Exclusive use on database is required

[111] Cannot write to read only file
[112] Index expression is too big (220 char maximum)
[113] Index interrupted. Index will be damaged if not completed
[114] Index damaged. REINDEX should be done before using data
[115] Invalid Invalid DIF File Header
[117] Invalid DIF Type Indicator
[118] Invalid DIF Character
[119] Invalid SYLK File Header
[120] Invalid SYLK File Dimension Bounds
[121] Invalid SYLK File Format
[122] Data catalog has not been established
[123] Invalid printer port
[124] Invalid printer redirection
[125] Printer is not ready
[126] Printer is not installed on port
[127] Not a valid VIEW file
[128] Unable to Skip
[129] Unable to Lock
[130] Record is not locked
[131] Database is encrypted
[132] Unauthorized log-in
[133] Unauthorized access level
[134] Not a valid QUERY file
[136] Unsupported path given
[137] Maximum record length exceeded

APPENDIX

C

A Large System in dBASE III Plus

C.1 INTRODUCTION TO THE SYSTEM

The system presented in this chapter is a working system. It was originally developed for a client in dBASE II and was subsequently converted to dBASE III Plus. The conversion was performed using the techniques given in Chapter 11 of this book. Care was taken to use as many of the good features of dBASE III Plus as was possible, including date variables. An outline of the structure of the system, a listing of the database file, and a copy of the documentation is included in this appendix.

C.2 AN OUTLINE SHOWING THE LOGICAL STRUCTURE OF THE SALES/RECEIVABLES/INVENTORY SYSTEM

SYSTEM	Main driver and menu
ACCOUNTI	Print the accounting report
BADCHECK	Driver for bad checks subsystem
BCENTER	Enter information for bad check
BCRESOLV	Resolve a bad check
BILLING	Driver for billing subsystem—can also change amount on last bill
MAKEBILL	Print the bills
ACCOUNTS	Charge accounts subsystem
CRACCOUN	Create a charge account
UPDATEAC	Change a charge account record
ACTSTATR	Print charge account status report
DEFAULT	Driver for default subsystem
DEFACT	Decide what action to take if an account is in default
DEFLRETT	Prepare letters for accounts in default
PRINTLET	Print letters for accounts in default
DISPUTE	Driver for account dispute subsystem
DISENTER	Enter a dispute
DISRES1	Resolve one dispute
DISRESAL	Resolve all old disputes
DELETE	Delete records by key or by date
FINDRECO	Display selected records on the screen
INVENTOR	Driver for inventory subsystem
ENTERINV	Enter a new inventory record
UPDATEIN	Change an inventory record

SENDINV	Move inventory from one location to another
RECINV	Record the receipt of moved inventory
TRDISCRP	Print the discrepancy report for items moved but not received in total
INVREPOR	Print the complete inventory report
PAYMENTS	Driver for purchases and payments
BUYCASH	Enter a cash purchase
BUYCHARG	Enter a charge purchase
MAKEPAYM	Enter a payment
INDEXES	Recreate all indexes

C.3 THE DATABASE FILES USED IN THE SYSTEM

Structure for database : C:ACCTFILE.dbf
Number of data records: 0
Date of last update : 11/07/86

Field	*Field Name*	*Type*	*Width*	*Dec*	*Description*
1	ACCTACCNO	Character	10		Account number
2	ACCTTYPACT	Character	20		Type of activity
3	ACCTDTACT	Date	8		Date of activity
4	ACCTAMT	Numeric	9	2	Dollar amount
** Total **			48		

Structure for database : C:ACCOUNTS.dbf
Number of data records: 0
Date of last update : 11/07/86

Field	*Field Name*	*Type*	*Width*	*Dec*	*Description*
1	ACCNO	Character	10		Account number
2	ACCCOMPANY	Character	25		Company name
3	ACCLNAME	Character	15		Last name of contact person
4	ACCFNAME	Character	10		First name of contact person
5	ACCPOBOX	Character	10		PO box number
6	ACCSTREET	Character	25		Street
7	ACCCITY	Character	15		City
8	ACCSTATE	Character	2		State

9	ACCZIP	Character	9		Zip code
10	ACCTYPE	Character	2		Type of account
11	ACCSTATUS	Character	3		Status of account
12	ACCCREDLIM	Numeric	6		Credit limit
13	ACCSECDEP	Character	25		Security deposit
14	ACCSPECACT	Character	25		Special action
15	ACCTOTCHRG	Numeric	9	2	Total charges due
16	ACCCARYOVR	Numeric	9	2	Payment carryover
17	ACCPAYMENT	Numeric	9	2	Payments pending
18	ACCTOTINT	Numeric	7	2	Total interest due
19	ACCYTDINT	Numeric	7	2	Year-to-date interest
20	ACCDTLACT	Date	8		Date of last activity
21	ACCDISCPER	Numeric	4	1	Discount percent
22	ACCBADCHNO	Character	6		Last bad check number
23	ACCMONARR	Numeric	3		Months in arrears
24	ACCOVER30	Numeric	9	2	Over 30
25	ACCOVER60	Numeric	9	2	Over 60
26	ACCOVER90	Numeric	9	2	Over 90
27	ACCBILLTYP	Character	3		Billing type
28	ACCMINPAY	Numeric	9	2	Minimum payment
29	ACCINTFLG	Character	1		Charge interest (Y/N)
** Total **			285		

Structure for database : C:BILLING.dbf
Number of data records: 0
Date of last update : 11/07/86

Field	*Field Name*	*Type*	*Width*	*Dec*	*Description*
1	BILLACCTNO	Character	10		Account number
2	BILLAMT	Numeric	9	2	Amount of bill
3	BILLDATE	Date	8		Date billed
** Total **			28		

Structure for database : C:CHARGES.dbf
Number of data records: 0
Date of last update : 11/07/86

Field	*Field Name*	*Type*	*Width*	*Dec*	*Description*
1	CHACCTNO	Character	10		Account number
2	CHTICKETNO	Character	10		Charge number
3	CHITEMNO	Character	20		Inventory item number

4	CHITEMDESC	Character	15		Item description
5	CHMANU	Character	25		Manufacturer's description
6	CHLOCATION	Character	15		Warehouse location
7	CHQTY	Numeric	6	1	Quantity
8	CHITEMPR	Numeric	9	2	Selling price
9	CHDOLLARS	Numeric	9	2	Dollar amount of charge
10	CHDATE	Date	8		Date of charge
11	CHDISPDATE	Date	8		Dispute date
12	CHDISPAMT	Numeric	9	2	Amount disputed
13	CHRESTYPE	Character	15		Type of resolution
14	CHRESREPTD	Character	1		Resolution reported (Y/N)
15	CHACTRESDT	Date	8		Actual resolution date
16	CHBPAID	Numeric	9	2	Amount paid so far
17	CHBPAIDDT	Date	8		Date of last payment
18	CHPOSTED	Character	1		Item description printed on a bill yet (Y/N)
** Total **			187		

Structure for database : C:INVENTOR.dbf
Number of data records: 0
Date of last update : 11/07/86

Field	*Field Name*	*Type*	*Width*	*Dec*	*Description*
1	INVITEMNO	Character	20		Item number
2	INVMANU	Character	25		Manufacturer's designation
3	INVLOC	Character	15		Location
4	INVDESC	Character	15		Description
5	INVUNITS	Character	5		Units
6	INVQTYPER	Numeric	4		Quantity per unit
7	INVQTYONH	Numeric	6	1	Quantity on hand
8	INVREORDPT	Numeric	4		Reorder point
9	INVREORDAM	Numeric	6		Reorder amount
10	INVCSTPERU	Numeric	9	2	Cost per unit
11	INVSELLPR	Numeric	9	2	Price per unit
** Total **			119		

Structure for database : C:LET1.dbf, LET2.dbf, and LET3.dbf
Number of data records: 0
Date of last update : 11/07/86

Field	*Field Name*	*Type*	*Width*	*Dec*	*Description*
1	LETACCNO	Character	10		Account number
2	LETLNAME	Character	15		Last name
3	LETFNAME	Character	10		First name
4	LETCOMPANY	Character	25		Company name
5	LETPOBOX	Character	10		PO box number
6	LETSTREET	Character	25		Street
7	LETADDRESS	Character	26		City, state, and Zip
8	LETTOTCHRG	Numeric	9	2	Total charges due
9	LETTOTINT	Numeric	9	2	Total interest due
10	LETTOTDUE	Numeric	9	2	Total amount due
** Total **			149		

Structure for database : C:NOTIFICA.dbf
Number of data records: 0
Date of last update : 11/07/86

Field	*Field Name*	*Type*	*Width*	*Dec*	*Description*
1	NOTACCTNO	Character	10		Account number
2	NOTTYPE	Character	1		Type of letter
3	NOTDATE	Date	8		Notification date
4	NOTSTATUS	Character	2		Status of default
5	NOTTOTDUE	Numeric	9	2	Total amount due
** Total **			31		

Structure for database : C:PAYMENTS.dbf
Number of data records: 0
Date of last update : 11/07/86

Field	*Field Name*	*Type*	*Width*	*Dec*	*Description*
1	PAYACCTNO	Character	10		Account number
2	PAYAMT	Numeric	9	2	Amount of payment
3	PAYDATE	Date	8		Date of payment
4	PAYCHECKNO	Character	6		Check number
** Total **			34		

Structure for database : C:TRANSFER.dbf
Number of data records: 0
Date of last update : 11/07/86

Field	Field Name	Type	Width	Dec	Description
1	TRSENDLOC	Character	15		Sending location
2	TRRECLOC	Character	15		Receiving location
3	TRITEMNO	Character	20		Item number
4	TRMANU	Character	25		Manufacturer's designation
5	TRDESC	Character	15		Item description
6	TRSENDDT	Date	8		Date sent
7	TRQTYSENT	Numeric	6		Quantity sent
8	TRUNITS	Character	5		Units
9	TRQTYPER	Numeric	4		Quantity per unit
10	TRCSTPERU	Numeric	9	2	Cost per unit
11	TRSELLPR	Numeric	9	2	Selling price
12	TRRECDT	Date	8		Date received
13	TRQTYREC	Numeric	6		Quantity received
** Total **			146		

C.4 DOCUMENTATION FOR THE SYSTEM

INTRODUCTION

The purpose of this software system is to allow you to gain a greater degree of control over accounts receivable and inventory. It has been designed by members of the organization and Nelson Dinerstein, and has been programmed by Nelson Dinerstein. The complete system, hardware and software, consists of the following:

1. The computer is the IBM PC/XT.
2. The printer is the Okidata Microline 84 with the Plug 'N Play Roms.
3. The SALES/RECEIVABLES/INVENTORY software is delivered on two disks. One disk contains the programs (written in dBASE III Plus) and the other disk contains the data files.
4. The dBASE III Plus system is delivered separately, on another disk.

The organization is responsible for the purchase of paper for the printer. Two types of paper are necessary:

1. 9½ x 11 (narrow), and

2. 14 x 11 (wide)

In addition, the organization is responsible for the purchase of additional disks for backup storage of programs and data. The appropriate disk type is:

5¼", dual sided, double density

These disks may be purchased in boxes of ten. The recommended disk type is:

DYSAN, 104/2D

Even the best quality new disks may not work. If a new disk does not work, it usually can be returned to the purchaser for a refund.

It is strongly recommended that backup copies of each disk be made on a regular basis. In particular, backup copies of the software disk that contains the data files for the system should be made at least daily. These backups are required, since there are several situations that might destroy the data on the disks. Some, but not all, of the situations that might destroy the disk itself or the data on the disk are:

1. A power failure while writing on the disk
2. Static electricity

It is also recommended that a backup of the data disk be made each time immediately before the billing routine is run. This insures that the billing process can be rerun in case of system failure, such as power failure or paper jamming in the printer.

In order to FORMAT a new disk for use on the computer, insert the disk to be formatted into the slot (drive A). Then run the FORMAT program to FORMAT the disk. After a disk has been formatted for use on the IBM PC/XT, it may be used without ever being formatted again.

The SALES/RECEIVABLES/INVENTORY System

The system is run as follows:

When prompted by the operating system (when C> appears on the screen), type DBASE SYSTEM

A menu will then appear on the screen. The purpose of the menu is to display the major functional areas on the screen and allow you to select the desired function. Note that whenever the system pauses with the cursor positioned after an entry prompt, you are expected to enter 1 character with no carriage return. You may then be presented with another menu in order to further refine the choice of action or action may start immediately, depending on the function selected.

The main menu allows the choice of the following major functional areas:

1. EXIT
   Terminate the current operation of the system.
2. ACCOUNTING REPORT
   Print the report showing all financial transactions since the last such report was printed.
3. BAD CHECKS
   Enter or resolve bad checks.
4. BILLING
   Modify a previous bill or produce complete billing information.
5. CHARGE ACCOUNTS
   Create a new charge account, modify an existing charge account record, or produce the charge account status report.
6. CHARGE ACCOUNT DEFAULT
   Decide on what action to take, based upon information in the charge account status report (see No. 5 above), prepare files to record names of people to receive letters notifying them of default of payment, and print the default letters.
7. CHARGE ACCOUNT DISPUTE
   Enter a disputed charge from a customer, resolve a specific dispute, or resolve all disputes over 30 days old.
8. DELETE RECORDS BY KEY OR BY DATE
   Delete one or more of the following types of records:
   A. Charge account
   B. Bill
   C. Charge ticket
   D. Inventory
   E. Inventory transfer
   F. Notification of default
   G. Payment
9. FIND RECORDS AND DISPLAY ON THE SCREEN
   Find and display on the screen all or part of each of the records noted in No. 8 above.

10. INVENTORY
    Enter a new inventory record, update an existing inventory record, transfer inventory from one location to another, enter the receipt of an inventory transfer, print a report showing all discrepancies between inventory sent and inventory received, and print a complete inventory report.
11. PAYMENTS/CASH PURCHASE/CHARGE
    Enter information for a cash purchase, a charge purchase, or a payment.
12. REINDEX THE FILES
    In case of a system error, reindex all the database files.

ACCOUNTING REPORT

The accounting report is produced automatically when item B is selected from the main menu. The report will include all financial information gathered since the last accounting report. When the report has been printed, you will be asked whether the report has been printed successfully. If so, the accounting information is removed from the system. If not, the report may be produced again. The accounting report is categorized by type of activity. For example, cash purchase, charge, payment and tax. The report contains the column headings:

1. Account number
2. Type of activity
3. Date of activity
4. Dollar amount

Narrow paper may be used to produce the report (9½ x 11).

BAD CHECKS

This module is invoked when item C is selected from the main menu. A new menu is presented on the screen, allowing you to enter new bad check information or to resolve an old bad check.

ENTRY OF BAD CHECK INFORMATION

Bad check information is entered in the form of a charge ticket, with "BAD CHECK" as the item description. If the customer already has an account, the charge ticket is posted to this account. If the customer does not already have a charge account, one is created with ACCOUNT

TYPE = BC and ACCOUNT STATUS = HLD. In this case, the charge ticket for the bad check is posted to the new (special) account. In either case, the bad check information is posted to the accounting file.

RESOLUTION OF BAD CHECK

To resolve a bad check, you will be prompted for the account number. If the account is located in the system, you will be prompted for the dollar amount of the resolution. This dollar amount is entered into the system as a payment and is posted to the accounting file. This payment then offsets (completely or partially) the previous charge ticket for the bad check.

BILLING

This module is invoked when item D is selected from the main menu. A new menu is presented on the screen, allowing you to produce the new billing information or to change the last billing amount on a bill already sent.

PRODUCE BILLING INFORMATION

The billing report may be printed on narrow paper. The date entered at the time that the system is first invoked becomes the billing date. If another date is desired, terminate the current session and restart a new session with the desired date. At the time that the billing information is produced, charges not yet paid are accumulated and payments received since the last billing but prior to the new billing date are applied (payments are not applied to the bills until the billing program is actually run). Interest is computed on unpaid charges (over 30 days old) and previous unpaid interest at a rate of 1.75% per month. There are two types of bills: REG and SCH, for regular and scheduled billing. SCH bills are the same as REG bills, except that a minimum expected payment is printed on the bill; interest is accumulated in the same manner in both types of bills. The "bills" produced in this manner are not meant to be the bills themselves, but rather to provide the information necessary to produce actual bills. The billing information includes the following information:

Account number

Company name

Individual's name

PO box

Address

Amount on previous bill

Payments received since or carried over from last billing

For each item charged since the last billing

- Item number
- Item description
- Quantity
- Item price
- Total charge amount
- Charge date

Total dollar charges since last billing

Interest accrued since last billing

Total amount due

Dollar amounts over 30, 60, and 90 days

Date due (arbitrarily chosen to be 15 days from the billing date)

If the billing type is SCH, the minimum expected payment and months in arrears is printed. In this case, if the minimum expected payment is not met, the number of consecutive such months is accumulated. If, at any time, the minimum expected payment is met, the number of months in arrears is reset to zero. If there was any activity for an account during the year, the December's billing will contain the year-to-date interest figure.

UPDATE THE AMOUNT ON A PREVIOUS BILL

It may occasionally be necessary to change the amount on the last bill to match changes made elsewhere in the system by the user. This may be required if the last bill is deleted, charges are modified, etc. Remember that the dollar amount of the last billing in the system provides the "amount of the previous bill" on the next bill.

CHARGE ACCOUNTS

This module is invoked when item E is selected from the main menu. A new menu is presented on the screen, allowing you to create a new charge account, modify information in an existing charge account record, or produce the charge account status report.

CREATE A NEW CHARGE ACCOUNT

To facilitate the entry of a new charge account record, a blank charge account record is presented on the screen. You may enter the appropriate information and may also backup to previous fields for corrections or additions. To backup to a previous field, enter CTRL-E. This is entered by holding down the CTRL button and typing the letter E. To advance to the next field, either fill the field with the required information or fill part of the field and type a RETURN. This method of entering and correcting records is called "full-screen editing." Corrections and additions can be made until the last field on the record has been terminated with a RETURN. Before a new record is entered, the user should decide the account type, account status, and billing type. The permissible choices are:

ACCOUNT TYPE

- BC = bad check
- RC = revolving charge
- SI = single item
- UN = old unpaid account

ACCOUNT STATUS

- CAN = cancelled
- HLD = hold for special action
- OVL = over the charge limit
- VAL = normal valid charge account

BILLING STATUS

- REG = regular billing
- SCH = minimum payment allowed

Some of the fields in the new charge account cannot be entered into the record at the time of creation. For example, TOTAL CHARGES (not including interest) and charges over 30/60/90 are to be maintained by the system to insure that the system is in balance. When creating a new account, the current charges will be zero. To enter charges, including old unpaid charges, enter a charge ticket through the appropriate module. It is recommended that charge tickets for old unpaid bills have a different numbering sequence than regular charge tickets. If you wish to start a new charge account for an old unpaid bill, you may enter old interest at the time of account creation, but remember to enter the charge separately. Also remember to enter the interest into both the INTEREST DUE and YTD INTEREST fields. After the records are created, the interest due and the YTD interest are maintained automatically by the system.

MODIFY AN ACCOUNT RECORD

To simplify the updating (modification) of an account record, the entire record is displayed on the screen. You may use the full-screen editing functions to move through the record to get to the fields where you wish to make modifications. Remember that the changing of any of the dollar values for charges, payments, interest and, over 30/60/90 days may cause the system to become unbalanced, so these must be done very carefully.

PRODUCE THE ACCOUNT STATUS REPORT

Wide paper is necessary for this report. For each charge account in the system, the following information is produced:

Account number

Company name

Individual name

Address

Account type

Account status

Balance due

Months in arrears

Level of last default sent

Date last default letter sent

Status of response to last default letter

Number of last unresolved bad check, if any

Dollar amount over 30/60/90 days old

CHARGE ACCOUNT DEFAULT

This module is invoked when item F is selected from the main menu. A new menu is presented on the screen, allowing you to take action on a charge account default, prepare files for the printing of default notification letters, or to actually print the default notification letters.

ACTION DECISION

Using the CHARGE ACCOUNT STATUS REPORT, you may determine further action to be taken in the event that an account is in default or in the event that the default has been resolved. It is recommended that you use the following when running this module:

LETTER TYPES

0 = send no letter, problem resolved

1 = send gentle reminder of default

2 = send stronger reminder of default

3 = send strongest reminder of default

STATUS TYPES

LS = letter sent

RS = last action resolved

If the status type for the last action is LS, then the implication is that the matter is not yet resolved. You must record (write down) the date that you made the action decision(s) for use in the next module.

PREPARE FILES FOR LETTERS

You will be prompted for the date that the action decisions were made. After you enter this date (make sure that you enter the date in the correct form), appropriate information for the printing of the letters will be prepared for all action decisions performed on the indicated date. Once the date has been entered, further processing in this module should be automatic.

PRINT DEFAULT LETTERS

Each of the required default letters, based on your action decisions and the preparation mentioned in the previous module, will be printed. Narrow paper is used here.

CHARGE ACCOUNT DISPUTE

This module is invoked when item G is selected from the main menu. A new menu is presented on the screen, allowing you to enter a disputed charge information, resolve a specific charge dispute, or resolve all charge disputes over 30 days old.

ENTER A DISPUTE FROM A CUSTOMER

You will be prompted for the ticket number of the charge, the date disputed and the disputed amount. The disputed amount will not appear on the billing until the dispute is resolved.

RESOLVE A SPECIFIC DISPUTE

You will be prompted for the original ticket number, the new charge amount (possibly the original amount, possibly less than the original amount), and the resolution date. The original dollar amount on the charge will be changed to reflect the new charge amount. The new charge amount will appear as part of the new billing, when the billing information is produced.

RESOLVE ALL DISPUTES OVER 30 DAYS OLD

Currently the law requires that you respond to all disputes in writing, with a letter that is not computer generated. The law also allows you, the creditor, to decide what action to take in the case of a disputed charge, after 30 days has elapsed from being notified of the dispute by the customer. In the event that you do not resolve a dispute harmoniously with the customer, after the passage of 30 days, you may ignore the dispute and re-enter it as part of the normal charges. The purpose of this module is to automatically resolve, at the original charge amount, any disputed but still unresolved charges that have been disputed over 30 days.

DELETE RECORDS BY KEY OR BY DATE

This module is invoked when item H is selected from the main menu. A new menu is presented on the screen, allowing you to specify which type of records are to be deleted. Having selected the record type to be deleted, you may be asked, depending on the type of record, how the deletion should be made: by record key or by date. Deletion by date actually deletes all records of the indicated type that are older than the date that you enter. All the records that you request to be deleted are first marked for deletion, but still remain in the files. After you have indicated all the desired deletions and exit from this module, the records are actually deleted from the files. The actual deletion process may be very time-consuming, depending on the size of the files involved, so this module should be run when you can afford the time. The records that may be deleted and the possible deletion methods are as follows:

RECORDS	DELETION TYPES ALLOWED
ACCOUNTS	By activity date or account number
BILLS	By date or account number and search for the particular bill
CHARGES	By date or ticket number
INVENTORY	By item number, manufacturer/special designator, and location
INVENTORY TRANSFER	By sending location, receiving location, item number and sending date, or by receiving date
NOTIFICATION OF DEFAULT	By date
PAYMENTS	By date

In addition to deletions as indicated above, it is possible to effect a deletion for the following records as indicated:

RECORDS	ADDITIONAL DELETION ACTIONS
NOTIFICATION OF DEFAULT	Perform a new default action with letter type=0 and status=RS
PAYMENT (specific)	Enter an appropriate charge ticket or bad check information

Important Notes on Deletions:

1. If an ACCOUNT record is deleted, all payments, charges, bills, and notification letters are also deleted.
2. If a BILL is deleted, it may be necessary to change the dollar amounts on the previous bill to keep the system in balance.
3. An unpaid CHARGE cannot be deleted until it is paid for. In the case that you really wish to delete an unpaid charge (you give up on ever collecting it), enter a (bogus) payment first, then delete it.
4. An INVENTORY TRANSFER record cannot be deleted until it has been received in the quantity sent. In the case that you really wish to

delete such a record, you may enter the (bogus) receipt first, and then adjust other inventory record(s) as necessary. Then you may delete it.

5. If you delete a payment record by date, make sure that the date used is at least older than the last date that billing information was produced.

FIND RECORDS AND DISPLAY ON THE SCREEN

This module is invoked when item I is selected from the main menu. A new menu is presented on the screen, allowing you to select any of the following records by the indicated methods:

RECORD TYPE	SELECTION METHOD
ACCOUNT	By account number, company name, or last name
BILLS	By account number
CHARGE TICKET	By account number or ticket number
DEFAULT NOTIFICATION	By account number
INVENTORY	By item number, by item number and manufacturer/special designator, by item number and location, or by item number, location and manufacturer/ special designator
INVENTORY TRANSFER	By sending location, receiving location, and item number
PAYMENT	By account number or check number

In the cases where more than one record is selected to be displayed on the screen, the screen is filled and then the output stops. To continue the output, type any key.

For each of the following records, the indicated fields are displayed on the screen:

ACCOUNT record select by account number

The complete record

ACCOUNT record selected by company name or last name

Account number

Company name

Last name

Credit limit

Total due (charges + interest − payments to date)

BILLS

Account number

Dollar amount of the bill

Date of the bill

CHARGE TICKET

Account number

Ticket number

Item description

Item cost

Charge date

Dispute date (if disputed)

Dispute resolved yet (Y/N)

DEFAULT NOTIFICATION LETTER

Account number

Letter type (0,1,2, or 3)

Date of letter

Status

Dollar amount in letter

INVENTORY

Item number

Manufacturer/special designator

Location

Description

Quantity on hand

Cost

Price

INVENTORY TRANSFER

Sending location

Receiving location

Item number

Manufacturer/special designator
Description
Date sent
Quantity sent
Units sent
Quantity per unit sent
Quantity received

PAYMENT
Account number
Dollar amount
Date
Check number

INVENTORY

This module is invoked when item J is selected from the main menu. A new menu is presented on the screen, allowing you to enter a new inventory record, update an existing inventory record, initiate an inventory transfer, receipt an inventory transfer, produce a report showing any discrepancies between inventory items transferred and inventory items received, and printing the complete inventory report, using wide paper.

NEW INVENTORY RECORD

To facilitate the entry of a new inventory record, the blank record is displayed on the screen waiting to be filled in. You may use the full screen editing features to enter the record.

UPDATE (MODIFY) AN EXISTING INVENTORY RECORD

You will be prompted for the item number, manufacturer/special designator, and location. If the record can be found, the existing record is displayed on the screen and the full-screen editing features may be used to make changes.

INITIATE AN INVENTORY TRANSFER (SEND)

You will be prompted for the item number, manufacturer/special designator, and location. If the inventory record can be found, it will be displayed on the screen for verification. If verification is successful, you will be prompted for quantity, date, and receiving location. In addition, you will be prompted for the type of transfer. The permissible transfer types are:

B = bulk transfer

C = compute the quantity transferred = quantity entered * count per unit. This would allow, for example, the transfer of one drum of 55 gallons as a 55 gallon transfer. In this case, the original inventory record would be decremented by one drum and the receiving inventory, when the items are actually received, would be incremented by 55 gallons.

RECEIPT OF AN INVENTORY TRANSFER (RECEIVE)

You will be prompted for the item number, the sending location, the receiving location, and the date sent. All inventory records that meet the criteria will be displayed on the screen, one by one. You will be asked to indicate which is the correct transfer record. If you indicate that one of the displayed records is the one that you wish to enter a receipt for, you will be prompted for quantity received and date received. If an inventory record for this item/manufacturer/location already exists for the receiving location, it will be updated. If such a record does not exist, a new one will be created and you will be prompted for reorder point and reorder amount.

PRODUCE TRANSFER DISCREPANCY REPORT

Wide paper will be needed for this report. The report will contain the following information for transfer records where the quantity sent does not equal the quantity received:

Sending location

Receiving location

Item number

Date sent

Date received

Manufacturer/special designator

Description

Quantity sent

Quantity received

Units received

Count per unit received

PRODUCE THE COMPLETE INVENTORY REPORT

Wide paper will be needed for this report. The report will contain the following information for each inventory item and will be sorted in order by item number:

Item number

Manufacturer/special designator

Location

Description

Units

Quantity per unit

Quantity on hand

Reorder point

Reorder amount

Cost per unit

Selling price

Total cost for items on hand

Total selling price for items on hand

PAYMENTS/CASH PURCHASE/CHARGE

This module is invoked when item K is selected from the main menu. A new menu is presented on the screen, allowing you to enter a payment on a bill, a cash purchase, or a charge purchase.

MAKE A PAYMENT ON A BILL (FOR A CHARGE ACCOUNT)

You will be prompted for account number, date of payment, dollar amount, and check number. If there is no check number (payment is made with cash) hit the RETURN key instead of entering the check number. Payments are recorded when entered, but are not applied to individual charges until the billing program is run.

CASH PURCHASE

You will be prompted for the inventory information: item number, manufacturer/special designator, and location. If the inventory item is on file, it is displayed on the screen for verification. If verified, the quantity on hand is decremented by the quantity sold. In either case, the sale amount and the tax are recorded in the accounting file.

CHARGE

This is similar to the CASH PURCHASE, except that the ticket number and charge date are asked for. In addition, the charge ticket is entered into the system.

REINDEX THE FILES

Errors in the hardware or software may, in unusual situations, cause the index files to be damaged. Use this function to recreate all the indexes used in the system. This function may take several minutes to complete.

STARTING UP THE SYSTEM

Because of the complexity of a software system such as this one, it is desirable to try the system first with a limited amount of data. This gives you the opportunity to be able to manually verify that the system does or does not work correctly. Then, when you are convinced that the system works correctly with a limited amount of data, gradually increase the amount of data in the system and verify again that the system works correctly. Finally, increase the amount of the data in the system to full capacity. This technique is most valuable for you personally to determine that the system works in the manner that you desire. Many organizations take three full accounting cycles (usually 3 months) to test out a new system and have the errors removed.

WARRANTY

Because of the nature of software construction, it must be assumed that any newly delivered software system will contain some errors, even though every effort has been made by the programmer to insure that the software is as error free as possible. In the event of errors or problems, feel free to contact me at any time. My current work telephone number is 555-1212. In case of errors, I will make every reasonable effort to correct the problem as quickly as possible.

C.5 THE LISTING OF THE PROGRAMS

The programs are listed here in alphabetical order, and the end of each program is distinctly marked.

```
* ACCOUNTING.PRG
CLEAR
? "INSERT NARROW PAPER IN THE PRINTER."
WAIT
CLEAR
SELECT C
USE ACCTFILE INDEX ACCTTYPA
REPORT FORM ACCOUNTI TO PRINTER
CLEAR
STORE SPACE(1) TO ANSWER
WAIT "WAS THE REPORT PRODUCED SUCCESSFULLY (Y/N):" TO ANSWER
IF UPPER(ANSWER) = "Y"
   ? "NOW DELETING ACCOUNTING INFO FROM SYSTEM"
   SET INDEX TO
   ZAP
   INDEX ON ACCTTYPA TO ACCTTYPA
ENDIF
RETURN
***************************** END OF PROGRAM ******************

* ACCOUNTS.PRG
DO WHILE .T.
```

```
        CLEAR
        @ 3,5 SAY "ACCOUNTS MODULE SELECTION CODE"
        @ 4,5 SAY "------------------------------"
        @ 5,10 SAY "A. EXIT"
        @ 6,10 SAY "B. CREATE A NEW ACCOUNT"
        @ 7,10 SAY "C. MODIFY AN ACCOUNT RECORD"
        @ 8,10 SAY "D. PRODUCE THE ACCOUNT STATUS REPORT"
        WAIT "ENTER YOUR SELECTION CODE:" TO CODE1
        DO CASE
                CASE CODE1 = "A"
                        RETURN
                CASE CODE1 = "B"
                        DO CRACCOUN
                CASE CODE1 = "C"
                        DO UPDATEAC
                CASE CODE1 = "D"
                        DO ACTSTATR
                OTHERWISE
                        @ 15,0 SAY "ILLEGAL SELECTION CODE."
                        WAIT
        ENDCASE
        CLEAR ALL
ENDDO
RETURN
***************************** END OF PROGRAM ******************

* ACTSTATR.PRG
SET DEVICE TO SCREEN
```

```
CLEAR
@ 1,0 SAY "INSERT WIDE PAPER IN THE PRINTER."
WAIT
CLEAR
SET DEVICE TO PRINT
SELECT A
USE ACCOUNTS INDEX ACCNO
SELECT F
USE NOTIFICA INDEX NOTACCTNO
STORE 60 TO MAXLINES
STORE 1 TO PAGENO
@ 0,0 SAY CHR(15)
@ 1,65 SAY "CHARGE ACCOUNT STATUS REPORT"
@ 2,76 SAY DATE()
@ 2,90 SAY "PAGE NO:"
@ 2,98 SAY PAGENO PICTURE "9999"
@ 4, 1 SAY "ACCOUNT NO"
@ 4,13 SAY "COMPANY"
@ 4,39 SAY "NAME"
@ 4,65 SAY "ADDRESS"
@ 4,131 SAY "TYPE"
@ 4,136 SAY "STATUS"
@ 4,143 SAY "BALANCE DUE"
@ 4,155 SAY "MONTHS IN ARREARS"
@ 4,173 SAY "LETTER"
@ 4,180 SAY "DATE"
@ 4,189 SAY "STATUS"
@ 4,196 SAY "BAD CHECK NO"
```

```
@ 4,209 SAY "LAST ACT"
@ 5, 1 SAY "----------"
@ 5,13 SAY "-------------------------"
@ 5,39 SAY "-------------------------"
@ 5,65 SAY "----------------------------------------------"+;
           "-------------------"
@ 5,131 SAY "----"
@ 5,136 SAY "------"
@ 5,143 SAY "-----------"
@ 5,155 SAY "-----------------"
@ 5,173 SAY "------"
@ 5,180 SAY "--------"
@ 5,189 SAY "------"
@ 5,196 SAY "------------"
@ 5,209 SAY "--------"
STORE 5 TO ROW
SELECT A
DO WHILE .NOT. EOF()
   STORE ACCNO TO MEMACCTNO
   STORE ROW + 1 TO ROW
   IF ROW > MAXLINES
      EJECT
      STORE PAGENO + 1 TO PAGENO
      @ 1,65 SAY "CHARGE ACCOUNT STATUS REPORT"
      @ 2,76 SAY DATE()
      @ 2,90 SAY "PAGE NO:"
      @ 2,98 SAY PAGENO
      @ 4, 1 SAY "ACCOUNT NO"
```

```
    @ 4,13 SAY "COMPANY"
    @ 4,39 SAY "NAME"
    @ 4,65 SAY "ADDRESS"
    @ 4,131 SAY "TYPE"
    @ 4,136 SAY "STATUS"
    @ 4,143 SAY "BALANCE DUE"
    @ 4,155 SAY "MONTHS IN ARREARS"
    @ 4,173 SAY "LETTER"
    @ 4,180 SAY "DATE"
    @ 4,189 SAY "STATUS"
    @ 4,196 SAY "BAD CHECK NO"
    @ 4,209 SAY "LAST ACT"
    @ 5, 1 SAY "----------"
    @ 5,13 SAY "-------------------------"
    @ 5,39 SAY "-------------------------"
    @ 5,65 SAY "-------------------------------------"+;
               "----------------------------"
    @ 5,131 SAY "----"
    @ 5,136 SAY "------"
    @ 5,143 SAY "-----------"
    @ 5,155 SAY "-----------------"
    @ 5,173 SAY "------"
    @ 5,180 SAY "--------"
    @ 5,189 SAY "------"
    @ 5,196 SAY "------------"
    @ 5,209 SAY "--------"
    STORE 6 TO ROW
ENDIF
```

```
@ ROW, 1 SAY ACCNO
@ ROW,13 SAY ACCCOMPANY
@ ROW,39 SAY TRIM(ACCLNAME)+" ,"+TRIM(ACCFNAME);
  PICTURE "XXXXXXXXXXXXXXXXXXXXXXXXX"
IF ACCPOBOX = SPACE(10)
   STORE TRIM(ACCSTREET)+","+TRIM(ACCCITY)+","+;
     TRIM(ACCSTATE)+","+TRIM(ACCZIP) TO MEMADDRESS
ELSE
   STORE "PO BOX:"+TRIM(ACCPOBOX)+","+TRIM(ACCSTREET)+;
     ","+TRIM(ACCCITY)+","+TRIM(ACCSTATE)+;
     ","+TRIM(ACCZIP) TO MEMADDRESS
ENDIF
@ ROW,65 SAY MEMADDRESS ;
   PICTURE ;
"XXXXXXXXXXXXXXXXXXXXXXXXXXXXXXXXXXXXXXXXXXXXXXXXXXXXXXXXXXXXXXXXXXX""
@ ROW,131 SAY ACCTYPE
@ ROW,136 SAY ACCSTATUS
@ ROW,143 SAY ACCTOTCHRG + ACCTOTINT - ACCPAYMENT - ACCCARYOVR
@ ROW,155 SAY ACCMONARR
IF ACCMONARR > 2
   @ ROW,169 SAY "*" PICTURE "X"
ENDIF
STORE ACCBADCHNO TO MEMBADCHNO
STORE ACCDTLACT TO MEMLASTACT
SELECT F
SEEK MEMACCTNO
IF .NOT. EOF()
   @ ROW,173 SAY NOTTYPE
```

```
      @ ROW,180 SAY NOTDATE
      @ ROW,189 SAY NOTSTATUS
   ENDIF
   @ ROW,196 SAY MEMBADCHNO
   @ ROW,209 SAY MEMLASTACT
   SELECT A
   STORE ROW+1 TO ROW
   @ ROW,11 SAY "OVER 30:"
   @ ROW,19 SAY ACCOVER30 PICTURE "999999.99"
   @ ROW,29 SAY "OVER 60:"
   @ ROW,39 SAY ACCOVER60 PICTURE "999999.99"
   @ ROW,49 SAY "OVER 90:"
   @ ROW,57 SAY ACCOVER90 PICTURE "999999.99"
   SKIP 1
ENDDO
@ 66,153 SAY CHR(18)
EJECT
SET DEVICE TO SCREEN
RETURN
***************************** END OF PROGRAM ******************

* BADCHECKS.PRG
DO WHILE .T.
   CLEAR
   @ 3,5 SAY "BAD CHECKS MODULE SELECTION CODE"
   @ 4,5 SAY "--------------------------------"
   @ 5,10 SAY "A. EXIT"
   @ 6,10 SAY "B. ENTER BAD CHECK INFORMATION"
```

```
   @ 7,10 SAY "C. RESOLVE A BAD CHECK"
   WAIT "ENTER YOUR SELECTION CODE:" TO CODE1
   DO CASE
      CASE CODE1 = "A"
         RETURN
      CASE CODE1 = "B"
         DO BCENTER
      CASE CODE1 = "C"
         DO BCRESOLV
      OTHERWISE
         @ 15,0 SAY  "ILLEGAL SELECTION CODE."
         WAIT
   ENDCASE
   CLOSE DATABASES
ENDDO
RETURN
***************************** END OF PROGRAM ******************

* BCENTER.PRG
CLEAR
SELECT A
USE ACCOUNTS INDEX ACCNO, ACCLNAME, ACCCOMPA
SELECT B
USE CHARGES INDEX CHACCTNO, CHTICKET
SELECT C
USE ACCTFILE INDEX ACCTTYPA
DO WHILE .T.
   CLEAR
```

```
STORE SPACE(1) TO ANSWER
WAIT "DO YOU WISH TO ENTER ANOTHER BAD CHECK (Y/N):" TO ANSWER
IF UPPER(ANSWER) <> "Y"
   RETURN
ENDIF
SELECT A
STORE SPACE(6) TO MEMCHECKNO
STORE 0 TO MEMAMT
CLEAR
@ 1,1 SAY "ENTER THE BAD CHECK NUMBER" GET MEMCHECKNO
@ 3,1 SAY "ENTER THE AMOUNT OF THE BAD CHECK" GET MEMAMT
READ
STORE SPACE(1) TO ANSWER
WAIT "DOES THE CLIENT ALREADY HAVE A CHARGE ACCOUNT (Y/N):" ;
  TO ANSWER
IF UPPER(ANSWER) <> "Y"
   SET DEVICE TO SCREEN
   CLEAR
   APPEND BLANK
   @  1, 1 SAY "NEW ACCOUNT ENTRY FORM FOR BAD CHECK"
   @  2, 1 SAY "------------------------------------"
   @  3, 1 SAY "ACCOUNT NUMBER"
   @  3,16 GET ACCNO
   @  5, 1 SAY "COMPANY NAME"
   @  5,16 GET ACCCOMPANY
   @  6, 1 SAY "LAST NAME"
   @  6,11 GET ACCLNAME
   @  6,29 SAY "FIRST NAME"
```

```
@  6,40 GET ACCFNAME
@  7, 1 SAY "PO BOX"
@  7, 8 GET ACCPOBOX
@  7,20 SAY "STREET"
@  7,27 GET ACCSTREET
@  8, 1 SAY "CITY"
@  8, 6 GET ACCCITY
@  8,23 SAY "STATE"
@  8,29 GET ACCSTATE
@  8,39 SAY "ZIP"
@  8,43 GET ACCZIP
@ 10, 1 SAY "ACCOUNT TYPE"
@ 10,30 SAY "ACCOUNT STATUS"
@ 10,60 SAY "BILLING TYPE"
@ 11, 1 SAY "------------"
@ 11,30 SAY "--------------"
@ 11,60 SAY "------------"
@ 12, 1 SAY "BC=BAD CHECK"
@ 12,30 SAY "CAN=CANCELLED"
@ 12,60 SAY "REG=REGULAR"
@ 13, 1 SAY "RC=REVOLVING CHARGE"
@ 13,30 SAY "HLD=HOLD FOR SPECIAL ACTION"
@ 13,60 SAY "SCH=BY PAY SCHEDULE"
@ 14, 1 SAY "SI=SINGLE ITEM"
@ 14,30 SAY "OVL=OVER THE CHARGE LIMIT"
@ 15, 1 SAY "UN=OLD UNPAID ACCOUNT"
@ 15,30 SAY "VAL=NORMAL CHARGE ACCOUNT"
REPLACE ACCTYPE WITH "BC", ACCSTATUS WITH "HLD", ACCTOTCHRG ;
```

```
        WITH MEMAMT, ACCSPECACT WITH "PAY BAD CHECK", ACCBADCHNO ;
        WITH MEMCHECKNO, ACCDTLACT WITH DATE(), ACCBILLTYP WITH "REG"
      @ 16, 1 SAY "TYPE OF ACCOUNT:"
      @ 16,17 SAY ACCTYPE
      @ 16,21 SAY "STATUS OF ACCOUNT:"
      @ 16,39 SAY ACCSTATUS
      @ 16,43 SAY "BILLING TYPE:"
      @ 16,56 SAY ACCBILLTYP
      @ 17, 1 SAY "CREDIT LIMIT"
      @ 17,13 GET ACCCREDLIM
      @ 17,21 SAY "DESCRIPTION OF SECURITY DEPOSIT"
      @ 17,53 GET ACCSECDEP
      @ 18, 1 SAY "SPECIAL ACTION REQUIRED:"
      @ 18,26 SAY ACCSPECACT
      @ 19, 1 SAY "INTEREST DUE"
      @ 19,14 GET ACCTOTINT
      @ 19,23 SAY "YTD INTEREST"
      @ 19,36 GET ACCYTDINT
      @ 20, 1 SAY "DATE OF LAST ACCOUNT ACTIVITY:"
      @ 20,31 SAY ACCDTLACT
      @ 21, 1 SAY "TOTAL CHARGES:"
      @ 21,18 SAY ACCTOTCHRG
      @ 23, 1 SAY "LAST BAD CHECK NUMBER:"
      @ 23,23 SAY ACCBADCHNO
      READ
      STORE ACCNO TO MEMACCTNO
   ELSE
      STORE SPACE(10) TO MEMACCTNO
```

```
    CLEAR
    @ 1,0 SAY "ENTER THE NUMBER OF THE ACCOUNT" GET MEMACCTNO
    READ
    SEEK MEMACCTNO
    IF EOF()
       @ 3,0 SAY "NO SUCH ACCOUNT NUMBER."
       WAIT
       LOOP
    ENDIF
    @ 3,0 SAY "COMPANY="+ACCCOMPANY
    @ 4,0 SAY "NAME    ="+TRIM(ACCFNAME)+" "+TRIM(ACCLNAME)
    STORE SPACE(1) TO ANSWER
    WAIT "IS THIS THE CORRECT ACCOUNT (Y/N):" TO ANSWER
    IF UPPER(ANSWER) <> "Y"
       LOOP
    ENDIF
    REPLACE ACCBADCHNO WITH MEMCHECKNO, ACCTOTCHRG WITH;
      ACCTOTCHRG + MEMAMT, ACCDTLACT WITH DATE()
ENDIF
STORE SPACE(6) TO MEMTICKETN
@ 6,1 SAY "ENTER THE TICKET NUMBER FOR THE CHARGE" ;
   GET MEMTICKETN
READ
SELECT B
APPEND BLANK
REPLACE CHACCTNO WITH MEMACCTNO, CHTICKETNO WITH MEMTICKETN,;
   CHITEMDESC WITH "BAD CH #"+MEMCHECKNO, CHDOLLARS WITH MEMAMT,;
   CHDATE WITH DATE()
```

```
   SELECT C
   APPEND BLANK
   REPLACE ACCTACCNO WITH MEMACCTNO, ACCTTYPACT WITH "BAD CHECK",;
     ACCTDTACT WITH DATE(), ACCTAMT WITH MEMAMT
ENDDO
RETURN
***************************** END OF PROGRAM ******************


* BCRESOLVE.PRG
SELECT A
USE ACCOUNTS INDEX ACCNO
SELECT C
USE ACCTFILE INDEX ACCTTYPA
SELECT D
USE PAYMENTS INDEX PAYACCTN, PAYCHECK
DO WHILE .T.
   CLEAR
   STORE SPACE(1) TO ANSWER
   WAIT "DO YOU WISH TO RESOLVE ANOTHER BAD CHECK (Y/N):" TO ANSWER
   IF UPPER(ANSWER) <> "Y"
      RETURN
   ENDIF
   STORE SPACE(10) TO MEMACCTNO
   CLEAR
   @ 1,0 SAY "ENTER THE ACCOUNT NUMBER:" GET MEMACCTNO
   READ
   SELECT A
   SEEK MEMACCTNO
```

```
IF EOF()
   @ 3,0 SAY "NO SUCH ACCOUNT."
   WAIT
   LOOP
ENDIF
@ 3,0 SAY "ACCOUNT NO="+ACCNO
@ 4,0 SAY "COMPANY   ="+ACCCOMPANY
@ 5,0 SAY "NAME      ="+TRIM(ACCFNAME)+" "+TRIM(ACCLNAME)
@ 6,0 SAY "ADDRESS   ="+TRIM(ACCSTREET)+","+TRIM(ACCCITY)+","+;
      TRIM(ACCSTATE)
STORE SPACE(1) TO ANSWER
WAIT "IS THIS THE CORRECT ACCOUNT (Y/N):" TO ANSWER
IF UPPER(ANSWER) <> "Y"
   LOOP
ENDIF
STORE 0 TO MEMAMT
STORE SPACE(6) TO MEMCHECKNO
@ 10,0 SAY "ENTER THE DOLLAR AMOUNT OF THE RESOLVED CHECK" ;
   GET MEMAMT
@ 11,0 SAY "ENTER THE CHECK NUMBER IF PAYMENT IS BY CHECK" ;
   GET MEMCHECKNO
READ
REPLACE ACCBADCHNO WITH SPACE(6), ACCPAYMENT WITH ACCPAYMENT ;
   + MEMAMT,ACCDTLACT WITH DATE()
SELECT D
APPEND BLANK
REPLACE PAYACCTNO WITH MEMACCTNO, PAYAMT WITH MEMAMT, PAYDATE WITH;
  DATE(), PAYCHECKNO WITH MEMCHECKNO
```

```
   SELECT C
   APPEND BLANK
   REPLACE ACCTACCNO WITH MEMACCTNO, ACCTTYPACT WITH ;
     "RESOLUTION OF BAD CHECK", ACCTDTACT WITH DATE(), ACCTAMT WITH;
     MEMAMT
ENDDO
RETURN
***************************** END OF PROGRAM *****************

* BILLING.PRG
SELECT E
USE BILLING INDEX BILLACCT
CLEAR
@  5, 5 SAY "SELECT BILLING MODE"
@  6, 5 SAY "-------------------"
@  7,10 SAY "A. PRODUCE BILLING INFO FROM CHARGES"
@  8,10 SAY "B. UPDATE A BILL AMOUNT TO CHANGE PREVIOUS "+;
               "BILL AMOUNT ON NEXT BILL"
WAIT "ENTER A SELECTION CODE:" TO CODE1
DO CASE
   CASE CODE1 = "A"
      DO MAKEBILL
   CASE CODE1 = "B"
      CLEAR
      DO WHILE .T.
         STORE SPACE(1) TO ANSWER
         WAIT "DO YOU WISH TO UPDATE ANOTHER BILL (Y/N):" TO ANSWER
         IF UPPER(ANSWER) <> "Y"
```

```
            RETURN
         ENDIF
         STORE SPACE(10) TO MEMACCTNO
         CLEAR
         @ 1,0 SAY "ENTER THE ACCOUNT NUMBER" GET MEMACCTNO
         READ
         SEEK MEMACCTNO
         IF EOF()
            @ 3,0 SAY "NO BILLS ON FILE FOR THIS ACCOUNT NUMBER"
            WAIT
            LOOP
         ENDIF
         @ 3,0 SAY "CURRENT BILL AMOUNT=" GET BILLAMT
         READ
      ENDDO
   OTHERWISE
      @ 15,0 SAY "ILLEGAL SELECTION CODE"
      WAIT
ENDCASE
RETURN
***************************** END OF PROGRAM ******************


* BUYCASH.PRG
SET DEVICE TO SCREEN
SELECT C
USE ACCTFILE INDEX ACCTTYPA
SELECT J
USE INVENTOR INDEX INVITMAN, INVITLOC
```

```
DO WHILE .T.
   CLEAR
   STORE SPACE(1) TO ANSWER
   WAIT "DO YOU WISH TO ENTER ANOTHER CASH TICKET (Y/N):" ;
      TO ANSWER
   IF UPPER(ANSWER) <> "Y"
      RETURN
   ENDIF
   CLEAR
   SELECT J
   STORE SPACE(20) TO MEMITEMNO
   STORE SPACE(25) TO MEMMANU
   STORE SPACE(15) TO MEMLOC
   STORE .F. TO OKKEY
   DO WHILE .NOT. OKKEY
      CLEAR
      @ 1, 1 SAY "ENTER THE ITEM NUMBER                    "
      @ 1,42 GET MEMITEMNO
      @ 2, 1 SAY "ENTER THE MANUFACTURER/SPECIAL DESIGNATOR"
      @ 2,42 GET MEMMANU
      @ 3, 1 SAY "ENTER THE LOCATION                       "
      @ 3,42 GET MEMLOC
      READ
      @ 6, 1 SAY "YOU HAVE ENTERED THE FOLLOWING:"
      @ 7, 5 SAY "ITEM NUMBER                 ="
      @ 7,37 SAY MEMITEMNO
      @ 8, 5 SAY "MANUFACTURER/SPECIAL DESIGNATOR="
      @ 8,37 SAY MEMMANU
```

```
      @ 9, 5 SAY "LOCATION                          ="
      @ 9,37 SAY MEMLOC
      STORE SPACE(1) TO ANSWER
      @ 11,0 SAY "IS THIS INFORMATION CORRECT (Y/N):" GET ANSWER
      READ
      IF UPPER(ANSWER) <> "Y"
         @ 15,0 SAY "PLEASE RE-ENTER"
         WAIT
      ELSE
         STORE .T. TO OKKEY
      ENDIF
   ENDDO
   STORE MEMITEMNO + MEMMANU + MEMLOC TO MEMKEY
   SEEK MEMKEY
   IF EOF()
      STORE 0 TO MEMUNITPR
      @ 15,0 SAY "NO INVENTORY RECORD ON FILE FOR GIVEN INFORMATION"
      @ 16,0 SAY "UNABLE TO UPDATE INVENTORY."
      STORE SPACE(1) TO ANSWER
      @ 17,0 SAY "DO YOU WISH TO CONTINUE (Y/N):" GET ANSWER
      READ
      IF UPPER(ANSWER) <> "Y"
         LOOP
      ENDIF
   ELSE
      CLEAR
      @  1, 1 SAY "UPDATE AN INVENTORY RECORD FOR CASH PAYMENT"
      @  2, 1 SAY "-------------------------------------------"
```

```
@  3, 1 SAY "INVENTORY ITEM NUMBER:"
@  3,24 SAY INVITEMNO
@  4, 1 SAY "MANUFACTURER OR SPECIAL DESIGNATOR:"
@  4,37 SAY INVMANU
@  5, 1 SAY "DESCRIPTION OF ITEM:"
@  5,21 SAY INVDESC
@  7, 1 SAY "LOCATION OF ITEM:"
@  7,19 SAY INVLOC
@  9, 1 SAY "UNITS:"
@  9, 7 SAY INVUNITS
@  9,19 SAY "COUNT PER UNIT:"
@  9,34 SAY INVQTYPER
@ 11, 1 SAY "QUANTITY ON HAND:"
@ 11,18 SAY INVQTYONH
@ 13, 1 SAY "REORDER POINT:"
@ 13,15 SAY INVREORDPT
@ 13,28 SAY "REORDER AMOUNT:"
@ 13,43 SAY INVREORDAM
@ 15, 1 SAY "UNIT COST:"
@ 15,15 SAY INVCSTPERU
@ 17, 1 SAY "SELLING PRICE:"
@ 17,15 SAY INVSELLPR
STORE SPACE(1) TO ANSWER
@ 19,0 SAY "IS THIS THE CORRECT RECORD (Y/N):" GET ANSWER
READ
IF UPPER(ANSWER) <> "Y"
   LOOP
ELSE
```

```
        STORE INVCSTPERU TO MEMUNITPR
        STORE INVDESC TO MEMDESC
    ENDIF
ENDIF
STORE 0 TO MEMQTY
STORE 0.00 TO MEMPRICE
STORE 0.00 TO MEMTAX
STORE DATE() TO MEMDATE
STORE .F. TO OKDATA
DO WHILE .NOT. OKDATA
    CLEAR
    @ 2, 1 SAY "QUANTITY SOLD                 "
    @ 2,27 GET MEMQTY
    READ
    @ 3, 1 SAY "SALES PRICE, EXCLUDING TAX"
    MEMPRICE = MEMQTY*INVSELLPR
    @ 3,27 GET MEMPRICE
    @ 4, 1 SAY "TAX                           "
    @ 4,27 GET MEMTAX
    @ 5, 1 SAY "DATE OF SALE                  "
    @ 5,27 GET MEMDATE
    READ
    @ 7, 1 SAY "YOU HAVE ENTERED THE FOLLOWING INFORMATION:"
    @ 9, 5 SAY "QUANTITY SOLD              ="
    @ 9,32 SAY MEMQTY
    @ 10,5 SAY "SALES PRICE, EXCLUDING TAX="
    @ 10,32 SAY MEMPRICE
    @ 11,5 SAY "TAX                        ="
```

```
    @ 11,32 SAY MEMTAX
    @ 12,5 SAY "DATE OF SALE              ="
    @ 12,32 SAY MEMDATE
    STORE SPACE(1) TO ANSWER
    @ 14,0 SAY "IS THIS INFORMATION CORRECT (Y/N):" GET ANSWER
    READ
    IF UPPER(ANSWER) <> "Y"
       @ 16,0 SAY "PLEASE RE-ENTER"
       WAIT
       LOOP
    ENDIF
    STORE .T. TO OKDATA
ENDDO
STORE MEMPRICE+MEMTAX TO MEMCHRGAMT
IF .NOT. EOF()
   REPLACE INVQTYONH WITH INVQTYONH-MEMQTY
ENDIF
SELECT C
APPEND BLANK
REPLACE ACCTACCNO WITH SPACE(10), ACCTTYPACT WITH ;
  "CASH PAYMENT", ACCTDTACT WITH MEMDATE, ACCTAMT WITH ;
  MEMPRICE
IF MEMTAX = 0
   LOOP
ENDIF
APPEND BLANK
REPLACE ACCTACCNO WITH SPACE(10), ACCTTYPACT WITH ;
  "TAX", ACCTDTACT WITH MEMDATE, ACCTAMT WITH MEMTAX
```

```
ENDDO
RETURN
***************************** END OF PROGRAM ******************


* BUYCHARGE.PRG
SET DEVICE TO SCREEN
SELECT A
USE ACCOUNTS INDEX ACCNO
SELECT B
USE CHARGES INDEX CHACCTNO, CHTICKET
SELECT C
USE ACCTFILE INDEX ACCTTYPA
SELECT J
USE INVENTOR INDEX INVITMAN
DO WHILE .T.
   CLEAR
   STORE SPACE(1) TO ANSWER
   WAIT "DO YOU WISH TO ENTER ANOTHER CHARGE TICKET (Y/N):" ;
      TO ANSWER
   IF UPPER(ANSWER) <> "Y"
      RETURN
   ENDIF
   CLEAR
   SELECT A
   STORE SPACE(10) TO MEMACCTNO
   CLEAR
   @ 1,1 SAY "ENTER THE CHARGE ACCOUNT NUMBER" GET MEMACCTNO
   READ
```

```
SEEK MEMACCTNO
IF EOF()
   @ 3,0 SAY "NO SUCH ACCOUNT NUMBER ON FILE."
   WAIT
   LOOP
ELSE
   @ 3,1 SAY "COMPANY       ="+ ACCCOMPANY
   @ 4,1 SAY  "NAME          ="+ TRIM(ACCLNAME)+', '+;
              TRIM(ACCFNAME)
   @ 5,1 SAY  "ACCOUNT TYPE  ="+ ACCTYPE
   @ 6,1 SAY  "ACCOUNT STATUS="+ ACCSTATUS
   @ 7,1 SAY  "CREDIT LIMIT  =  "+ STR(ACCCREDLIM,9,2)
   @ 8,1 SAY  "UNPAID CHARGES="+ STR(ACCTOTCHRG+ACCTOTINT-;
               ACCPAYMENT-ACCCARYOVR,9,2)
   @ 9,1 SAY  "OVER 30       =  "+ STR(ACCOVER30,9,2)
   @ 10,1 SAY  "OVER 60       =  "+ STR(ACCOVER60,9,2)
   @ 11,1 SAY  "OVER 90       =  "+ STR(ACCOVER90,9,2)
   @ 12,1 SAY   "DISCOUNT %    ="+ STR(ACCDISCPER,9,2)
   STORE SPACE(1) TO ANSWER
   @ 14,0 SAY "DO YOU WISH TO ENTER THE CHARGE (Y/N):" ;
       GET ANSWER
   READ
   IF UPPER(ANSWER) <> "Y"
      LOOP
   ENDIF
ENDIF
STORE SPACE(20) TO MEMITEMNO
STORE SPACE(25) TO MEMMANU
```

```
STORE SPACE(15) TO MEMLOC
STORE .F. TO OKKEY
DO WHILE .NOT. OKKEY
   CLEAR
   @ 1, 1 SAY "ENTER THE ITEM NUMBER                        "
   @ 1,42 GET MEMITEMNO
   @ 2, 1 SAY "ENTER THE MANUFACTURER/SPECIAL DESIGNATOR"
   @ 2,42 GET MEMMANU
   @ 3, 1 SAY "ENTER THE LOCATION                           "
   @ 3,42 GET MEMLOC
   READ
   @ 6, 1 SAY "YOU HAVE ENTERED THE FOLLOWING:"
   @ 7, 5 SAY "ITEM NUMBER                    ="
   @ 7,37 SAY MEMITEMNO
   @ 8, 5 SAY "MANUFACTURER/SPECIAL DESIGNATOR="
   @ 8,37 SAY MEMMANU
   @ 9, 5 SAY "LOCATION                       ="
   @ 9,37 SAY MEMLOC
   STORE SPACE(1) TO ANSWER
   WAIT "IS THIS INFORMATION CORRECT (Y/N):" TO ANSWER
   IF UPPER(ANSWER) <> "Y"
      ? "PLEASE RE-ENTER"
     WAIT
   ELSE
     STORE .T. TO OKKEY
   ENDIF
ENDDO
STORE MEMITEMNO + MEMMANU + MEMLOC TO MEMKEY
```

```
SELECT J
SEEK MEMKEY
IF EOF()
   STORE 0 TO MEMUNITPR
   ? "NO INVENTORY RECORD ON FILE FOR GIVEN INFORMATION"
   ? "UNABLE TO UPDATE INVENTORY."
   STORE SPACE(1) TO ANSWER
   WAIT "DO YOU WISH TO CONTINUE (Y/N):" TO ANSWER
   IF UPPER(ANSWER) = "Y"
       CLEAR
       STORE SPACE(15) TO MEMDESC
       @ 1,1 SAY "ENTER THE ITEM DESCRIPTION" GET MEMDESC
       READ
   ELSE
      LOOP
   ENDIF
 ELSE
    CLEAR
    @  1, 1 SAY "UPDATE AN INVENTORY RECORD FOR CHARGE"
    @  2, 1 SAY "-------------------------------------"
    @  3, 1 SAY "INVENTORY ITEM NUMBER:"
    @  3,24 SAY INVITEMNO
    @  4, 1 SAY "MANUFACTURER OR SPECIAL DESIGNATOR:"
    @  4,37 SAY INVMANU
    @  5, 1 SAY "DESCRIPTION OF ITEM:"
    @  5,21 SAY INVDESC
    @  7, 1 SAY "LOCATION OF ITEM:"
    @  7,19 SAY INVLOC
```

```
  @  9, 1 SAY "UNITS:"
  @  9, 7 SAY INVUNITS
  @  9,19 SAY "COUNT PER UNIT:"
  @  9,34 SAY INVQTYPER
  @ 11, 1 SAY "QUANTITY ON HAND:"
  @ 11,18 SAY INVQTYONH
  @ 13, 1 SAY "REORDER POINT:"
  @ 13,15 SAY INVREORDPT
  @ 13,28 SAY "REORDER AMOUNT:"
  @ 13,43 SAY INVREORDAM
  @ 15, 1 SAY "UNIT COST:"
  @ 15,15 SAY INVCSTPERU
  @ 17, 1 SAY "SELLING PRICE:"
  @ 17,15 SAY INVSELLPR
  STORE SPACE(1) TO ANSWER
  WAIT "IS THIS THE CORRECT RECORD (Y/N):" ;
     TO ANSWER
  IF UPPER(ANSWER) <> "Y"
     LOOP
   ELSE
    STORE INVCSTPERU TO MEMUNITPR
    STORE INVDESC TO MEMDESC
  ENDIF
ENDIF
STORE SPACE(10) TO MEMTICKET
STORE 0 TO MEMQTY
STORE 0.00 TO MEMPRICE
STORE 0.00 TO MEMTAX
```

```
STORE DATE() TO MEMDATE
STORE .F. TO OKDATA
DO WHILE .NOT. OKDATA
   CLEAR
   @ 1, 1 SAY "TICKET NUMBER             "
   @ 1,27 GET MEMTICKET
   @ 2, 1 SAY "QUANTITY SOLD             "
   @ 2,27 GET MEMQTY
   READ
   MEMPRICE = MEMQTY*INVSELLPR
   @ 3, 1 SAY "SALES PRICE, EXCLUDING TAX"
   @ 3,27 GET MEMPRICE
   @ 4, 1 SAY "TAX                       "
   @ 4,27 GET MEMTAX
   @ 5, 1 SAY "DATE OF SALE              "
   @ 5,27 GET MEMDATE
   READ
   @ 7, 1 SAY "YOU HAVE ENTERED THE FOLLOWING INFORMATION:"
   @ 8, 5 SAY "TICKET NUMBER             ="
   @ 8,32 SAY MEMTICKET
   @ 9, 5 SAY "QUANTITY SOLD             ="
   @ 9,32 SAY MEMQTY
   @ 10,5 SAY "SALES PRICE, EXCLUDING TAX="
   @ 10,32 SAY MEMPRICE
   @ 11,5 SAY "TAX                       ="
   @ 11,32 SAY MEMTAX
   @ 12,5 SAY "DATE OF SALE              ="
   @ 12,32 SAY MEMDATE
```

```
   STORE SPACE(1) TO ANSWER
   @ 14,0 SAY "IS THIS INFORMATION CORRECT (Y/N)" GET ANSWER
   READ
   IF UPPER(ANSWER) <> "Y"
      @ 15,0 SAY "PLEASE RE-ENTER"
      WAIT
      LOOP
   ENDIF
   STORE .T. TO OKDATA
ENDDO
STORE MEMPRICE+MEMTAX TO MEMCHRGAMT
IF FOUND()
   REPLACE INVQTYONH WITH INVQTYONH-MEMQTY
ENDIF
SELECT C
APPEND BLANK
REPLACE ACCTACCNO WITH MEMACCTNO, ACCTTYPACT WITH ;
  "CHARGE", ACCTDTACT WITH MEMDATE, ACCTAMT WITH ;
  MEMPRICE
IF MEMTAX <> 0
   APPEND BLANK
   REPLACE ACCTACCNO WITH MEMACCTNO, ACCTTYPACT WITH ;
     "TAX", ACCTDTACT WITH MEMDATE, ACCTAMT WITH MEMTAX
ENDIF
SELECT A
SEEK MEMACCTNO
IF EOF()
   @ 20,0 SAY "UNABLE TO FIND ACCOUNT RECORD. CAN NOT "+;
```

```
              "ADD CHARGE TO RECORD."
      WAIT
   ELSE
      REPLACE ACCTOTCHRG WITH ACCTOTCHRG + MEMPRICE ;
        + MEMTAX, ACCDTLACT WITH MEMDATE
   ENDIF
   SELECT B
   APPEND BLANK
   REPLACE CHACCTNO WITH MEMACCTNO,CHTICKETNO WITH MEMTICKET,;
     CHITEMNO WITH MEMITEMNO,CHITEMDESC WITH MEMDESC,CHMANU ;
     WITH MEMMANU,CHLOCATION WITH MEMLOC
   REPLACE CHQTY WITH MEMQTY,CHDOLLARS WITH MEMCHRGAMT,CHDATE ;
     WITH MEMDATE
ENDDO
RETURN
***************************** END OF PROGRAM ******************


* CRACCOUN.PRG
SET DEVICE TO SCREEN
SELECT A
USE ACCOUNTS INDEX ACCNO, ACCLNAME, ACCCOMPA
DO WHILE .T.
   CLEAR
   STORE SPACE(1) TO ANSWER
   WAIT "DO YOU WISH TO ENTER ANOTHER NEW ACCOUNT (Y/N):" ;
      TO ANSWER
   IF UPPER(ANSWER) <> "Y"
      RETURN
```

```
ENDIF

CLEAR

APPEND BLANK

@  1, 1 SAY "NEW ACCOUNT ENTRY FORM"

@  2, 1 SAY "----------------------"

@  3, 1 SAY "ACCOUNT NUMBER"

@  3,16 GET ACCNO

@  5, 1 SAY "COMPANY NAME"

@  5,16 GET ACCCOMPANY

@  6, 1 SAY "LAST NAME"

@  6,11 GET ACCLNAME

@  6,29 SAY "FIRST NAME"

@  6,40 GET ACCFNAME

@  7, 1 SAY "PO BOX"

@  7, 8 GET ACCPOBOX

@  7,20 SAY "STREET"

@  7,27 GET ACCSTREET

@  8, 1 SAY "CITY"

@  8, 6 GET ACCCITY

@  8,23 SAY "STATE"

@  8,29 GET ACCSTATE

@  8,39 SAY "ZIP"

@  8,43 GET ACCZIP

@ 10, 1 SAY "ACCOUNT TYPE"

@ 10,30 SAY "ACCOUNT STATUS"

@ 10,60 SAY "BILLING TYPE"

@ 11, 1 SAY "------------"

@ 11,30 SAY "--------------"
```

```
@ 11,60 SAY "------------"
@ 12, 1 SAY "BC=BAD CHECK"
@ 12,30 SAY "CAN=CANCELLED"
@ 12,60 SAY "REG=REGULAR"
@ 13, 1 SAY "RC=REVOLVING CHARGE"
@ 13,30 SAY "HLD=HOLD FOR SPECIAL ACTION"
@ 13,60 SAY "SCH=BY PAY SCHEDULE"
@ 14, 1 SAY "SI=SINGLE ITEM"
@ 14,30 SAY "OVL=OVER THE CHARGE LIMIT"
@ 15, 1 SAY "UN=OLD UNPAID ACCOUNT"
@ 15,30 SAY "VAL=NORMAL CHARGE ACCOUNT"
@ 16, 1 SAY "TYPE OF ACCOUNT"
@ 16,17 GET ACCTYPE
@ 16,21 SAY "STATUS OF ACCOUNT"
@ 16,38 GET ACCSTATUS
@ 16,43 SAY "BILLING TYPE"
@ 16,56 GET ACCBILLTYP
@ 16,61 SAY "MIN PMT"
@ 16,68 GET ACCMINPAY
@ 17, 1 SAY "CREDIT LIMIT"
@ 17,13 GET ACCCREDLIM
@ 17,21 SAY "DESCRIPTION OF SECURITY DEPOSIT"
@ 17,53 GET ACCSECDEP
@ 18, 1 SAY "SPECIAL ACTION REQUIRED"
@ 18,25 GET ACCSPECACT
@ 19, 1 SAY "INTEREST DUE"
@ 19,14 GET ACCTOTINT
@ 19,23 SAY "YTD INTEREST"
```

```
   @ 19,36 GET ACCYTDINT
   @ 20, 1 SAY "DATE OF LAST ACCOUNT ACTIVITY"
   @ 20,31 GET ACCDTLACT
   @ 21, 1 SAY "DISCOUNT PERCENT"
   @ 21,18 GET ACCDISCPER
   @ 23, 1 SAY "LAST BAD CHECK NUMBER"
   @ 23,23 GET ACCBADCHNO
   @ 23,31 SAY "MONTHS IN ARREARS"
   @ 23,48 GET ACCMONARR
   READ
ENDDO
RETURN
***************************** END OF PROGRAM *****************

* DEFACT.PRG
CLEAR
? "TODAY'S DATE IS THE DATE USED TO RECORD THE ACTION "
? "DECISIONS THAT YOU ARE ABOUT TO MAKE,"
? "AND WILL BE REQUIRED LATER AS INPUT, WHEN"
? "YOU PREPARE THE FILES FOR THE DEFAULT LETTERS."
?
WAIT
SELECT F
USE NOTIFICA INDEX NOTACCTN
SELECT A
USE ACCOUNTS INDEX ACCNO
DO WHILE .T.
   CLEAR
```

```
STORE SPACE(1) TO ANSWER
WAIT "DO YOU WISH TO TAKE ANOTHER ACTION (Y/N):" TO ANSWER
IF UPPER(ANSWER) <> "Y"
   RETURN
ENDIF
STORE SPACE(10) TO MEMACCTNO
CLEAR
@ 1,1 SAY "ENTER THE ACCOUNT NUMBER" GET MEMACCTNO
READ
SELECT A
SEEK MEMACCTNO
IF EOF()
   @ 3,0 SAY "NO ACCOUNT RECORD FOR THIS ACCOUNT NUMBER."
   WAIT
   LOOP
ENDIF
@ 4,1 SAY "ACCOUNT NUMBER=" + ACCNO
@ 5,1 SAY "COMPANY NAME  =" + ACCCOMPANY
@ 6,1 SAY "NAME          =" + TRIM(ACCLNAME)+", "+TRIM(ACCFNAME)
STORE SPACE(1) TO ANSWER
WAIT "IS THIS THE CORRECT RECORD (Y/N):" TO ANSWER
IF UPPER(ANSWER) <> "Y"
   LOOP
ENDIF
STORE ACCTOTCHRG + ACCTOTINT TO MEMTOTDUE
SELECT F
STORE .F. TO OKLETTER
DO WHILE .NOT. OKLETTER
```

```
   CLEAR
   @ 1,1 SAY "LETTER TYPES"
   @ 2,1 SAY "------------"
   @ 3,1 SAY "0=MATTER RESOLVED, TAKE NO FURTHER ACTION"
   @ 4,1 SAY "1=MILD      WARNING"
   @ 5,1 SAY "2=STRONG    WARNING"
   @ 6,1 SAY "3=STRONGEST WARNING"
   STORE SPACE(1) TO MEMLETTYPE
   @ 8,0 SAY "ENTER LETTER TYPE" GET MEMLETTYPE
   READ
   IF MEMLETTYPE <> "0" .AND. MEMLETTYPE <> "1" .AND. ;
      MEMLETTYPE <> "2" .AND. MEMLETTYPE <> "3"
      @ 10,0 SAY "ILLEGAL LETTER TYPE"
      WAIT
   ELSE
      STORE .T. TO OKLETTER
   ENDIF
ENDDO
STORE .F. TO OKSTATUS
DO WHILE .NOT. OKSTATUS
   CLEAR
   @ 1,1 SAY "STATUS TYPES"
   @ 2,1 SAY "------------"
   @ 3,1 SAY "LS=LETTER SENT"
   @ 4,1 SAY "RS=LAST ACTION RESOLVED"
   STORE SPACE(2) TO MEMSTATUS
   @ 6,0 SAY "ENTER NEW STATUS" GET MEMSTATUS
   READ
```

```
      IF MEMSTATUS <> "LS" .AND. MEMSTATUS <> "RS"
         @ 10,0 SAY "ILLEGAL STATUS TYPE"
         WAIT
      ELSE
         STORE .T. TO OKSTATUS
      ENDIF
   ENDDO
   APPEND BLANK
   REPLACE NOTACCTNO WITH MEMACCTNO, ;
     NOTTYPE WITH MEMLETTYPE, NOTDATE WITH DATE(), NOTSTATUS WITH;
     MEMSTATUS, NOTTOTDUE WITH MEMTOTDUE
ENDDO
RETURN
***************************** END OF PROGRAM *****************


* DEFAULT.PRG
DO WHILE .T.
   CLEAR
   @ 3,5 SAY "DEFAULT MODULE SELECTION CODE"
   @ 4,5 SAY "-----------------------------"
   @ 5,10 SAY "A. EXIT"
   @ 6,10 SAY "B. ACTION DECISION"
   @ 7,10 SAY "C. PREPARE FILES FOR LETTERS"
   @ 8,10 SAY "D. PRINT LETTERS"
   WAIT "ENTER YOUR SELECTION CODE:" TO CODE1
   DO CASE
      CASE CODE1 = "A"
         RETURN
```

```
      CASE CODE1 = "B"
         DO DEFACT
      CASE CODE1 = "C"
         DO DEFLETTE
      CASE CODE1 = "D"
         DO PRINTLET
      OTHERWISE
         @ 15,0 SAY "ILLEGAL SELECTION CODE."
         WAIT
   ENDCASE
   CLEAR ALL
ENDDO
RETURN
***************************** END OF PROGRAM ******************

* DEFLETTERS.PRG
SET DEVICE TO SCREEN
CLEAR
? "NOW CLEARING OUT OLD DATA FROM FILES."
SELECT A
USE ACCOUNTS INDEX ACCNO
SELECT F
USE NOTIFICA INDEX NOTACCTN
SELECT G
USE LET1
ZAP
SELECT H
USE LET2
```

```
ZAP
SELECT I
USE LET3
ZAP
CLEAR
STORE CTOD("  /  /  ") TO MEMDATE
@ 1,0 SAY ;
   "ENTER THE DATE OF THE ACTION DECISIONS IN THE FORM MM/DD/YY" ;
   GET MEMDATE
READ
STORE DATE() TO MEMTDATE
CLEAR
? "NOW PLACING DATA IN FILES TO BE USED LATER TO PRODUCE LETTERS."
SELECT F
DO WHILE .NOT. EOF()
   STORE NOTACCTNO TO MEMACCTNO
   STORE NOTTYPE TO MEMLETTYPE
   IF MEMDATE = NOTDATE
      SELECT A
      SEEK MEMACCTNO
      IF EOF()
         @ 1,1 SAY "UNABLE TO FIND ACCOUNT RECORD WITH "+;
                   "ACCOUNT NUMBER=" + MEMACCTNO
         WAIT
         SELECT F
         SKIP 1
         LOOP
      ELSE
```

```
STORE ACCCOMPANY TO MEMCOMPANY
STORE ACCLNAME TO MEMLNAME
STORE ACCFNAME TO MEMFNAME
STORE ACCPOBOX TO MEMPOBOX
STORE TRIM(ACCSTREET) TO MEMSTREET
STORE TRIM(ACCCITY)+","+TRIM(ACCSTATE)+" "+;
      TRIM(ACCZIP) TO MEMADDRESS
STORE ACCTOTCHRG TO MEMTOTCHRG
STORE ACCTOTINT TO MEMTOTINT
STORE ACCTOTCHRG + ACCTOTINT TO MEMTOTDUE
DO CASE
   CASE MEMLETTYPE = "1"
      SELECT G
   CASE MEMLETTYPE = "2"
      SELECT H
   CASE MEMLETTYPE = "3"
      SELECT H
   OTHERWISE
      SELECT F
      SKIP 1
      LOOP
ENDCASE
APPEND BLANK
REPLACE LETACCNO WITH MEMACCTNO, LETPOBOX WITH;
  MEMPOBOX, LETLNAME WITH MEMLNAME, LETFNAME WITH;
  MEMFNAME, LETSTREET WITH MEMSTREET
REPLACE LETADDRESS WITH MEMADDRESS,LETTOTCHRG WITH;
  MEMTOTCHRG, LETTOTINT WITH MEMTOTINT, LETTOTDUE ;
```

```
          WITH MEMTOTDUE, LETCOMPANY WITH MEMCOMPANY
      ENDIF
   ENDIF
   SELECT F
   SKIP 1
ENDDO
RETURN
***************************** END OF PROGRAM ******************

* DELETE.PRG
SELECT A
USE ACCOUNTS
SELECT B
USE CHARGES
SELECT C
USE TRANSFER
SELECT D
USE PAYMENTS
SELECT E
USE BILLING
SELECT F
USE NOTIFICA
SELECT J
USE INVENTOR
SET DEVICE TO SCREEN
STORE .F. TO DELACCT
STORE .F. TO DELCHARGE
STORE .F. TO DELPAY
```

```
STORE .F. TO DELNOTICE
STORE .F. TO DELBILL
STORE .F. TO DELINV
STORE .F. TO DELTRANS
DO WHILE .T.
   CLEAR
   @ 1,0 SAY "THIS PROCEDURE MAY BE VERY TIME CONSUMING, "+;
             "SINCE IT INVOLVES"
   @ 2,0 SAY "REFORMATING ALL FILES IN WHICH DELETIONS OCCUR."
   @  5, 5 SAY "RECORD THAT CAN BE DELETED"
   @  6, 5 SAY "--------------------------"
   @  7,10 SAY "A. EXIT AND REFORMAT FILES"
   @  8,10 SAY "B. ACCOUNT"
   @  9,10 SAY "C. BILL"
   @ 10,10 SAY "D. CHARGE"
   @ 11,10 SAY "E. INVENTORY"
   @ 12,10 SAY "F. INVENTORY TRANSFER"
   @ 13,10 SAY "G. NOTIFICATION OF DEFAULT"
   @ 14,10 SAY "H. PAYMENT"
   WAIT "ENTER A SELECTION CODE:" TO MODE
   DO CASE
      CASE MODE = "A"
         * PERFORM THE PACKS AND RE-INDEXING
         IF DELACCT
            SELECT A
            SET INDEX TO
            PACK
            INDEX ON ACCNO TO ACCNO
```

```
   INDEX ON ACCCOMPANY TO ACCCOMPA
   INDEX ON ACCLNAME TO ACCLNAME
ENDIF
IF DELCHARGE
   SELECT B
   SET INDEX TO
   PACK
   INDEX ON CHACCTNO TO CHACCTNO
   INDEX ON CHTICKETNO TO CHTICKET
ENDIF
IF DELPAY
   SELECT D
   SET INDEX TO
   PACK
   INDEX ON PAYACCTNO TO PAYACCTN
   INDEX ON PAYCHECKNO TO PAYCHECK
ENDIF
IF DELNOTICE
   SELECT F
   SET INDEX TO
   PACK
   INDEX ON NOTACCTNO+;
      STR(30000000-YEAR(NOTDATE)*10000+MONTH(NOTDATE)*100;
      +DAY(NOTDATE),8) TO NOTACCTN
ENDIF
IF DELBILL
   SELECT E
   SET INDEX TO
```

```
      PACK
      INDEX ON BILLACCTNO+;
        STR(30000000-YEAR(BILLDATE)*10000+MONTH(BILLDATE)*100;
        +DAY(BILLDATE),8) TO BILLACCT
   ENDIF
   IF DELINV
      SELECT J
      SET INDEX TO
      PACK
      INDEX ON INVITEMNO+INVMANU+INVLOC TO INVITMAN
      INDEX ON INVITEMNO+INVLOC TO INVITLOC
   ENDIF
   IF DELTRANS
      SELECT C
      SET INDEX TO
      PACK
      INDEX ON TRSENDLOC+TRRECLOC+TRITEMNO+DTOC(TRSENDDT) ;
         TO TRLOCITD
   ENDIF
   RETURN
CASE MODE = "B"
   * DELETE ACCOUNT RECORD
   CLEAR
   @  5, 5 SAY "DELETION MODES FOR CHARGE ACCOUNTS"
   @  6, 5 SAY "----------------------------------"
   @  7,10 SAY "A. BY ACCOUNT NUMBER"
   @  8,10 SAY "B. BY DATE (ALL PREVIOUS TO DATE)"
   WAIT "ENTER A SELECTION CODE:" TO CODE1
```

```
IF CODE1 <> "A" .AND. CODE1 <> "B"
   @ 10,0 SAY "ILLEGAL MODE SELECTION CODE"
   WAIT
   LOOP
ENDIF
IF CODE1 = "A"
   CLEAR
   SELECT A
   SET INDEX TO ACCNO
   STORE SPACE(10) TO MEMACCTNO
   @ 1,1 SAY "ENTER THE ACCOUNT NUMBER" GET ;
      MEMACCTNO
   READ
   SEEK MEMACCTNO
   IF EOF()
      @ 3,0 SAY "NO ACCOUNT RECORD FOR GIVEN NUMBER"
      WAIT
      LOOP
   ENDIF
   DELETE NEXT 1
   STORE .T. TO DELACCT
   SELECT B
   SET INDEX TO CHACCTNO
   SEEK MEMACCTNO
   IF .NOT. EOF()
       DO WHILE .NOT. EOF() .AND. CHACCTNO = MEMACCTNO
      DELETE NEXT 1
      SKIP 1
```

```
      STORE .T. TO DELCHARGE
    ENDDO
  ENDIF
  SELECT D
  SET INDEX TO PAYACCTN
  SEEK MEMACCTNO
  IF .NOT. EOF()
    DO WHILE .NOT. EOF() .AND. PAYACCTNO = MEMACCTNO
      DELETE NEXT 1
      SKIP 1
      STORE .T. TO DELPAY
    ENDDO
  ENDIF
  SELECT F
  SET INDEX TO NOTACCTN
  SEEK MEMACCTNO
  IF .NOT. EOF()
    DO WHILE .NOT. EOF() .AND. NOTACCTNO = MEMACCTNO
      DELETE NEXT 1
      SKIP 1
      STORE .T. TO DELNOTICE
    ENDDO
  ENDIF
  SELECT E
  SET INDEX TO BILLACCT
  SEEK MEMACCTNO
  IF .NOT. EOF()
    DO WHILE .NOT. EOF() .AND. BILLACCTNO = MEMACCTNO
```

```
            DELETE NEXT 1
            SKIP 1
            STORE .T. TO DELBILL
           ENDDO
         ENDIF
         SELECT A
         SET INDEX TO
         SELECT B
         SET INDEX TO
         SELECT D
         SET INDEX TO
         SELECT F
         SET INDEX TO
         SELECT E
         SET INDEX TO
      ENDIF
      IF CODE1 = "B"
        STORE CTOD("  /  /  ") TO MEMDATE
        CLEAR
        @ 1,1 SAY "ENTER THE DATE IN THE FORM MM/DD/YY"
        @ 2,1 SAY "ALL ACCOUNTS WITH LAST ACTIVITY PREVIOUS TO"
        @ 3,1 SAY "THIS DATE WILL BE DELETED." GET MEMDATE
        READ
        SELECT A
        SET INDEX TO
        GOTO TOP
        DO WHILE .NOT. EOF()
         IF YEAR(ACCDTLACT) <> 0 .AND. ACCDTLACT < MEMDATE
```

```
    STORE ACCNO TO MEMACCTNO
DELETE NEXT 1
STORE .T. TO DELACCT
SELECT B
SET INDEX TO CHACCTNO
SEEK MEMACCTNO
IF .NOT. EOF()
  DO WHILE .NOT. EOF() .AND. CHACCTNO = MEMACCTNO
      DELETE NEXT 1
      SKIP 1
      STORE .T. TO DELCHARGE
ENDDO
ENDIF
SELECT D
SET INDEX TO PAYACCTN
SEEK MEMACCTNO
IF .NOT. EOF()
  DO WHILE .NOT. EOF() .AND. PAYACCTNO = MEMACCTNO
      DELETE NEXT 1
      SKIP 1
      STORE .T. TO DELPAY
      ENDDO
ENDIF
SELECT F
SET INDEX TO NOTACCTN
SEEK MEMACCTNO
IF .NOT. EOF()
  DO WHILE .NOT. EOF() .AND. NOTACCTNO = MEMACCTNO
```

```
          DELETE NEXT 1
          SKIP 1
          STORE .T. TO DELNOTICE
         ENDDO
       ENDIF
       SELECT E
       SET INDEX TO BILLACCT
       SEEK MEMACCTNO
       IF .NOT. EOF()
         DO WHILE .NOT. EOF() .AND. BILLACCTNO = MEMACCTNO
          DELETE NEXT 1
          SKIP 1
          STORE .T. TO DELBILL
         ENDDO
       ENDIF
    ENDIF
    SELECT A
    SKIP 1
   ENDDO
   SELECT A
   SET INDEX TO
   SELECT B
   SET INDEX TO
   SELECT D
   SET INDEX TO
   SELECT F
   SET INDEX TO
   SELECT E
```

```
         SET INDEX TO
      ENDIF
   CASE MODE = "C"
      * DELETE BILL
      CLEAR
      @  5, 5 SAY "DELETION MODES"
      @  6, 5 SAY "--------------"
      @  7,10 SAY "A. BY ACCOUNT NUMBER AND SEARCH"
      @  8,10 SAY "B. BY DATE (ALL PREVIOUS TO DATE)"
      WAIT "ENTER A MODE:" TO CODE1
      IF CODE1 <> "A" .AND. CODE1 <> "B"
         @ 10,0 SAY  "ILLEGAL MODE SELECTION CODE"
         WAIT
         LOOP
      ENDIF
      IF CODE1 = "A"
         CLEAR
         @ 1,1 SAY "WHEN THE MOST RECENT BILL IS DELETED, "
         @ 2,1 SAY "THE PREVIOUS BILL IS USED TO PRODUCE "
         @ 3,1 SAY "THE PREVIOUS BALANCE ON THE NEXT BILL."
         @ 4,1 SAY "IF NECESSARY, CHANGE THE BILLING AMOUNT "
         @ 5,1 SAY "ON THE PREVIOUS BILL."
         STORE SPACE(10) TO MEMACCTNO
         @ 7,1 SAY "ENTER THE ACCOUNT NUMBER" GET ;
            MEMACCTNO
         READ
         SELECT E
         SET INDEX TO BILLACCT
```

```
    SEEK MEMACCTNO
    IF EOF()
       @ 10,0 SAY "NO BILLING RECORDS FOR THIS ACCOUNT"
       WAIT
       LOOP
    ENDIF
    DO WHILE .NOT. EOF() .AND. MEMACCTNO = BILLACCTNO
       CLEAR
       @ 1,1 SAY "AMOUNT OF BILL="
       @ 1,16 SAY BILLAMT
       STORE BILLDATE TO MEMBDT
       @ 2,1 SAY "DATE OF BILL="+DTOC(MEMBDT)
       STORE SPACE(1) TO ANSWER
       @ 5,0 SAY "DO YOU WISH TO DELETE THIS BILL (Y/N)" ;
             GET ANSWER
       READ
       IF UPPER(ANSWER) = "Y"
          DELETE NEXT 1
          STORE .T. TO DELBILL
       ENDIF
       SKIP 1
    ENDDO
ENDIF
IF CODE1 = "B"
  STORE CTOD("  /  /  ") TO MEMDATE
  CLEAR
  @ 1,1 SAY "ENTER THE DATE IN THE FORM MM/DD/YY"
  @ 2,1 SAY "ALL BILLS PREVIOUS TO THIS DATE WILL BE "+;
```

```
              "DELETED" GET MEMDATE
      READ
      SELECT E
      SET INDEX TO
      GOTO TOP
      DO WHILE .NOT. EOF()
       IF BILLDATE < MEMDATE
          DELETE NEXT 1
          STORE .T. TO DELBILL
       ENDIF
       SKIP 1
      ENDDO
    ENDIF
  CASE MODE = "D"
    * DELETE CHARGE
    CLEAR
    ? "TO DELETE AN UNPAID CHARGE, MAKE A PAYMENT FIRST"
    @  5, 5 SAY "DELETION MODES FOR PAID CHARGES"
    @  6, 5 SAY "-------------------------------"
    @  7,10 SAY "A. BY TICKET NUMBER"
    @  8,10 SAY "B. BY DATE (ALL PREVIOUS TO DATE)"
    WAIT "ENTER A MODE:" TO CODE1
    IF CODE1 <> "A" .AND. CODE1 <> "B"
       @ 10,0 SAY "ILLEGAL MODE SELECTION CODE"
       WAIT
       LOOP
    ENDIF
    IF CODE1 = "A"
```

```
        CLEAR
        STORE SPACE(10) TO MEMTICKETN
        @ 1,1 SAY "ENTER THE TICKET NUMBER" GET MEMTICKETN
        READ
        SELECT B
        SET INDEX TO CHTICKET
        SEEK MEMTICKETN
        IF EOF()
           @ 5,0 SAY "NO RECORD FOR GIVEN TICKET NUMBER"
           WAIT
           LOOP
        ENDIF
        IF CHBPAID >= CHDOLLARS .AND. (CHRESREPTD = ;
          "Y" .OR. CHRESREPTD = " ")
           DELETE NEXT 1
           STORE .T. TO DELCHARGE
        ELSE
           @ 5,0 SAY "CHARGE NOT PAID YET OR DISPUTED"
           @ 6,0 SAY "CAN NOT DELETE"
           WAIT
           LOOP
        ENDIF
    ENDIF
    IF CODE1 = "B"
      STORE CTOD("  /  /  ") TO MEMDATE
      CLEAR
      @ 1,1 SAY "ENTER THE DATE IN THE FORM MM/DD/YY"
      @ 2,1 SAY "ALL PAID CHARGES PREVIOUS TO THIS DATE WILL"
```

```
        @ 3,1 SAY "BE DELETED" GET MEMDATE
        READ
        SELECT B
        SET INDEX TO
        GOTO TOP
        DO WHILE .NOT. EOF()
         IF CHBPAID < CHDOLLARS
            SKIP 1
            LOOP
         ENDIF
         IF YEAR(CHDATE) <> 0 .AND. CHDATE < MEMDATE
            DELETE NEXT 1
            STORE .T. TO DELCHARGE
         ENDIF
         SKIP 1
      ENDDO
    ENDIF
CASE MODE = "E"
    * DELETE INVENTORY
    CLEAR
    STORE SPACE(20) TO MEMITEMNO
    STORE SPACE(25) TO MEMMANU
    STORE SPACE(15) TO MEMLOC
    @ 1,1 SAY "ENTER THE ITEM NUMBER" GET MEMITEMNO
    @ 2,1 SAY "ENTER THE MFCTR/SPEC DESIGNATOR" GET MEMMANU
    @ 3,1 SAY "ENTER THE LOCATION" GET MEMLOC
    READ
    STORE MEMITEMNO + MEMMANU + MEMLOC TO MEMKEY
```

```
    SELECT J
    SET INDEX TO INVITMAN
    SEEK MEMKEY
    IF EOF()
       @ 5,0 SAY "NO RECORD FOR GIVEN INFORMATION"
       WAIT
    ELSE
       DELETE NEXT 1
       STORE .T. TO DELINV
    ENDIF
 CASE MODE = "F"
    * DELETE INVENTORY TRANSFER
    CLEAR
    @ 1,1 SAY "AN INVENTORY TRANSFER CAN BE DELETED ONLY "+;
              "AFTER IT HAS BEEN RECEIVED."
    @ 2,1 SAY "TO DELETE A TRANSFER WHICH HAS NOT BEEN "+;
              "RECEIVED YET, ENTER THE RECEIPT "
    @ 3,1 SAY "AND, IF NECESSARY, UPDATE THE APPROPRIATE "+;
              "INVENTORY."
    @  6, 5 SAY "RECEIVED INVENTORY TRANSFER DELETION MODES"
    @  7, 5 SAY "------------------------------------------"
    @  8,10 SAY "A. BY SENDING LOCATION, RECEIVING LOCATION"
    @  9,10 SAY "     ITEM NUMBER AND SENDING DATE"
    @ 10,10 SAY "B. BY RECEIVING DATE (ALL PREVIOUS TO DATE)"
    WAIT "ENTER A MODE:" TO CODE1
    IF CODE1 <> "A" .AND. CODE1 <> "B"
       @ 12,0 SAY "ILLEGAL MODE SELECTION CODE"
       WAIT
```

```
   LOOP
ENDIF
IF CODE1 = "A"
   CLEAR
   STORE SPACE(15) TO MEMSLOC
   STORE SPACE(15) TO MEMRLOC
   STORE SPACE(20) TO MEMITEMNO
   STORE CTOD("  /  /  ") TO MEMDATE
   @ 1,1 SAY "ENTER THE SENDING LOCATION" GET MEMSLOC
   @ 2,1 SAY "ENTER THE RECEIVING LOCATION" GET MEMRLOC
   @ 3,1 SAY "ENTER THE ITEM NUMBER" GET MEMITEMNO
   @ 4,1 SAY "ENTER THE SENDING DATE IN THE FORM MM/DD/YY" ;
             GET MEMDATE
   READ
   STORE MEMSLOC+MEMRLOC+MEMITEMNO+DTOC(MEMDATE) TO MEMKEY
   SELECT C
   SET INDEX TO TRLOCITD
   SEEK MEMKEY
   IF EOF()
      @ 6,0 SAY "NO TRANSFER RECORD FOR GIVEN INFO"
      @ 7,0 SAY "UNABLE TO DELETE"
      WAIT
      LOOP
   ENDIF
   IF  TRQTYSENT <= TRQTYREC
      DELETE NEXT 1
      STORE .T. TO DELTRANS
   ELSE
```

```
        @ 6,0 SAY "UNABLE TO DELETE TRANSFER RECORD."
        @ 7,0 SAY "QTY RECEIVED < QTY SENT."
        WAIT
        LOOP
     ENDIF
  ENDIF
  IF CODE1 = "B"
    CLEAR
    STORE CTOD("  /  /  ") TO MEMDATE
    @ 1,1 SAY "ENTER THE DATE IN THE FORM MM/DD/YY"
    @ 2,1 SAY  "ALL TRANSFERS RECEIVED PREVIOUS TO THIS "+;
               "DATE WILL"
    @ 3,1 SAY "BE DELETED" GET MEMDATE
    READ
    SELECT C
    SET INDEX TO
    GOTO TOP
    DO WHILE .NOT. EOF()
     IF TRQTYREC < TRQTYSENT
        SKIP 1
        LOOP
     ENDIF
     IF YEAR(TRRECDT) <> 0 .AND. TRRECDT < MEMDATE
        DELETE NEXT 1
        STORE .T. TO DELTRANS
     ENDIF
     SKIP 1
  ENDDO
```

```
   ENDIF
CASE MODE = "G"
   * DELETE DEFAULT NOTIFICATION
   CLEAR
   @ 1,1 SAY "TO DELETE THE LAST LETTER RECORD, PERFORM "+;
             "A DEFAULT ACTION, AND CHOOSE AN"
   @ 2,1 SAY "APPROPRIATE LETTER TYPE."
   STORE SPACE(1) TO ANSWER
   WAIT "DO YOU WISH TO DELETE ALL LETTER RECORDS "+;
        "PREVIOUS TO A SPECIFIC DATE (Y/N):" TO ANSWER
   IF UPPER(ANSWER) <> "Y"
      LOOP
   ENDIF
   CLEAR
   STORE CTOD("  /  /  ") TO MEMDATE
   @ 1,1 SAY "ENTER THE DATE IN THE FORM MM/DD/YY"
   @ 2,1 SAY "ALL TRANSFERS RECEIVED PREVIOUS TO THIS DATE "+;
             "WILL"
   @ 3,1 SAY "BE DELETED" GET MEMDATE
   READ
   SELECT F
   SET INDEX TO
   GOTO TOP
   DO WHILE .NOT. EOF()
     IF YEAR(NOTDATE) <> 0 .AND. NOTDATE < MEMDATE
      DELETE NEXT 1
      STORE .T. TO DELNOTICE
     ENDIF
```

```
      SKIP 1
    ENDDO
CASE MODE = "H"
    * DELETE PAYMENT
    CLEAR
    @ 1,1 SAY "TO DELETE A SPECIFIC PAYMENT, ENTER AN "+;
              "APPROPRIATE ADDITIONAL CHARGE OR ENTER"
    @ 2,1 SAY "BAD CHECK INFORMATION."
    STORE SPACE(1) TO ANSWER
    WAIT "DO YOU WISH TO DELETE OLD PAYMENTS BY DATE (Y/N):" ;
      TO ANSWER
    IF UPPER(ANSWER) <> "Y"
       LOOP
    ENDIF
    CLEAR
    STORE CTOD("  /  /  ") TO MEMDATE
    @ 1,1 SAY "ENTER THE DATE IN THE FORM MM/DD/YY"
    @ 2,1 SAY "ALL PAYMENMTS PREVIOUS TO THIS DATE WILL"
    @ 3,1 SAY "BE DELETED" GET MEMDATE
    READ
    SELECT D
    SET INDEX TO
    GOTO TOP
    DO WHILE .NOT. EOF()
      IF YEAR(PAYDATE) <> 0 .AND. PAYDATE < MEMDATE
        DELETE NEXT 1
        STORE .T. TO DELPAY
      ENDIF
```

```
          SKIP 1
        ENDDO
     OTHERWISE
        @ 20,0 SAY "ILLEGAL MODE"
        WAIT
   ENDCASE
ENDDO
RETURN
***************************** END OF PROGRAM ******************

* DISENTER.PRG
SELECT A
USE ACCOUNTS INDEX ACCNO
SELECT B
USE CHARGES INDEX CHTICKET
SELECT C
USE ACCTFILE INDEX ACCTTYPA
DO WHILE .T.
   CLEAR
   STORE SPACE(1) TO ANSWER
   WAIT "DO YOU WISH TO ENTER ANOTHER DISPUTE (Y/N):" TO ANSWER
   IF UPPER(ANSWER) <> "Y"
      RETURN
   ENDIF
   CLEAR
   STORE SPACE(10) TO MEMTICKETN
   @ 1,0 SAY "ENTER THE TICKET NUMBER FOR THE ORIGINAL CHARGE" ;
      GET MEMTICKETN
```

```
READ
SELECT B
SEEK MEMTICKETN
IF EOF()
   @ 3,0 SAY "NO SUCH TICKET NUMBER."
   WAIT
   LOOP
ENDIF
CLEAR
@ 3,1 SAY  "ACCOUNT NUMBER="+CHACCTNO
@ 4,1 SAY  "ITEM NUMBER   ="+CHITEMNO
@ 5,1 SAY  "MANU/DESIG    ="+CHMANU
@ 6,1 SAY  "LOCATION      ="+CHLOCATION
@ 7,1 SAY  "DESCRIPTION   ="+CHITEMDESC
@ 8,1 SAY  "QUANTITY      ="+STR(CHQTY,6)
@ 9,1 SAY  "AMOUNT CHARGED="+STR(CHDOLLARS,7,2)
STORE SPACE(1) TO ANSWER
WAIT "IS THIS THE CORRECT TICKET (Y/N):" TO ANSWER
IF UPPER(ANSWER) <> "Y"
   LOOP
ENDIF
STORE 0.00 TO MEMDISPAMT
@ 12,1 SAY "ENTER THE DOLLAR PORTION OF THE CHARGE THAT "+;
   "IS DISPUTED" GET MEMDISPAMT
READ
IF MEMDISPAMT > CHDOLLARS
   @ 15,1 SAY "ERROR: THE AMOUNT DISPUTED IS GREATER THAN "+;
      "THE CHARGE AMOUNT."
```

```
      WAIT
      LOOP
   ENDIF
   STORE CTOD("  /  /  ") TO MEMDATE
   @ 14, 1 SAY "ENTER THE DISPUTE DATE IN THE FORM MM/DD/YY" ;
      GET MEMDATE
   READ
   STORE CHACCTNO TO MEMACCTNO
   REPLACE CHDISPDATE WITH MEMDATE, CHDISPAMT WITH MEMDISPAMT, ;
     CHRESREPTD WITH "N", CHRESTYPE WITH SPACE(15)
   SELECT A
   SEEK MEMACCTNO
   IF EOF()
      @ 16,1 SAY "UNABLE TO FIND CHARGE ACCOUNT RECORD FOR "+;
          "ACCOUNT=" + MEMACCTNO
      WAIT
      LOOP
   ENDIF
   REPLACE ACCTOTCHRG WITH ACCTOTCHRG - MEMDISPAMT
   SELECT C
   APPEND BLANK
   REPLACE ACCTACCNO WITH MEMACCTNO, ACCTTYPACT WITH "CHARGE DISPUTE",;
     ACCTDTACT WITH MEMDATE, ACCTAMT WITH MEMDISPAMT
ENDDO
RETURN
***************************** END OF PROGRAM *****************


* DISPUTE.PRG
```

```
DO WHILE .T.
   CLEAR
   @ 3,5 SAY "DISPUTE MODULE SELECTION CODE"
   @ 4,5 SAY "--------------------------------"
   @ 5,10 SAY "A. EXIT"
   @ 6,10 SAY "B. ENTER A DISPUTE FROM CUSTOMER"
   @ 7,10 SAY "C. RESOLVE A SPECIFIC DISPUTE"
   @ 8,10 SAY "D. RESOLVE ALL DISPUTES OVER 30 DAYS OLD"
   WAIT "ENTER YOUR SELECTION CODE:" TO CODE1
   DO CASE
      CASE CODE1 = "A"
         RETURN
      CASE CODE1 = "B"
         DO DISENTER
      CASE CODE1 = "C"
         DO DISRES1
      CASE CODE1 = "D"
         DO DISRESAL
      OTHERWISE
         @ 15,0 SAY "ILLEGAL SELECTION CODE."
         WAIT
   ENDCASE
   CLEAR ALL
ENDDO
RETURN
****************************** END OF PROGRAM ******************


* DISRES1.PRG
```

```
SELECT A
USE ACCOUNTS INDEX ACCNO
SELECT B
USE CHARGES INDEX CHTICKET
SELECT C
USE ACCTFILE INDEX ACCTTYPA
DO WHILE .T.
   CLEAR
   STORE SPACE(1) TO ANSWER
   WAIT "DO YOU WISH TO RESOLVE ANOTHER DISPUTE (Y/N):" TO ;
       ANSWER
   IF UPPER(ANSWER) <> "Y"
      RETURN
   ENDIF
   STORE SPACE(10) TO MEMTICKETN
   CLEAR
   @ 1,1 SAY "ENTER THE TICKET NUMBER FOR THE ORIGINAL CHARGE" ;
      GET MEMTICKETN
   READ
   SELECT B
   SEEK MEMTICKETN
   IF EOF()
      @ 3,0 SAY "NO SUCH TICKET NUMBER."
      WAIT
      LOOP
   ENDIF
   CLEAR
   @ 3,1 SAY  "ACCOUNT NUMBER ="+CHACCTNO
```

```
@ 4,1 SAY  "ITEM NUMBER     ="+CHITEMNO
@ 5,1 SAY  "MANU/DESIG      ="+CHMANU
@ 6,1 SAY  "LOCATION        ="+CHLOCATION
@ 7,1 SAY  "DESCRIPTION     ="+CHITEMDESC
@ 8,1 SAY  "QUANTITY        ="+STR(CHQTY,6)
@ 9,1 SAY  "AMOUNT  CHARGED="+STR(CHDOLLARS,7,2)
@ 10,1 SAY  "AMOUNT DISPUTED="+STR(CHDISPAMT,7,2)
STORE SPACE(1) TO ANSWER
WAIT "IS THIS THE CORRECT TICKET (Y/N):" TO ANSWER
IF UPPER(ANSWER) <> "Y"
   LOOP
ENDIF
IF CHDISPAMT = 0 .OR. CHRESREPTD = "Y"
   @ 12,1 SAY "THIS CHARGE NOT DISPUTED, SO CAN NOT RESOLVE."
   WAIT
   LOOP
ENDIF
STORE 0.00 TO MEMNEWCHAR
STORE CTOD("  /  /  ") TO MEMDATE
@ 12,1 SAY "ENTER THE NEW CHARGE AMOUNT (INCLUDING TAX), "+;
           "AFTER RESOLUTION OF DISPUTE"
@ 13,60 GET MEMNEWCHAR
@ 14,1 SAY "ENTER THE RESOLUTION DATE IN THE FORM MM/DD/YY" ;
    GET MEMDATE
READ
STORE CHACCTNO TO MEMACCTNO
STORE CHDISPAMT TO MEMDISPAMT
STORE CHDOLLARS TO MEMDOLLARS
```

```
* COMPUTE DIFFERENCE BETWEEN ORIGINAL CHARGE AND RESOLVED
*         CHARGE
STORE CHDOLLARS-MEMNEWCHAR TO MEMDIFAMT
IF CHDOLLARS < MEMNEWCHAR
   @ 15,1 SAY "UNABLE TO RESOLVE THE DISPUTE: THE NEW "+;
         "CHARGE AMOUNT CAN"
   @ 16,1 SAY "NOT BE GREATER THAN THE ORIGINAL CHARGE AMOUNT."
   WAIT
   LOOP
ENDIF
IF MEMDISPAMT < MEMDIFAMT
   @ 18,1 SAY "UNABLE TO RESOLVE THE DISPUTE: THE "+;
              "DIFFERENCE BETWEEN"
   @ 19,1 SAY "THE ORIGINAL AND THE NEW CHARGES IS "+;
              "GREATER THAN THE DISPUTED AMOUNT."
   WAIT
   LOOP
ENDIF
* REPLACE CHDOLLARS WITH MEMNEWCHAR IS INCORRECT
REPLACE CHACTRESDT WITH MEMDATE, ;
  CHRESTYPE WITH "AGREEMENT W/CUS", CHRESREPTD WITH "Y"
SELECT A
SEEK MEMACCTNO
IF EOF()
   @ 21,1 SAY "UNABLE TO FIND CHARGE ACCOUNT RECORD "+;
              "FOR ACCOUNT=" + MEMACCTNO
   WAIT
   LOOP
```

```
   ENDIF
   REPLACE ACCTOTCHRG WITH ACCTOTCHRG+MEMDISPAMT-MEMDOLLARS;
     +MEMNEWCHAR,ACCPAYMENT WITH ACCPAYMENT + MEMDIFAMT
   SELECT C
   APPEND BLANK
   REPLACE ACCTACCNO WITH MEMACCTNO, ACCTTYPACT WITH ;
     "CHARGE RESOLUTION",ACCTDTACT WITH MEMDATE, ;
     ACCTAMT WITH MEMDIFAMT
ENDDO
RETURN
****************************** END OF PROGRAM ******************
```

```
* DISRESAL.PRG
CLEAR
SELECT A
USE ACCOUNTS INDEX ACCNO
SELECT B
USE CHARGES INDEX CHTICKET
SELECT C
USE ACCTFILE INDEX ACCTTYPA
SELECT B
DO WHILE .NOT. EOF()
   IF CHDISPAMT = 0 .OR. CHRESREPTD = "Y"
      SKIP 1
      LOOP
   ENDIF
   * SKIP THIS RECORD IF NOT DUE TO BE RESOLVED YET
   IF CHDISPDATE + 31 > DATE()
```

```
      SKIP 1
      LOOP
   ENDIF
   STORE CHACCTNO TO MEMACCTNO
   STORE CHDISPAMT TO MEMDISPAMT
   REPLACE CHACTRESDT WITH DATE(), CHRESTYPE WITH ;
     "AUTO RESOLUTION",CHRESREPTD WITH "Y"
   SELECT A
   SEEK MEMACCTNO
   IF EOF()
      ? "UNABLE TO FIND CHARGE ACCOUNT RECORD FOR ACCOUNT=",;
         MEMACCTNO
      WAIT
      LOOP
   ENDIF
   REPLACE ACCTOTCHRG WITH ACCTOTCHRG+MEMDISPAMT
   SELECT C
   APPEND BLANK
   REPLACE ACCTACCNO WITH MEMACCTNO, ACCTTYPACT WITH "AUTO CH RES",;
     ACCTDTACT WITH DATE(), ACCTAMT WITH MEMDISPAMT
   SELECT B
   SKIP 1
ENDDO
RETURN
***************************** END OF PROGRAM ******************


* ENTERINV.PRG
SET DEVICE TO SCREEN
```

```
SELECT J
USE INVENTOR INDEX INVITMAN, INVITLOC
DO WHILE .T.
   CLEAR
   STORE SPACE(1) TO ANSWER
   WAIT "DO YOU WISH TO ENTER ANOTHER NEW INVENTORY "+;
        "RECORD(Y/N):" TO ANSWER
   IF UPPER(ANSWER) <> "Y"
      RETURN
   ENDIF
   CLEAR
   APPEND BLANK
   @  1, 1 SAY "ENTER A NEW INVENTORY RECORD"
   @  2, 1 SAY "----------------------------"
   @  3, 1 SAY "INVENTORY ITEM NUMBER"
   @  3,23 GET INVITEMNO
   @  4, 1 SAY "MANUFACTURER OR SPECIAL DESIGNATOR"
   @  4,36 GET INVMANU
   @  5, 1 SAY "DESCRIPTION OF ITEM"
   @  5,21 GET INVDESC
   @  7, 1 SAY "LOCATION OF ITEM"
   @  7,18 GET INVLOC
   @  9, 1 SAY "UNITS"
   @  9, 7 GET INVUNITS
   @  9,19 SAY "COUNT PER UNIT"
   @  9,34 GET INVQTYPER
   @ 11, 1 SAY "QUANTITY ON HAND"
   @ 11,18 GET INVQTYONH
```

```
   @ 13, 1 SAY "REORDER POINT"
   @ 13,15 GET INVREORDPT
   @ 13,28 SAY "REORDER AMOUNT"
   @ 13,43 GET INVREORDAM
   @ 15, 1 SAY "UNIT COST"
   @ 15,15 GET INVCSTPERU
   @ 17, 1 SAY "SELLING PRICE"
   @ 17,15 GET INVSELLPR
   READ
ENDDO
RETURN
****************************** END OF PROGRAM ******************
```

```
* FILEEMPT.PRG
USE ACCOUNTS
   ZAP
USE CHARGES
   ZAP
USE PAYMENTS
   ZAP
USE NOTIFICATION
   ZAP
USE BILLING
   ZAP
USE INVENTORY
   ZAP
USE TRANSFER
   ZAP
```

```
USE ACCTFILE
   ZAP
USE LET1
   ZAP
USE LET2
   ZAP
USE LET3
   ZAP
DO INDEXES
RETURN
***************************** END OF PROGRAM ******************

* FINDRECO.PRG
SELECT A
USE ACCOUNTS
SELECT B
USE CHARGES
SELECT C
USE TRANSFER
SELECT D
USE PAYMENTS
SELECT E
USE BILLING
SELECT F
USE NOTIFICA
SELECT J
USE INVENTOR
SET DEVICE TO SCREEN
```

```
DO WHILE .T.
   CLEAR
   STORE SPACE(1) TO ANSWER
   WAIT "DO YOU WISH TO FIND ANOTHER RECORD (Y/N):" TO ANSWER
   IF UPPER(ANSWER) <> "Y"
      RETURN
   ENDIF
   CLEAR
   @  5, 5 SAY "RECORD SELECT"
   @  6, 5 SAY "-------------"
   @  7,10 SAY "A. ACCOUNT"
   @  8,10 SAY "B. BILL"
   @  9,10 SAY "C. CHARGE TICKET"
   @ 10,10 SAY "D. DEFAULT NOTIFICATION"
   @ 11,10 SAY "E. INVENTORY"
   @ 12,10 SAY "F. INVENTORY TRANSFER"
   @ 13,10 SAY "G. PAYMENT"
   WAIT "ENTER A SELECTION CODE:" TO CODE1
   DO CASE
      CASE CODE1 = "A"
         CLEAR
         @  5, 5 SAY "ACCOUNT RECORD SELECTION"
         @  6, 5 SAY "------------------------"
         @  7,10 SAY "A. BY ACCOUNT NUMBER"
         @  8,10 SAY "B. BY COMPANY NAME"
         @  9,10 SAY "C. BY LAST NAME"
         WAIT "ENTER A SELECTION CODE:" TO CODE2
         IF CODE2 <> "A" .AND. CODE2 <> "B" .AND. CODE2 <> "C"
```

```
   @ 12,0 SAY "ILLEGAL SELECTION CODE"
   WAIT
   LOOP
ENDIF
IF CODE2 = "A"
   CLEAR
   STORE SPACE(10) TO MEMACCTNO
   @ 1,1 SAY "ENTER THE ACCOUNT NUMBER" GET MEMACCTNO
   READ
   SELECT A
   SET INDEX TO ACCNO
   SEEK MEMACCTNO
   IF EOF()
   @ 3,0 SAY "NO ACCOUNT RECORD FOR GIVEN NUMBER"
   WAIT
   LOOP
ENDIF
CLEAR
@  1, 1 SAY "ACCOUNT RECORD"
@  2, 1 SAY "--------------"
@  3, 1 SAY "ACCOUNT NUMBER:"
@  3,17 SAY ACCNO
@  4, 1 SAY "COMPANY NAME:"
@  4,16 SAY ACCCOMPANY
@  5, 1 SAY "LAST NAME:"
@  5,11 SAY ACCLNAME
@  5,29 SAY "FIRST NAME:"
@  5,40 SAY ACCFNAME
```

```
@  6, 1 SAY "PO BOX:"
@  6, 8 SAY ACCPOBOX
@  6,20 SAY "STREET:"
@  6,27 SAY ACCSTREET
@  7, 1 SAY "CITY:"
@  7, 6 SAY ACCCITY
@  7,23 SAY "STATE:"
@  7,29 SAY ACCSTATE
@  7,39 SAY "ZIP:"
@  7,43 SAY ACCZIP
@ 8, 1 SAY "ACCOUNT TYPE"
@ 8,30 SAY "ACCOUNT STATUS"
@ 8,60 SAY "BILLING TYPE"
@ 9, 1 SAY "------------"
@ 9,30 SAY "--------------"
@ 9,60 SAY "------------"
@ 10, 1 SAY "BC=BAD CHECK"
@ 10,30 SAY "CAN=CANCELLED"
@ 10,60 SAY "REG=REGULAR"
@ 11, 1 SAY "RC=REVOLVING CHARGE"
@ 11,30 SAY "HLD=HOLD FOR SPECIAL ACTION"
@ 11,60 SAY "SCH=BY PAY SCHEDULE"
@ 12, 1 SAY "SI=SINGLE ITEM"
@ 12,30 SAY "OVL=OVER THE CHARGE LIMIT"
@ 13, 1 SAY "UN=OLD UNPAID ACCOUNT"
@ 13,30 SAY "VAL=NORMAL CHARGE ACCOUNT"
@ 14, 1 SAY "TYPE OF ACCOUNT:"
@ 14,17 SAY ACCTYPE
```

```
@ 14,21 SAY "STATUS OF ACCOUNT:"
@ 14,39 SAY ACCSTATUS
@ 14,44 SAY "BILLING TYPE:"
@ 14,57 SAY ACCBILLTYP
@ 14,61 SAY "MIN PMT:"
@ 14,69 SAY ACCMINPAY
@ 15, 1 SAY "CREDIT LIMIT:"
@ 15,14 SAY ACCCREDLIM
@ 15,24 SAY "DESC. OF SECURITY DEPOSIT:"
@ 15,50 SAY ACCSECDEP
@ 16, 1 SAY "SPECIAL ACTION REQUIRED:"
@ 16,25 SAY ACCSPECACT
@ 17, 1 SAY "TOTAL UNPAID CHARGES:"
@ 17,23 SAY ACCTOTCHRG
@ 17,35 SAY "TOTAL PAYMENTS:"
@ 17,50 SAY ACCPAYMENT+ACCCARYOVR
@ 18, 1 SAY "INTEREST DUE:"
@ 18,14 SAY ACCTOTINT
@ 18,23 SAY "YTD INTEREST:"
@ 18,36 SAY ACCYTDINT
@ 19, 1 SAY "DATE OF LAST ACCOUNT ACTIVITY:"
@ 19,31 SAY ACCDTLACT
@ 19,42 SAY "DISCOUNT PERCENT:"
@ 19,59 SAY ACCDISCPER
@ 20, 1 SAY "OVER 30:"
@ 20, 9 SAY ACCOVER30
@ 20,20 SAY "OVER 60:"
@ 20,28 SAY ACCOVER60
```

```
   @ 20,38 SAY "OVER 90:"
   @ 20,46 SAY ACCOVER90
   @ 21, 1 SAY "LAST BAD CHECK NUMBER:"
   @ 21,23 SAY ACCBADCHNO
   @ 21,31 SAY "MONTHS IN ARREARS:"
   @ 21,49 SAY ACCMONARR
   WAIT
ELSE
IF CODE2 = "B"
   CLEAR
   STORE SPACE(25) TO MEMCOMPANY
   @ 1,1 SAY "ENTER THE COMPANY NAME" GET MEMCOMPANY
   READ
   SELECT A
   SET INDEX TO ACCCOMPANY
   SEEK MEMCOMPANY
   IF EOF()
      @ 3,0 SAY "NO RECORD FOR GIVEN COMPANY"
      WAIT
      LOOP
   ENDIF
   STORE 20 TO MAXLINES
   CLEAR
   @ 3, 1 SAY "ACCOUNT NO"
   @ 3,12 SAY "COMPANY"
   @ 3,38 SAY "NAME"
   @ 3,59 SAY "CREDIT LIM"
   @ 3,70 SAY "TOTAL DUE"
```

```
@ 4, 1 SAY "----------"
@ 4,12 SAY "-------------------------"
@ 4,38 SAY "--------------------"
@ 4,59 SAY "----------"
@ 4,70 SAY "---------"
STORE 4 TO ROW
DO WHILE .NOT. EOF() .AND. MEMCOMPANY = ACCCOMPANY
  IF ROW + 1 > MAXLINES
   WAIT
   CLEAR
   @ 3, 1 SAY "ACCOUNT NO"
   @ 3,12 SAY "COMPANY"
   @ 3,38 SAY "NAME"
   @ 3,59 SAY "CREDIT LIM"
   @ 3,70 SAY "TOTAL DUE"
   @ 4, 1 SAY "----------"
   @ 4,12 SAY "-------------------------"
   @ 4,38 SAY "--------------------"
   @ 4,59 SAY "----------"
   @ 4,70 SAY "---------"
   STORE 4 TO ROW
  ENDIF
STORE ROW + 1 TO ROW
@ ROW, 1 SAY ACCNO
@ ROW,12 SAY ACCCOMPANY
@ ROW,38 SAY TRIM(ACCFNAME)+" "+TRIM(ACCLNAME);
  PICTURE "XXXXXXXXXXXXXXXXXXXX"
@ ROW,59 SAY ACCCREDLIM
```

```
    @ ROW,70 SAY ACCTOTCHRG+ACCTOTINT-ACCPAYMENT;
      PICTURE "999999.99"
    SKIP 1
    ENDDO
    WAIT
ELSE
IF CODE2 = "C"
    CLEAR
    STORE SPACE(15) TO MEMLNAME
    @ 1,1 SAY "ENTER THE LAST NAME" GET MEMLNAME
    READ
    SELECT A
    SET INDEX TO ACCLNAME
    SEEK MEMLNAME
    IF EOF()
       @ 3,0 SAY "NO RECORD FOR GIVEN LAST NAME"
       WAIT
       LOOP
    ENDIF
    STORE 20 TO MAXLINES
    CLEAR
    @ 3, 1 SAY "ACCOUNT NO"
    @ 3,12 SAY "COMPANY"
    @ 3,38 SAY "NAME"
    @ 3,59 SAY "CREDIT LIM"
    @ 3,70 SAY "TOTAL DUE"
    @ 4, 1 SAY "----------"
    @ 4,12 SAY "------------------------"
```

```
@ 4,38 SAY "--------------------"
@ 4,59 SAY "----------"
@ 4,70 SAY "---------"
STORE 4 TO ROW
DO WHILE .NOT. EOF() .AND. MEMLNAME = ACCLNAME
  IF ROW + 1 > MAXLINES
   WAIT
   CLEAR
   @ 3, 1 SAY "ACCOUNT NO"
   @ 3,12 SAY "COMPANY"
   @ 3,38 SAY "NAME"
   @ 3,59 SAY "CREDIT LIM"
   @ 3,70 SAY "TOTAL DUE"
   @ 4, 1 SAY "----------"
   @ 4,12 SAY "-------------------------"
   @ 4,38 SAY "--------------------"
   @ 4,59 SAY "----------"
   @ 4,70 SAY "---------"
   STORE 4 TO ROW
  ENDIF
  STORE ROW + 1 TO ROW
  @ ROW, 1 SAY ACCNO
  @ ROW,12 SAY ACCCOMPANY
  @ ROW,38 SAY TRIM(ACCFNAME)+" "+TRIM(ACCLNAME);
    PICTURE "XXXXXXXXXXXXXXXXXXXX"
  @ ROW,59 SAY ACCCREDLIM
  @ ROW,70 SAY ACCTOTCHRG+ACCTOTINT-ACCPAYMENT;
    PICTURE "999999.99"
```

```
          SKIP 1
        ENDDO
        WAIT
     ENDIF
     ENDIF
     ENDIF
  CASE CODE1 = "B"
     CLEAR
     STORE SPACE(10) TO MEMACCTNO
     @ 1,1 SAY "ENTER THE ACCOUNT NUMBER" GET MEMACCTNO
     READ
     SELECT E
     SET INDEX TO BILLACCTDT
     SEEK MEMACCTNO
     IF EOF()
        @ 3,0 SAY "NO BILLS FOR THIS ACCOUNT"
        WAIT
        LOOP
     ENDIF
     STORE 20 TO MAXLINES
     CLEAR
     @ 3, 1 SAY "ACCOUNT NO"
     @ 3,12 SAY "AMOUNT OF BILL"
     @ 3,27 SAY "DATE OF BILL"
     @ 4, 1 SAY "----------"
     @ 4,12 SAY "--------------"
     @ 4,27 SAY "------------"
     STORE 4 TO ROW
```

```
      DO WHILE .NOT. EOF() .AND. MEMACCTNO = BILLACCTNO
         IF ROW+1 > MAXLINES
            WAIT
            CLEAR
            @ 3, 1 SAY "ACCOUNT NO"
            @ 3,12 SAY "AMOUNT OF BILL"
            @ 3,27 SAY "DATE OF BILL"
            @ 4, 1 SAY "----------"
            @ 4,12 SAY "--------------"
            @ 4,27 SAY "------------"
            STORE 4 TO ROW
         ENDIF
         STORE ROW + 1 TO ROW
         @ ROW, 1 SAY BILLACCTNO
         @ ROW,12 SAY BILLAMT
         @ ROW,27 SAY BILLDATE
         SKIP 1
      ENDDO
      WAIT
   CASE CODE1 = "C"
      CLEAR
      @  3, 5 SAY "CHARGE TICKET SELECTION MODE"
      @  4, 5 SAY "----------------------------"
      @  5,10 SAY "A. BY ACCOUNT NUMBER"
      @  6,10 SAY "B. BY TICKET NUMBER"
      WAIT "ENTER A SELECTION CODE:" TO CODE2
      IF CODE2 <> "A" .AND. CODE2 <> "B"
         @ 10,0 SAY "ILLEGAL SELECTION CODE"
```

```
   WAIT
   LOOP
ENDIF
IF CODE2 = "A"
   CLEAR
   STORE SPACE(10) TO MEMACCTNO
   @ 1,1 SAY "ENTER THE ACCOUNT NUMBER" GET MEMACCTNO
   READ
   SELECT B
   SET INDEX TO CHACCTNO
   SEEK MEMACCTNO
   IF EOF()
      @ 3,0 SAY "NO CHARGES FOR THIS ACCOUNT"
      WAIT
      LOOP
   ENDIF
   STORE 20 TO MAXLINES
   CLEAR
   @ 3, 1 SAY "ACCOUNT NO"
   @ 3,12 SAY "TICKET  NO"
   @ 3,23 SAY "ITM DESCRIPTION"
   @ 3,39 SAY "ITEM COST"
   @ 3,49 SAY "CH DATE"
   @ 3,58 SAY "DISP DATE"
   @ 3,68 SAY "RESOLVED YET"
   @ 4, 1 SAY "----------"
   @ 4,12 SAY "----------"
   @ 4,23 SAY "---------------"
```

```
@ 4,39 SAY "---------"
@ 4,49 SAY "--------"
@ 4,58 SAY "---------"
@ 4,68 SAY "------------"
STORE 4 TO ROW
DO WHILE .NOT. EOF() .AND. MEMACCTNO = CHACCTNO
   IF ROW+1 > MAXLINES
      WAIT
      CLEAR
      @ 3, 1 SAY "ACCOUNT NO"
      @ 3,12 SAY "TICKET  NO"
      @ 3,23 SAY "ITM DESCRIPTION"
      @ 3,39 SAY "ITEM COST"
      @ 3,49 SAY "CH DATE"
      @ 3,58 SAY "DISP DATE"
      @ 3,68 SAY "RESOLVED YET"
      @ 4, 1 SAY "----------"
      @ 4,12 SAY "----------"
      @ 4,23 SAY "---------------"
      @ 4,39 SAY "---------"
      @ 4,49 SAY "--------"
      @ 4,58 SAY "---------"
      @ 4,68 SAY "------------"
      STORE 4 TO ROW
   ENDIF
   STORE ROW + 1 TO ROW
   @ ROW, 1 SAY CHACCTNO
   @ ROW,12 SAY CHTICKETNO
```

```
      @ ROW,23 SAY CHITEMDESC
      @ ROW,39 SAY CHDOLLARS
      @ ROW,49 SAY CHDATE
      @ ROW,58 SAY CHDISPDATE
      IF YEAR(CHDISPDATE) <> 0 .AND. ;
        (CHRESREPTD = "N" .OR. CHRESREPTD = " ")
         @ ROW,68 SAY "N" PICTURE "X"
      ELSE
      IF YEAR(CHDISPDATE) <> 0 .AND. ;
        CHRESREPTD = "Y"
         @ ROW,68 SAY "Y" PICTURE "X"
      ENDIF
      ENDIF
      SKIP 1
   ENDDO
   WAIT
ENDIF
IF CODE2 = "B"
   CLEAR
   STORE SPACE(10) TO MEMTICKETN
   @ 1,1 SAY "ENTER THE TICKET NUMBER" GET MEMTICKETN
   READ
   SELECT B
   SET INDEX TO CHTICKETNO
   SEEK MEMTICKETN
   IF EOF()
      @ 3,0 SAY "NO RECORD FOR THIS TICKET NUMBER"
      WAIT
```

```
   LOOP
ENDIF
CLEAR
@ 3, 1 SAY "ACCOUNT NO"
@ 3,12 SAY "TICKET  NO"
@ 3,23 SAY "ITM DESCRIPTION"
@ 3,39 SAY "ITEM COST"
@ 3,49 SAY "CH DATE"
@ 3,58 SAY "DISP DATE"
@ 3,68 SAY "RESOLVED YET"
@ 4, 1 SAY "----------"
@ 4,12 SAY "----------"
@ 4,23 SAY "---------------"
@ 4,39 SAY "---------"
@ 4,49 SAY "--------"
@ 4,58 SAY "---------"
@ 4,68 SAY "------------"
@ 5, 1 SAY CHACCTNO
@ 5,12 SAY CHTICKETNO
@ 5,23 SAY CHITEMDESC
@ 5,39 SAY CHDOLLARS
@ 5,49 SAY CHDATE
@ 5,58 SAY CHDISPDATE
IF YEAR(CHDISPDATE) <> 0 .AND. ;
  (CHRESREPTD = "N" .OR. CHRESREPTD = " ")
   @ 5,68 SAY "N" PICTURE "X"
ELSE
IF YEAR(CHDISPDATE) <> 0 .AND. ;
```

```
        CHRESREPTD = "Y"
         @ 5,68 SAY "Y" PICTURE "X"
      ENDIF
      ENDIF
      WAIT
   ENDIF
CASE CODE1 = "D"
   CLEAR
   STORE SPACE(10) TO MEMACCTNO
   @ 1,1 SAY "ENTER THE ACCOUNT NUMBER" GET MEMACCTNO
   READ
   SELECT F
   SET INDEX TO NOTACCTN
   SEEK MEMACCTNO
   IF EOF()
      @ 3,0 SAY "NO DEFAULT LETTERS FOR THIS ACCOUNT"
      WAIT
      LOOP
   ENDIF
   STORE 20 TO MAXLINES
   CLEAR
   @  3, 1 SAY "ACCOUNT NO"
   @  3,12 SAY "LETTER TYPE"
   @  3,24 SAY "DATE"
   @  3,33 SAY "STATUS"
   @  3,40 SAY "DOLLARS"
   @  4, 1 SAY "----------"
   @  4,12 SAY "-----------"
```

```
@  4,24 SAY "--------"
@  4,33 SAY "------"
@  4,40 SAY "---------"
STORE 4 TO ROW
DO WHILE .NOT. EOF() .AND. MEMACCTNO = NOTACCTNO
   IF ROW+1 > MAXLINES
      WAIT
      CLEAR
      @  3, 1 SAY "ACCOUNT NO"
      @  3,12 SAY "LETTER TYPE"
      @  3,24 SAY "DATE"
      @  3,33 SAY "STATUS"
      @  3,40 SAY "DOLLARS"
      @  4, 1 SAY "----------"
      @  4,12 SAY "-----------"
      @  4,24 SAY "--------"
      @  4,33 SAY "------"
      @  4,40 SAY "---------"
      STORE 4 TO ROW
   ENDIF
   STORE ROW + 1 TO ROW
   @ ROW, 1 SAY NOTACCTNO
   @ ROW,12 SAY NOTTYPE
   @ ROW,24 SAY NOTDATE
   @ ROW,33 SAY NOTSTATUS
   @ ROW,40 SAY NOTTOTDUE
   SKIP 1
ENDDO
```

```
    ? "TYPE ANY KEY TO CONTINUE"
    WAIT TO CONTINUE
CASE CODE1 = "E"
    * FIND INVENTORY RECORD
    CLEAR
    @  3, 5 SAY "INVENTORY RECORD SELECTION CODES"
    @  4, 5 SAY "--------------------------------"
    @  6,10 SAY "A. BY ITEM NUMBER"
    @  7,10 SAY "B. BY ITEM NUMBER AND"
    @  8,10 SAY "      MANUFACTURER/SPECIAL DESIGNATOR"
    @  9,10 SAY "C. BY ITEM NUMBER AND LOCATION"
    @ 10,10 SAY "D. BY ITEM NUMBER, LOCATION AND"
    @ 11,10 SAY "      MANUFACTURER/SPECIAL DESIGNATOR"
    ? "ENTER A SELECTION CODE"
    WAIT TO CODE2
    IF CODE2 <> "A" .AND. CODE2 <> "B" .AND.;
       CODE2 <> "C" .AND. CODE2 <> "D"
       ? "ILLEGAL SELECTION CODE."
       ? "TYPE ANY KEY TO CONTINUE."
       WAIT TO CONTINUE
       LOOP
    ENDIF
    CLEAR
    STORE 20 TO MAXLINES
    STORE SPACE(20) TO MEMITEMNO
    @ 1,1 SAY "ENTER THE ITEM NUMBER" GET MEMITEMNO
    READ
    IF CODE2 = "A" .OR. CODE2 = "B" .OR. CODE2 = "C"
```

```
IF CODE2 = "A"
 SELECT J
 SET INDEX TO INVITLOC
 STORE MEMITEMNO TO MEMKEY
ELSE
IF CODE2 = "B"
 SELECT J
 SET INDEX TO INVITMANLOC
 STORE SPACE(25) TO MEMMANU
 @ 2,1 SAY "ENTER THE MFCTR/SPECIAL DESIGNATOR" GET MEMMANU
 READ
 STORE MEMITEMNO + MEMMANU TO MEMKEY
ELSE
IF CODE2 = "C"
 SELECT J
 SET INDEX TO INVITLOC
 STORE SPACE(15) TO MEMLOC
 @ 2,1 SAY "ENTER ITEM LOCATION" GET MEMLOC
 READ
 STORE MEMITEMNO + MEMLOC TO MEMKEY
ENDIF
ENDIF
ENDIF
 SEEK MEMKEY
 IF EOF()
    @ 5,0 SAY "NO INVENTORY RECORD FOR THIS ITEM"
    WAIT
    LOOP
```

```
ENDIF
CLEAR
@ 2, 1 SAY "ITEM NUMBER="
@ 2,13 SAY MEMITEMNO
@ 4, 1 SAY "MFCTR. OR SPEC DESIG"
@ 4,22 SAY "LOCATION"
@ 4,38 SAY "DESCRIPTION"
@ 4,54 SAY "QOH"
@ 4,61 SAY "COST"
@ 4,71 SAY "PRICE"
@ 5, 1 SAY "--------------------"
@ 5,22 SAY "---------------"
@ 5,38 SAY "---------------"
@ 5,54 SAY "------"
@ 5,61 SAY "---------"
@ 5,71 SAY "---------"
STORE 5 TO ROW
IF CODE2 = "A"
DO WHILE .NOT. EOF() .AND. MEMITEMNO = INVITEMNO
   IF ROW+1 > MAXLINES
      ? "TYPE ANY KEY TO CONTINUE"
      WAIT TO CONTINUE
      CLEAR
      @ 2, 1 SAY "ITEM NUMBER="
      @ 2,13 SAY MEMITEMNO
      @ 4, 1 SAY "MFCTR. OR SPEC DESIG"
      @ 4,22 SAY "LOCATION"
      @ 4,38 SAY "DESCRIPTION"
```

```
            @ 4,54 SAY "QOH"
            @ 4,61 SAY "COST"
            @ 4,71 SAY "PRICE"
            @ 5, 1 SAY "--------------------"
            @ 5,22 SAY "---------------"
            @ 5,38 SAY "---------------"
            @ 5,54 SAY "------"
            @ 5,61 SAY "---------"
            @ 5,71 SAY "---------"
            STORE 5 TO ROW
        ENDIF
        STORE ROW + 1 TO ROW
        @  ROW, 1 SAY INVMANU
        @  ROW,22 SAY INVLOC
        @  ROW,38 SAY INVDESC
        @  ROW,54 SAY INVQTYONH PICTURE "999999"
        @  ROW,61 SAY INVCSTPERU
        @  ROW,71 SAY INVSELLPR
        SKIP 1
    ENDDO
    ENDIF
    IF CODE2 = "B"
    DO WHILE .NOT. EOF() .AND. MEMITEMNO = INVITEMNO;
       .AND. MEMMANU = INVMANU
        IF ROW+1 > MAXLINES
            ? "TYPE ANY KEY TO CONTINUE"
            WAIT TO CONTINUE
            CLEAR
```

```
        @ 2, 1 SAY "ITEM NUMBER="
        @ 2,13 SAY MEMITEMNO
        @ 4, 1 SAY "MFCTR. OR SPEC DESIG"
        @ 4,22 SAY "LOCATION"
        @ 4,38 SAY "DESCRIPTION"
        @ 4,54 SAY "QOH"
        @ 4,61 SAY "COST"
        @ 4,71 SAY "PRICE"
        @ 5, 1 SAY "--------------------"
        @ 5,22 SAY "---------------"
        @ 5,38 SAY "---------------"
        @ 5,54 SAY "------"
        @ 5,61 SAY "---------"
        @ 5,71 SAY "---------"
        STORE 5 TO ROW
     ENDIF
     STORE ROW + 1 TO ROW
     @  ROW, 1 SAY INVMANU
     @  ROW,22 SAY INVLOC
     @  ROW,38 SAY INVDESC
     @  ROW,54 SAY INVQTYONH PICTURE "999999"
     @  ROW,61 SAY INVCSTPERU
     @  ROW,71 SAY INVSELLPR
     SKIP 1
  ENDDO
  ENDIF
  IF CODE2 = "C"
  DO WHILE .NOT. EOF() .AND. MEMITEMNO = INVITEMNO;
```

```
        .AND. MEMLOC = INVLOC
     IF ROW+1 > MAXLINES
        ? "TYPE ANY KEY TO CONTINUE"
        WAIT TO CONTINUE
        CLEAR
        @ 2, 1 SAY "ITEM NUMBER="
        @ 2,13 SAY MEMITEMNO
        @ 4, 1 SAY "MFCTR. OR SPEC DESIG"
        @ 4,22 SAY "LOCATION"
        @ 4,38 SAY "DESCRIPTION"
        @ 4,54 SAY "QOH"
        @ 4,61 SAY "COST"
        @ 4,71 SAY "PRICE"
        @ 5, 1 SAY "--------------------"
        @ 5,22 SAY "---------------"
        @ 5,38 SAY "---------------"
        @ 5,54 SAY "------"
        @ 5,61 SAY "---------"
        @ 5,71 SAY "---------"
        STORE 5 TO ROW
     ENDIF
     STORE ROW + 1 TO ROW
     @  ROW, 1 SAY INVMANU
     @  ROW,22 SAY INVLOC
     @  ROW,38 SAY INVDESC
     @  ROW,54 SAY INVQTYONH PICTURE "999999"
     @  ROW,61 SAY INVCSTPERU
     @  ROW,71 SAY INVSELLPR
```

```
        SKIP 1
      ENDDO
      ENDIF
      WAIT
   ENDIF
   IF CODE2 = "D"
      CLEAR
      STORE SPACE(25) TO MEMMANU
      STORE SPACE(15) TO MEMLOC
      @ 1,1 SAY "ENTER THE MFCTR/SPECIAL DESIGNATOR" GET ;
                MEMMANU
      @ 2,1 SAY "ENTER ITEM LOCATION" GET MEMLOC
      READ
      STORE MEMITEMNO + MEMMANU + MEMLOC TO MEMKEY
      SELECT J
      SET INDEX TO INVITMANLOC
      SEEK MEMKEY
      IF EOF()
         @ 5,0 SAY "NO INVENTORY RECORD FOR THIS ITEM"
         WAIT
         LOOP
      ENDIF
      CLEAR
      @ 2, 1 SAY "ITEM NUMBER="
      @ 2,13 SAY MEMITEMNO
      @ 4, 1 SAY "MFCTR. OR SPEC DESIG"
      @ 4,22 SAY "LOCATION"
      @ 4,38 SAY "DESCRIPTION"
```

```
        @ 4,54 SAY "QOH"
        @ 4,61 SAY "COST"
        @ 4,71 SAY "PRICE"
        @ 5, 1 SAY "--------------------"
        @ 5,22 SAY "---------------"
        @ 5,38 SAY "---------------"
        @ 5,54 SAY "------"
        @ 5,61 SAY "---------"
        @ 5,71 SAY "---------"
        @  6, 1 SAY INVMANU
        @  6,22 SAY INVLOC
        @  6,38 SAY INVDESC
        @  6,54 SAY INVQTYONH PICTURE "999999"
        @  6,61 SAY INVCSTPERU
        @  6,71 SAY INVSELLPR
        ? "TYPE ANY KEY TO CONTINUE."
        WAIT TO CONTINUE
        LOOP
     ENDIF
  CASE CODE1 = "F"
     CLEAR
     STORE SPACE(15) TO MEMSENDLOC
     STORE SPACE(15) TO MEMRECLOC
     STORE SPACE(20) TO MEMITEMNO
     @ 1,1 SAY "ENTER THE SENDING LOCATION" ;
           GET MEMSENDLOC
     @ 2,1 SAY "ENTER THE RECEIVING LOCATION" ;
           GET MEMRECLOC
```

```
@ 3,1 SAY "ENTER THE INVENTORY ITEM NUMBER" ;
      GET MEMITEMNO
READ
STORE MEMSENDLOC + MEMRECLOC + MEMITEMNO TO MEMKEY
SELECT C
SET INDEX TO TRLOCITD
SEEK MEMKEY
IF EOF()
   @ 5,0 SAY "NO INVENTORY TRANSFERS FOR GIVEN "+;
             "LOCATIONS AND ITEM"
   WAIT
   LOOP
ENDIF
STORE 20 TO MAXLINES
CLEAR
@  2, 1 SAY "SENDING LOC="
@  2,13 SAY MEMSENDLOC
@  2,30 SAY "RECEIVING LOCATION="
@  2,49 SAY MEMRECLOC
@  3, 1 SAY "ITEM NO="
@  3, 9 SAY MEMITEMNO
@  4, 1 SAY "MANUFAC. OR SPEC DESIG"
@  4,27 SAY "DESCRIPTION"
@  4,43 SAY "DATE"
@  4,52 SAY "QTY S"
@  4,59 SAY "UNITS"
@  4,65 SAY "QTY/UN"
@  4,72 SAY "QTY R"
```

```
@  5, 1 SAY "-------------------------"
@  5,27 SAY "---------------"
@  5,43 SAY "--------"
@  5,52 SAY "------"
@  5,59 SAY "-----"
@  5,65 SAY "------"
@  5,72 SAY "------"
STORE 5 TO ROW
DO WHILE .NOT. EOF() .AND. MEMSENDLOC = TRSENDLOC .AND.;
  MEMRECLOC = TRRECLOC .AND. MEMITEMNO = TRITEMNO
   IF ROW+1 > MAXLINES
      WAIT
      CLEAR
      @  2, 1 SAY "SENDING LOC="
      @  2,13 SAY MEMSENDLOC
      @  2,30 SAY "RECEIVING LOCATION="
      @  2,49 SAY MEMRECLOC
      @  3, 1 SAY "ITEM NO="
      @  3, 9 SAY MEMITEMNO
      @  4, 1 SAY "MANUFAC. OR SPEC DESIG"
      @  4,27 SAY "DESCRIPTION"
      @  4,43 SAY "DATE"
      @  4,52 SAY "QTY S"
      @  4,59 SAY "UNITS"
      @  4,65 SAY "QTY/UN"
      @  4,72 SAY "QTY R"
      @  5, 1 SAY "-------------------------"
      @  5,27 SAY "---------------"
```

```
            @  5,43 SAY "--------"
            @  5,52 SAY "------"
            @  5,59 SAY "-----"
            @  5,65 SAY "------"
            @  5,72 SAY "------"
            STORE 5 TO ROW
         ENDIF
         STORE ROW + 1 TO ROW
         @ ROW, 1 SAY TRMANU
         @ ROW,27 SAY TRDESC
         @ ROW,43 SAY TRSENDDT
         @ ROW,52 SAY TRQTYSENT
         @ ROW,59 SAY TRUNITS
         @ ROW,65 SAY TRQTYPER
         @ ROW,72 SAY TRQTYREC
         SKIP 1
      ENDDO
      WAIT
   CASE CODE1 = "G"
      * FIND PAYMENT RECORD
      CLEAR
      @  5, 5 SAY "PAYMENT SELECTION MODES"
      @  6, 5 SAY "----------------------"
      @  7,10 SAY "A. BY ACCOUNT NUMBER"
      @  8,10 SAY "B. BY CHECK NUMBER"
      WAIT " ENTER A SELECTION CODE:" TO CODE2
      IF CODE2 <> "A" .AND. CODE2 <> "B"
         @ 10,0 SAY "ILLEGAL SELECTION CODE"
```

```
   WAIT
   LOOP
ENDIF
IF CODE2 = "A"
   CLEAR
   STORE SPACE(10) TO MEMACCTNO
   @ 1,1 SAY "ENTER THE ACCOUNT NUMBER" GET MEMACCTNO
   READ
   SELECT D
   SET INDEX TO PAYACCTNO
   SEEK MEMACCTNO
   IF EOF()
      @ 3,0 SAY "NO PAYMENT RECORDS FOR THIS ACCOUNT"
      WAIT
      LOOP
   ENDIF
   CLEAR
   STORE 20 TO MAXLINES
   @  4, 1 SAY "ACCOUNT NO"
   @  4,12 SAY "AMOUNT"
   @  4,22 SAY "DATE"
   @  4,31 SAY "CHECK NUMBER"
   @  5, 1 SAY "----------"
   @  5,12 SAY "---------"
   @  5,22 SAY "--------"
   @  5,31 SAY "------------"
   STORE 5 TO ROW
   DO WHILE .NOT. EOF() .AND. MEMACCTNO = PAYACCTNO
```

```
            IF ROW+1 > MAXLINES
               WAIT
               CLEAR
               @  4, 1 SAY "ACCOUNT NO"
               @  4,12 SAY "AMOUNT"
               @  4,22 SAY "DATE"
               @  4,31 SAY "CHECK NUMBER"
               @  5, 1 SAY "----------"
               @  5,12 SAY "---------"
               @  5,22 SAY "--------"
               @  5,31 SAY "------------"
               STORE 5 TO ROW
            ENDIF
            STORE ROW+1 TO ROW
            @ ROW,1 SAY PAYACCTNO
            @ ROW,12 SAY PAYAMT
            @ ROW,22 SAY PAYDATE
            @ ROW,31 SAY PAYCHECKNO
            SKIP 1
         ENDDO
         WAIT
      ENDIF
      IF CODE2 = "B"
         CLEAR
         STORE SPACE(6) TO MEMCHECKNO
         @ 1,1 SAY "ENTER THE CHECK NUMBER" GET MEMCHECKNO
         READ
         SELECT D
```

```
SET INDEX TO PAYCHECKNO
SEEK MEMCHECKNO
IF EOF()
   @ 3,0 SAY "NO PAYMENT RECORDS FOR THIS CHECK NUMBER"
   WAIT
   LOOP
ENDIF
CLEAR
STORE 20 TO MAXLINES
@  4, 1 SAY "ACCOUNT NO"
@  4,12 SAY "AMOUNT"
@  4,22 SAY "DATE"
@  4,31 SAY "CHECK NUMBER"
@  5, 1 SAY "----------"
@  5,12 SAY "---------"
@  5,22 SAY "--------"
@  5,31 SAY "------------"
STORE 5 TO ROW
DO WHILE .NOT. EOF() .AND. MEMCHECKNO = PAYCHECKNO
   IF ROW+1 > MAXLINES
      WAIT
      CLEAR
      @  4, 1 SAY "ACCOUNT NO"
      @  4,12 SAY "AMOUNT"
      @  4,22 SAY "DATE"
      @  4,31 SAY "CHECK NUMBER"
      @  5, 1 SAY "----------"
      @  5,12 SAY "---------"
```

```
                @  5,22 SAY "--------"
                @  5,31 SAY "------------"
                STORE 5 TO ROW
             ENDIF
             STORE ROW+1 TO ROW
             @ ROW,1 SAY PAYACCTNO
             @ ROW,12 SAY PAYAMT
             @ ROW,22 SAY PAYDATE
             @ ROW,31 SAY PAYCHECKNO
             SKIP 1
          ENDDO
          WAIT
       ENDIF
    OTHERWISE
       @ 20, 0 SAY "ILLEGAL RECORD SELECTION CODE."
       WAIT
   ENDCASE
ENDDO
RETURN
***************************** END OF PROGRAM *****************

* INDEXES.PRG
USE ACCOUNTS
   INDEX ON ACCNO TO ACCNO
   INDEX ON ACCCOMPANY TO ACCCOMPA
   INDEX ON ACCLNAME   TO ACCLNAME
USE CHARGES
   INDEX ON CHACCTNO   TO CHACCTNO
```

```
   INDEX ON CHTICKETNO TO CHTICKET
USE PAYMENTS
   INDEX ON PAYACCTNO  TO PAYACCTN
   INDEX ON PAYCHECKNO TO PAYCHECK
USE NOTIFICATION
   INDEX ON NOTACCTNO+;
     STR(30000000-YEAR(NOTDATE)*10000+MONTH(NOTDATE)*100;
     +DAY(NOTDATE),8) TO NOTACCTN
USE BILLING
   INDEX ON BILLACCTNO+;
     STR(30000000-YEAR(BILLDATE)*10000+MONTH(BILLDATE)*100;
     +DAY(BILLDATE),8) TO BILLACCT
USE INVENTORY
   INDEX ON INVITEMNO+INVMANU+INVLOC TO INVITMAN
   INDEX ON INVITEMNO+INVLOC         TO INVITLOC
USE TRANSFER
   INDEX ON TRSENDLOC+TRRECLOC+TRITEMNO+DTOC(TRSENDDT) ;
      TO TRLOCITD
USE ACCTFILE
   INDEX ON ACCTTYPACT TO ACCTTYPA
RETURN
***************************** END OF PROGRAM ******************


* INVENTOR.PRG
SET DEVICE TO SCREEN
DO WHILE .T.
   CLEAR
   @  5, 1 SAY "SELECT A LETTER CODE"
```

```
@  6, 1 SAY "------------"
@  7, 5 SAY "A. EXIT"
@  8, 5 SAY "B. ENTER A NEW INVENTORY RECORD"
@  9, 5 SAY "C. UPDATE AN EXISTING INVENTORY RECORD"
@ 10, 5 SAY "D. ENTER AN INVENTORY TRANSFER RECORD"
@ 11, 5 SAY "E. ACCEPT AN INVENTORY TRANSFER"
@ 12, 5 SAY "F. PRODUCE TRANSFER DISCREPANCY REPORT"
@ 13, 5 SAY "G. PRODUCE COMPLETE INVENTORY REPORT"
WAIT "ENTER A SELECTION CODE:" TO CODE1
DO CASE
   CASE CODE1 = "A"
      RETURN
   CASE CODE1 = "B"
      DO ENTERINV
   CASE CODE1 = "C"
      DO UPDATEIN
   CASE CODE1 = "D"
      DO SENDINV
   CASE CODE1 = "E"
      DO RECINV
   CASE CODE1 = "F"
      DO TRDISCRP
   CASE CODE1 = "G"
      DO INVREPOR
   OTHERWISE
      @ 15,0 SAY "ILLEGAL CODE SELECTED"
      WAIT
ENDCASE
```

```
   CLEAR ALL
ENDDO
RETURN
****************************** END OF PROGRAM ******************

* INVREPOR.PRG
CLEAR
? "INSERT WIDE PAPER IN THE PRINTER."
? "TYPE ANY KEY TO CONTINUE."
WAIT
CLEAR
SET DEVICE TO PRINT
@ 0,0 SAY CHR(15)
SELECT J
USE INVENTOR INDEX INVITMAN
REPORT FORM INVENTOR TO PRINT
@ 66,153 SAY CHR(18)
SET DEVICE TO SCREEN
RETURN
****************************** END OF PROGRAM ******************

* MAKEBILLS.PRG
* MEMLASTCHR = CHARGES FROM LAST BILL
* MEMTOTCHRG = CHARGES FROM LAST BILL OR OLD CHARGES
*              - PAYMENTS APPLIED
* MEMOLDINT  = INTEREST FROM LAST BILL OR OLD INTEREST
*              - PAYMENTS APPLIED
* MEMPAYMENT = CURRENT TOTAL PAYMENTS FROM ACCOUNTS FILE,
```

```
*               INCLUDING OLD CREDITS
* MEMPAYAMT  = REMAINDER OF PAYMENTS AND CREDITS TO BE APPLIED TO
*               BILL
* MEMPAYINT  = AMOUNT OF PAYMENTS APPLIED TO OLD INTEREST
* MEMNCHRG   = CHARGES SINCE LAST BILL
* MEMINTRATE = ACTUAL INTEREST RATE ON UNPAID BILLS
* MEMINTST   = NEW INTEREST ON UNPAID CHARGES
* MEMINTOINT = INTEREST ON OLD UNPAID INTEREST
* MEMTOTBPD  = TOTAL OF PAYMENTS TO CHARGES APPLIED THIS BILLING
* MEMNTOTCHR = NEW TOTAL CHARGES
* MEMTOTDUE  = NEW BILL TOTAL
* MEMBILLDT  = DATE OF BILL IN ORIGINAL MM/DD/YY FORM
* MEMOVER30  = PART OF BILL OVER 30 DAYS OLD
* MEMOVER60  = PART OF BILL OVER 60 DAYS OLD
* MEMOVER90  = PART OF BILL OVER 90 DAYS OLD
* MEMBILLTYP = TYPE OF BILLING: REG = REGULAR;
*                                SCH = BY SCHEDULE
*                                       (MIN MONTHLY PAYMENTS)
* MEMMINPAY  = MINIMUM PAYMENT EXPECTED IF BILLING TYPE = SCH
* MEMCDOLLAR = DOLLAR AMOUNT OF CHARGE
* MEMTPBAL   = TOTAL PREVIOUS BALANCE (CHARGES + INTEREST)
* MEMTPC     = TOTAL PAYMENTS AND CREDITS FOR BILLING PERIOD
* MEMTPCAPP  = TOTAL PAYMENTS AND CREDITS FOR BILLING PERIOD
*               ACTUALLY APPLIED TO BILLS
* MEMTCHRG   = TOTAL NEW CHARGES FOR BILLING PERIOD
* MEMTINT    = TOTAL NEW INTEREST FOR BILLING PERIOD
* MEMINTFLG  = INTEREST INDICATOR FOR CURRENT ACCOUNT
*               (ACCUMULATE INT Y OR N)
```

```
* MEMCARYOVR = CREDITS AND PAYMENTS CARRIED OVER FROM LAST
*              BILLING
* MEMTCOVR   = TOTAL CREDITS AND PAYMENTS CARRIED OVER FROM
*              LAST BILLING
MEMINTRATE = .0175
MAXROWS    =  25
SELECT A
USE ACCOUNTS INDEX ACCNO
SELECT B
USE CHARGES INDEX CHACCTNO
SELECT E
USE BILLING INDEX BILLACCT
STORE 0 TO MEMPAYINT
STORE 0 TO MEMTPBAL
STORE 0 TO MEMTPC
STORE 0 TO MEMTPCAPP
STORE 0 TO MEMTCHRG
STORE 0 TO MEMTINT
STORE 0 TO MEMTCOVR
STORE DATE() TO MEMDATE
STORE MEMDATE TO MEMBILLDT
* SET NUMBER OF DAYS UNTIL BILL IS DUE
STORE 15 TO MEMBILLDAY
SET DEVICE TO PRINT
SELECT A
CLEAR
MEMOK = .F.
DO WHILE .NOT. MEMOK
```

```
STORE 1 TO PAGENO
@ 4,21 SAY "PAGE NO:"
@ 4,29 SAY "99"
@ 5, 6 SAY "XXXXXXXXXXXXXXXXXXXXXXXXXXXXXXXXXX"
@ 6,6 SAY "XXXXXXXXXXXXXXXXXXXXXXXXXXXXXXXXXX"
@ 6,55 SAY DATE() PICTURE "XXXXXXXX"
@ 6,68 SAY DATE() PICTURE "XXXXXXXX"
@ 6,81 SAY "XXXXXXX"
@ 7, 6 SAY "PO BOX:"
@ 7,13 SAY "XXXXXXXXXX"
@ 8,6 SAY "XXXXXXXXXXXXXXXXXXXXXXXXXXXXXXXXXX"
@ 9, 6 SAY "XXXXXXXXXXXXXXXXXXXXXXXXXXXXXXXXXX"
@ 10,56 SAY "XXXXXXX"
@ 14, 21 SAY "PREVIOUS BALANCE DUE:"
@ 14, 52 SAY "999999.99"
@ 14, 68 SAY "P BAL"
@ 14, 76 SAY "999999.99"
@ 15, 21 SAY "PAYMENTS/CREDITS"
@ 15, 52 SAY "999999.99"
@ 15, 68 SAY "PAYMENT" PICTURE "XXXXXXX"
@ 15, 76 SAY "999999.99"
STORE 16 TO ROW
DO WHILE ROW <= 40
   @ ROW, 0 SAY "XXXXXXXX"
   @ ROW,10 SAY "XXXXXXXX"
   @ ROW,21 SAY "XXXXXXXXXXXXXXX"
   @ ROW,38 SAY "QTY=" PICTURE "XXXX"
   @ ROW,42 SAY "9999.9"
```

```
  @ ROW,52 SAY "999999.99"
  @ ROW,68 SAY "XXXXXXX"
  @ ROW,76 SAY "999999.99"
  STORE ROW+1 TO ROW
ENDDO
@ 41, 21 SAY "NEW CHARGES"
@ 41, 52 SAY "999999.99"
@ 41, 68 SAY "NEW CH:"
@ 41, 76 SAY "999999.99"
@ 42,21 SAY "INTEREST FOR THIS PERIOD:"
@ 42,52 SAY "999999.99"
@ 42,68 SAY "INTREST"
@ 42,76 SAY "999999.99"
@ 45, 0 SAY "999999.99"
@ 45,13 SAY "999999.99"
@ 45,26 SAY "999999.99"
@ 45,39 SAY "999999.99"
@ 45,52 SAY "999999.99"
@ 45,76 SAY "999999.99"
@ 47, 0 SAY "MIN PAYMENT:"
@ 47,12 SAY "999999.99"
@ 47,30 SAY "DATE DUE:"
@ 47,39 SAY "XXXXXXXX"
@ 47,48 SAY "YTD INT:"
@ 47,56 SAY "999999.99"
@ 47,69 SAY "DATE DUE:"
@ 47,78 SAY "XXXXXXXX"
@ 48, 0 SAY "MONTHS IN ARREARS:"
```

```
  @ 48,19 SAY "9999"
  @ 48,68 SAY "MONTHS ARREARS:"
  @ 48,85 SAY "9999"
  EJECT
  WAIT "PRINTER ALIGNED CORRECTLY (Y/N)" TO ANSWER
  IF UPPER(ANSWER) = "Y" .OR. ANSWER = SPACE(1)
    MEMOK = .T.
  ENDIF
ENDDO
? "PROCESSING OF THE BILLS HAS STARTED"
DO WHILE (.NOT. EOF())
  STORE 0 TO ITEMCOUNT
  STORE 0 TO MEMNCHRG
  STORE 0 TO MEMINTRST
  STORE 0 TO MEMOVER30
  STORE 0 TO MEMOVER60
  STORE 0 TO MEMOVER90
  STORE ACCNO TO MEMACCTNO
  STORE ACCTOTCHRG TO MEMTOTCHRG
  STORE ACCTOTCHRG TO MEMLASTCHR
  STORE ACCTOTINT TO MEMOLDINT
  STORE ACCMINPAY TO MEMMINPAY
  STORE ACCBILLTYP TO MEMBILLTYP
  STORE ACCINTFLG TO MEMINTFLG
  * NEXT IS TOTAL PAYMENT RECEIVED SINCE LAST BILL
  STORE ACCPAYMENT+ACCCARYOVR TO MEMPAYMENT
  STORE ACCCARYOVR TO MEMCARYOVR
  STORE MEMTCOVR + MEMCARYOVR TO MEMTCOVR
```

```
STORE MEMTPC+MEMPAYMENT TO MEMTPC
* NEXT IS AMOUNT TO BE APPLIED TO PAYMENT OF CHARGES
STORE MEMPAYMENT TO MEMPAYAMT
* IF TOTAL CHARGES = 0, AND NO PAYMENTS, NO BILL PRODUCED
IF ACCTOTCHRG + ACCTOTINT = 0 .AND. ACCPAYMENT = 0 .AND. ;
  (MONTH(MEMBILLDT) <> 1 .OR. YEAR(ACCDTLACT) <> ;
  YEAR(MEMBILLDT)-1)
  SKIP 1
  LOOP
ENDIF
STORE 1 TO PAGENO
@ 4,21 SAY "PAGE NO:"
@ 4,29 SAY PAGENO PICTURE "99"

IF ACCLNAME <> SPACE(15)
  @ 5, 6 SAY TRIM(ACCLNAME)+","+TRIM(ACCFNAME) PICTURE ;
    "XXXXXXXXXXXXXXXXXXXXXXXXXXXXXXXXXXX"
ENDIF
IF MEMACCTNO <> SPACE(10)
  @ 6,6 SAY ACCCOMPANY PICTURE ;
     "XXXXXXXXXXXXXXXXXXXXXXXXXXXXXXXXXXX"
ENDIF
@ 6,55 SAY DATE() PICTURE "XXXXXXXX"
@ 6,68 SAY DATE() PICTURE "XXXXXXXX"
@ 6,81 SAY MEMACCTNO PICTURE "XXXXXXX"
IF ACCPOBOX <> SPACE(10)
  @ 7, 6 SAY "PO BOX:"
  @ 7,13 SAY ACCPOBOX
```

```
ENDIF
IF ACCSTREET <> SPACE(25)
  @ 8,6 SAY ACCSTREET
ENDIF
@ 9, 6 SAY TRIM(ACCCITY)+", "+TRIM(ACCSTATE)+" "+TRIM(ACCZIP) ;
    PICTURE "XXXXXXXXXXXXXXXXXXXXXXXXXXXXXXXXXX"
@ 10,56 SAY MEMACCTNO PICTURE "XXXXXXX"

* OBTAIN BALANCE DUE AND DATE OF BILLING, FROM PREVIOUS BILL
SELECT E
SEEK MEMACCTNO
IF EOF()
  STORE 0 TO MEMPREVBAL
  STORE CTOD("  /  /  ") TO MEMPRVBDT
ELSE
  STORE BILLAMT TO MEMPREVBAL
  STORE BILLDATE TO MEMPRVBDT
ENDIF
STORE MEMTPBAL+MEMPREVBAL TO MEMTPBAL
@ 14, 21 SAY "PREVIOUS BALANCE DUE:"
@ 14, 52 SAY MEMPREVBAL PICTURE "999999.99"
@ 14, 68 SAY "P BAL"
@ 14, 76 SAY MEMPREVBAL PICTURE "999999.99"
@ 15, 21 SAY "PAYMENTS/CREDITS"
@ 15, 52 SAY MEMPAYMENT PICTURE "999999.99"
@ 15, 68 SAY "PAYMENT" PICTURE "XXXXXXX"
@ 15, 76 SAY MEMPAYMENT PICTURE "999999.99"
STORE 16 TO ROW
```

```
* SUBTRACT REMAINDER OF PAYMENTS FROM OLD INTEREST
STORE 0 TO MEMPAYINT
IF MEMPAYAMT > 0 .AND. MEMPAYAMT <= MEMOLDINT
  STORE MEMOLDINT - MEMPAYAMT TO MEMOLDINT
  STORE MEMPAYAMT TO MEMPAYINT
  STORE 0 TO MEMPAYAMT
ELSE
IF MEMPAYAMT > 0 .AND. MEMPAYAMT > MEMOLDINT
  STORE MEMPAYAMT - MEMOLDINT TO MEMPAYAMT
  STORE MEMOLDINT TO MEMPAYINT
  STORE 0 TO MEMOLDINT
ENDIF
ENDIF
* EXAMINE CHARGES
SELECT B
SEEK MEMACCTNO
IF .NOT. EOF()
  * APPLY PAYMENTS DIRECTLY TO CHARGES AND PRINT ITEMS ON BILL
  DO WHILE (.NOT. EOF()) .AND. CHACCTNO = MEMACCTNO
    IF CHBPAID >= CHDOLLARS
      SKIP 1
      LOOP
    ELSE
      IF CHRESREPTD = "Y" .OR. CHRESREPTD = " "
        STORE CHDOLLARS TO MEMCDOLLAR
      ELSE
        STORE CHDOLLARS - CHDISPAMT TO MEMCDOLLAR
      ENDIF
```

```
IF MEMPAYAMT >= 0 .AND. MEMCDOLLAR-CHBPAID <= ;
  MEMPAYAMT .AND. MEMCDOLLAR <> CHBPAID
  STORE MEMPAYAMT-(MEMCDOLLAR-CHBPAID) ;
    TO MEMPAYAMT
  REPLACE CHBPAID WITH MEMCDOLLAR, ;
    CHBPAIDDT WITH DATE()
ELSE
IF MEMPAYAMT >= 0 .AND. MEMCDOLLAR-CHBPAID > ;
  MEMPAYAMT .AND. MEMCDOLLAR <> CHBPAID
  REPLACE CHBPAID WITH CHBPAID + ;
    MEMPAYAMT, CHBPAIDDT WITH DATE()
  STORE 0 TO MEMPAYAMT
ENDIF
ENDIF
STORE CHDATE TO MEMCHDT
* SEE IF CHARGE HAS ALREADY BEEN POSTED
* (REPORTED AS CHARGE ITEM ON A PREVIOUS BILL)
IF CHPOSTED <> "Y"
  STORE ROW+1 TO ROW
  IF ROW > MAXROWS
    EJECT
    STORE PAGENO+1 TO PAGENO
    @ 4,21 SAY "PAGE NO:"
    @ 4,29 SAY PAGENO PICTURE "99"
    IF ACCLNAME <> SPACE(15)
      @ 5, 6 SAY TRIM(ACCLNAME)+","+TRIM(ACCFNAME) PICTURE ;
        "XXXXXXXXXXXXXXXXXXXXXXXXXXXXXXXXXXX"
    ENDIF
```

```
    IF MEMACCTNO <> SPACE(10)
      @ 6,6 SAY ACCCOMPANY PICTURE ;
          "XXXXXXXXXXXXXXXXXXXXXXXXXXXXXXXXXXX"
    ENDIF
    @ 6,55 SAY DATE() PICTURE "XXXXXXXX"
    @ 6,68 SAY DATE() PICTURE "XXXXXXXX"
    @ 6,81 SAY MEMACCTNO PICTURE "XXXXXXX"
    IF ACCPOBOX <> SPACE(10)
      @ 7, 6 SAY "PO BOX:"
      @ 7,13 SAY ACCPOBOX
    ENDIF
    IF ACCSTREET <> SPACE(25)
      @ 8,6 SAY ACCSTREET
    ENDIF
    @ 9, 6 SAY TRIM(ACCCITY)+", "+TRIM(ACCSTATE)+" "+;
      TRIM(ACCZIP) PICTURE ;
      "XXXXXXXXXXXXXXXXXXXXXXXXXXXXXXXXXXX"
    @ 10,57 SAY MEMACCTNO PICTURE "XXXXXXX"
    STORE 14 TO ROW
  ENDIF
  @ ROW, 0 SAY CHTICKETNO PICTURE "XXXXXXXX"
  @ ROW,10 SAY CHDATE PICTURE "XXXXXXXX"
  @ ROW,21 SAY CHITEMDESC PICTURE "XXXXXXXXXXXXXXX"
  @ ROW,38 SAY "QTY=" PICTURE "XXXX"
  @ ROW,42 SAY CHQTY PICTURE "9999.9"
  @ ROW,52 SAY MEMCDOLLAR PICTURE "999999.99"
  @ ROW,68 SAY CHTICKETNO PICTURE "XXXXXXX"
  @ ROW,76 SAY MEMCDOLLAR PICTURE "999999.99"
```

```
        * IF THIS CHARGE NOT YET POSTED,
        * ACCUMULATE AMOUNT AND POST
        STORE MEMNCHRG+MEMCDOLLAR TO MEMNCHRG
        REPLACE CHPOSTED WITH "Y"
      ENDIF
    ENDIF
    * IF NOT PAID OFF YET, COMPUTE INTEREST
    IF CHBPAID < MEMCDOLLAR .AND. MEMBILLDT-MEMCHDT > 30
      STORE MEMCDOLLAR-CHBPAID TO MEMDOLLARS
      STORE MEMINTRST+MEMDOLLARS*MEMINTRATE TO MEMINTRST
      IF MEMCHDT+60<=MEMBILLDT .AND. MEMCHDT+90>MEMBILLDT
      STORE MEMOVER30+(MEMCDOLLAR-CHBPAID) TO MEMOVER30
      ELSE
      IF MEMCHDT+90<=MEMBILLDT .AND. MEMCHDT+120>MEMBILLDT
      STORE MEMOVER60+(MEMCDOLLAR-CHBPAID) TO MEMOVER60
      ELSE
      IF MEMCHDT+120<=MEMBILLDT
      STORE MEMOVER90+(MEMCDOLLAR-CHBPAID) TO MEMOVER90
      ENDIF
      ENDIF
      ENDIF
    ENDIF
    SKIP 1
  ENDDO
ENDIF
* COMPUTE NEW TOTAL CHARGES, AFTER PAYMENTS
* MEMPAYMENT = ORIGINAL PAYMENT AMOUNT TO BE APPLIED TO THE
*               BILL
```

```
* MEMPAYAMT  = AMOUNT THAT CAN BE APPLIED TO EACH REMAINING
*              CHARGE
* MEMPAYNT   = AMOUNT THAT WAS APPLIED TO THE OLD INTEREST DUE
* ((MEMPAYMENT - MEMPAYAMT) - MEMPAYINT) = TOTAL AMOUNT
*              APPLIED ONLY TO THE CHARGES.
STORE MEMTOTCHRG - ((MEMPAYMENT - MEMPAYAMT) - MEMPAYINT) TO ;
   MEMTOTCHRG
* END OF NEW TOTAL CHARGES COMPUTATION
@ 41, 21 SAY "NEW CHARGES"
@ 41, 52 SAY MEMNCHRG PICTURE "999999.99"
@ 41, 68 SAY "NEW CH:"
@ 41, 76 SAY MEMNCHRG PICTURE "999999.99"

STORE MEMTCHRG+MEMNCHRG TO MEMTCHRG
* AT THIS POINT, MEMINTRST IS INTEREST ONLY ON UNPAID CHARGES
* WITHOUT COMPUTING INTEREST ON REMAINDER OF THE UNPAID
*   PREVIOUS BALANCE
STORE ROUND(MEMINTRST,2) TO MEMINTRST

* COMPUTE INTEREST ON OLD UNPAID INTEREST
STORE MEMINTRATE*MEMOLDINT TO MEMINTOINT
STORE ROUND(MEMINTOINT,2) TO MEMINTOINT
* COMPUTE INTEREST FOR THIS PERIOD
STORE MEMINTOINT + MEMINTRST TO MEMNTOTINT
* IF NOT SUPPOSED TO ACCUMULATE NEW INTEREST ON THIS ACCOUNT,
*   SET NEW INTEREST TO 0
* THIS IS DONE IF COMPANY IS IN BANKRUPTCY OR IF FAVORED ACCOUNT
IF MEMINTFLG = "N"
```

```
  STORE 0 TO MEMNTOTINT
ENDIF
@ 42,21 SAY "INTEREST FOR THIS PERIOD:"
@ 42,52 SAY MEMNTOTINT PICTURE "999999.99"
@ 42,68 SAY "INTREST"
@ 42,76 SAY MEMNTOTINT PICTURE "999999.99"
STORE MEMTINT+MEMNTOTINT TO MEMTINT
* COMPUTE NEW TOTAL INTEREST = OLD INTEREST + INTEREST FOR THIS ;
*    PERIOD
STORE MEMOLDINT + MEMNTOTINT TO MEMNTOTINT
* COMPUTE AMOUNT OF PAYMENTS ACTUALLY APPLIED TO CURRENT BILL
STORE MEMPAYMENT - MEMPAYAMT TO MEMTOTBPD
STORE MEMTPCAPP+MEMTOTBPD TO MEMTPCAPP
* COMPUTE NEW TOTAL CHARGES
STORE MEMTOTCHRG TO MEMNTOTCHR
* COMPUTE NEW BALANCE DUE
STORE MEMNTOTCHR + MEMNTOTINT TO MEMTOTDUE
@ 45, 0 SAY MEMTOTDUE-MEMOVER30-MEMOVER60-MEMOVER90 ;
    PICTURE "999999.99"
@ 45,13 SAY MEMOVER30 PICTURE "999999.99"
@ 45,26 SAY MEMOVER60 PICTURE "999999.99"
@ 45,39 SAY MEMOVER90 PICTURE "999999.99"
@ 45,52 SAY MEMTOTDUE PICTURE "999999.99"
@ 45,76 SAY MEMTOTDUE PICTURE "999999.99"

IF MEMBILLTYP = "SCH"
  @ 47, 0 SAY "MIN PAYMENT:"
  @ 47,12 SAY ACCMINPAY PICTURE "999999.99"
```

```
ENDIF
STORE MEMBILLDT+MEMBILLDAY TO MEMDATEDUE
* UPDATE APPROPRIATE RECORDS NOW THAT ALL PAYMENTS HAVE BEEN
*   APPLIED TO
* CHARGES AND INTEREST HAS BEEN COMPUTED
SELECT E
APPEND BLANK
REPLACE BILLACCTNO WITH MEMACCTNO, BILLAMT WITH MEMTOTDUE, ;
  BILLDATE WITH MEMBILLDT
SELECT A
STORE 0 TO MEMMONARR
IF MEMBILLTYP = "SCH"
  IF MEMMINPAY > MEMPAYMENT
    STORE ACCMONARR + 1 TO MEMMONARR
  ELSE
    STORE 0 TO MEMMONARR
  ENDIF
ENDIF
REPLACE ACCPAYMENT WITH 0, ACCCARYOVR WITH MEMPAYMENT-MEMTOTBPD, ;
 ACCTOTCHRG WITH MEMNTOTCHR, ACCMONARR WITH MEMMONARR, ;
 ACCTOTINT WITH MEMNTOTINT, ACCYTDINT WITH ACCYTDINT + ;
 MEMNTOTINT - MEMOLDINT
REPLACE ACCOVER30 WITH MEMOVER30, ACCOVER60 WITH MEMOVER60, ;
  ACCOVER90 WITH MEMOVER90
@ 47,30 SAY "DATE DUE:"
```

```
  @ 47,39 SAY MEMDATEDUE PICTURE "XXXXXXXX"
  IF MONTH(MEMBILLDT) = 12
    @ 47,48 SAY "YTD INT:"
    @ 47,56 SAY ACCYTDINT PICTURE "999999.99"
    REPLACE ACCYTDINT WITH 0
  ENDIF
  @ 47,69 SAY "DATE DUE:"
  @ 47,78 SAY MEMDATEDUE PICTURE "XXXXXXXX"
  IF MEMBILLTYP = "SCH"
    @ 48, 0 SAY "MONTHS IN ARREARS:"
    @ 48,19 SAY MEMMONARR PICTURE "9999"
    @ 48,68 SAY "MONTHS ARREARS:"
    @ 48,85 SAY MEMMONARR PICTURE "9999"
  ENDIF
  SKIP 1
  EJECT
ENDDO
@ 6, 6 SAY "SUMMARY OF BILLING"
@ 6,55 SAY DATE() PICTURE "XXXXXXXX"
@ 15, 1 SAY "TOTAL OF PREVIOUS CHARGES AND INTEREST:"
@ 15,40 SAY MEMTPBAL PICTURE "9999999.99"
@ 16, 1 SAY "PAYMENTS AND CREDITS RECEIVED          :"
@ 16,40 SAY MEMTPC-MEMTCOVR PICTURE "9999999.99"
@ 17, 1 SAY "PAYMENTS AND CREDITS CARRIED OVER      :"
@ 17,40 SAY MEMTCOVR PICTURE "9999999.99"
```

```
@ 18, 1 SAY "NEW CHARGES                          :"
@ 18,40 SAY MEMTCHRG PICTURE "9999999.99"
@ 19, 1 SAY "NEW INTEREST                         :"
@ 19,40 SAY MEMTINT PICTURE "9999999.99"
@ 20,40 SAY "----------"
@ 21, 1 SAY "TOTAL RECEIVABLES, MINUS CARRY OVER   :"
@ 21,40 SAY MEMTPBAL-MEMTPC+MEMTCHRG+MEMTINT PICTURE ;
   "9999999.99"

@ 25, 1 SAY "PAYMENTS ACTUALLY APPLIED TO ACCOUNTS:"
@ 25,40 SAY MEMTPCAPP PICTURE "9999999.99"
@ 26,1 SAY  "CREDITS ACCUMULATED TOWARDS NEXT BILL:"
@ 26,40 SAY MEMTPC-MEMTPCAPP PICTURE "9999999.99"
EJECT
SET DEVICE TO SCREEN
? "PROCESSING OF THE BILLS HAS BEEN COMPLETED."
WAIT
RETURN
****************************** END OF PROGRAM ******************


* MAKEPAYM.PRG
SET DEVICE TO SCREEN
SELECT A
USE ACCOUNTS INDEX ACCNO, ACCLNAME, ACCCOMPA
SELECT C
USE ACCTFILE INDEX ACCTTYPA
SELECT D
```

```
USE PAYMENTS INDEX PAYACCTN, PAYCHECK
DO WHILE .T.
   CLEAR
   STORE SPACE(1) TO ANSWER
   WAIT "DO YOU WISH TO ENTER ANOTHER PAYMENT (Y/N):" TO ANSWER
   IF UPPER(ANSWER) <> "Y"
      RETURN
   ENDIF
   CLEAR
   STORE SPACE(10) TO MEMACCTNO
   @ 1,1 SAY "ENTER THE ACCOUNT NUMBER" GET MEMACCTNO
   READ
   SELECT A
   SEEK MEMACCTNO
   IF EOF()
      @ 3,0 SAY "NO ACCOUNT FOR GIVEN ACCOUNT NUMBER."
      WAIT
      LOOP
   ELSE
      CLEAR
      @ 5,1 SAY "ACCOUNT NUMBER="+ ACCNO
      @ 6,1 SAY "COMPANY NAME  ="+ ACCCOMPANY
      @ 7,1 SAY "CONTACT NAME  ="+ TRIM(ACCLNAME)+", "+;
            TRIM(ACCFNAME)
      STORE SPACE(1) TO ANSWER
      @ 8,0 SAY "IS THIS THE CORRECT ACCOUNT (Y/N):" GET ANSWER
      READ
      IF UPPER(ANSWER) <> "Y"
```

```
   LOOP
ENDIF
STORE CTOD("  /  /  ") TO MEMDATE
STORE 0.00 TO MEMPAYAMT
STORE SPACE(6) TO MEMCHECKNO
STORE .F. TO OKINPUT
DO WHILE .NOT. OKINPUT
   CLEAR
   @ 1, 1 SAY "DATE OF PAYMENT IN FORM MM/DD/YY"
   @ 1,33 GET MEMDATE
   @ 2, 1 SAY "AMOUNT OF PAYMENT                "
   @ 2,33 GET MEMPAYAMT
   @ 3, 1 SAY "CHECK NUMBER                     "
   @ 3,33 GET MEMCHECKNO
   READ
   @ 5, 1 SAY "YOU HAVE ENTERED THE FOLLOWING:"
   @ 6, 5 SAY "DATE OF PAYMENT  ="
   @ 6,23 SAY MEMDATE
   @ 7, 5 SAY "AMOUNT OF PAYMENT="
   @ 7,23 SAY MEMPAYAMT
   @ 8, 5 SAY "CHECK NUMBER     ="
   @ 8,23 SAY MEMCHECKNO
   STORE SPACE(1) TO ANSWER
   @ 10,0 SAY "IS THIS INFORMATION CORRECT (Y/N)" ;
       GET ANSWER
   READ
   IF UPPER(ANSWER) <> "Y"
      @ 12,0 SAY "WILL NOT ENTER THIS DATA"
```

```
          WAIT
        ELSE
          STORE .T. TO OKINPUT
        ENDIF
      ENDDO
      REPLACE ACCPAYMENT WITH ACCPAYMENT+MEMPAYAMT, ACCDTLACT ;
        WITH MEMDATE
      SELECT D
      APPEND BLANK
      REPLACE PAYACCTNO WITH MEMACCTNO, PAYAMT WITH MEMPAYAMT,;
        PAYDATE WITH MEMDATE, PAYCHECKNO WITH MEMCHECKNO
      SELECT C
      APPEND BLANK
      REPLACE ACCTACCNO WITH MEMACCTNO, ACCTTYPACT WITH ;
        "PAYMENT",ACCTDTACT WITH MEMDATE, ACCTAMT WITH MEMPAYAMT
   ENDIF
ENDDO
RETURN
****************************** END OF PROGRAM ******************


* PAYMENTS.PRG
DO WHILE .T.
   CLEAR
   @ 3,5 SAY "CASH/CHARGE/PAYMENT MODULE SELECTION CODE"
   @ 4,5 SAY "-----------------------------------------------------"
   @ 5,10 SAY "A. EXIT"
   @ 6,10 SAY "B. ENTER CASH TICKET"
   @ 7,10 SAY "C. ENTER CHARGE TICKET"
```

```
   @ 8,10 SAY "D. MAKE A PAYMENT ON A BILL"
   WAIT "ENTER YOUR SELECTION CODE:" TO CODE1
   DO CASE
      CASE CODE1 = "A"
         RETURN
      CASE CODE1 = "B"
         DO BUYCASH
      CASE CODE1 = "C"
         DO BUYCHARG
      CASE CODE1 = "D"
         DO MAKEPAYM
      OTHERWISE
         @ 15,0 SAY "ILLEGAL SELECTION CODE."
         WAIT
   ENDCASE
   CLOSE DATABASES
ENDDO
RETURN
***************************** END OF PROGRAM ******************

* PRINTLET.PRG
SET DEVICE TO PRINT
SELECT G
USE LET1
DO WHILE .NOT. EOF()
   STORE 5 TO ROW
   @ ROW+1,28 SAY "COMPANY NAME"
   @ ROW+2,28 SAY "ADDRESS"
```

```
@ ROW+3,28 SAY "TELEPHONE"
@ ROW+4,35 SAY DATE()
STORE 14 TO ROW
@ ROW, 1 SAY TRIM(LETFNAME)+" "+TRIM(LETLNAME)
STORE ROW + 1 TO ROW
IF LETCOMPANY <> SPACE(25)
   @ ROW,1 SAY LETCOMPANY
   STORE ROW+1 TO ROW
ENDIF
IF LETPOBOX <> SPACE(10)
   @ ROW, 1 SAY "PO BOX:"
   @ ROW, 8 SAY LETPOBOX
   STORE ROW + 1 TO ROW
ENDIF
IF LETSTREET <> SPACE(25)
   @ ROW, 1 SAY LETSTREET
   STORE ROW + 1 TO ROW
ENDIF
@ ROW, 1 SAY LETADDRESS
STORE ROW + 1 TO ROW
@ ROW, 1 SAY "ACCOUNT NO:"
@ ROW,12 SAY LETACCNO
STORE ROW + 4 TO ROW
@ ROW, 1 SAY "DEAR FRIEND:"
STORE ROW +  4 TO ROW
@ ROW, 1 SAY "     Our records show that we have not received "+;
             "a recent payment from you."
STORE ROW + 2 TO ROW
```

```
@ ROW, 1 SAY "Since you are a valued customer, we certainly "+;
            "hope that this is merely an "
STORE ROW + 2 TO ROW
@ ROW, 1 SAY "oversight on your part.  In fact, if you have "+;
            "already sent in payment, "
STORE ROW + 2 TO ROW
@ ROW, 1 SAY "please disregard this notice.  We would "+;
            "appreciate your taking action on"
STORE ROW + 2 TO ROW
@ ROW, 1 SAY "this matter within 15 days."
STORE ROW + 2 TO ROW
@ ROW, 1 SAY "     For your records, total unpaid charges to date is:"
@ ROW,58 SAY LETTOTCHRG
STORE ROW + 1 TO ROW
@ ROW, 1 SAY "                         total unpaid interest is       :"
@ ROW,58 SAY LETTOTINT
STORE ROW + 1 TO ROW
@ ROW,58 SAY "---------"
STORE ROW + 1 TO ROW
@ ROW, 1 SAY "                                   TOTAL AMOUNT DUE     $"
@ ROW,58 SAY LETTOTDUE
STORE ROW + 6 TO ROW
@ ROW,40 SAY "Sincerely,"
STORE ROW + 4 TO ROW
@ ROW,40 SAY "Tom Smith"
STORE ROW + 1 TO ROW
@ ROW,40 SAY "Manager"
STORE ROW + 2 TO ROW
```

```
   @ ROW, 1 SAY "THIS NOTICE IS USED FOR CHARGE ACCOUNTS, OLD "+;
                 "UNPAID BILLS AND BAD"
   STORE ROW + 1 TO ROW
   @ ROW, 1 SAY "CHECKS.  IF YOU HAVE ANY QUESTIONS, PLEASE CONTACT ME."
   EJECT
   SKIP 1
ENDDO
USE LET2
DO WHILE .NOT. EOF()
   STORE 5 TO ROW
   @ ROW+1,28 SAY "Company name"
   @ ROW+2,28 SAY "Address"
   @ ROW+3,28 SAY "Telephone"
   @ ROW+4,35 SAY DATE()
   STORE 14 TO ROW
   @ ROW, 1 SAY TRIM(LETFNAME)+" "+TRIM(LETLNAME)
   STORE ROW + 1 TO ROW
   IF LETCOMPANY <> SPACE(25)
      @ ROW,1 SAY LETCOMPANY
      STORE ROW+1 TO ROW
   ENDIF
   IF LETPOBOX <> SPACE(10)
      @ ROW, 1 SAY "PO BOX:"
      @ ROW, 8 SAY LETPOBOX
      STORE ROW + 1 TO ROW
   ENDIF
   IF LETSTREET <> SPACE(25)
      @ ROW, 1 SAY LETSTREET
```

```
   STORE ROW + 1 TO ROW
ENDIF
@ ROW, 1 SAY LETADDRESS
STORE ROW + 1 TO ROW
@ ROW, 1 SAY "ACCOUNT NO:"
@ ROW,12 SAY LETACCNO
STORE ROW + 4 TO ROW
@ ROW, 1 SAY "DEAR FRIEND:"
STORE ROW +  4 TO ROW
@ ROW, 1 SAY "     Our records show that we have not received "+;
             "payment from you for at"
STORE ROW + 2 TO ROW
@ ROW, 1 SAY "least two months.  Since you are a valued "+;
             "customer, we certainly hope"
STORE ROW + 2 TO ROW
@ ROW, 1 SAY "that this is merely an oversight on your part.  "+;
             "In fact, if you have "
STORE ROW + 2 TO ROW
@ ROW, 1 SAY "already sent in payment, please disregard this "+;
             "notice.  We would "
STORE ROW + 2 TO ROW
@ ROW, 1 SAY "appreciate your taking action on this matter "+;
             "within 15 days."
STORE ROW + 2 TO ROW
@ ROW, 1 SAY "     If you are having difficulty making "+;
             "payments on your account, please"
STORE ROW + 2 TO ROW
@ ROW, 1 SAY "contact me so that a payment schedule can be arranged."
```

```
   STORE ROW + 2 TO ROW
   @ ROW, 1 SAY "     For your records, total unpaid charges to date is:"
   @ ROW,58 SAY LETTOTCHRG
   STORE ROW + 1 TO ROW
   @ ROW, 1 SAY "                        total unpaid interest is       :"
   @ ROW,58 SAY LETTOTINT
   STORE ROW + 1 TO ROW
   @ ROW,58 SAY "---------"
   STORE ROW + 1 TO ROW
   @ ROW, 1 SAY "                                  TOTAL AMOUNT DUE     $"
   @ ROW,58 SAY LETTOTDUE
   STORE ROW + 6 TO ROW
   @ ROW,40 SAY "Sincerely,"
   STORE ROW + 4 TO ROW
   @ ROW,40 SAY "Tom Smith"
   STORE ROW + 1 TO ROW
   @ ROW,40 SAY "Manager"
   STORE ROW + 2 TO ROW
   @ ROW, 1 SAY "THIS NOTICE IS USED FOR CHARGE ACCOUNTS, OLD "+;
             "UNPAID BILLS AND BAD"
   STORE ROW + 1 TO ROW
   @ ROW, 1 SAY "CHECKS.  IF YOU HAVE ANY QUESTIONS, PLEASE CONTACT ME."
   EJECT
   SKIP 1
ENDDO
USE LET3
DO WHILE .NOT. EOF()
   STORE 5 TO ROW
```

```
@ ROW+1,28 SAY "Company name"
@ ROW+2,28 SAY "Address"
@ ROW+3,28 SAY "Telephone"
@ ROW+4,35 SAY DATE()
STORE 14 TO ROW
@ ROW, 1 SAY TRIM(LETFNAME)+" "+TRIM(LETLNAME)
STORE ROW + 1 TO ROW
IF LETCOMPANY <> SPACE(25)
   @ ROW,1 SAY LETCOMPANY
   STORE ROW+1 TO ROW
ENDIF
IF LETPOBOX <> SPACE(10)
   @ ROW, 1 SAY "PO BOX:"
   @ ROW, 8 SAY LETPOBOX
   STORE ROW + 1 TO ROW
ENDIF
IF LETSTREET <> SPACE(25)
   @ ROW, 1 SAY LETSTREET
   STORE ROW + 1 TO ROW
ENDIF
@ ROW, 1 SAY LETADDRESS
STORE ROW + 1 TO ROW
@ ROW, 1 SAY "ACCOUNT NO:"
@ ROW,12 SAY LETACCNO
STORE ROW + 4 TO ROW
@ ROW, 1 SAY "Dear Mr/Ms"
@ ROW,12 SAY TRIM(LETLNAME)+":"
STORE ROW +  4 TO ROW
```

```
@ ROW, 1 SAY "     As you have been informed, we are "+;
             "maintaining a past due account"
STORE ROW + 2 TO ROW
@ ROW, 1 SAY "in your name in the amount of $"
@ ROW,32 SAY LETTOTDUE
@ ROW,42 SAY "."
STORE ROW + 2 TO ROW
@ ROW, 1 SAY "     We previously gave you fifteen (15) days "+;
             "to respond and/or remit"
STORE ROW + 2 TO ROW
@ ROW, 1 SAY "the amount due.  Your neglect in this matter "+;
             "leaves us no other choice"
STORE ROW + 2 TO ROW
@ ROW, 1 SAY "but to turn this matter over to our attorney "+;
              "for legal action.  May you"
STORE ROW + 2 TO ROW
@ ROW, 1 SAY "be aware that if such action is necessary, "+;
             "we would sue for attorney's"
STORE ROW + 2 TO ROW
@ ROW, 1 SAY "fees and costs of court which can be expensive.  "+;
             "It would thus be to your"
STORE ROW + 2 TO ROW
@ ROW, 1 SAY "distinct financial advantage to take care of "+;
             "this matter immediately."
STORE ROW + 2 TO ROW
@ ROW, 1 SAY "     This is your final opportunity - no further "+;
             "notices or letters will"
STORE ROW + 2 TO ROW
```

```
   @ ROW, 1 SAY "be sent to you.  You are hereby given five (5) "+;
             "days from the date of this"
   STORE ROW + 2 TO ROW
   @ ROW, 1 SAY "letter to pay the amount in full."
   STORE ROW + 6 TO ROW
   @ ROW,40 SAY "Sincerely,"
   STORE ROW + 4 TO ROW
   @ ROW,40 SAY "Tom Smith"
   STORE ROW + 1 TO ROW
   @ ROW,40 SAY "Manager"
   STORE ROW + 2 TO ROW
   EJECT
   SKIP 1
ENDDO
SET DEVICE TO SCREEN
RETURN
***************************** END OF PROGRAM *****************


* RECINV.PRG
SELECT J
USE INVENTOR INDEX INVITMAN, INVITLOC
SELECT C
USE TRANSFER INDEX TRLOCITD
DO WHILE .T.
   CLEAR
   STORE SPACE(1) TO ANSWER
   WAIT "DO YOU WISH TO RECEIPT ANOTHER INVENTORY SHIPMENT(Y/N):" ;
         TO ANSWER
```

```
IF UPPER(ANSWER) <> "Y"
   RETURN
ENDIF
SELECT C
STORE SPACE(20) TO MEMITEMNO
STORE SPACE(15) TO MEMSENDLOC
STORE SPACE(15) TO MEMRECLOC
STORE CTOD("  /  /  ") TO MEMSENDDT
CLEAR
@ 1,1 SAY "ENTER THE INVENTORY ITEM NUMBER" GET MEMITEMNO
@ 2,1 SAY "ENTER THE LOCATION OF THE SENDER" GET MEMSENDLOC
@ 3,1 SAY "ENTER THE LOCATION OF THE RECEIVER" GET MEMRECLOC
@ 4,1 SAY "ENTER THE DATE SENT IN THE FORM MM/DD/YY" GET ;
           MEMSENDDT
READ
STORE MEMSENDLOC+MEMRECLOC+MEMITEMNO+DTOC(MEMSENDDT) TO MEMKEY
SEEK MEMKEY
IF EOF()
   @ 7,0 SAY "NO INVENTORY TRANSFER RECORD ON FILE FOR "+;
             "GIVEN INFORMATION"
   WAIT
   LOOP
ELSE
   STORE "N" TO ANSWER
   STORE .F. TO FOUND
   DO WHILE (.NOT. EOF()) .AND. (.NOT. FOUND) .AND. ;
     MEMSENDLOC = TRSENDLOC .AND.  MEMRECLOC = TRRECLOC .AND. ;
     MEMITEMNO = TRITEMNO .AND. MEMSENDDT = TRSENDDT
```

```
CLEAR
* DISPLAY THE TRANSFER RECORD
@  1, 1 SAY "INVENTORY TRANSFER RECORD"
@  2, 1 SAY "-------------------------"
@  3, 1 SAY "SENDING LOCATION:"
@  3,19 SAY TRSENDLOC
@  3,37 SAY "RECEIVING LOCATION:"
@  3,57 SAY TRRECLOC
@  5, 1 SAY "INVENTORY ITEM NUMBER:"
@  5,24 SAY TRITEMNO
@  6, 1 SAY "MANUFACTURER OR SPECIAL DESIGNATION:"
@  6,38 SAY TRMANU
@  7, 1 SAY "DESCRIPTION:"
@  7,14 SAY TRDESC
@  9, 1 SAY "DATE SENT:"
@  9,12 SAY TRSENDDT
@  9,24 SAY "QUANTITY SENT:"
@  9,39 SAY TRQTYSENT
@  9,47 SAY "QUANTITY REC:"
@  9,60 SAY TRQTYREC
@ 10, 1 SAY "UNITS:"
@ 10, 8 SAY TRUNITS
@ 10,20 SAY "COUNT PER UNIT:"
@ 10,36 SAY TRQTYPER
@ 12, 1 SAY "UNIT COST:"
@ 12,12 SAY TRCSTPERU
@ 13, 1 SAY "SELLING PRICE:"
@ 13,16 SAY TRSELLPR
```

```
* END OF RECORD DISPLAY
STORE SPACE(1) TO ANSWER
WAIT "IS THIS THE CORRECT RECORD (Y/N):" TO ANSWER
IF UPPER(ANSWER) <> "Y"
   SKIP 1
ELSE
   STORE .T. TO FOUND
ENDIF
ENDDO
IF .NOT. FOUND
   @ 20,0 SAY "UNABLE TO LOCATE TRANSFER RECORD"
   WAIT
   LOOP
ELSE
   STORE 0 TO MEMQTY
   STORE CTOD("  /  /  ") TO MEMRECDT
   @ 15,1 SAY "ENTER THE QUANTITY RECEIVED" ;
      GET MEMQTY
   @ 16,1 SAY "ENTER THE DATE RECEIVED IN THE FORM MM/DD/YY";
     GET MEMRECDT
   READ
   REPLACE TRRECDT WITH MEMRECDT, TRQTYREC WITH MEMQTY
   STORE TRDESC TO MEMDESC
   STORE TRUNITS TO MEMUNITS
   STORE TRQTYPER TO MEMQTYPER
   STORE TRCSTPERU TO MEMCSTPERU
   STORE TRSELLPR TO MEMSELLPR
   STORE TRMANU TO MEMMANU
```

```
    SELECT J
    STORE MEMITEMNO+MEMMANU+MEMRECLOC TO MEMKEY
    SEEK MEMKEY
    IF EOF()
       CLEAR
       @ 1,1 SAY "NOT ABLE TO LOCATE EXISTING INVENTORY "+;
          "RECORD IN RECEIVING LOCATION."
       @ 2,1 SAY "WILL NOW CREATE A NEW INVENTORY RECORD."
       STORE 0 TO MEMREORDPT
       STORE 0 TO MEMREORDAM
       @ 4,1 SAY "ENTER REORDER POINT FOR NEW RECORD" ;
           GET MEMREORDPT
       @ 5,1 SAY "ENTER REORDER AMOUNT FOR NEW RECORD" ;
           GET MEMREORDAM
       READ
       APPEND BLANK
       REPLACE INVITEMNO WITH MEMITEMNO, INVMANU WITH MEMMANU,;
        INVLOC WITH MEMRECLOC, INVDESC WITH MEMDESC, INVUNITS ;
        WITH MEMUNITS,INVQTYPER WITH MEMQTYPER
       REPLACE INVQTYONH WITH MEMQTY,INVREORDPT WITH MEMREORDPT,;
        INVREORDAM WITH MEMREORDAM,INVCSTPERU WITH MEMCSTPERU, ;
        INVSELLPR WITH MEMSELLPR
    ELSE
       REPLACE INVQTYONH WITH INVQTYONH+MEMQTY,;
         INVCSTPERU WITH MEMCSTPERU, INVSELLPR WITH ;
         MEMSELLPR
    ENDIF
 ENDIF
```

```
   ENDIF
ENDDO
RETURN
***************************** END OF PROGRAM ******************


* SENDINV.PRG
SELECT J
USE INVENTOR INDEX INVITMAN
SELECT C
USE TRANSFER INDEX TRLOCITD
SET DEVICE TO SCREEN
DO WHILE .T.
   CLEAR
   SELECT J
   STORE SPACE(1) TO ANSWER
   WAIT "DO YOU WISH TO TRANSFER ANOTHER INVENTORY ITEM (Y/N):" ;
         TO ANSWER
   IF UPPER(ANSWER) <> "Y"
      RETURN
   ENDIF
   CLEAR
   STORE SPACE(20) TO MEMITEMNO
   STORE SPACE(25) TO MEMMANU
   STORE SPACE(15) TO MEMSENDLOC
   @ 1,1 SAY  "ENTER THE INVENTORY ITEM NUMBER" GET MEMITEMNO
   @ 2,1 SAY  "ENTER THE MANUFACTURER/SPECIAL DESIGNATOR" GET ;
              MEMMANU
   @ 3,1 SAY  "ENTER THE SENDING LOCATION" GET MEMSENDLOC
```

```
READ
STORE MEMITEMNO + MEMMANU + MEMSENDLOC TO MEMKEY
SEEK MEMKEY
IF EOF()
   @ 5,0 SAY "NO INVENTORY RECORD EXISTS FOR GIVEN INFORMATION"
   WAIT
ELSE
   * DISPLAY RECORD FOR VISUAL CHECK
   CLEAR
   @  1, 1 SAY "INVENTORY RECORD"
   @  2, 1 SAY "----------------"
   @  3, 1 SAY "INVENTORY ITEM NUMBER:"
   @  3,23 SAY INVITEMNO
   @  4, 1 SAY "MANUFACTURER OR SPECIAL DESIGNATOR:"
   @  4,36 SAY INVMANU
   @  5, 1 SAY "DESCRIPTION OF ITEM:"
   @  5,21 SAY INVDESC
   @  7, 1 SAY "LOCATION OF ITEM:"
   @  7,18 SAY INVLOC
   @  9, 1 SAY "UNITS:"
   @  9, 7 SAY INVUNITS
   @  9,19 SAY "COUNT PER UNIT:"
   @  9,34 SAY INVQTYPER
   @ 11, 1 SAY "QUANTITY ON HAND:"
   @ 11,18 SAY INVQTYONH
   @ 13, 1 SAY "REORDER POINT:"
   @ 13,15 SAY INVREORDPT
   @ 13,28 SAY "REORDER AMOUNT:"
```

```
@ 13,43 SAY INVREORDAM
@ 15, 1 SAY "UNIT COST:"
@ 15,15 SAY INVCSTPERU
@ 17, 1 SAY "SELLING PRICE:"
@ 17,15 SAY INVSELLPR
* END OF RECORD DISPLAY
STORE SPACE(1) TO ANSWER
WAIT "IS THIS THE CORRECT RECORD (Y/N):" TO ANSWER
IF UPPER(ANSWER) <> "Y"
   LOOP
ENDIF
STORE INVDESC TO MEMDESC
STORE INVQTYPER TO MEMQTYPER
STORE INVCSTPERU TO MEMCSTPERU
STORE INVSELLPR TO MEMSELLPR
CLEAR
STORE 0 TO MEMQTY
@ 1, 1 SAY "ENTER THE QUANTITY TO BE TRANSFERRED" GET MEMQTY
READ
IF MEMQTY > INVQTYONH
   @ 2, 0 SAY "NOT POSSIBLE TO TRANSFER MORE THAN QTY ON HAND."
   WAIT
   LOOP
ENDIF
STORE CTOD("  /  /  ") TO MEMDATE
@ 3,1 SAY "ENTER DATE OF TRANSFER IN FORM MM/DD/YY" GET ;
      MEMDATE
READ
```

```
STORE SPACE(1) TO MEMTYPTRAN
DO WHILE MEMTYPTRAN <> "B" .AND. MEMTYPTRAN <> "C"
   @ 5,1 SAY "IF THE TRANSFER IS BY BULK, ENTER THE LETTER B"
   @ 6,1 SAY "IF THE TRANSFER IS TO BE COMPUTED "+;
             "(QTY*COUNT PER UNIT), ENTER THE LETTER C" ;
             GET MEMTYPTRAN
   READ
ENDDO
STORE SPACE(15) TO MEMRECLOC
@ 8,1 SAY "ENTER THE RECEIVING LOCATION" GET MEMRECLOC
READ
REPLACE INVQTYONH WITH INVQTYONH - MEMQTY
IF MEMTYPTRAN = "C"
   STORE SPACE(15) TO MEMUNITS
   @ 10,1 SAY "ENTER THE UNITS DESIGNATION FOR RECEIVER" ;
      GET MEMUNITS
   READ
   STORE MEMQTY*INVQTYPER TO MEMQTY
   STORE MEMCSTPERU/MEMQTYPER TO MEMCSTPERU
   STORE MEMSELLPR/MEMQTYPER TO MEMSELLPR
   STORE 1 TO MEMQTYPER
ELSE
   STORE INVUNITS TO MEMUNITS
ENDIF
@ 13,0 SAY "WHEN THE TRANSFER IS ACKNOWLEDGED, THE "+;
          "INVENTORY AT THE RECEIVING LOCATION WILL BE "+;
          "UPDATED."
@ 15,0 SAY "THE INVENTORY AT THE SENDING LOCATION WILL "+;
```

```
                "BE UPDATED NOW."
      WAIT
      SELECT C
      APPEND BLANK
      REPLACE TRSENDLOC WITH MEMSENDLOC, TRRECLOC WITH MEMRECLOC, ;
        TRITEMNO WITH MEMITEMNO, TRMANU WITH MEMMANU, TRSENDDT WITH ;
        MEMDATE, TRQTYSENT WITH MEMQTY, TRUNITS WITH MEMUNITS
      REPLACE TRDESC WITH MEMDESC, TRCSTPERU WITH MEMCSTPERU, ;
        TRSELLPR WITH MEMSELLPR, TRQTYPER WITH MEMQTYPER
   ENDIF
ENDDO
RETURN
***************************** END OF PROGRAM *****************

* SYSTEM.PRG
SET TALK OFF
SET SAFETY OFF
SET STATUS OFF
DO WHILE .T.
   CLEAR
   @  3, 1 SAY "SALES, RECEIVABLES, AND INVENTORY SYSTEM"
   @  4, 1 SAY "----------------------------------------"
   @  5, 5 SAY "A. EXIT FROM THE SYSTEM"
   @  6, 5 SAY "B. ACCOUNTING REPORT"
   @  7, 5 SAY "C. BAD CHECKS"
   @  8, 5 SAY "D. BILLING"
   @  9, 5 SAY "E. CHARGE ACCOUNTS"
   @ 10, 5 SAY "F. CHARGE ACCOUNT DEFAULT"
```

```
@ 11, 5 SAY "G. CHARGE ACCOUNT DISPUTE"
@ 12, 5 SAY "H. DELETE RECORDS BY KEY OR BY DATE"
@ 13, 5 SAY "I. FIND RECORDS AND DISPLAY ON SCREEN"
@ 14, 5 SAY "J. INVENTORY"
@ 15, 5 SAY "K. PAYMENTS/CASH PURCHASE/CHARGE"
@ 16, 5 SAY "L. REINDEX ALL OF THE FILES"
WAIT "ENTER YOUR LETTER CODE SELECTION:" TO CODE
DO CASE
   CASE CODE = "A"
      ? "NORMAL TERMINATION OF RECEIVABLES/INVENTORY SYSTEM"
      QUIT
   CASE CODE = "B"
      DO ACCOUNTI
   CASE CODE = "C"
      DO BADCHECK
   CASE CODE = "D"
      DO BILLING
   CASE CODE = "E"
      DO ACCOUNTS
   CASE CODE = "F"
      DO DEFAULT
   CASE CODE = "G"
      DO DISPUTE
   CASE CODE = "H"
      DO DELETE
   CASE CODE = "I"
      DO FINDRECO
   CASE CODE = "J"
      DO INVENTOR
```

```
      CASE CODE = "K"
         DO PAYMENTS
      CASE CODE = "L"
         DO INDEXES
      OTHERWISE
         ? "ILLEGAL LETTER CODE SELECTED"
         WAIT
   ENDCASE
   CLEAR ALL
ENDDO
RETURN
***************************** END OF PROGRAM ******************



* TRDISCRPT.PRG
CLEAR
? "INSERT WIDE PAPER IN THE PRINTER."
? "TYPE ANY KEY TO CONTINUE."
WAIT
CLEAR
SET DEVICE TO PRINT
@ 0,0 SAY CHR(15)
SELECT C
USE TRANSFER INDEX TRLOCITD
REPORT FORM TRDISCRE TO PRINT
@ 66,150 SAY CHR(18)
SET DEVICE TO SCREEN
RETURN
***************************** END OF PROGRAM ******************
```

```
* UPDATEACCT.PRG
SET DEVICE TO SCREEN
SELECT A
USE ACCOUNTS INDEX ACCNO, ACCLNAME, ACCCOMPA
DO WHILE .T.
   CLEAR
   STORE SPACE(1) TO ANSWER
   WAIT "DO YOU WISH TO UPDATE ANOTHER ACCOUNT (Y/N):" TO ANSWER
   IF UPPER(ANSWER) <> "Y"
      RETURN
   ENDIF
   CLEAR
   STORE SPACE(10) TO MEMACCTNO
   @ 1,0 SAY "ENTER THE ACCOUNT NUMBER" GET MEMACCTNO
   READ
   SEEK MEMACCTNO
   IF EOF()
      @ 3,0 SAY "NO RECORD ON FILE FOR THE GIVEN ACCOUNT NUMBER"
      WAIT
      LOOP
   ELSE
      CLEAR
      @  1, 1 SAY " ACCOUNT UPDATE FORM"
      @  2, 1 SAY "---------------------"
      @  3, 1 SAY "ACCOUNT NUMBER:"
      @  3,17 SAY ACCNO
      @  5, 1 SAY "COMPANY NAME"
```

```
@  5,16 GET ACCCOMPANY
@  6, 1 SAY "LAST NAME"
@  6,11 GET ACCLNAME
@  6,29 SAY "FIRST NAME"
@  6,40 GET ACCFNAME
@  7, 1 SAY "PO BOX"
@  7, 8 GET ACCPOBOX
@  7,20 SAY "STREET"
@  7,27 GET ACCSTREET
@  8, 1 SAY "CITY"
@  8, 6 GET ACCCITY
@  8,23 SAY "STATE"
@  8,29 GET ACCSTATE
@  8,39 SAY "ZIP"
@  8,43 GET ACCZIP
@ 10, 1 SAY "ACCOUNT TYPE"
@ 10,30 SAY "ACCOUNT STATUS"
@ 10,60 SAY "BILLING TYPE"
@ 11, 1 SAY "------------"
@ 11,30 SAY "--------------"
@ 11,60 SAY "------------"
@ 12, 1 SAY "BC=BAD CHECK"
@ 12,30 SAY "CAN=CANCELLED"
@ 12,60 SAY "REG=REGULAR"
@ 13, 1 SAY "RC=REVOLVING CHARGE"
@ 13,30 SAY "HLD=HOLD FOR SPECIAL ACTION"
@ 13,60 SAY "SCH=BY PAY SCHEDULE"
```

```
@ 14, 1 SAY "SI=SINGLE ITEM"
@ 14,30 SAY "OVL=OVER THE CHARGE LIMIT"
@ 15, 1 SAY "UN=OLD UNPAID ACCOUNT"
@ 15,30 SAY "VAL=NORMAL CHARGE ACCOUNT"
@ 16, 1 SAY "TYPE OF ACCOUNT"
@ 16,17 GET ACCTYPE
@ 16,21 SAY "STATUS OF ACCOUNT"
@ 16,38 GET ACCSTATUS
@ 16,43 SAY "BILLING TYPE"
@ 16,56 GET ACCBILLTYP
@ 16,61 SAY "MIN PMT"
@ 16,68 GET ACCMINPAY
@ 17, 1 SAY "CREDIT LIMIT"
@ 17,13 GET ACCCREDLIM
@ 17,21 SAY "DESCRIPTION OF SECURITY DEPOSIT"
@ 17,53 GET ACCSECDEP
@ 18, 1 SAY "SPECIAL ACTION REQUIRED"
@ 18,25 GET ACCSPECACT
@ 19, 1 SAY "TOTAL UNPAID CHARGES"
@ 19,23 GET ACCTOTCHRG
@ 19,35 SAY "TOTAL PAYMENTS"
@ 19,50 GET ACCPAYMENT
@ 19,63 SAY "CARRY"
@ 19,69 GET ACCCARYOVR
@ 20, 1 SAY "INTEREST DUE"
@ 20,14 GET ACCTOTINT
@ 20,23 SAY "YTD INTEREST"
@ 20,36 GET ACCYTDINT
```

```
      @ 20,50 SAY "ACCUMULATE INTEREST (Y/N)"
      @ 20,76 GET ACCINTFLG
      @ 21, 1 SAY "DATE OF LAST ACCOUNT ACTIVITY"
      @ 21,31 GET ACCDTLACT
      @ 21,42 SAY "DISCOUNT PERCENT"
      @ 21,59 GET ACCDISCPER
      @ 22, 1 SAY "OVER 30"
      @ 22, 8 GET ACCOVER30
      @ 22,19 SAY "OVER 60"
      @ 22,26 GET ACCOVER60
      @ 22,37 SAY "OVER 90"
      @ 22,45 GET ACCOVER90
      @ 23, 1 SAY "LAST BAD CHECK NUMBER"
      @ 23,23 GET ACCBADCHNO
      @ 23,31 SAY "MONTHS IN ARREARS"
      @ 23,48 GET ACCMONARR
      READ
   ENDIF
ENDDO
RETURN
****************************** END OF PROGRAM ******************


* UPDATEIN.PRG
SET DEVICE TO SCREEN
SELECT J
USE INVENTOR INDEX INVITMAN, INVITLOC
DO WHILE .T.
   CLEAR
```

```
STORE SPACE(1) TO ANSWER
WAIT "DO YOU WISH TO UPDATE ANOTHER INVENTORY "+;
      "RECORD(Y/N):" TO ANSWER
IF UPPER(ANSWER) <> "Y"
   RETURN
ENDIF
CLEAR
STORE SPACE(20) TO MEMITEMNO
STORE SPACE(25) TO MEMMANU
STORE SPACE(15) TO MEMLOC
@ 1,1 SAY "ENTER THE ITEM NUMBER" GET MEMITEMNO
@ 2,1 SAY "ENTER THE MANUFACTURER/SPECIAL DESIGNATOR" ;
          GET MEMMANU
@ 3,1 SAY "ENTER THE LOCATION" GET MEMLOC
READ
STORE MEMITEMNO + MEMMANU + MEMLOC TO MEMKEY
SEEK MEMKEY
IF EOF()
   @ 5,0 SAY "NO INVENTORY RECORD ON FILE FOR GIVEN INFORMATION"
   WAIT
   LOOP
ELSE
   CLEAR
   @  1, 1 SAY "UPDATE AN EXISTING INVENTORY RECORD"
   @  2, 1 SAY "-----------------------------------"
   @  3, 1 SAY "INVENTORY ITEM NUMBER:"
   @  3,24 SAY INVITEMNO
   @  4, 1 SAY "MANUFACTURER OR SPECIAL DESIGNATOR:"
```

```
        @  4,37 SAY INVMANU
        @  5, 1 SAY "DESCRIPTION OF ITEM"
        @  5,21 GET INVDESC
        @  7, 1 SAY "LOCATION OF ITEM:"
        @  7,19 SAY INVLOC
        @  9, 1 SAY "UNITS"
        @  9, 7 GET INVUNITS
        @  9,19 SAY "COUNT PER UNIT"
        @  9,34 GET INVQTYPER
        @ 11, 1 SAY "QUANTITY ON HAND"
        @ 11,18 GET INVQTYONH
        @ 13, 1 SAY "REORDER POINT"
        @ 13,15 GET INVREORDPT
        @ 13,28 SAY "REORDER AMOUNT"
        @ 13,43 GET INVREORDAM
        @ 15, 1 SAY "UNIT COST"
        @ 15,15 GET INVCSTPERU
        @ 17, 1 SAY "SELLING PRICE"
        @ 17,15 GET INVSELLPR
        READ
    ENDIF
ENDDO
RETURN
```

C.6 SOME COMMENTS ON THE SYSTEM

Since this system was converted from dBASE II to dBASE III Plus, you should expect to see an occasional carry over from dBASE II programming. Two examples are: a single FSE program is not used for the entry and modification of database records, and there is some duplication of data already in other database files. This system does not have a separate FSE program, since I developed this technique after I wrote the original version of this system, and some data was duplicated to speed up the execution of potentially slow dBASE II programs. For examples of FSE programs, see CUSTFSE.PRG, INVFSE.PRG, and ORDFSE.PRG in Chapter 6. Note how these FSE programs are called from both entry and modification programs. For a discussion of the pros and cons of duplication of data in databases, see Chapter 7.

INDEX

D

E

F

G

H

I

J

K

L

Here's how to receive your free catalog and save money on your next book order from Scott, Foresman and Company

Simply mail in the response card below to receive your free copy of our latest catalog featuring computer and business books. After you've looked through the catalog and you're ready to place your order, attach the coupon below to receive $1.00 off the catalog price of Scott, Foresman and Company Professional Publishing Group computer and business books.

☐ YES, please send me my *free* catalog of your latest computer and business books! I am especially interested in

☐ IBM
☐ MACINTOSH
☐ AMIGA
☐ APPLE IIc, IIe, IIGS
☐ COMMODORE
☐ Programming
☐ Business Applications
☐ Networking/Telecommunications
☐ Other ______________________

Name (please print) ______________________

Company ______________________

Address ______________________

City ______________ State ________ Zip ________

Mail response card to: Scott, Foresman and Company
Professional Publishing Group
1900 East Lake Avenue
Glenview, IL 60025

PUBLISHER'S COUPON   NO EXPIRATION DATE

SAVE $1.00

Limit one per order. Good only on Scott, Foresman and Company Professional Publishing Group publications. Consumer pays any sales tax. Coupon may not be assigned, transferred, or reproduced. Coupon will be redeemed by Scott, Foresman and Company, Professional Publishing Group, 1900 E. Lake Ave., Glenview, IL 60025.

Customer's Signature ______________________